Religion Returns to the Public Square

Religion Returns to the Public Square
Faith and Policy in America

Edited by

Hugh Heclo

and

Wilfred M. McClay

Woodrow Wilson Center Press
Washington, D.C.

The Johns Hopkins University Press
Baltimore and London

EDITORIAL OFFICES

Woodrow Wilson Center Press
Woodrow Wilson International Center for Scholars
One Woodrow Wilson Plaza
1300 Pennsylvania Avenue, N.W.
Washington, D.C. 20004-3027
Telephone 202-691-4010
www.wilsoncenter.org

ORDER FROM:

The Johns Hopkins University Press
Hampden Station
P.O. Box 50370
Baltimore, Maryland 21211
Telephone 1-800-537-5487
www.jhupbooks.com

Printed in the United States of America on acid-free paper ∞

2 4 6 8 9 7 5 3 1

Library of Congress Cataloging-in-Publication Data

Religion returns to the public square: faith and policy in America / edited by
Hugh Heclo and Wilfred M. McClay.
p. cm.
Includes bibliographical references and index.
ISBN 0-8018-7194-8 (hardcover : alk. paper)—ISBN 0-8018-7195-6
(pbk. : alk. paper)
1. Religion and politics—United States. I. Heclo, Hugh. II. McClay,
Wilfred M.
BL2525.F34 2002
322'.1'0973—dc21 2002151344

ABOUT THE CENTER

The Center is the living memorial of the United States of America to the nation's twenty-eighth president, Woodrow Wilson. Congress established the Woodrow Wilson Center in 1968 as an international institute for advanced study, "symbolizing and strengthening the fruitful relationship between the world of learning and the world of public affairs." The Center opened in 1970 under its own board of trustees.

In all its activities the Woodrow Wilson Center is a nonprofit, nonpartisan organization, supported financially by annual appropriations from the Congress, and by the contributions of foundations, corporations, and individuals. Conclusions or opinions expressed in Center publications and programs are those of the authors and speakers and do not necessarily reflect the views of the Center staff, fellows, trustees, advisory groups, or any individuals or organizations that provide financial support to the Center.

For Michael J. Lacey

With thee conversing I forget all time . . .

—John Milton

and Susan Nugent

They at her coming sprung,
And, touched by her fair tendance, gladlier grew.

—John Milton

Contents

Foreword

E.J. Dionne Jr.

Religion, if it is taken seriously, must inevitably become a public matter. It is public in the narrowest sense: Those who believe that a tradition or a form of spirituality is true and valid cannot help but have their own public behavior shaped by its inspirations and demands. It is public in sociological terms: Those who share spiritual beliefs inevitably come together in community. Many religions and spiritual traditions may honor—but are not sustained by—hermits and spiritual virtuosos who go off into the wilderness. Because the rest of us live in community under some set of public norms, religion is thus inevitably public in the political sense. All serious traditions develop views of what is right and just. Some traditions might choose to apply their insights about justice to society as a whole. Others might be interested in narrower goals: the establishment of rules and conditions that allow their particular tradition to survive and prosper. In either case, public religion and, in the broadest sense, political religion is inevitable.

These claims may seem commonsensical, but they are not uncontroversial because they are all premised on the idea of taking religion *seriously*.

That is not what everyone does, and certainly not all intellectuals. As Wilfred McClay argues in these pages, certain forms of secularism would confine religion "to a sort of cultural red light district, along with other unfortunate frailties and vices to which we are liable." In this view, "religion is tolerated as a form of irrationality" and religious people "are left free to believe what they wish, and even to act in private on their beliefs, as long as they do not trouble the rest of us with them, or bestir the proverbial horses."

This thoughtful volume makes a large contribution toward bestirring the hostile and the indifferent to the intellectual power and seriousness of what José Casanova calls "public religion." It is a book that describes the trend evoked in its title—the return of religion to the public square—but is itself evidence of this change in our public life. The effort to shove religion to the margin of public life, to impose what Casanova calls "an incapacitating 'gag rule'" on religious citizens, has failed. This does not mean that religious freedom is in jeopardy. On the contrary, the new movement to defend religion's public role is aimed at expanding the sphere of liberty. Defending the public role of religious citizens would, in fact, be harder absent the advances in religious freedom over the last four decades. Whatever their areas of agreement and disagreement, all of the authors here are sensitive to the reality of religious pluralism and to the special responsibilities religious citizens have in a republic based on the freedoms of speech, association, and worship. Their call for taking religion's public role seriously is rooted in democratic republicanism, not theocracy.

The core argument that runs through the book is well stated by Hugh Heclo in his introduction: "Whether we like it or not, the connections between religion and public policy choices are profound and unavoidable. Government policy and religious matters are not the same thing, but neither do they exist in isolation from each other. The two are distinct but not separate from each other." The two domains intertwine, Heclo says, "because both claim to give authoritative answers to important questions about how people should live."

Or as the philosopher Jean Bethke Elshtain has put it elsewhere: "Separation of church and state is one thing. Separation of religion and politics is another thing altogether. Religion and politics flow back and forth in American civil society all the time—always have, always will. How could it be otherwise?"[1] Exactly how this happens, and when, raises interesting, complex, and important questions. The essays in this book live up that standard of interest, complexity, and importance.

If you believe, as I do, that we are at a new stage in our great national debate over religious liberty, these essays provide an immensely useful step forward in the debates and struggles of what I call the third stage in our history of grappling with the demands and obligations of religious liberty.[2]

To oversimplify matters dealt with in much richer detail in this book: The first stage might be seen as a time of White Protestant hegemony, and it lasted well into the 20th Century. "Protestant hegemony" sounds like a terribly negative phrase. I don't mean it that way. American Protestantism—and I say this as a Catholic—deserves credit for helping shape our heritage of religious liberty. Protestantism also shaped our national character and our nation's identity to the point that American Jews and Catholics, Muslims and Sihks, Buddhists, Hindus, atheists—just about all of us—are more than a little bit Protestant. That's something my friends in the Vatican used to note with some frustration when I was covering them as a journalist in the mid-1980s.

Our nation drew upon this shared Protestant spirit to connect people to one another and to the institutions of their common democracy. Lincoln's Second Inaugural Address may have been one of the finest statements of this shared identity.

If not everyone shared in this Protestant identity in a theological sense, everyone did more or less identify with the institutions it upheld. And it was one of the great virtues of this American Protestantism that it underwrote religious toleration and liberty. It is that commitment to religious liberty that allowed Catholics and Jews and then Muslims and many others to settle here—and, ultimately, helped unsettle Protestant dominance.

White Protestant hegemony in America—the first stage—began to erode with the Scopes trial and the end of Prohibition, arguably the last political project to unite mainline and fundamentalist Protestants. But the formal dominance of Protestantism was repealed in the 1960s, with, it must be said, the strong support of many moderate and progressive Protestants themselves. Thus began the second stage.

The second stage involved a hard push for separation, including many of the relevant court decisions such as the ban on public school prayer. It was no accident that all this occurred as the country was coming to terms with its historic treatment of minorities.

John F. Kennedy's election as president marked the full entry of Roman Catholics into the mainstream of American civic life. The civil rights movement sought to right historic wrongs done to African Americans. The era swept away long-standing barriers to Jews and brought the effective end of restrictive covenants. It led to new movements to defend the rights of immigrants from Latin America, Asia, and the Caribbean. Their numbers became even larger after the liberalization of immigration laws in 1965. In their racial diversity, these groups brought with them religious diversity as well. All this brought the pervasively white and Protestant ethos in government-financed institutions and society into question.

The third stage of the debate, which we are going through now, reflects a concern over whether the push to reduce Protestant Christianity's public role may have had the effect of marginalizing faith's public role altogether.

Religious conservatives certainly played a key role in this challenge. They decried the growing "secularization" of America and engaged in what sociologist Nathan Glazer has called a "defensive offensive." It was meant to restore the consensus on values that existed—or at least was presumed to exist—before the 1960s.[3] Naturally and reasonably, those dismayed by the religious right saw separation as a bulwark against the growing influence of organizations such as the Christian Coalition and the Moral Majority.

But it's worth noting that most of the religious conservatives insisted that their goal was not the creation of a Christian nation—even though some in their ranks talked that way—but to preserve their own culture and faith commitments. The Christian conservatives cast themselves as a beleaguered minority suffering under the oppression of Washington and Hollywood. In a sense, as Glazer has written in another context, "we're all multiculturalists now." Ralph Reed, the Christian conservative leader was careful in his choice of words in describing his movement's goals. He said the Christian Right sought "a place at the table." He did not propose to take ownership of the table, or to drive others away from the table. You might argue that the phrase "a place at the table," especially when used by a leader of the religious conservative movement, represents the true triumph of religious pluralism.

In sum: The third stage of our debate involves an effort to preserve the great gains in religious liberty that characterized the second stage and yet also to protect religion's free exercise and its role in our culture. Today's commotion is the product of a vigorous renegotiation of religion's public role. At its heart is the concern raised by Stephen Carter. He wondered if our nation was replacing old prejudices of race and religion with a new prejudice against belief itself.[4] That, of course, is a concern that runs throughout this volume.

Perhaps the clearest symbol of the difference between the second stage and the third is the sharp contrast between the way John F. Kennedy treated his faith as a public issue, and how Joe Lieberman treated his.

Both men, of course, broke barriers as representatives of minority religions—as non-Protestants—in public life. But John Kennedy made the case for his own election on the grounds that his religion was *not important at all* to his role as a politician. His central assertion, politically necessary at the time, was that if ever his faith came into conflict with the Constitution or the public interest, he would resign. And, in truth, few outside the most anti-Catholic quarters—and certainly no one who actually knew Kennedy, as Arthur Schlesinger has written—believed that was even remotely possible.

Joe Lieberman's approach could not have been more different. He praised God in public. He thanked God for his new public role. He spoke at length about the importance of his faith and about the legitimacy of a politician bringing his or her faith to the public arena. Unlike Kennedy, Lieberman said: *My religion is really, really important to me.* He joked that as a result of all this, he became known as "Holy Joe," a title he said his mother quite liked but that he did not like at all.

Now notice something else here: In order to win acceptance from Protestants, especially evangelical Protestants, it was absolutely essential for John Kennedy to play *down* his faith. But when Joe Lieberman played *up* his faith and spoke of God, it was said that doing so—doing exactly the opposite of what John F. Kennedy did—was aimed at winning over *the very same groups* of evangelical Protestants (or perhaps their children and grandchildren). In Kennedy's case, Protestants feared he was too Catholic—that his religion would be too important to him. In Lieberman's case, conservative evangelicals worried that Democrats weren't religious enough, and Lieberman sought to reassure them.

It's important, of course, to remember the Kennedy story in understanding the growing movement over the last half-century to privatize religion. While I share the view of many of the authors represented here that privatizing religion can, indeed, promote a "gag rule" on the religiously engaged, the impulse to privatize had some honorable motives. Many Americans who experienced the Kennedy campaign—not to mention the Al Smith campaign in 1928—never again wanted what seemed like a patent religious test to be applied to a candidate for public office. If "public religion" came to mean public discrimination against a particular faith, many Americans said a very loud "No!" And they were right.

Similarly, many Americans—perhaps especially Mainline Protestants—reacted to the rise of the Christian Right in the 1970s and 1980s with unease and alarm. For many progressive Christians, the Christian conservatives seemed to be subordinating the Christian message to a very particular political agenda. Where, they asked, did anything Jesus said point to a reduction in the capital gains tax? But this itself was a religious reaction. What the moment required was a fierce and honest debate among religious voices about what their traditions required, not a flat rejection of religious voices altogether.

The problem lay not in the question about capital gains taxes, which was entirely fair, but in a response suggesting that all links between religion and politics should be sundered. In fact, Mainline Protestantism (and social justice Catholicism and Judaism) had long insisted on a strong link between the religious and public realms. To cite the names Reinhold Niebuhr, Abraham Joshua Heschel, John Courtney Murray, and Martin Luther King Jr. is to underscore the essential role religious voices played in our public life over the last century. The understandable reaction against the Christian Right in many quarters had the unfortunate side effect of proposing something untenable: that because of what was wrong with the religious right, religious voices should simply retreat from the public square. That was not about to happen—and, as this volume makes clear, it should not happen.

Let us be honest: Religion can create community, and it can divide communities. It can lead to searing self-criticism, and it can promote a pompous self-satisfaction. It can encourage dissent and conformity, generosity and narrow-mindedness. It can engender both righteous behavior and self-righteousness. Its very best and very worst forms can be inward-looking. Religion's finest hours have been the times when intense belief led to social transformations, yet some of its darkest days have entailed the translation of intense belief into the ruthless imposition of orthodoxy.

But the history of the United States, despite many outbreaks of prejudice, nativism, and self-congratulation, is in large part a history of religion's role as a prod to social justice, inclusion, and national self-criticism.

This volume is dedicated to Michael Lacey and Susan Nugent, and for the very best of reasons. Susan's generous spirit and vast abilities have long been invaluable to the Wilson Center and, in particular, its pathbreaking work in American intellectual history. She has been singly responsible for organizing numerous conferences, shepherding manuscripts through the editing process, and helping to ensure that this very publication saw the light of day. With grace and a gift of clear thinking, she makes the most difficult tasks look easy. Her thoughtfulness is always a blessing, and especially so in the sensitive area of religion and public life.

Mike Lacey has spent a lifetime insisting that intellectuals should take faith seriously, and that the faithful should engage the intellectual world. This commitment is fashionable now, but Mike pursued it when it wasn't. People who know Mike are deeply indebted to him—and I'm certainly one of those—but so are many who never met him, and yet have been inspired by the work that Mike has done and sponsored. Mike has always insisted that a proper understanding of the United States requires our being alive to the role religion plays in shaping who we are and what we do. This volume bears Mike's imprint throughout and is a reflection of his passion. Americans who are religious and Americans who want to understand religion owe him, as a well-known politician would put it, big time.

Notes

1. Jean Bethke Elshtain, "The Clinton Scandal and the Culture of the Therapeutic," in E. J. Dionne Jr. and John J. DiIulio Jr., eds., *What's God Got to Do With the American Experiment?"* (Washington: Brookings Institution Press, 2000), 101. See also Peter Steinfels, "Holy Waters: Plunging into the Sea of Faith-Based Initiatives," in E.J. Dionne Jr. and Ming Hsu Chen, eds., *Sacred Places, Civic Purposes: Should Government Help Faith-Based Charity* (Washington, D.C.: Brookings Institution Press, 2002), 327–37.

2. A more condensed version of this argument appeared in Dionne and DiIulio, 115–20.

3. Nathan Glazer, "Fundamentalism: A Defensive Offensive," in Richard John Neuhaus and Michael Cromartie, eds., *Piety and Politics: Evangelicals and Fundamentalists Confront the World"* (Washington: Ethics and Public Policy Center, 1987), 250–51.

4. Stephen L. Carter, *The Culture of Disbelief: How American Law and Politics Trivialize Religious Devotion* (New York: Doubleday, 1994).

Acknowledgments

The book that follows is meant to be less a thesis-driven tract than a suggestive contribution to a national conversation—a conversation that is already well under way. Hence, it is especially necessary for the editors to thank the wide variety of individuals and institutions that contributed to make it possible.

First and foremost, we wish to express our thanks to the Woodrow Wilson International Center for Scholars, a jewel of Washington's intellectual life, and one of the few places in that city, or anywhere else, where academic scholars and policymakers regularly meet and draw upon one another's knowledge for the furtherance of the public good. It would be hard to imagine a more appropriate memorial to Woodrow Wilson's public career—or a better context for the kind of inquiry this book attempts. In addition to providing material support for this project, the Wilson Center provided us with the venue for two public conferences, in February 2000 and April 2001, respectively, where preliminary versions of the papers offered herein were presented and discussed. We greatly appreciate the interest and support that Lee Hamilton, the Center's director; Philippa Strum, director of United States Studies; and others on the Wilson staff have shown for this project and others relating to the role of religion in public life.

The inspirational force behind the book is the Wilson Center's longtime director of United States Studies, Michael J. Lacey, who has recently retired from that position after thirty years of invaluable service. Although his name does not appear on the title page or in the table of contents, he was as much the editor of this volume as the two named editors. It is therefore fitting that the book should bear a grateful dedication to him. Without the benefit of his fertile mind, as well as his energy, vision, imagination, and gentle prodding, the project would surely never have gotten off the ground. As those who know him will attest, Mike is one of the world's great conversationalists—a man of catholic interests with a career-long dedication to the study of bureaucracy, national planning, reform, liberal political thought, welfare economics, and the institutional use of statistics, among many other subjects. Less well known, but just as integral to his makeup, are his Catholic interests, which have included a deep and growing engagement with the theological works of Bernard Lonergan. It took a capacious, multitasking mind like Mike's first to conceive of, and then convince us of, the value of a book about faith and policy in America. We hope the results will measure up to the standards of the one who inspired them.

Thanks are also due to Donald L. Critchlow, a former Wilson Center fellow, professor of history at St. Louis University and editor of the *Journal of Policy History.* His invitation to Hugh Heclo to guest edit a special issue of his journal led to the commissioning of six of the essays appearing herein. That issue, entitled "Religion, Politics, and Public Policy," appeared in Spring 2001, as volume 13, number 1 of the *JPH*. We appreciate Don's willingness to permit expanded, refined, and updated versions of those essays to appear in this book, along with others that were commissioned to complement them.

We are also pleased to acknowledge significant financial support coming from the Pew Charitable Trusts, which has done so much, in so many ways, to support the intelligent consideration of the relationship between religious faith and public policy in America. Pew's support, conveyed through their Christian Scholars Program, helped underwrite some of the expenses associated with the second of our Wilson Center conferences.

Valuable commentary and editorial advice came from, among others, Peter Steinfels, R. Laurence Moore, E.J. Dionne Jr., John Noonan, Philip Selznick, Samuel Beer, Marc Landy, as well as the editor of the *Wilson Quarterly,* Steve Lagerfeld, and the editorial staff of Woodrow Wilson Center Press, including director Joe Brinley and editor Yamile Kahn.

Last but not least, we want to thank Susan Nugent, program assistant to the United States Studies Division at the Wilson Center, whose amazing combination of boundless warmth and relentless efficiency made short and exceedingly pleasant work of the onerous logistical problems associated with organizing two conferences, a journal volume, and a published book.

Part I

The Big Picture

1

An Introduction to Religion and Public Policy

Hugh Heclo

Mention religion and public policy in the same breath and controversies about abortion, school prayer, the death penalty, and stem cell research will most likely jump to mind. This is because these are important, well-publicized public choices that arouse the religious consciences of many Americans. However, such issues are also particular instances of a much larger subject. That subject is the profound, troubled, and inescapable interaction between religious faith and government action in the United States. It is the topic of this book.

One hundred years ago, advanced thinkers were all but unanimous in dismissing religion as an outmoded, childish survival from humanity's mental infancy. Today what is being outgrown is the idea that modern man will outgrow religion. Contrary to the expectations of Sigmund Freud, Max Weber, John Dewey, and a host of others, religion has not be-

The author thanks James L. Heft, S.M., for his especially helpful comments on the first draft of this chapter.

come a vestigial remain of premodern culture. If anything, Americans at the dawn of the twenty-first century are more willing to contemplate a public place for religion than they had been for the past one or two generations. In this book we ask: What does it mean for religion to "reenter the public square?" What will it find there? What harm and what good might it do? A useful point of entry into the complex interaction between religion and public choice in the United States is to think historically about our present situation.

Glancing Backward

For most of American history, religion and public policy was not a subject that seemed to need much discussion. The widespread presumption was that there was, or should be, a direct correspondence between Americans' religious commitments and their government's public policy choices. When the oldest of today's Americans were born (which is to say in the days of William Jennings Bryan, William McKinley, and Theodore Roosevelt), the "public-ness" of religion was taken for granted in a national political culture dominated by Protestants. It was widely assumed that the United States was a Christian nation and should behave itself accordingly. Of course, exactly what that meant in practice could arouse vigorous argument when it came to such issues as alcohol control, labor legislation, child welfare, and foreign colonization. Nevertheless, it was essentially in a self-confident Protestant party system and moralistic political culture that any dissenters had to find their place.[1]

Those days are long past. During the twentieth century, religion increasingly came to be regarded as a strictly private matter of personal concern. It was this theme that presidential candidate John F. Kennedy articulated in 1960 as he reassured a national convocation of Baptist ministers about his Catholicism (a problem that only thirty years earlier had torpedoed the candidacy of New York governor Al Smith). Kennedy was widely applauded for the enlightened view that his religion and church teachings on public issues were a private matter unrelated to actions in public office. Intellectual elites in particular were convinced that such "privatization" of religion was a natural accompaniment of modernization in any society. By the middle of the twentieth century, Supreme Court decisions were also erecting a so-called wall of separation between church and state that was nationwide and stronger than anything known heretofore among the state governments. National bans on state-mandated prayer (1962) and Bible reading in public schools (1963) soon followed.

However, even while Kennedy spoke and Supreme Court justices wrote, there were strong crosscurrents at work. Martin Luther King Jr. and many other civil rights activists asserted the very opposite of any disconnection between religious convictions and public policy claims. King's crusade against segregation and larger agenda for social justice was explicitly based on Christian social obligations, duties seen as flowing from belief in the person of Jesus Christ.[2] Similarly, after the 1960s, the United States along with many countries around the world witnessed a political revival of largely conservative "fundamentalist" religious movements. These, according to prevailing academic theories, were supposed to have disappeared with the steam engine.[3] The horror of the September 11, 2001, terrorist attacks showed in the most public way imaginable that modernization was not relegating religion to an isolated sphere of private belief. Religious convictions could still terrorize. They could also comfort a nation and inspire beautiful acts of compassion.

Meanwhile, the dominating influences in American culture—universities, elite media, leaders in arts and letters—did move in the predicted direction during much of the twentieth century. What, at midcentury, had been mere embarrassment with old-fashioned religious belief had, by century's end, often become hostility to a Fundamentalist Christianity that believed in revealed truth.[4] Noting that the people of India live in the most religious society in the world and that Sweden is the most secularized society, sociologist Peter Berger has offered the provocative view that the United States can be usefully thought of as a society of Indians ruled by an elite of Swedes.[5]

From Secularization to Public Religion

In contemporary discussions of religion and public affairs, the master concept has been the idea of secularization. This volume will have much to say about secularization, but first it might help to offer a brief background.

The term itself derives from the Latin word *saeculum*, meaning "world" or "age." In a very general way, the idea of the secular directs our attention to the place and time of this world. In that sense, it presupposes a demarcation between the sacred and profane. Similarly, secularization is the corresponding process of attending more to what is worldly, as opposed to things religious and beyond time. For example, in the Catholic Church brothers, sisters, and priests who take the three vows of poverty, chastity, and obedience and live in communities are called "religious." Conversely, men ordained as diocesan priests, who do not take the vow of poverty or live in communities, work daily with the people of their parishes and are called "secular" priests. In calling the latter secular, the Catholic Church emphasizes their involvement in the day-to-day lives of ordinary people, the laity. When religious or diocesan priests leave the priesthood, they undergo "laicization." Another, more modern meaning of secular emerged at the time of the Protestant Reformation, when not only Catholic assets but also traditional church functions (charity, almshouses, education, etc.) were increasingly taken over by the political state.

This history provided the materials out of which the young social sciences of the latter nineteenth century developed their theories of secularization that dominated much of twentieth-century thinking. In this new scientific view of society, all human activity should be analyzed as historical phenomena, rooted in place and time, one thing unfolding out of another. Religion itself was just another human activity that should be understood historically. In other words, religion was an evolutionary social function moving from more primitive to higher forms. In this way, the idea of secularization became very tightly bound up with understandings of modernization and its outgrowing of religion.

As the twentieth century dawned, the "secularization" that religious traditionalists considered an abrupt wrong turn was viewed by leading modernists as a benign, progressive evolution of belief systems. Secular political organizations were replacing the welfare, educational, and other social functions of medieval religious institutions. So too, science and enlightened humanitarianism would provide the new creed that would displace religious superstitions. As society modernized, religion would more and more retreat to private zones of personal belief, while policymaking would deal with worldly affairs in a scientific manner neutral and indifferent to religious faith. Religion could rest comfortably in the modern state and do its individual soul work. Public life could proceed peacefully, safeguarded from passionate clashes over religious truth.

All of this, in very crude terms, is what became known as the secularization thesis. To be modern meant to replace childish fables of miracles with scientific knowledge of the world. It meant to disabuse the mind of religious superstitions and recognize the psychological needs that prompt humankind to create religious commitments in the first place. A modern person might still call things sacred, but it was his or her private call. In public life, the spell of enchantment was now said to be broken, or soon would be.

However, something happened on the way to privatizing religion. Speaking very schematically, the twentieth century appears to have witnessed a two-phase movement. For about the first two-thirds of the century, secularization seemed to predominate. In the last third of the century, the picture changed considerably. Religion refused to stay in the private ghetto to which modernity had assigned it. From the Islamic revolution in Iran, to the Catholic Church in communist Eastern Europe, to the Religious Right in the United States, religion reengaged with political history. The sociologist José Casanova has surveyed this resurgence of "public religion" and observes: "During the entire decade of the 1980s it was hard to find any serious political conflict anywhere in the world that did not show behind it the not-so-hidden hand of religion. . . . We are witnessing the 'deprivatization' of religion in the modern world."[6]

Moreover, this "going public" of religion was not an expression of new religious movements or quasi-religions of modern humanism. Rather, it was a reentry into the political arena of precisely those traditional religions—the so-called vestigial survivals—that secular modernity was supposed to have made obsolete. How can we best think about this thing called public religion in a time when government policies are becoming ever more prominent in people's lives? Like the people themselves, many policy choices seem to be both secular and religious.[7] In any case, at the beginning of the twenty-first century there can be no doubt that religion is a "public" as well as a private activity.

Ordinary Americans continue to declare a devotion to religion that is unique in comparison with other industrial nations. At the beginning of the twenty-first century, nine out of ten Americans say they believe in God and pray at least once week. Six in ten claim to attend religious services at least once a month (and 43 percent weekly). Religious nonbelief is a distinctly minority position (only 7 percent acknowledge being atheists, agnostics, or have no religious preferences and never attend religious services). Nonbelief is also hugely unpopular. Large majorities claim they would vote for their party's presidential candidate if that person were female (92 percent), black (95 percent), Jewish (92 percent), or even homosexual (59 percent)—but not if he or she were an atheist (49 percent). In the summer of 2002 a political firestorm greeted a decision by the 9th U.S. Circuit Court of Appeals that the words "under God" (which Congress added to the Pledge of Allegiance in 1954) violated the separation of church and state. As the hapless court backed down, polls showed 87 percent of Americans supported keeping God in the Pledge and 54 percent thought government should *not* avoid promoting religion.[8]

After declining sharply between the mid-1960s and late 1970s, the percentage of Americans saying religion is very important to them gradually increased to roughly two-thirds in 2001. At the same time, seven in ten Americans want to see religion's influence on American society increase and an ever larger proportion is concerned about the moral condition of the nation (and this includes two-thirds of young Americans seventeen to thirty-five years old).[9] By general agreement, the common culture has become coarser and more salacious, more given to profanity, gambling, pornography, the glorification of violence, and the like. Given the widespread criticism of America's moral tone, one may well wonder who is making this popular culture so popular.

It is probably no coincidence that the meaning of religious belief itself has been changing in recent decades. A great many Americans find that the search for "spirituality" is more important than traditional religious doctrines, confessional creeds, or church denominations.[10] Though most Americans say they want religion to play a greater public role to help check the poor moral condition of the nation, only one in four says that religious doctrines provide the basis for individual moral judgments about right and wrong. Even among born-again Christians, fewer than half say they base their moral views on specific teachings of the Bible. To claim that there are absolute moral truths (a view rejected by three out of four American adults in the 1990s) or that one religious faith is more valid than another has become widely regarded as something akin to spiritual racism.

The new cornerstone belief is that moral truths depend on what individuals choose to believe relative to their individual circumstances. Human choice has become the trump value and judgmentalism the chief sin. Thus for that large majority of Americans who want religion to become more influential in American society, three-fourths say it does not matter to them which religion it is that becomes more influential. Similarly, between 80 and 90 percent of Americans identify themselves as Christians, but most of these Christian believers dismiss some of the central beliefs of that religion as Christianity has been heretofore understood.[11] Richard John Neuhaus has aptly summarized the situation: "To say that America is a Christian nation is like saying it's an English-speaking nation. There are not many people who speak the language well, but when they are speaking a language poorly, it is the English language they are speaking."[12]

What all this means for politics and public policy is a mystery left to be examined. Americans both want and distrust religious convictions in the public arena. Unlike activists in religious groups, more than 60 percent of Americans want elected officials to compromise rather than vote their religious beliefs, even on issues such as abortion, the death penalty, and gay rights. In recent decades, Americans generally have become more open to having religion talked about in the public arena, but 70 percent also think that when political leaders talk about their faith they are just saying what people want to hear.

Most people surveyed are willing to see religious leaders speak out more on public issues, but they also do not care much if they do. In the spring of 2001, as President George W. Bush's faith-based initiatives were gaining publicity, three-quarters of Americans expressed strong support for the idea of such groups receiving government funds to provide social services. However, the same proportion opposed government-funded religious groups hiring only those people who shared their faith-based beliefs. But then again, most Americans opposed funding American religious groups that were Muslim or Buddhist, and even Mormons were marginal. Here is crooked timber indeed for building a framework for religion and public policy.

This thumbnail sketch hints at a wonderfully rich story about religion and democracy in modern America. Unfortunately, it is a story that has been ignored and even suppressed in public school textbooks and university curricula. Both educational venues were largely purged of "God-talk" after the mid-twentieth century—itself a revealing development. So sparse has been the sowing of traditional religious information that one could accurately designate younger cohorts of Americans passing through the school system as a "seedless" generation.[13] A less polite term for this strange, religiously lobotomized view of culture would be heathen. It leaves the public sector of life feeling like (in Søren Kierkegaard's phrase) "a kind of gigantic something, an abstract and deserted void which is everything and nothing."[14] The premise of this book is that such ignorance is a sandy and extraordinarily dangerous foundation on which to build an American future. The intersection of religion with public affairs is a powerful, culture-shaping force. Never mind thinking outside the box. Americans have been losing the capacity to think inside the box.

An Overview

Our aim in the following pages is to step back from isolated controversies and consider the larger transactions between religion and public policy. What has happened between these domains in the century just ended and what does this portend for the years ahead? The following chapters focus on how the influence of religion has been, and ought to be, accommodated in the conduct of public policy. Although this is a large subject, public policy is not all of public life and the religious influences we write about are certainly not all of American religion. Christianity is the religion this book discusses at length because it is the one that was most directly connected with important policy issues during the past century. In 2001 the Gallup poll found 82 percent of Americans described themselves as Christian, down slightly from the 89 percent in 1947 when the polling question was first asked. In comparison, only 10 percent of Americans put themselves into all non-Christian faith categories and 8 percent reported being non-believers.[15] Protestants and Catholics have dominated the American story, but as we also shall see in subsequent chapters, Islam has to be a growing presence in public thinking.

Likewise, there are specific policy issues this book does not address. For example, abortion, assisted suicide, and genetic engineering are important subjects where people's religious beliefs cut deeply into the public choices that must be made. These controversies remain in the background of this volume so that we can focus on the broader political engagements between secular and religious commitments within which such particular debates take place.

To appreciate what the following chapters do have to say, it is useful to be more explicit about the common categories Americans typically have in mind, even if vaguely, when they confront this book's topic. Probably the first thing that comes to our minds is the idea about separation of church and state. Often, the average citizen even invokes judicial language (which we will be surprised to find is not in the Constitution) about "a wall of separation between church and state." Visualizing the public square, the easiest things for us to perceive are the structures—a church building here, a government building there, both separate institutions. And that, Americans have long believed, is as it should be.

However, if the wall metaphor has not blinded us, even casual observation also shows us that there is more than this going on in the public square. Perched atop an ostensible wall of separation between church and state structures, we watch a public forum where religion and politics are anything but separated. There are not two kinds of people in the forum, some religious and some political. There are only citizens there, and they are expressing themselves both religiously and politically as they jostle together. Yet when we look still more carefully, we realize there is more than just expressive behavior going on. Religious, nonreligious, and antireligious ideas are at work in people's heads. And from these outlooks, people in the public square are constructing definitions of problems and selecting concrete measures to deal with them, collectively, as a people. Religious and nonreligious ideas are becoming intermixed through enacted programs on behalf of some vision of the social order.

Church and state, religion and politics, ideas and social action—these are crosscutting features that we often sense as present in the public square, even if they are categories that can remain unconscious and thus unarticulated. They suggest a schema that may be helpful in thinking about the chapters to follow. Major interactions between religion and public policy seem to occur across three domains.[16]

The first domain is *institutional.* Here attention focuses on the way organized structures of religion and government impinge on each other and together on society. It is a perspective that comes most naturally to Americans because it is genetically encoded, so to speak, with their nation's constitutional understanding of itself. The bland phrase "separation of church and state" conceals what was the historically unique and most audacious thing about the U.S. experiment in self-government: the commitment to a free exercise of religion.[17] It is on this institutional level, with national and then state government, that one encounters the contests over government sponsorship of religious organizations and disputed infringements on groups claiming the unfettered exercise of religious liberties. Less obviously, it is also where one finds religious and public agencies grinding against each other in the conduct of such things as educational and welfare policies.

The second dimension of interconnectedness between religion and public policy can be termed *behavioral.* By this, one means nothing grander than the idea that religious attachments move people to act in public ways (e.g., voting, community organizing, and other political activities). It is important to notice that there is a direct, though paradoxical, link between these first and second dimensions. The hands-off distancing between religious and government institutions has meant that religion in the United States could be a free-forming and immensely rich resource for the nation's politics. The astute observer Alexis de Tocqueville concluded that his American informants were correct—the main reason religion held great sway over their country was the separation of church and state: "By diminishing the apparent power of religion one increased its real strength."[18] Since Tocqueville's visit in 1831, Americans in religious association have created and sustained movements promoting the abolition of slavery, women's rights, prison and asylum reform, child welfare, worker protection, mothers' pensions, liquor regulation, racial desegregation, and civil rights legislation. People moved to political action through religious affiliations have also been an important resource in more routine party politics and elections.

The third dimension of connections between religion and public policy is more difficult to put into words. But one senses, almost instinctively, that something very important is still missing if we simply give an account of organized institutions and politically relevant behavior. Lacking a better term, we might call this third sphere *philosophical*, understanding this as broad policy outlooks on the social order. Here one is trying to appreciate the intersection of religion and policymaking where ideas and modes of thought are expressed in programmatic courses of action. It is the realm people are operating in when they speak about culture wars in the schools, the work ethic in welfare, or the need for a moral clarity in foreign policy. It is the basis on which some people cringe and others rejoice in anticipation when a presidential candidate talks about his personal relationship with Jesus Christ. The cringers know that religion can mask all manner of hypocritical mischief in public affairs, and the rejoicers know that it can yield principled striving for a better world. Both are right.

Far from being about abstract thought experiments, this philosophical level ties back into the first two domains we have been discussing. Consider that early American policy philosophy contending for separation of church and state. In keeping the new national government out of religious matters, the formal Constitution was constructed, as some have described it, as a "godless" document.[19] This is not because religion was unimportant to the society but because it was extraordinarily important. As a matter of prudent political predictions—in the behavioral dimension noted above—the Founders understood why the Constitution had best keep essentially silent on matters of religion and God. In general, the dangers of political division based on religion were fresh in historic memories of Europe's religious wars. More particularly, the fragile coalition behind the proposed Constitution would be endangered by any statements about religion and devotion to God that might compete with the abundant state and local government dealings on the subject.

Yet, in relating calculations of political behavior and institutional design, the Founders were also drawing on a deeper set of philosophical understandings already present in society. These were ideas about individual conscience identified with Protestantism, and they had been tested and refined during decades-long encounters among concrete communities of religious believers and dissenters in the colonies all along the Atlantic seaboard. Thus behind the separating of church and state loomed an emerging cultural commitment to the free exercise of religion. This state-limiting, free exercise norm was mainly a religious achievement pursued in search of genuine religiosity. Generally speaking, champions of religious liberty were not secular philosophers but religious people who were convinced that religion could never be authentic if it was directly or indirectly coerced through government.[20]

The point, then, is that institutional, behavioral, and philosophical categories are three interrelated perspectives important to the subject matter of this book. The reader encounters their connections in every one of the following chapters, although the emphasis differs as the chapters proceed from the more general to the more specific policy perspectives. The state, political society, and civil society can be distinguished. They can be studied apart. But they are lived together in the one life of the nation. How are we to understand what this life has become? When religion reenters the public square, what will it find there?

Part I of this book consists of three chapters that look at the "big picture." These chapters focus on core features of the institutional confrontation between religion and public authority: secularism, constitutional doctrine, and the very idea of a public religion.

In chapter 2, Wilfred McClay describes the confrontation between modern secularist and religious commitments in the United States. Religion—beleaguered by its confrontation with a militant secularism in the twentieth century—is reentering a public square where such secular thinking has itself become passive and is on the defensive. Even postmodernists find it lame. To be sure, the so-called culture wars express genuine conflicts about very important things. However, they are not total wars. The time is ripe for rejecting an assertive secularism that has functioned in the public square as a kind of antireligious religion. Instead, McClay identifies a second concept of secularism that offers constructive hope and deserves support in the years ahead, not least of all because its antitheocratic vigilance can be a boon to religion. Secularism rightly understood will disadvantage illiberal versions of any religion—Christian, Muslim, or other—and that is as it should be in American democracy. However, this democracy will also need the clear and present voice of orthodox religion to sustain what is truly human in a society of stunning technological changes.

Religion reenters a public square where the institutional rules of engagement between religious claims and the secular state are made and unmade in the courts. This judge-made view of public religion is a twentieth-century phenomenon growing out of changing views of what the Constitution requires. In chapter 3, Charles Reid surveys this development of constitutional doctrine. His point of departure is an early-twentieth-century America that may seem like a different country, where religious freedoms were routinely subordinated to the interests of a self-proclaimed "Christian nation." The post–World War II era brought a flowering of protections for individual religious liberty demanded by national courts, usually against the desires of the states. However, there also developed a deepening morass of judicial efforts to eradicate any trace of government support for religion. Today, religion reenters a public square where, on the one hand, judicial reasoning about religious liberty is becoming incoherent and, on the other hand, there is near unanimous doctrinal confusion about what the separation of church and state means and requires.

In this legally messy public forum, how can an ordinary citizen get his or her bearings for thinking about the political role of religion? In chapter 4, José Casanova considers the essential meanings of a "public religion." Religion can be seen engaged in public roles with respect to the state, political society, and civil society. It is in this third sphere—in participating in the civic forum's open debate about public affairs and the common good—that religion needs to be de-privatized. There was a time when Americans hoped for a homogeneous moral consensus built around a kind of national civil religion. The battles over America's public schools as islands of secularity show that time is gone. Instead, a morally pluralistic, globally dependent American society will now have to strive for a working consensus through democratic contests about normative principles of public policy. Though it took several centuries, Catholics in America had to learn to do that kind of public business.

Casanova argues that the public Catholicism that emerged after the Second Vatican Council exemplifies the kind of public religion that is called for in modern America. Though some see an impending clash of civilizations in global politics, "a new experiment in intercivilizational encounters and accommodation between all the world religions is taking place at home." In the American setting, Muslims and adherents of other world religions face two options. They can adopt the older Catholic strategy of withdrawing into a defensive subculture trying to protect itself from corrosive Americanization. Alternatively, they can follow the newer path of Catholicism and organize themselves to be a public, self-assertive cultural option in a nation that is becoming the "first new global society." The choice is clear. Islam is already moving on the second path to become a public religion in the nation's political debates and one of the alternatives for being religiously American. Like Judaism and Catholic and Protestant Christianity before them, world religions are being Americanized in the new world and in the process are both transforming American religion and challenging traditionalist adherents of the religions in their international homelands.

Part II of the book focuses on religion in political action. Here the emphasis shifts from larger institutional perspectives to religious behavior in U.S. political processes (recalling, of course, that the courts discussed in part I are also part of that process).

In chapter 5, Wilson Carey McWilliams describes a developing revolution in American political society. The United States is well on its way to abandoning the historical view that saw religion as the basis for a moral community underpinning orderly self-government. Unlike the Founders, today's politicians are more apt to talk about the vague "faith" aspects of religion rather than about religion as a standard of right public action. The moral coherence and authority the Founders expected from the religious orientation of "good citizens" has dissolved on a variety of fronts. With moral principles now assumed to be tentative commitments based on personal choice and preferences, we—unlike the Founders—have good reason to be more welcoming of religious faith in the public square. However, that means tolerating, not merely watery faith-talk, but historical religious faiths that prophetically confront American society's feeble moral conversation. Such traditional religions confront our political choices with the claim that human beings have natural limits and high obligations that are not matters of mere personal preference. Against the prevailing penchant for tiptoeing around personal sensitivities, McWilliams upholds a more authentic debate and morally educational public role for religious believers.

The way American politics works, such believers are not isolated individuals but instead appear in the public square trailing clouds of collective partisanship. In chapter 6, James Reichley describes the party politics through which Americans have been religiously grouped and gained public influence. History shows that rather than destabilizing democracy, religion has been an enduring source of partisan competition. Northern Protestants have supplied much of the base for the Republican Party, whereas Catholics and Southern Protestants have done much the same for the Democratic Party. However, since the mid-twentieth century, many religious groups have changed their familiar alignments. Mainline Protestant denominations have increasingly split between liberal leaderships and moderate to conservative laities. Having been influenced by social issues such as abortion, Catholics now are only marginally Democratic. Despite some neoconservative defections to the Republicans, Jews remain heavily Democratic. The growing number of Muslim voters seem to be quite unsettled between the two parties. Most dramatically of all, Evangelical Protestants have switched from being politically passive and Democratic to becoming militant and Republican.

At the same time, cutting across religious groups is a deepening divergence between traditionalists and modernists. Traditionalists from each religion are finding common cause in resisting what they see as the growing influence of godless secularism. Wider than any gender gap today is the religious gap between Republicans and Democrats, the former disproportionately supported by religiously observant voters and the latter by nonchurchgoing Americans.

Historically, Protestants have been the dominant religious voice in American politics. In chapter 7, D.G. Hart examines the most visible form of religious political activism—the "Christian Right"—and does so within the larger context of Protestantism's troubled engagement with political society during the twentieth century. As McClay describes two kinds of secularism, Hart distinguishes Evangelical and liturgical Protestantism to offer two paths for conservative religion reentering the public square. The Evangelical Christian Right has pursued the first path in recent decades and fallen into an either/or impasse that fits strangely well with the agenda of militant secularists. Along this line of thinking, either the public square must welcome religion (serving Evangelicals' Bible-based political program for American society) or it must exclude religion (serving the nonbelievers' substitute "religion" of secular humanism).

Hart advocates the second path of liturgical Protestantism. Down this path, conservative Protestants can see politics as a legitimate means for restraining evil but as secondary to the church's holy calling and certainly not as a means for Christianizing American public life. Down this path, conservative Christians can hope to avoid the twentieth-century mistakes of mainline Protestants and enter the public square without allowing politics to distort their Christian faith.

Part III of the book is devoted to policy applications in thinking about public religion. The notion of "applications" should not be misconstrued as mere technical policy details. The applications in view are essentially ideas put into action for particular domains of public policy.

In chapter 8, John Coleman takes us deeper into modern American Catholicism—in other words, into the paradigmatic public religion sketched by Casanova in chapter 4. Coleman analyzes the ideas, organization, and methods of the Catholic Church and its specific engagements in public policy debate. Thus what the McClay and Hart chapters have to commend, respectively, in negative secularism and liturgical Protestantism, we can see taking concrete form outside the once-dominant Protestant political order.

Coleman's discussion of Catholic welfare programs leads us into two specific domains of domestic policy. Welfare (or "charity" as it would have been known in earlier centuries) and education have been the two central domains wherein the transformation of public roles occurred between church and state during the past five hundred years of modern "secularization." Here, of course, we confine ourselves to the twentieth-century American experience. In chapter 9, Stanley Carlson-Thies presents an overall account of public welfare policy and carries us into the current debate over government support for faith-based institutions. With this we see religion reentering the public square to reverse six decades of national policy developments.

Chapter 10 examines trends in exactly the opposition direction (what McClay calls "positive secularism"). Here, Charles Glenn offers a clear and provocative critique of our religion-free public school policies. He describes the movement of public schools from symbols of moral unity to islands of secularity beyond anything to be found in the U.S. military, the halls of Congress, or the courts themselves. It is a story of public philosophies and political behavior interacting to produce an institutional framework that all but casts religion as its enemy. If Glenn is correct, major changes of a truly pluralistic nature must lie ahead for public education in the United States.

The volume ends with religion in a public square that looks outward to the world. Chapter 11 takes up the much neglected connection between Americans' religious commitments and the nation's foreign policy. William Martin describes the long-standing involvement of religious forces with the U.S. role in the world. Far from being a thing of the past, religion properly understood is an essential asset for effective international statecraft. Not only religious leaders but unassuming groups of religiously motivated citizens can and do draw on the best of their religious traditions to promote policies of compassion, truthfulness, justice, and reconciliation. Moreover, America's religious freedom and vitality, growing out of the toleration established by separation of church and state, offers a constructive example to other religious peoples around the world. In such a world—with or without the threat of terrorism—authentic religion refuses to stay something private and confined inside people's heads and hearts. It demands to be engaged in the public choices that lie in government hands. It invites others to see that the United States has much more to offer the rest of the world than secular materialism.

This, then, is a bird's-eye view of the following chapters. However, it leaves us with the question: Why should a person make the effort to inquire into what these chapters have to say? The easiest thing to do is to adopt one of the popular intellectual shortcuts to escape the complexities of this subject. On the one hand, a person might cling to a simplistic formula that says religion and public policy really ought not to mix. On the other hand, one could strike a pose of worldly wisdom and claim the issue is simply a matter of religious groups' self-interested struggles for political power. The problem is that the first of these intellectual shortcuts is an illusion and the second is a lie that obscures real and growing challenges to the conduct of the public's business.

The Inescapable Coupling

Whether we like it or not, the connections between religion and public policy choices are profound and unavoidable. Government policy and religious matters are not the same thing, but neither do they exist in isolation from each other. The two are distinct but not separate.

The two domains intertwine because both claim to give authoritative answers to important questions about how people should live. Both are concerned with the pursuit of values in an obligational way. To put it another way, both religion and public policies deal in "oughts" and do so in terms of commands rather than idle suggestions or passing speculations.

Obviously, religion tells people how they should live. It can be less obvious that public policy also presents directives for living out some answers and not others. It does so because policy represents certain choices for society, and those choices are backed up by the coercive power of government. Like it or not, modern government policy is invariably in the business of mandating, promoting, discouraging, or prohibiting some ways of life and not others. Even adopting the comforting principle of "neutrality" involves bestowing approval and disapproval. Indifference is itself a way of taking sides. It can amount to a de facto claim that something is *not* a moral issue. The point, then, is that in a very deep, substantive way, the City of God and the City of Man are inescapably engaged in transactions with each other.[21] Our book is about the changing terms and meaning of that engagement in the United States.

Nevertheless, it is also obvious that religion and policy are not the same thing. Religion points toward matters of ultimate meaning understood as humans stand in relation to the sacred and supernatural. Religion—concerned with what is timeless, unchanging, and holy—is about the Absolute, or it is about nothing. In contrast, the courses of action pursued by government—its policies—are societal engagements with the here and now. Its meanings are proximate. At least in democratic (as opposed to totalitarian) government, policymaking acknowledges itself to be contingent, potentially erroneous, and changeable.

But exactly at this point we risk falling into another trap of simplistic, stereotyped thinking about our subject. Are religious people therefore to be seen as the ones who make absolutist pronouncements and the irreligious mind as the only one capable of tolerance? Is serious religion necessarily intolerant and are godless people the ones who can be counted on to engage the diverse public audience with persuasion rather than with asserting dogma? Not at all. This way of parsing the subject obscures too many of the spiritual possibilities in religion. It also obscures the inhumane possibilities in any godless morality that might be championed by secular Pharisees. It denies the possibility of a religious faith that, sensing the eternal and transcendent, renders relative and contingent all human institutions and claims to truth—including dogmatic religiousness as a form of idolatry.[22] It is possible for religion to foster toleration. It was, after all, Baptist voters in his district who gave the winning margin to elect James Madison to the new Congress, where he promised to introduce the Bill of Rights that enshrined religious freedom.

Likewise, if there can be contingent, humbling dimensions to lived religion, there can also be absolutist assumptions and dogmatically imposed faith surrounding supposedly contingent, secular policies. It is precisely the prideful claim that humankind is the center of the universe and that the purposes of the Almighty coincide with our human purposes that orthodox religion most relentlessly denounces. Religion and policy mark a continuous flash point in public life because the two touch precisely along that horizon where the great thing needful is to keep relative things relative and absolutes absolute.[23]

In modern intellectual circles, a fashionable strategy for pursuing the decoupling of religion from policy debate has been to argue for "dialogic neutrality." According to this view, religious conviction may be the motivation, but in democratic debate religionists must learn to translate and give publicly accessible reasons for their policy claims, reasons that are secular inasmuch as they can be shared beyond one's particular religious grouping. As the philosopher Richard Rorty has put it, "The main reason religion needs to be privatized, is that, in political discussion with those outside the relevant community, it is a conversation stopper." In this view, a comment to the effect that "Christian discipleship requires that I oppose abortion" is equivalent to someone else saying "Reading pornography is the only pleasure I get out of life these days." Rorty argues that both elicit the same response in the public sphere: "So what? We weren't talking about your private life."[24]

On the other side are those who claim, with justification, that the dominant commitment to translation, far from being dialogically neutral, amounts to a demand that religious believers be other than themselves and act publicly as if their faith is of no real consequence.[25] By accommodating only secular reasoning, religious believers will not only adapt and translate themselves out of any meaningful democratic existence. By doing so, they can also create a shriveled "public" that has no room or even awareness of theological grounds for discussing serious normative issues.

In this debate about public debate, one is essentially encountering a contest over the practical meanings of religion. At the beginning of the twentieth century, William James anticipated the basic outlines of this contest in his famous work *The Varieties of Religious Experience.* James rejected the intellectually fashionable "survival theory" that religion is merely fading superstitions held over from premodern times. Instead, he found religious life arising from an awareness of one's personal connection with a transcendent reality mediated through the subconscious self. Although James's book is now remembered mainly for this seminal interpretation that allegedly privatized religion, he in fact had much more to say.

James's conclusion was to draw a sharp contrast between what he called "universalistic supernaturalism" and "piecemeal" supernaturalism." The former basically corresponds to a view that some today would call spirituality. It sees an abstract, ideal dimension separate from the world of phenomena. At most, it is an illuminator, provider of meaning, a source of sensibilities to the facts already given elsewhere in nature. Piecemeal supernaturalism sees a transcending but imminent power that is all that, plus a postulator of new facts in the world as well. It filters through and bursts into the world of phenomena at particular points. It enters into the flat level of historic experience and interpolates itself piecemeal between distinct portions of nature with facts of its own. And these facts are dispositive for guiding practical conduct in the world.

The claim for dialogical neutrality fits comfortably with a view of religion as universalist supernaturalism. If this sounds too abstract, we need only reflect upon the way contemporary politicians use religion, a theme that will be developed in chapter 9. To be sure faith, and even Jesus, is invoked. The problem is that the God who is brought into the public sphere does not seem to count for much. No policy consequences seem to follow.

In contrast, piecemeal supernaturalism insists on the scandal of doing religion in public. William James left no doubt where he stood in this contest over the meaning of religion:

> In this universalistic way of taking the ideal world, the essence of practical religion seems to me to evaporate. Both instinctively and for logical reasons, I find it hard to believe that principles can exist which make no difference in facts. But all facts are particular facts, and the whole interest of the question of God's existence seems to me to lie in the consequences for particulars which that existence may be expected to entail. That no concrete particular of experience should alter its complexion in consequence of a God being there seems to me an incredible proposition.[26]

In other words, to orthodox believers God can never be dialogically neutral.

If nothing else, these introductory comments should raise warning flags: Thinking about religion and public policy requires thinking in complex rather than simplistic ways. Doing so means harkening to what might be taken as a prime commandment of all religions—to "pay attention"—that is, to look past the surface of things and not assume that what meets the eye is all that is going on. Religion in politics is sometimes full of hypocrisy and hate. It is also sometimes full of light and life.

A Timely Retrospective

Brute facts are looming that make it particularly worthwhile just now to pause and take stock of recent history regarding religion and public policy. The first fact is the ever-expanding role of national policy in Americans' lives. During the course of the twentieth century, struggles over federal policy increasingly served to define the American political and cultural order.[27] In other words, conceptions of who we are as a people more and more were translated into arguments about what Washington should do, or stop doing. Abortion is the obvious example, but to see the point one need only to consider our thinking about race, the role of women, crime, free speech, economic security in old age, how our children are to be educated, or people's relation to the natural environment, to mention just a few.

Reflecting this trend, academics and then the public after the 1950s began to make unprecedented use of the term "policy" as a category for understanding American political life. However, the century as a whole germinated, nourished, and spread the modern syndrome of "policy-mindedness"—an addiction to the idea that everything preying on the public mind requires government to do or stop doing something. In this situation, almost any human activity can be seen as charged with policy relevance, from the design of toilets to sexual innuendo in the workplace (filigrees of environmental policy and civil rights policy, respectively). Like it or not, our cultural discussions and decisions are now policy-embedded.

Second, it is good to take stock now because technological advances have brought our nation to the point where profoundly important public choices are becoming inescapable. Of course, scientific knowledge has been accumulating over many centuries of human investigation of the natural world. Particularly in the late twentieth century, however, much of modern society's earlier investment in basic research cumulated in technological applications able to affect human life on a massive scale. For example, in 1827 the existence of the human egg was first discovered, and only in the middle of the twentieth century was the DNA structure of life discovered. Since then, momentous applications of this accumulated knowledge have come in a crashing rush. By 1978, the first "test tube" (in vitro-fertilized) human baby was born. By the 1990s, the first mammals had been cloned, human manipulation of "designer genes" had begun, and the first financial markets for human egg donors had developed.

Other scientific advances are requiring portentous decisions about artificial intelligence and the reconstitution of the human brain, the meaning and prolongation of death, organ regeneration and human manipulation of the structures of life, the reconstruction of matter at the atomic level of nanotechnology—to mention only a few issues. Americans' rather loosely religious, all-tolerant spiritual questing is occurring in a technological society that demands public policy choices with ever more far-reaching consequences for the meaning of human life.

Likewise, scaling up in the other direction to global life, only since the mid-twentieth century has the growing technological impact of modern society on the environment become known. At the end of the 1950s, Rachel Carson offered the first dramatic account of humanity's disastrous impact on life and the earth.[28] Within eight years, human beings saw the first pictures from space of their common Earth home. The point is not simply that issues such as ozone depletion, species extinction, and global warming have never been thought about before our own times. The point is that these are examples of portentous matters that people have never before had to deal with as objects of collective decisionmaking—which is to say as matters of public policy.

Inescapably, the extent to which ethics leads or lags behind technology is now measured in the particular policy decisions produced by our political system. Those most knowledgeable about twenty-first-century science and technology are often the ones most worried. In accepting the Templeton Prize for 2000, the distinguished scientist Freeman Dyson observed that science and religion must come together to make decisions about humanity's fate. Likewise, in offering a melancholic reflection on the meaning of his own work, Bill Joy, the founder and chief scientist of Sun Microsystems, describes how the transformative power of new technology forces us "to confront the issue of what we are to become. . . . Science is providing possibilities but no useful limits."[29] If all this is so, there is no escaping a future where religious faith intertwines with the politics of policymaking.

Here is a powerful case for the timeliness of this volume's topic. Modern technological civilization is the first with such outward reach, bringing all societies within a common destiny; and it is also the first with such penetrating inwardness, putting the very structures of life and matter into human hands. This is more than information overload. Driven by the apparently unstoppable momentum of scientific and technological know-how, it is a specter of policy choices drenched in religious and cultural implications as to what humankind is and how we should live. One might say many things about this technology trap. That it is going to go away is not one of those things.

Finally, in a time of growing cultural diversity, it is especially important to pause and search for common understandings of what has been happening to us. Without some minimally shared memory, it is difficult even to have an "us." On the one hand, twentieth-century America experienced declining geographic and class differences. The churning of advertising and consumption in a single mass market has homogenized material life throughout the fifty states.[30] On the other hand, however, with uniformity in this dimension has come greater acceptance of variation in the realm of cultural meanings and values. Slogans such as "identity politics," "culture wars," "inclusiveness," and "political correctness" have become common in recent decades. Their widespread use reflects how much affirmations of diversity have supplanted earlier assumptions about a cultural core. "Multiculturalism" is simply the way of labeling a host of changes in demographics, group self-consciousness, and educational philosophy. With Muslims outnumbering Presbyterians in today's United States, multiculturalism is more than faddish academic terminology. Nominal Christians still outnumber non-Christian believers eight to one, but America is becoming a more truly multifaith, post-Christian society.[31]

Thus while we wrote in 2000, beyond the arbitrariness of turnover in a century's calendar, there are three substantive reasons why now is a good time for citizens to take stock of interrelations between religion and public policy. Begin with a vast political society that more and more defines itself by self-consciously making collective decisions about what to do and not do. Add a technological imperative that expands this society's policy agenda to raise ever more profound questions—the nature of life, brains, reproduction, death, and the sustainability of humankind's earthly existence. Policy-mindedness and the technology trap together would be challenge enough, but to these we must add the third feature: an increasingly fragmented sense of cultural identities among the self-governing people who are called upon to oversee those decisions. These three observations imply that the interaction of religion and public policy will be, to say the very least, a growing challenge in the years ahead.

In this light, we have tried to produce benchmark essays that any citizen can consult to gain a fair and usable idea of the twentieth century's "big picture" concerning American religion and public policy. More particularly, we hope the results will be broadly educational for the coming generation of young believers and nonbelievers who will have to deal with each other and with the implications of this history in the next century.

The Wages of Entanglement

Many people consider it disturbing, if not downright dangerous, to invoke religious commitments in matters of public policy. There are good reasons to think this way. Because religion makes claims about ultimate truth, compromise can be not only difficult; it may be interpreted as sinning against God. Yet, compromise is what makes peaceful politics possible. Thus mixing religion and policymaking opens pathways to intolerance, persecution, and bloody-mindedness in the body politic. The mixture stirs the modern mind's vague but potent memories of crusades, inquisitions, and religious wars. It was to this dominant understanding of religion that John Lennon could appeal in his popular song "Imagine" describing an ideal future: "Imagine there's no countries/ It isn't hard to do/ Nothing to kill or die for/ No religion too/ Imagine all the people/ living life in peace."

People are probably less likely to recognize the opposite danger that policy engagement poses for religious persons. Far from being intolerant of error, political engagement can encourage crass expediency, duplicity, and hypocrisy (not to mention a focus on the allurements of fund-raising).[32] Even if religious folk avoid these snares, such high-minded people are easily exploitable. Writing about the fall of the Roman Empire, Edward Gibbon observed that for philosophers all religions are false and for common people they are all true. But, he said, for politicians all religions are useful.

In other words, mixing religion and policy is likely to call forth not only worldly knaves and naive saints but also the worst of crossbreeds: knaves who appear saintly. A subtler, frequently overlooked danger for the religious outlook is that policy engagement often reveals unanswerable puzzles and contradictions among "God's people." This in turn may not only shake the faith of believers. It is also likely to deepen doubts among religious skeptics and supply abundant ammunition to those who are actively hostile to all religion. Thus, on all these counts, it is only prudent to recognize that, as one of our authors has said, when religion touches politics, politics touches back.

Growing as they do out of centuries of hard experience, these first two major points are far from groundless worries. Nevertheless, there are also reasons to welcome the mixture of religion and public policy. There can be a benefit to religion itself, because engagement with policy concerns gives concrete meaning to otherwise abstract commitments. Apart perhaps from passing mystic encounters, it seems that to be in touch with the universal one has to be connected to the concrete, or as it was put more succinctly, faith without works is dead. Seeking to influence the policies that will guide their society is an important way for people of faith to live out their beliefs. This is especially true in a system of self-government where religious consciences can never be purely public or private.

There are also gains for society in acknowledging and positively valuing the mixture of religion in public policy debates. For one thing, with modern policies touching ever more profound issues of life, there is a dangerous narrow-mindedness in dismissing religious perspectives as if policymakers had finally settled the great questions of human existence. Without religion mixed into the policy conversation, society runs the risk of falling for false claims of moral "neutralism"—the too easy reassurance that policy choices depend merely on technical knowledge or popular convenience. Neutralism is itself based on fundamental assumptions, beliefs, and leaps of faith. Having to confront bodies of overtly religious people whose fundamental assumptions are out in public can do much to bring the hidden secular assumptions of policymaking to light.

There is more at stake, however, than a tolerant open forum and better public debate process. Religion adds something vitally important to the content of what is being said. It asserts that there is a transcendent purpose that gives meaning to who human beings are and what they do. The religious voice insists that God-inspired standards be taken seriously in the way a society governs itself, that questions of right and wrong, better or worse are more than matters of passing opinion. By its nature, religion rejects fainthearted stabs at real virtue and is ferociously opposed to easy excuses about nobody being perfect. Religion insists that leaders and everyone else measure up rather than adjust the yardstick.

However, the point is not simply that religion is a valuable foundation for moral behavior, thus preventing liberty from descending into license. Religion can also have overarching value for the very humanity of society. It is a religious outlook that contends for both the immortal grandeur and the fallenness of humankind—a God-imaged part of the creation raised above the natural world but not above God. It champions this view, not as poetic metaphor, but as an essential conviction about the factual reality of human existence. The way of orthodox religion elevates the narrow ridge between essential human worth and essential human humility. On the one hand, if human beings live no more meaningfully and die as conclusively as animals, they are unlikely to possess any qualitative, intrinsic difference in value from animals. On the other hand, if humanity is its own god, what may it not do? Neither of these is a happy thought when it comes to the life and death issues that rushing technological changes pose for modern public policy.

Thus, religion stirs up troublesome and deep issues in public debate. Nevertheless, it seems far healthier to have such trouble in a modern developed democracy than not to have it. Religion contends that action in history is meaningful beyond any passing material concerns. If traditional religion is absent from the public arena, human beings can be counted on to invoke secular religions to try to satisfy their quests for meaning.

There have indeed been crusades, inquisitions, and religious wars in past centuries, but men and women have also been raised to extraordinary achievements by authentic religious teachings. Religion's unworldly ideals have the capacity to sober us with the shocking realization of how far we fall short of what is holy, Secular faiths can't even recognize the gap. As G.K. Chesterton foretold in 1905, "the permanent and urgent danger of fanaticism is from the men who have worldly ideals. . . . The ideal which intoxicates most is the least idealistic kind of ideal."[33] Twentieth century history, not the premodern history of religious inquisitions, carries the most relevant warning for today's Americans. Throughout the century just ended, a succession of anti-democratic and anti-theistic political ideologies exploited people's yearning for meaning and social idealism. It was an atheistic faith in humankind as creator of our own grandeur that lay at the heart of communism, fascism, and all the horrors they unleashed for the twentieth century. And it was adherents of traditional historical religions—such as Martin Niemöller, G.K. Chesterton, C.S. Lewis, Dietrich Bonhoeffer, Karl Barth, Reinhold Niebuhr, and Martin Buber—who warned most clearly of the tragedy to come from humanity's self-deification and the hubris of attempting to build our own version of the New Jerusalem on Earth. Such warning voices may be at least as valuable in the high-technology world of the twenty-first century.

If religion is to have a place in public life, the question naturally arises of how to accommodate it. Some extremely thoughtful people have recognized the stunning power over all life of humankind's technology and have decided that it renders obsolete 2,500 years of ethical discourse. For them, one or another form of paternalistic guardianship seems the only way out.[34] In contrast, the faith of American democracy is in people's ability to talk their way through their problems, but rarely with final closure. Of course, the democratic conversation is at times contradictory, shortsighted, and base. But it need not be that, and the great religions can enrich that conversation about the kind of people we will become. Unfortunately, while political activists have sharpened their slogans against each other in the values debate and culture wars, ordinary Americans seem infantile in discussing the public claims of religious conviction. A recent report on religion and public life puts the point ever so politely: "This study and other opinion research do suggest that many Americans have not thought very carefully about the implications and potential downsides of many of their views."[35]

In examining what has happened in the interactions of religion and public policy, the following chapters seek to integrate accounts of both theory and practice. We have tried, not always successfully, to avoid the academic inclination to force the history of ideas and events into two separate compartments. Too often, the result is intelligence divided against itself. On one side, the academic temptation is to weave elaborate but abstract interpretative theories that are out of touch with concrete social realities. If they were honest, many academics could not recognize their own lives in their theories. On the other side, practical-minded realists are tempted to rummage through the politics of policymaking—who gets what, when, how—to show yet again that self-interest rules, as if in such struggles no larger meanings for individuals and society were at stake. The problem is that self-interest is not self-defining.

Probably the most helpful way to think about the subject matter of this volume lies in the response given by the English philosopher Alfred North Whitehead to a student who asked: Which is more important, ideas or events? Neither, was Whitehead's answer. What matters most are ideas about events. The following chapters teach that these idea-event linkages are the work, not simply of intellectual theorists, but of a people's historical existence together. This includes their life together in light of their understandings about God. The core of history is not a series of naked events but a sequence of essential attitudes toward events, attitudes that are themselves a product of collective memory handed down from one generation to the next.[36] Without this, a people cease to be a people.

The authors of the following chapters do not shrink from presenting their own ideas about the meaning of events and recommending future choices. They do so, however, after giving a great deal of attention to how we got to where we are. Why should a person care about this history? It is a reasonable question. For a reasonable answer, one can do no better than invoke the thinking of an American who, toward the end of his life, seemed to embody an almost mystic union of religious and political sensibilities. As the great bloodletting to come gathered momentum, in 1858 Abraham Lincoln sought perspective: "If we could first know where we are, and whither we are tending, we could then better judge what to do and how to do it."[37] This remains good advice: First pay attention and try to know where you are. We hope this volume will help contribute to that more careful thinking.

Notes

1. Sydney E. Ahlstrom, *A Religious History of the American People* (New Haven, Conn.: Yale University Press, 1972), 776.

2. Richard Lischer, *The Preacher King* (New York: Oxford University Press, 1995).

3. José Casanova, *Public Religions in the Modern World* (Chicago: University of Chicago Press, 1994); early findings from the American Academy of Arts and Sciences's five-volume publication on worldwide fundamentalism appear in Martin E. Marty and R. Scott Appleby, *The Glory and the Power: The Fundamentalist Challenge to the Modern World* (Boston: Beacon Press, 1992).

4. George M. Marsden, *The Soul of the American University: From Protestant Establishment to Established Nonbelief* (New York: Oxford University Press, 1994).

5. Cited by Richard John Neuhaus in *First Things*, June–July 2001, 72.

6. Casanova, *Public Religions*, 3, 5. The about-face in secularization theories is well illustrated in Peter L. Berger, ed., *The Desecularization of the World: Resurgent Religion and World Politics* (Washington, D.C.: Ethics and Public Policy Center, 1999).

7. As one of leading scholars of religion put it, ours is a "religio-secular, operative-passional, sacro-secular life and society"; Martin E. Marty, "The Sacred and Secular in American History," in *Transforming Faith: The Sacred and Secular in Modern American History*, ed. M.L. Bradbury and James B. Gilbert (Westport, Conn.: Greenwood Publishing, 1989), 1, 8.

8. *Washington Post*, June 30, 2002, A8.

9. The various statistics in this section can be gleaned from Steve Farkas et al., *For Goodness Sake: Why So Many Want Religion to Play a Greater Role in American Life* (New York: Public Agenda Foundation, 2001); Pew Forum on Religion and Public Life, *American Views on Religion, Politics, and Public Policy*. (Washington, D.C.: Pew Research Center for the People and the Press, 2001); and George Barna and Mark Hatch, *Boiling Point* (Ventura, Calif.: Regal Books, 2001).

10. Robert Wuthnow, *After Heaven: Spirituality in America since the 1950s* (Berkeley: University of California Press, 1998); and David G. Myers, *The American Paradox: Spiritual Hunger in an Age of Plenty* (New Haven, Conn.: Yale University Press, 2000); Philip Rieff, *The Triumph of the Therapeutic: Uses of Faith after Freud* (New York: Harper and Row, 1966); Paul C. Vitz, *Psychology as Religion: The Cult of Self-Worship* (Grand Rapids, Mich.: Eerdmans Publishing, 2nd ed., 1994).

11. Although a little more than eight in ten Americans claim to be Christians, only three in ten hold that salvation is a gift of God through faith in Jesus Christ, as opposed to something earned through good works. For this and similar findings, see Barna and Hatch, *Boiling Point*, chapter nine, "What Americans Really Believe."

12. *First Things,* June–July 2001, 72.

13. George Barna, *Third Millenium Teens* (Ventura, Calif.: Regal Books, 2002).

14. Søren Kierkegaard, *The Present Age* (London: Oxford University Press, 1940), 41.

15. Gregg Esterbrook, "Religion in America: The New Ecumenicalism," *Brookings Review*, winter 2002, 46.

16. The schema is adapted from Mark Noll's introduction in *Religion and American Politics*, ed. Mark A. Noll (New York: Oxford University Press, 1990).

17. John T. Noonan Jr., *The Lustre of Our Country: The American Experience of Religious Freedom* (Berkeley: University of California Press, 1998).

18. Alexis de Tocqueville, *Democracy in America*, ed. J.P. Mayer and Max Lerner (New York: Harper & Row, 1966), 273.

19. Isaac Kramnick and R. Laurence Moore, *The Godless* Constitution (New York: Norton, 1996). Explanations for the Constitution's godless language are examined historically by John F. Wilson, "Religion, Government, and Power in the New American Nation," in Noll, *Religion*, 77–91; and Daniel L. Dreisbach, "In Search of a Christian Commonwealth," *Baylor Law Review* 48, no. 4 (1996): 927–1000.

20. See Noonan, *Lustre of Our Country.*

21. Deeper interpretations of the historical transformation in these transactions cannot be dealt with here. A provocative account is Marcel Gauchet, *The Disenchantment of the World: A Political History of Religion* (Princeton, N.J.: Princeton University Press, 1997). For a valuable counterpoint, see Charles Taylor's foreword to this volume, as well as his *Sources of the Self* (Cambridge, Mass.: Harvard University Press, 1989) and *A Catholic Modernity? Charles Taylor's Marianist Award Lecture* (Oxford: Oxford University Press, 1999).

22. See Glenn Tinder, *Tolerance and Community* (Columbia: University of Missouri Press, 1995), chap. 3.

23. This is exactly the viewpoint Richard Niebuhr identified behind the Founders' commitment to religious freedom. See his 1939 lecture, "The Limitation of Power and Religious Liberty," reproduced in *Religion & Values in Public Life*, 3, no. 2 (1995): 1-3.

24. Richard Rorty, *Philosophy and Social Hope* (New York: Penguin Books, 2000), 169ff. In a less provocative vein, the case is set out in Kent Greenawalt, *Private Convictions and Political Choice* (New York: Oxford University Press, 1995).

25. This case is well developed in Stephen L. Carter, *The Culture of Disbelief: How American Laws and Politics Trivialize Religious Devotion* (New York: Basic Books, 1993). Others would confine the requirement for secular reasoning to the adoption of coercive policies on others. See Robert Audi and Nicholaw Wolterstorff, *Religion in the Public Square: The Place of Religious Convictions in Political Debate* (Lanham, Md.: Rowman & Littlefield, 1997).

26. William James, *The Varieties of Religious Experience* (New York: Modern Library, 1929 [first published 1902]), chap. 20. The quotation is taken from pp. 511–12.

27. For an important argument about the way federal government growth helped catalyze religious conflicts, see Robert Wuthnow, *The Restructuring of American Religion: Society and Faith since World War II* (Princeton, N.J.: Princeton University Press, 1988).

28. Rachel Carson, *Silent Spring* (Boston: Houghton Mifflin, 1962), which first appeared as a series of articles in the *New Yorker.*

29. "Why the Future Doesn't Need Us," *Wired* Magazine, April 2000, at http://www.wired.com/wired/archive/8.04/joy/html.

30. Frank Levy, *The New Dollars and Dreams* (New York: Russell Sage, 1998).

31. Richard E. Wentz, *The Culture of Religious Pluralism* (Boulder, Colo.: Westview Press, 1997).

32. For a recent recognition of this danger from two leaders of the Religious Right, see Cal Thomas and Ed Dobson, *Blinded by Might* (Grand Rapids, Mich.: Zondervan, 1999).

33. G.K. Chesterton, "Heretics," appearing in *The Collected Works of G.K. Chesterton* (San Francisco: Ignatius Press, 1986), vol. I, 176.

34. Hans Jonas, *The Imperative of Responsibility* (Chicago: Chicago University Press, 1984).

35. Farkas, *For Goodness' Sake*, 45.

36. Maurice Friedman, *Martin Buber's Life and Work: The Middle Years 1923–1945*, vol. 2 (New York: E.P. Dutton, 1983), 137.

37. Acceptance speech before the Republican Party state convention, Springfield, Ill., June 16, 1858.

2

Two Concepts of Secularism

Wilfred M. McClay

Looking back over the century just ended, it is not easy to assess the status and prospects of secularism and the secular ideal in the United States. As is so often the case in American history, when one sets out in search of the simple and obvious, one soon comes face to face with a crowd of paradoxes. The psychologist Erik Erikson once observed that Americans have a talent for sustaining opposites, and he could hardly have been more right. Such Janus-faced doubleness, or multiplicity, is virtually the American *specialité de la maison.*[1]

Consider a few examples. The American Revolution was, as Samuel Johnson delighted in pointing out, led by valiant freedom fighters—who were also the owners of slaves.[2] It would be hard to imagine a nation whose self-conception has been more firmly wedded to moralistic idealism—or to unabashed materialism.[3] The same nation that worships a high-octane, near-anarchic style of individualism is also the nation that in practice puts a stiflingly high premium on social conformity—even if the standard being conformed to is one tailor-made to look fashionably anarchic, like a pair of hand-faded, designer-torn blue jeans, purchased off the rack.[4]

More to our present purpose, consider another American paradox: that the vanguard nation of technological innovation, the world's principal exemplar of capitalism's powerful and inexorable "creative destruction," is also the industrial world's principal bastion of religious faith and practice—a nation that continues to sustain remarkably high levels of traditional religious belief and affiliation, even as it careens merrily down the whitewater rapids of modernity.[5]

This last paradox is doubly perplexing, because it simply was not supposed to be possible. Sociologists from Max Weber to Peter Berger were convinced that secularization was merely one inevitable facet of that great and powerful monolith called "modernization," and hence they trusted that secularization would come along bundled with a comprehensive package: urbanization, rationalization, professionalization, functional differentiation, bureaucratization, and all the rest.[6] If by "secularism" we mean a perspective that dismisses the very possibility of a transcendent realm of being, or regards the existence or nonexistence of such a realm as entirely irrelevant to the concerns of the visible, material world, then, according to the social scientists, we should have expected religious belief and practices to wither away by now, as the forces of modernization gathered strength. The taboos and superstitions of the great world religions may have transmitted a useful kernel of moral teaching. But their supernaturalism and irrationality were vestiges of the human race's childhood, properly doomed to the ash heap of history. Our growing mastery of the terms of human existence would seem to make it more and more inevitable that this world can, and should, be understood entirely on its own terms, through the exercise of human rationality. Secularity in all its fullness would arrive as naturally as adulthood.

Needless to say, we did not require the events of September 11, 2001, to tell us that these expectations have not been realized. The world we contemplate at the dawning of the twenty-first century remains vibrantly, energetically, and at times maniacally religious, in ways large and small, good and bad, superficial and profound, now as much as ever. If the "secularization theory" long promoted by social-scientific students of religion has been fatally undermined, as many believe it now has been, the unanticipated resiliency of religious faith in twentieth-century America could certainly be regarded as exhibit A, the single most arresting demonstration of the theory's inadequacy.[7]

How Secular Is America?

And yet, one should not admit this claim of persistent religious faith too quickly. Perhaps, one might argue, it is still too early to call the secularization thesis a complete failure in describing the United States. Perhaps the religious efflorescence we see at present is merely defensive and compensatory, an anxious and fleeting reaction against modernization's incursions, a shallow therapeutic response to passing stresses, or an atavistic reflex that will fade, atrophy, and eventually die. Indeed, in many respects, one could say that the United States has never been more thoroughly under the command of secular, and even militantly secular, ideas. The nation's elite culture, particularly as one sees it mirrored in the mass media and academe, is now almost entirely committed to a standard of antiseptically secular discourse, as denatured and delocalized as a Midwestern radio announcer's voice, in which the rational and value-neutral language of science and therapy has displaced the value-laden language of religion.[8] In addition, a steady stream of Supreme Court decisions since the 1940s have had the cumulative effect of severely circumscribing the opportunity for any public manifestation of traditional religious symbols and sentiments, thereby helping to create what has been called "the naked public square."[9]

Perhaps, to continue in this vein, the United States has lagged far behind Western Europe in completing the historically inevitable movement toward a purer form of secularity—but it is getting there just the same. True, it still is home to organized religious groups of surprising size and strength, and conflicts over the treatment of religious issues by, for example, the public schools seem as endemic as ever. But the influence of these conditions has been more than balanced by the affirmation of a "godless" Constitution and a growing structure of laws that effectively contain religion's influence upon public life.

Religious expression has not been stamped out, and there is no need to do so. Instead, it has been pushed to the margins, confined to a sort of cultural red light district, along with all the other unfortunate frailties and vices to which we are liable. Religion is tolerated as a form of irrationality to which fragile human beings, in this transitional stage of human history, are still unfortunately prone.[10] People are left free to believe what they wish, and even to act in private on their beliefs, as long as they do not trouble the rest of us with them, or bestir the proverbial horses. The point is to confine those beliefs entirely to the private realm, and deny them exposure and leverage in public affairs. Some who hold to this view offer themselves as friends of religion. Others are skeptics, or even avowed enemies.

But both are united in the belief that a "naked public square" is the price we must pay for the nonestablishment and liberty embodied in the First Amendment.

That, as I say, is where the secularizing view of recent history would take us. But there is another way of seeing matters, one that seems more plausible. In this latter view, secularism's seeming hold over the moment is illusory, unpopular, elitist, and doomed to fail. In this view, the claim that religious liberty can only be advanced by the federal imposition of a naked public square has come to seem as absurd as the Vietnam-era tactic of destroying villages in order to save them. On the contrary, in this view, religion has responded to the challenge of secularism with a vigorous defense of its appropriate role as an essential player in public life—one that, whatever one thinks of it, shows no sign of going away quietly.

Indeed, there is a growing sense that—in a postmodern world dominated by immense bureaucratic governments and sprawling transnational business corporations that are neither effectively accountable to national law nor answerable to any well-established code of behavior—religion is an indispensable counterweight and resource for upholding human dignity and moral order, for "speaking truth to power." Modernity, argues sociologist José Casanova, runs the risk of being "devoured by the inflexible, inhuman logic of its own creations," unless it restores a "creative dialogue" with the very religious traditions it has eviscerated and abandoned.[11]

Perhaps no event in the past quarter-century has given more credibility to this view than the profound influence of the Roman Catholic Church in engineering the downfall of communism in parts of the former Soviet empire; and no modern religious leader has been more keenly alert to the public uses of his faith than the current pope.[12] But even on strictly American grounds, there is plentiful evidence that publicly vigorous religious beliefs and practices have survived all efforts to suppress or supersede them, and are now ascendant.

One can gauge the extent of this not only by recourse to Gallup, Roper, and Barna polls but by examining shifts in public discourse. Ever since the election of Jimmy Carter in 1976, the taboo on public expression of religious sentiments by U.S. political leaders seems to have been steadily eroding, to the extent that in the 2000 presidential campaign candidates publicly invoked God and Jesus Christ at a pace not seen since the days of William Jennings Bryan.[13]

Perhaps even more indicative of change was the fact that all the candidates, Republican and Democratic alike, as well as President Bill Clinton himself, warmly endorsed the efforts of what are called "faith-based" organizations for the provision of social-welfare services.[14] Indeed, Clinton himself, although remaining an object of inexhaustible scorn for religious conservatives, again and again successfully invoked biblical and quasi-biblical language in his administration, not the least in his own self-defense.[15] Cynics may chuckle at such manipulations, or at the candidates' professions of faith; others may object strenuously to them, as inappropriate to public settings. But such rhetorical gestures are a form of recognition. One cannot successfully appeal to a standard, even if one does it entirely ritualistically, if that standard is not widely acknowledged as legitimate.

The signs are amply reflected, too, in a long list of developments in the realms of law and governance. President Clinton enthusiastically signed into law the Religious Freedom Restoration Act (RFRA), a 1993 bill buttressing the "free exercise" clause of the First Amendment, and commanding support from a collection of constituency groups so universal as to be almost surreal, ranging from Concerned Women for America and the Christian Coalition to the National Council of Churches and the American Civil Liberties Union.[16] When the Supreme Court struck down RFRA, the outcry against them came from Right and Left alike. The 1997 federal welfare reform legislation included an option for "charitable choice," which opens up the system to the provision of public social welfare services by openly religious organizations, operating on a contract basis but supported directly by tax revenues. President George W. Bush has attempted, albeit without resounding success as of this writing, to translate this new openness to nonsecular service organizations into a wider role for faith-based initiatives in solving social problems.

As always, a significant number of flash points have clustered around issues relating to public schooling. Perhaps the most notable of these was the Kansas Board of Education's decision in August 1999 to omit details relating to evolutionary theory from its optional teaching standards and standardized tests, a move that ignited a frenzy of accusation and ridicule, somewhat out of proportion to what the board had actually done.[17] But that controversy was, in a sense, a sideshow, when compared with the more significant incremental changes under way. The growing popularity of school-choice initiatives, a form of experimentation against which the public education lobby has fought with Alamo-like ferocity, promises to level the playing field for competition between religious and nonreligious schools.[18]

The Supreme Court's *Agostini* and *Zelman* decisions eased the country away from the strict taboo against public support for parochial and other sectarian schools, and its *Rosenberger* decision put college-campus religious organizations on the same footing as nonreligious organizations, with the same access to student activity fees.[19] Public schools and federal judges are asserting the importance of posting the Ten Commandments in their respective venues, while school districts in Alabama and Texas fight for the right to have student-led prayers at graduations and football games.[20] Not all these measures will succeed, and not all of them ought to. But the trend toward a reassertion of religious expression in education seems clear.

More generally, there seems to have been a rededication to the notion that U.S. religious life occupies a place of central importance in the nation's makeup. Even scholarly and popular writing on American history and politics has in recent years vigorously reasserted the centrality of religion in public life, and specifically in the founding of the country.[21] And the specter of religious persecution in the rest of the world, especially (though not exclusively) the persecution of Christians, has become a central galvanizing proposition for a growing number of American Evangelicals and Roman Catholics, whose religious convictions lead them to put pressure upon policymakers who must deal with such prominent offenders as China and Indonesia.[22]

And some things have never changed, even with secularism's impressive victories in the courts and halls of government and academe. Prayers are still uttered at the commencement of congressional sessions. God's name appears on our currency and in the oaths we take in court. Chaplains are still employed by Congress and the armed services. The tax-exempt status of religious institutions remains intact and unassailable. Belief in God remains astonishingly pervasive, and church and synagogue attendance rates remain high, at least relative to other Western countries.[23] President Clinton freely invoked his God and his faith, and carried his Bible around on a regular basis, without eliciting complaints from the American Civil Liberties Union. And his successor, George W. Bush, is arguably the most openly Evangelical Protestant president in modern American history, a leader who has not hesitated to use the language of good and evil in his presidential rhetoric.

In the national reaction to the September 11 attacks, no event was more powerfully significant as a national rallying point than the service for the National Day of Prayer and Remembrance, held on September 14 at Washington

National Cathedral, and attended by former presidents Clinton, George H.W. Bush, Carter, and Gerald Ford, former vice president Al Gore, and almost the entire Washington political establishment, including cabinet officers, senators and members of Congress, military officials, and members of the diplomatic corps.[24] Whatever one makes of these phenomena, the point is that this is still not an entirely secular country, one sanitized of any form of public sanction for religious faith.

An Uneasy Throne

One could easily continue in this vein. Yet the partisans of the secularizing view will likely not be persuaded. They may well respond that the majority's professed belief in God is thinner than skim milk. Such evidence simply illustrates Karl Marx's gibe about how revolutions tend to get mired down in the language of the ancien régime—but that no one should be thereby fooled into thinking that the secularizing revolution has ground to a halt.[25] The now-dominant secularism might seem to be conceding a good deal of ground to religion. But this actually serves to consolidate its rule, its advocates would argue, by seeming to show flexibility and give on relatively small points of language and symbolism.

Such flexibility can actually serve to sugar-coat more consequential social changes, which, once they have taken root, will eventually empty the old moral and theological language of all meaning. As the drama of President Clinton's impeachment amply demonstrated, the stern moralism once associated with American Protestantism is likely a thing of the distant past. It costs nothing, and means less, for a U.S. politician these days to genuflect in the direction of "religion," particularly if that religion is increasingly vague, nonspecific, diluted, and morally undemanding. Such gestures, in the secularizing view, are merely the verbal tics of a civilization in transition. A robust and entrenched secularism has nothing to fear from them.

Such a view has some truth in it. But it underestimates the importance of words and gestures as markers of legitimacy. And the very fact of such genuflection, even if that is all that it is, may nevertheless indicate how precarious and shallowly rooted are all the secularist advances. No one builds pedestals to the God of scientific rationality or the Comtean Religion of Humanity, although there is a booming trade in crystals, pyramids, horoscopes, and psychics. Indeed, even the public prestige of science has receded somewhat in our own day, as a consequence of science's growing politicization, its blizzard of inflated and conflicting claims about matters such as health and diet, and the public's fears, both founded and unfounded, that scientific and technological innovation has become a frighteningly impersonal, unconstrained juggernaut that lacks any sense of moral proportionality or ultimate ends.

The fact of the matter is that secularism in our day can claim no energizing vision and no revolutionary élan, not as in the past. Instead, it sits passive and inert, heavily dependent upon the missteps and excesses of the Religious Right or some similar foe to make its case, stir up its fading enthusiasm, and rally its remaining troops. Secularism sits uneasy upon its throne, a monarch that dares not speak in its proper name, and dares not openly propound its agenda, if indeed it still has one. For all its gains, it seems peculiarly on the defense, old and quaint, a tenured radical who has ascended to the endowed chair of culture only to spend its days shoring up the principle of *stare decisis*. Its victory, if that is what it has enjoyed, has not come without cost. For better or worse, the élan vital has gravitated elsewhere. These days it is rather more fashionable to be "spiritual" than to be secular.

There is no more powerful if indirect indication of secularism's rule—and the precariousness of that rule—than the challenge to it being mounted by a growing, intellectually sophisticated, and more and more ecumenical conservative religious counterculture.[26] This counterculture—which first emerged in reaction to the Supreme Court's 1973 decision in *Roe v. Wade* and the subsequent liberalization of abortion laws—includes in its membership a number of unaffiliated "fellow travelers" but is mainly made up of theological and moral conservatives drawn from the full range of organized denominations: Catholic, Jewish, and mainline and Evangelical Protestant.

Such a movement, particularly as embodied in Richard John Neuhaus's influential journal *First Things*, would have been inconceivable at any time in the past (i.e., before there was the perception of a powerful and entrenched secularist enemy to hold such a coalition together). In the past, the most conservative Catholics, Jews, and Protestants would have been the least likely to seek out common ground, and bracket their many differences, large and small, for the sake of presenting a unified front. That they are now willing to do so, with growing enthusiasm and commitment, is a tribute not only to their sophistication but also to the overriding effects of the secularist agenda.[27] It was once the case that to be ecumenical one had to be a liberal; but that is no longer true. There is now perceived to be something much larger than the historical differentia of the respective faiths at stake in the current struggles. That "something" is what we have come to call the "culture wars."

Postsecular Restlessness

The dynamics of culture wars should not, however, conceal the fact that the reaction against secularism in recent years is by no means restricted to political or cultural conservatives. Prominent liberals—such as the journalist E.J. Dionne, the law professor Stephen Carter, the theologian Harvey Cox, the psychologist Robert Coles, and the political theorist William Connolly—all have written against the inadequacies of a purely secular worldview.[28] They may offer the most powerful evidence of all for the decoupling of secularism from modernization, because they take the position, which is a less and less uncommon one on the political and cultural left, that a progressive or modernizing agenda need not be a secularizing one.[29]

At the same time, we should take note of a different but more and more influential critique emerging from the perspectives of academic postmodernism and postcolonialism, where Western secularism's claims to universal truth and impersonal rationality are increasingly held suspect, even condemned, as a form of cognitive imperialism. As a result, the claims of religion, especially "indigenous" religion, are no longer so easily bracketed as private and subjective. Indeed, in the postmodern dispensation, where knowledge is to be understood as something always rooted in, and inseparable from, the discourse of particular communities, religious assertions have as good a claim as anything else, and a better one than most, to the mantle of "truth."[30]

To be sure, such postmodernists tend to leave Christianity out of their formulations, considering it too much a part of the Western universalist hegemony. But nevertheless one can see a fascinating convergence of what might very loosely be called "fundamentalist" and "postmodern" perspectives, each very hostile to secularism, in the emergence of "postliberal" Christian theologies.[31] Such approaches to theology draw heavily upon recent literary theory and communitarian social thought, and they seek to reaffirm the authority of sacred texts. In that sense they strongly resemble American-style Protestant Fundamentalism or Evangelicalism. But they deal with the question of the sacred text's factual truth, an issue central to Fundamentalists and modernists alike, by choosing to bracket it or set it aside, stressing instead the text's deep embeddedness in the life of the sacred community. In other words, they assert the primacy of the "narrative" dimension of a sacred religious text—the fact that, to a believer, this sacred text embodies "our story," the story that has constituted "us" and in which "we" believe. Embrace of that story is a precondition of discourse itself. Hence one looks to the sacred text's narrative power, rather than its character as an inerrant textbook, as the source of its authority.

Although such an outlook may seem to concede a great deal of territory to the secular worldview, in fact it takes a stand that is potentially just as radical and challenging as that of Fundamentalism. For Christian "narrative theologians," the Bible, and not the world, is *the* primary reality through whose filter everything else has to be seen to be properly understood. They reason that, because the sacred narrative has in effect created the very discursive environment within which we operate, it has a primacy that cannot be subjected to anterior acts of rational examination and debunking. It is, for the believer, the functional equivalent of *cogito ergo sum*. "We" cannot get outside it, for to do so would be, as C.S. Lewis once neatly put it, as absurd as the scent trying to critique the rose.

It is not that there was or was not a literal Garden of Eden; such a question is beside the point. It is that "we" are constrained to see the world through *that* story of the Fall. The only alternative to doing so is the adoption of some *other* story—Buddhist, Darwinist, animist, whatever—as primary, because there is literally no world without a story, no Archimedean reality upon which one can stand outside such stories. Even the option of choice is not really open, because it implies—falsely—that there is some extra-linguistic phone booth one can duck into, however briefly, to make the change. The prison house of language and the structures of religious plausibility turn out to be one and the same thing.

Where this kind of thinking will take us in years to come is uncertain. As is so often the case in postmodernist efforts, one has the sense that the arguments are more forensically clever than profound, and may prove to have little staying power outside the hothouse of academe. The rise of radical Islamist movements with violent intentions toward the West seems to have elicited a fresh appreciation for Western virtues of tolerance and pluralism, and a diminished enthusiasm for postmodernism and postcolonialism. But that may prove to be only a temporary interruption of a long-term trend. In any event, their appearance underscores the fundamental point here being made. They suggest a restlessness with the regime of garden-variety Western secularism, in this case expressed from a position that cannot be called conservative in any traditional sense of the word—a position that has absorbed the insights of the Enlightenment and then gone far, far beyond them.

Reconstruing Our Conflicts

So let me again stress that not everything we see in the challenges to secularism can be made to take the shape of a culture war, particularly as seen and construed by the respective combatants. It is good to keep that in mind. But a great deal of it does fit the culture-war pattern, and it is also good to keep that in mind. Defenders of religion see an aggressive, arrogant, and all-but-triumphant secularism, which controls academe, the media, and the federal courts, and thereby largely controls public discourse. Secularists and their allies see in their opponents an incipient religious reaction, a dangerous cultural regression, a "return of the repressed" that would obliterate scientific inquiry and demolish individual liberty, and take us back to the Middle Ages. There is nothing imaginary about these conflicts. But there is nothing inevitable about their being couched in such extreme terms.

As the twenty-first century dawns, we want to find a way of construing our cultural conflict that faces the facts of social division without becoming a self-fulfilling prophecy of war.[32] The obstacles to this are formidable. There are, as sociologist James Davison Hunter has pointed out, structural considerations built into the institutional frameworks in which these national debates are now conducted, which tend to polarize the debates, harden lines of division, and accentuate the most extreme positions of either camp in order to mobilize both donors and troops.[33] The way we do public policy these days does not tend to make such dialogue very productive. For one thing, as I pointed out above, it makes it difficult to reckon with the fact that there are "liberal" believers and "conservative" secularists, and that such positions have legitimacy and integrity, rather than merely serving as forms of intellectual draft dodging, or ways of hiding out from the sterner alternatives on offer.

So the concept of "culture wars" may well further the very things it describes. But the most recent usage of the term, traceable back to Hunter's 1991 book of that name, has also had conceptual benefits. By granting the dignity of a rough parity to both sides, the term has helped us to see that the struggle between modernization and its discontents is not merely the battle of light against darkness, progress against backwardness, but does indeed have many of the qualities of a confessional struggle, pitting genuine and deeply held worldviews against one another—a struggle in which there is plenty of light and darkness, virtue and vice, to go around. Moreover, the culture-war model suggests that the conflicts described are not mere illusions or anxieties to be soothed away by therapy, or differences that can be finessed or coopted by a generous Madisonian pluralism.

To describe the conflict as a "culture war" is to insist that we are experiencing genuine conflicts over genuine things, and that the effort to simply split the differences among the U.S. population, by counseling a nonspecific moderation and prudential wisdom, and by following the utilitarian principle that one should give the least possible displeasure to the largest possible number, may have the effect of denying the moral urgency of what is at stake for the "hard" minorities on either both side.[34] Majorities can be wrong. And in this particular conflict, the stakes are high. The battle is being fought over nothing less than who will get to occupy the commanding heights of American life, and thereby define the nature and limits of the culture.

The Problem of Establishment

To speak of "commanding heights" is to raise the question of whether the United States is, or should be, an officially secular nation. In a sense, therefore, it is also to raise the question of whether there is a de facto U.S. religious establishment. This has always been a tangled and complex subject. Officially, of course, there never has been such an establishment. There are, as everyone knows, two "clauses" expressing the First Amendment's view of religion: a free exercise clause, and a nonestablishment clause. The two clauses are part of a single vision, because they compliment and mutually support one another, nonestablishment being a necessary precondition for free exercise, and free exercise being the surest way of ensuring the perpetuation of nonestablishment.[35]

But of the two, nonestablishment is surely the harder provision to observe and perpetuate. It is not hard to understand why this should be so. Just as nature abhors a vacuum, so the polity naturally seeks to have some unifying and binding principles to serve as a basis for its fundamental cohesion. There has to be a "final say" in a durable political order, and it is hard to keep a final say potent and vigorous with nothing more than an avowedly neutral proceduralism.[36] On the contrary: Everything we know about the functioning of a healthy political entity suggests to us the need for governing assumptions, legitimating myths, and foundational narratives to support it.

This is so partly because the neutrality of any procedure tends always to become suspect unless it can periodically be squared with, and refreshed by, reference to broader constitutional and moral principles. We need a *reason* to stay a "we." In the unpredictable and often chaotic flow of events, we need to have an ideal pattern or founding vision to look back to as a point of reference. Even neutrality relies upon certain prior axiomatic commitments, which are not themselves subject to procedural review. Otherwise we are, in Robert Frost's useful image, playing tennis without a net. No rules, no game.

In this respect, the radical and conservative critics of pluralism are right to point out that pluralism is not nearly as neutral or wide open as it pretends to be, because in practice it alters every available position to conform to its own image, thereby creating an unacknowledged criterion of public acceptability to which all other truth claims are discreetly subordinated.[37] When one begins to replace talk about competing principles or worldviews with talk about how certain positions deserve a "place at the table," eventually every religious position will be evaluated less for its truth than for its good manners. Such a concession is especially unsatisfying when one is speaking of questions of ultimate meaning and ultimate value, the questions that form the traditional subject matter of religion. The more reflective among us, contemplating this scene, will begin to ask: Is it not more revealing, and more important, to ask who sets the table, selects the guest list, and prepares and serves the food? Is secularism the real host of every such party? And the keeper of the pantry?

Beneath such interesting questions, however, is a deeper one. The historian George Marsden has argued that those in American academe have during the past hundred years merely exchanged one orthodoxy for another, granting today the same kind of commanding status to a strictly secular understanding of human existence that yesterday we granted to the Protestant Christian orthodoxy that secularism overthrew.[38] This would be remarkable, if true. Is there now a regnant secularist orthodoxy, which, though it usually rules genially and tolerantly, as in its dinner party mode, is ultimately intolerant of threatening deviations from its norms, as one can see in academe's suppression of explicit religious discourse and religious perspectives in scholarly discourse, not to mention hiring and promotion; or in its ferocious antagonism to the mere presentation of religious perspectives regarding human origins?

And, to phrase the question a little differently—more theoretically than empirically—is this the inevitable tendency of secularism, to become over time just as domineering and triumphalist, as comprehensive and crusading, as the religious faiths it once opposed? Is it accurate to speak of secularism as a kind of substitute religion, a reservoir of ultimate beliefs about ultimate things that stands, in that sense, in a continuum with, and in competition with, conventional orthodox religious faiths? Or is secularism more rightly understood as something quite distinct from, and more modest than, religion? Have we, caught as we are in a culture-war dynamic of secularism versus desecularization, perhaps lost sight of this distinctive quality of secularism, when it is rightly understood?

It gives an entirely different cast to this question if one looks for a moment beyond the Western world—the West being, as Peter Berger again and again has pointed out, the only part of the world where the juggernaut of secularization has been triumphant—and considers parts of the world where the connotations of the word "secularism" are rather different, though reminiscent of issues the West has not really faced since the days of its own wars of religion. The cultural crisis of the Islamic world as it struggles with its lingering theocratic tendencies perhaps presents the most obvious example of such troubles. But, to indicate how widespread the problem is, consider the following example, a *New York Times* news story dated December 6, 1999, dispatched from India.

On that day, the *Times* reported, police arrested dozens of activists who had gathered in the northern Indian temple town of Ayodhya to protest against, and mark the memory of, the demolition of a sixteenth-century Muslim mosque by Hindu zealots seven years before. That earlier event had sparked massive riots all over the country, leaving 3,000 people dead, and has remained a simmering issue ever since, a fresh contribution to the long, poisonous history of Hindu-Moslem relations in South Asia. Both Hindu and Islamic organizations put on demonstrations for the occasion, even though the Indian government had by law prohibited the assembly of more than four people on the anniversary day of the mosque's destruction. Ever since its destruction, militant Hindu groups, which refer to December 6 as "Victory Day," have been pushing to have a temple built on the Ganges Valley site, which they believe to be the birthplace of the god-king Rama. Muslims, however, have vowed to rebuild the mosque, carrying signs that read, "The jihad will go on." Meanwhile, miles away in Delhi, 300 activists from an organization called "Citizens for Secularism" marked December 6 with a march protesting the mosque's demolition.

Other examples could as easily be adduced. But this story neatly illustrates a simple point. What is meant by "secularism" will depend upon the cultural and historical context in which one is using the word.[39] In the context of contemporary American society, it means one thing: the demystified and disenchanted worldview of a postreligious society. But in the title of the Indian protesters' organization, Citizens for Secularism, it means something else. Not an antireligious worldview imposed by the state, but rather an antitheocratic understanding of a *secular* state that is fully compatible with the practice of religion—a hard-won achievement that is now so axiomatic in the West as to be virtually taken for granted even by the strongest proponents of religious revivalism.

This is not what we would normally call "secularism" in the West. When religious leaders complain of the mass media's secular prejudices, or when opponents of religion speak of "secular humanism," this is not what they mean. But that is precisely why I have found it valuable to insist upon using the word "secularism" in as broad a sense as possible in what follows, even if doing so has the effect of rendering equivocal and problematic a word that seems, at first blush, to be pretty clear in its meaning. For in preserving certain possibilities in words, one can also preserve their possibility in practice—among which is the possibility that there can be such a thing as "secularism rightly understood." Indeed, the Indian protesters' understanding of secularism is regarded favorably by most thoughtful religionists in the West, as a vital instrument to refine and restrain the expression of religious commitments, and to protect religious devotees from their own all-too-human tendencies toward fanaticism and blindness—traits that their own faiths themselves predict will reliably manifest themselves.

To be antitheocratic is then by no means to oppose religion. On the contrary, one can argue—as did Alexis de Tocqueville, the godfather of all "rightly understood" words—that the American tradition of antitheocracy has by and large proven to be a very great boon to religion, practically and morally, and essential to the maintenance of healthy religious commitments.[40] The extreme difficulty experienced by the nations of South Asia, and by nearly all the Islamic countries of the world, in establishing and sustaining such a bifurcation of commitments, suggests the crucial importance entailed in coming to understand secularism in a more nuanced way than is now the international norm.

Two Secularisms

How then are we to find the right balance in these matters, preserving what is good in secularism without ceding to it more than is its due? Recognizing that there is more than one way of dividing a pie, and many more than two ways of understanding the word "secularism," let me attempt to distinguish between two broadly distinct ways of understanding the concept, only one of which is an enemy of religion. There is, on the one hand, a way of understanding the secular idea as an opponent of established belief-including a *nonreligious* establishment—and a protector of the rights of free exercise and free association. On the other hand, one can understand the secular ideal as a proponent of established *unbelief* and a protector of strictly individual expressive rights, a category that includes rights of religious expression.

The former view is a fairly minimal, even "negative" understanding of secularism, as a freedom "from" establishmentarian imposition. For it, the idiom of secularism is merely a provisional lingua franca that serves to facilitate communication and commerce among different kinds of belief, rather than some new "absolute" language, an Esperanto of postreligious truth. The latter view, conversely, is the more robust, more assertive, more "positive" understanding of secularism with which we began this essay—the one that affirms secularism as an ultimate and alternative faith that rightfully supersedes the tragic blindnesses and destructive irrationalities of the historical religions, at least as far as activity in the public realm is concerned. By understanding religious liberty as a subcategory of individual expressive liberty, it confines religion to a strictly private sphere, where it can do little public harm or good.

The first of these two concepts of secularism, "negative" secularism, sounds almost identical to the language of the First Amendment. This fact in turn suggests that it is at least theoretically possible for there to be such a thing as a nonestablished secular order, one that is equally respectful of religionists and nonreligionists alike. Such an order preserves a core insistence upon the freedom of the uncoerced individual conscience. But it has a capacious understanding of the religious needs of humanity, and therefore it does not presume that the religious impulse should be understood as a merely individual matter—as if religion were nothing more than the private, individual way that each of us speaks to ourselves about the "mystery of human life."[41] On the contrary, it would insist that religion is also a social institution, for whose flourishing the rights of free association—by which we mean the right of co-religionists to form moral communities, which can congregate and include or exclude others from their ranks precisely as they please—are just as important as the rights of individual expression. It insists that pluralism is a necessary concomitant of liberalism, precisely because we are social creatures, whose social existence is a prior condition of all else that we value.

It might also be pointed out that the distinction between negative and positive understandings of secularism can be found neatly paralleled by competing understandings of the scope and meaning of the secular activity we call "science." There has been a powerful tendency since the advent of modern science to see its claims as competitive with, and ultimately triumphant over, those of traditional religion. Such a tendency may have been just as bad for science as it was for religion, tending to inflate the claims of science into a reductive scientism, replete with the declaration of metaphysical and cosmological certitudes that science, as such, has difficulty sustaining on its own terms.

A more modest, negative understanding of science sees it as an inherently tentative and provisional form of knowledge, defined by strict adherence to certain procedural norms involving the formulation of hypotheses, and the careful conduct of observable and replicable experiments to test those hypotheses. Such an activity is unable by its very nature to affirm or deny untestable claims about the nature of ultimate reality. To the extent that science appears to presume naturalism or atheism or the like, it may indeed be required to presume them methodologically—but not ontologically. It is not the business of science, for example, to confirm or deny the possibility of supernatural miracles. Such a carefully limited understanding gives the magnificent achievements of Western science their full measure of respect, without obliging us to construe science as a form of metaphysics and sworn enemy of religion.

Such subtle distinctions have generally been lost on the more militant secularists, which we will call the establishmentarian or "positive" secularists. Marx knew precisely what he was doing in attacking religion, but it is not so clear in the minds of today's positive secularists. In many cases, they honestly cannot imagine that they are imposing anything on anyone, which is why they consistently style themselves heroic defenders of civil liberties—or, more modestly, just People for the American Way. Indeed, that organizational name, whose breathtakingly self-aggrandizing qualities surely match any parallel offenses committed by the late and unlamented Moral Majority, perfectly expresses the unstated presumptions of our informal secular establishment. Their efforts have been aimed at creating and enforcing the naked public square. Such a regime seeks, under the guise of separating church and state, to exclude religious thought and discourse from any serious participation in public life, and to confine religious belief and practice, as much as possible, to the realm of private predilection and individual taste.

So we return to a key question: Is secularism itself a kind of faith, our new established religion? Or is it, rightly understood, something very different from religion, something cognitively distinct from religion, in just the way that science as a mode of inquiry and understanding is distinct from religion? Is there thus a way we can enjoy the fruits of secularity without making it into a substitute orthodoxy, a new establishment that has the distinction of being an establishment, not of a religion but of irreligion?

Two Liberties

My use of the modifiers "negative" and "positive" here will no doubt remind some readers of Isaiah Berlin's essay "Two Concepts of Liberty," to whose title I have shamelessly alluded in my own.[42] But I have not done so merely for literary effect. I believe there is value in exploring further the dichotomy that Berlin devised for our consideration, and seeking out any parallels or analogies his essay may suggest to us, by way of clarifying the concepts of secularism. Such parallels in fact arise almost immediately. Berlin set out in his great essay to explore the "permissible limits of coercion" in political life.[43] Our concern here is not at all dissimilar, because it deals with the appropriate limits of what I have called "establishment," which is itself a kind of moral and intellectual boundary. But the essay's suggestiveness does not stop there. It can be traced to the very heart of the essay, and Berlin's distinction between *negative* liberty, which designates a freedom from external interference, a freedom to be left alone, and *positive* liberty, which means a freedom to be self-governing and self-directed, to be "one's own master."

Stated thus—as freedom from meddling, versus freedom to be one's own boss—the two concepts of liberty may not seem very different. But as Berlin brilliantly demonstrated, each concept of liberty had implications buried within it that would ultimately cause the two to diverge sharply and arrive at very different destinations, with very different consequences. Negative liberty is freedom *from*; it involves warding off potential hindrances and guarding privacy, in the interest of creating the maximum "free area for action." It embodies the classical-liberal understanding of liberty, which seeks, to the fullest extent possible within the requirements of civil society, to preserve an essential zone of inviolable personal freedom, comprising those freedoms "which a man cannot give up without offending against the essence of his human nature."[44]

Berlin acknowledged that negative liberty would likely tend to lead over time to various kinds of inequality, and that it did not necessarily promote or mesh with conceptions of democracy or self-government. But he nevertheless chose to affirm negative liberty in the strongest terms, echoing the vision of John Stuart Mill: "To threaten a man with persecution . . . to block before him every door but one, no matter how noble the prospect upon which it opens, or how benevolent the motives of those who arrange this, is to sin against the truth that he is a man, a being with a life of his own to live."[45]

Positive liberty had aims that were higher and nobler. It sought more than merely getting government off one's back and other people out of one's way. Instead, it sought to free human beings to fulfill the most exalted elements of their nature. But it also was far more dangerous than negative liberty in Berlin's eyes, because its pursuit could so easily lead to authoritarian or totalitarian political arrangements. The logic by which Berlin arrived at this conclusion is especially relevant to our present purposes. He emphasized that, for human beings to become masters of themselves, they had to be self-overcoming and resolved to subdue the elements of recalcitrance or false consciousness, sloth, or appetite in their makeup, bringing them under the control of their rational faculties and "better selves."

This meant the practice of relentless self-coercion, in the name of a "higher freedom," precisely the sort of activity we would call self-discipline. But what starts out as self-coercion may in time become hard to distinguish from external coercion, because, as Berlin observed, "We recognize that it is . . . at times justifiable to coerce men in the name of some goal (let us say, justice or public health) which they would, if they were more enlightened, themselves pursue, but do not, because they are blind or ignorant or corrupt."[46] Such coercion is, of course, part and parcel of the rearing of children and the protection of dependents. But also for adults, there are times when we may have to be compelled by others to see the light, and even, to echo Rousseau's chilling phrase, be forced to be free.

By means of precisely such arguments, however, the door is opened for all manner of coercion in the name of honoring the "true self" and freeing it from illusion, from being "ruled by myths," and from various forms of "heteronomy," which meant for Berlin (as for Mill) "being dominated by outside factors in a direction not necessarily willed by the agent." Positive liberty seeks the maximum measure of rational self-direction and self-control; it seeks to say, "I can do what I will with my own."[47] Its ultimate goal is, to repeat, much more than a mere freedom from interference. It aspires to nothing short of a godlike state of autonomy and self-mastery. In so doing, it relies upon the demystifying power of modern science, both natural science and social science, to expose and dissolve the fears and illusions that support human irrationality. It thereby serves to illuminate the world with brilliant rays of absolute rational clarity.

Many of the greatest thinkers of the nineteenth century, men such as Auguste Comte and Karl Marx, were partisans of various forms of "positive liberty." They believed that "to understand the world is to be freed," but that most people are "enslaved by despots—institutions or beliefs or neuroses—which can be removed only by being analyzed and understood." Most of us live our lives "imprisoned by evil spirits which we have ourselves . . . created, and can exorcize them only by becoming conscious and acting appropriately."[48] Ye shall know the truth—and it is a scientific, secular, and naturalistic truth, to be sure—and that truth shall make you free.

But the very beliefs that enable one to penetrate the fog of irrationalist obfuscation that surrounds us can also tempt one "to ignore the actual wishes of men or societies, to bully, oppress, torture them in the name, and on behalf, of their 'real' selves, in the secure knowledge that whatever is the true goal of man . . . must be identical with his freedom—the free choice of his 'true,' albeit often submerged and inarticulate, self."[49] In the end, the ideal of positive liberty seemed to Berlin too dangerous—too arrogant and presumptuous, too prone to monism and "final solutions," too controlling and depersonalizing—to be endorsed. Hence his preference for negative liberty, and the pluralism it engenders, as "a truer and more humane ideal than the goals of those who seek in the great, disciplined, authoritarian structures the ideal of 'positive' self-mastery."[50]

Pluralism was, of course, the central political and social idea of Berlin's entire career. There are many goods in the world, he constantly asserted, and they are not necessarily in harmony with one another, or compatible with one another; indeed, they may even be mutually exclusive, without thereby ceasing to be good. Liberty, for example, exists in palpable tension with other goods such as equality, justice, happiness, security, and order. Therefore a political order that grants the greatest possible scope to the full variety of human goods is far preferable to an order that insists narrowly, tyrannically, upon only one. The consecrated life may represent a beautiful and noble ambition, perhaps the highest goal to which we can aspire as human beings. But it is not so unless we feel inwardly called to it. And it makes a very bad, very pernicious basis for political philosophy. If there is any place where the case for separating spheres, and the need to articulate secular principles, would seem to be airtight, it is here.

The Promise of Negative Secularism

Berlin's essay "Two Concepts of Liberty" remains, even after nearly a half-century, a rich and suggestive analysis, whose implications and ramifications extend far beyond the range of what Berlin himself could possibly have envisioned. Indeed, one is surprised to discover how adequately, if entirely unintentionally, its structure seems to describe the beleaguered state of religion today, as it struggles to evade the grip of a militant secularism. It is safe to say that Berlin, a secular Jew writing in 1958, could have had no such thing in mind. And yet his way of dividing up the concept of liberty also proves to be remarkably congruent with the different strains of secularism. Negative secularism, the secularism of nonestablishment, has many of the same virtues as negative liberty—an openness to diverse perspectives, whether religious or nonreligious, a commitment to free inquiry, free expression, and free association, and a "freedom from" the coerciveness of any "official" perspective, including that of militant secularism.

By the same token, positive secularism, the secularism of established unbelief, proves to have many of the same pitfalls as positive liberty. In affirming the secular ideal as an ultimate and alternative comprehensive faith, positive secularism also in effect embraces the dangerous ideal of self-mastery—an ideal that is quintessentially secular. In so doing, it also embraces an obligation to dispel the damaging misconceptions that prey on the minds of others, and to liberate them from the spell of priests, televangelists, and other purveyors of illusion. This will help them to discover their "true selves," of whose existence they had hitherto perhaps been ignorant, and help them along in the direction of greater and greater "autonomy." Whether this takes the form of coercion or not, the fact remains that positive secularism has all the sinister features of a crusading ideal—the very sort of ideal that Berlin warned against.

Standing athwart such transforming zeal, Berlin offered the following observation in the penultimate paragraph of his essay—words that form the culminating stroke in his defense of pluralism, but which well express the irreducible role and inescapable importance of religious faith in human existence:

> In the end, men choose between ultimate values; they choose as they do, because their life and thought are determined by fundamental moral categories and concepts that are, at any rate over large stretches of time and space, a part of their being and thought and sense of their own identity; part of what makes them human.[51]

And, one might add, whether or not Berlin had the persistence of religion in mind in writing these words, he could hardly have offered a more apt description of the reasons why a vibrantly pluralistic religious life in the United States is the only one compatible with the fullest possible respect for the dignity of the human person. For what is religion if not the most powerful of all expressions of ultimate values—values that, if truth be told, choose us, as much as we choose them? What positive secularizers have been pleased to regard with fear and contempt, or as an immense burden from which our "better selves" need liberation, negative secularizers regard as an essential (and inviolable) element in the warp and woof of our humanity.

This understanding of two secularisms may help explain the paradoxical situation with which I began this chapter, in which secularism seems at one and the same time both victor and vanquished. Because, in a sense, both assertions are true. Americans have by and large accepted the concept of negative secularism, and the fundamental respect for the human person that undergirds it, as an essential basis for peaceful coexistence in a religiously pluralistic society. To a large extent, any large-scale religious revivalism or enthusiasm the United States is likely to see in the years to come will have accepted the prior restraint that negative secularism imposes, and done so as a precondition of its very existence.

Indeed, the articulation of a well-considered theological basis for understanding and respecting "others" who are outside one's own tradition will be an essential element of those religions that hope to have the strongest public presence.[52] The signs are that religious activity and expression in the United States will continue to grow in strength and numbers in the years to come—but will do so largely within the container of a negative-secularist understanding of the world. The return of religious faith is not likely to be a fearsome "return of the repressed," at least not in the United States. For this, we can thank the very liberal tradition whose inadequacies religion has returned to correct.[53]

It follows, then, that religious faiths must undergo some degree of adaptation in accommodating themselves to negative secularism. They must, as it were, learn their table manners, and learn how to behave around strangers. But there is more to it than that. The key question adherents of those faiths must ask is whether such an adaptation represents a compromise of their faith, or a deepening and clarifying of it. And the answer may be a surprising one for those who think only in terms of the "war of science and religion" and the triumph of positive secularism, or who assume that all adaptation is mere trimming or acculturation.

It is true that the problem of how to adapt to negative secularism may pose insuperable obstacles for the most intransigent religious outlooks and traditions, if they have a rigid, poorly developed understanding of the "world," and of its relationship to the ultimate. They will, for that very reason, be all the more resistant to an adaptation that would, in their eyes, concede authority to the world over against their own traditions and sacred texts. Indeed, one of the most profound and consequential questions facing the twenty-first century is whether Islam will be able to achieve such an adaptation.[54] There is an inevitable tendency to equate the strength of a religious tradition with the extent of its intransigence.

But that need not be universally the case. If one may speak for a moment only of the Christian faith, the effects of such adaptation would seem to be largely positive, and an important "development of doctrine."[55] The principal effect is to remind Christians of something that they sometimes have lost sight of: that their faith *affirms* the world. It does not affirm the world as an absolute good, sufficient unto itself, nor as an exclusive focus for one's energies—nor without the qualifier that all Christians are obliged to renounce the world as the ultimate audience before which the drama of their lives is played.[56] But the world is a very great good nonetheless, and one whose goodness and order are inherent, because it is a world endowed by a Creator God with harmony, beauty, intelligibility, and usefulness that have not been entirely erased by the effects of human sin. The human inhabitants of that world, even the most thoroughly unregenerate among them, still bear the *imago Dei*, and all are the beneficiaries of what is called "common grace," which means that they remain fully capable of the finest acts of nobility, justice, love, and wisdom.

Because the activities of non-Christians have a full share of this inherent dignity found in the world, they therefore warrant Christians' respect and admiration, even when their activities proceed from non-Christian premises. It is not only an observable fact but a theologically sustainable truth that admirable qualities of mind and soul are not the exclusive property of one's co-religionists, and are not withheld from the nonbelieving artist, thinker, or politician. Nor should a religiously inspired thinker imagine that the only audience is among his or her own kind, and that devotion to God requires that one forswear a secular idiom that will be accessible to all. That is what the logic of a fuller understanding of the world entails, and makes possible.

Therefore the quality of mind we call "humanism" should not be seen as the sinister offspring of positive secularism, but as the lively child of a negative secularism, one that takes an soberly affirmative view of the natural potential inherent in human reason and imagination. "It is vital," writes cultural critic Ken Myers, that Christians "not regard art or science or the humanities to be evangelism carried out by other means." Nor, one might add, should complete withdrawal into gnostic otherworldliness, or any other form of extreme renunciation, be a collective goal either, although they frequently have been resorted to throughout the history of Christianity. (Indeed, as Isaiah Berlin has pointed out, they represent the ascetic form of "positive" liberty.)[57]

Instead, argues Myers, the purpose of these human pursuits, like the purpose of government and politics, is "simply to maintain fallen yet rich human life on the planet."[58] Even the famous biblical command to "Render unto Caesar what is Caesar's" represents a real commitment by the Christian to the legitimate scope of even the most unbelieving political rulers, and therefore the intrinsic worthiness and dignity, from the Christian perspective, of the worldly task of political governance.[59] It may be that Christianity is uniquely equipped for this task, and for sustaining an affirmation of the world that nevertheless asserts the priority of what lies beyond the world, precisely because it is so intrinsically ambivalent about the relationship between the immanent and the transcendent. But the task of adapting to a negative-secular order faces all the world's religions, if they are to bring any of their resources to bear effectively on the task of living in the next century.

Yet from this follows a final observation, which I fear may run the risk of restoring the very knotty complexity I have tried to unravel, but which I must at least touch upon. Given negative secularism's implicit respect for the world on its own terms, is it not necessary that we be prepared to endorse some set of normative standards inherent in nature—inherent limits and boundaries from which negative secularism derives its sense of the world's orderliness, regularities, and moral economy? And, to go to the heart of the matter, how much longer can it be meaningful to speak of the liberty of the individual person, when we are rapidly approaching the point where that liberty is taken to include the sovereign right to do whatever one wants with the human body, including the comprehensive genetic or pharmacological refashioning of it?

Is the very concept of individual liberty even intelligible under such circumstances, unless we can presume some measure of fixity and givenness in the agent-person? Does the very concept of liberty evaporate when its triumph is too complete, just as an economic competition becomes transformed into something different when one party prevails and becomes monopolistic? Is there any reason powerful enough to persuade us not to tinker with that fixity, and thereby risk making ourselves into the first post-human creatures—any reason, that is, other than the Judeo-Christian understanding of the human person as a created being whose dignity and fundamental characteristics are a divine endowment from that Creator? Where, in the traditions of either form of secularism, does one find an adequate defense against such temptation?

Such questions not only take us even further away from positive secularism. They also may force us to reconsider the necessity of something resembling a religious establishment. They suggest the possibility that secularism cannot ever exist entirely as a nonestablished order—that is, without the assumption of an orderly and *given* world undergirding it. This is not just a matter of the need for some kind of social and political axioms and norms. It is also a matter of having the right axioms. For without something like the Judeo-Christian conception of the created order superintending the works of secular society, and the notion that the individual person has an inviolable dignity simply because he or she is created by God, there may be no effective way of containing the powerful impulses that would work to fatally undermine that order. We see the first inklings of this possibility in the ease with which unexceptionable interventions, such as cosmetic surgery or the use of drugs to treat severe psychological disorders, blur into more questionable ones, such as gender "reassignment" and the pharmacological remaking of the self, with nary a bright line in sight to be drawn, except arbitrarily.[60]

Whether it knows it or not, the world-affirming work of secularism has always tacitly depended upon the social existence of its opposite number—a belief in the givenness and rightness of an orderly nature, whose scope and majesty are too great to be overcome by the human will. Paradoxically, belief in the existence of considerations beyond the reach of the "world" have served to give the world its solidity, undergird the possibility of human dignity, and discipline the human will. Our dignity is in overcoming—and in not overcoming. What can take their place in an era of ubiquitous plasticity?

Berlin seemed to recognize something like this later in his life—that both positive and negative liberty must somehow be confined within a certain radius.[61] He of course believed those confinements could be arrived at entirely by conventional means, and he continued to the end to reject emphatically any notion of universally valid norms. To have believed otherwise, he thought, would have violated his understanding of pluralism, a principle to which he was, so to speak, monistically committed. But it may not be so easy for us. The weakest, most disappointing points in Berlin's work reliably come at those moments when he is forced to appeal to a vague traditional standard of "those principles that most people have accepted for a very long time," rather than commit the unpardonable sin of proclaiming an absolute.

Perhaps Berlin could not see the extent to which this rather English reliance upon the residuum of Western cultural practice as a counterweight to liberty—and by extension, to secularism—made presumptions that we can no longer presume, and no longer rely upon. He resisted monism, the one truth. But at the beginning of the twenty-first century, perhaps even negative secularism needs to presume something stronger than mere convention, if it is to survive and thrive. If so, that will be one of the features sharply distinguishing the century we have now entered from the one we have left behind.

Notes

1. Erik H. Erikson, *Childhood and Society* (New York: Norton, 1950), 285; and Michael G. Kammen, *People of Paradox: An Inquiry Concerning the Origins of American Civilization* (New York: Knopf, 1972).

2. "How is it," asked Samuel Johnson in his 1775 anti-American tract *Taxation Not Tyranny*, "that we hear the loudest *yelps* for liberty among the drivers of negroes?" For a more systematic investigation of his insight, see Edmund S. Morgan, *American Slavery, American Freedom: The Ordeal of Colonial Virginia* (New York: Norton, 1975).

3. James B. Twitchell, *Lead Us Into Temptation: The Triumph of American Materialism* (New York: Columbia University Press, 1999); John Harmon McElroy, *American Beliefs: What Keeps a Big Country and a Diverse People United* (Chicago: Ivan R. Dee, 1999).

4. Wilfred M. McClay, *The Masterless: Self and Society in Modern America* (Chapel Hill: University of North Carolina Press, 1994); and "The Hipster and the Organization Man," *First Things*, May 1994, 23–30.

5. For a useful compendium of polling data regarding Americans' religious beliefs and practices, see D. Michael Lindsay and George Gallup Jr., *Surveying the Religious Landscape: Trends in U.S. Beliefs* (Atlanta: Morehouse, 2000). Up-to-the-moment polling data of a similar character are also readily available at the Website of the Gallup Organization http://www.gallup.com. See, e.g., the survey press release for May 6, 1999, which states that nine in ten of Americans pray to God, and three of four do so on a daily basis. "Creative destruction" is the coinage of the Austrian-American economist Joseph Schumpeter, in his *Capitalism, Socialism, and Democracy* (New York: Harper & Brothers, 1950), 81–86.

6. See, e.g., Max Weber, *Economy and Society: An Outline of Interpretive Sociology*, trans. Claud Wittich (Berkeley: University of California Press, 1979), and Emile Durkheim, *The Elementary Forms of Religious Life*, trans. Karen Fields (New York:

Free Press, 1995). An especially important formulation of the secularization theory is Peter Berger, *The Sacred Canopy: Elements of a Sociological Theory of Religion* (New York: Doubleday, 1967).

7. A succinct but useful recent examination of the perdurability of religious faith, a book that represents a reversal of the position that the author put forward in his earlier work, cited above, is Peter L. Berger, ed., *The Desecularization of the World: Resurgent Religion and World Politics* (Grand Rapids, Mich.: Eerdmans and Ethics and Public Policy Center, 1999). Also see Theodore Caplow et al., *All Faithful People: Change and Continuity in Middletown's Religion* (Minneapolis: University of Minnesota Press, 1983); Andrew Greeley, *Unsecular Man: The Persistence of Religion* (New York: Schocken, 1972); and David Martin, *The Religious and the Secular: Studies in Secularization* (London: Routledge and Kegan Paul, 1969).

8. Stephen L. Carter has been especially effective in bringing this condition into relief, in such works as *The Culture of Disbelief: How American Law and Politics Trivialize Religious Devotion* (New York: Basic Books, 1993), and his 1995 Massey Lectures at Harvard, *The Dissent of the Governed: A Meditation on Law, Religion, and Loyalty* (Cambridge, Mass.: Harvard University Press, 1998).

9. A useful guide to the relevant Supreme Court decisions, with excerpts and commentary beginning with *Cantwell v. Connecticut* (1940) and carrying the story up to and including *Lee v. Weisman* (1992), is Terry Eastland, ed., *Religious Liberty in the Supreme Court: The Cases That Define the Debate over Church and State* (Grand Rapids, Mich.: Eerdmans and Ethics and Public Policy Center, 1993). See also Marvin E. Frankel and Eric Foner, *Faith and Freedom: Religious Liberty in America* (New York: Hill & Wang, 1995). Required reading is Richard John Neuhaus's highly influential *The Naked Public Square: Religion and Democracy in America*, 2d ed. (Grand Rapids, Mich.: Eerdmans, 1986).

10. A perspective reflected in, among others, Wendy Kaminer, *Sleeping with Extra-Terrestrials: The Rise of Irrationalism and Perils of Piety* (New York: Pantheon, 1999); Isaac Kramnick and R. Laurence Moore, *The Godless Constitution: The Case against Religious Correctness* (New York: Norton, 1996); and Frederick Clarkson, *Eternal Hostility: The Struggle between Theocracy and Democracy* (Monroe, Maine: Common Courage Press, 1997).

11. José Casanova, *Public Religions in the Modern World* (Chicago: University of Chicago Press, 1994), 234.

12. On the influence of Roman Catholicism in Eastern and Central Europe, see especially the work of George Weigel, including *The Final Revolution: The Resistance Church and the Collapse of Communism* (New York: Oxford University Press, 1992), and his biography of John Paul II, *Witness to Hope* (New York: Cliff Street Books, 1999).

13. Jeffrey Rosen, "Is Nothing Secular?" *New York Times Magazine*, Jan. 20, 2000, 40–45. For some historical perspective on the provenance of such professions see Michael Novak, "Faith in Search of Votes," *New York Times*, Dec. 19, 1999, A25.

14. An excellent overview of these matters can be found in Charles Glenn, *The Ambiguous Embrace: Government and Faith-Based Schools and Social Agencies* (Princeton, N.J.: Princeton University Press, 2000). Also see Stanley W. Carlson-Thies and James W. Skillen, eds., *Welfare in America: Christian Perspectives on a Policy in Crisis* (Grand Rapids, Mich.: Eerdmans, 1996). An exemplary work by a prominent advocate of faith-based charities is Amy L. Sherman, *Restorers of Hope: Reaching the Poor in Your Community with Church-Based Ministries That Work* (New York: Crossway, 1997).

15. An interesting and ideologically diverse examination of Clinton's use of religious language arises out of the essays in *Judgment Day at the White House: A Critical Declaration Exploring Moral Issues and the Political Use and Abuse of Religion*, ed. Gabriel Fackre (Grand Rapids, Mich.: Eerdmans, 1999). See also J. Philip Wogaman, *From the Eye of the Storm: A Pastor to the President Speaks Out* (Louisville: Westminster/John Knox Press, 1998).

16. For a skeptical view of the meaning of RFRA, see Wilfred M. McClay, "The Worst Decision Since Dred Scott?" *Commentary*, Oct. 1997, 52–54.

17. See Robert E. Hemenway, "The Evolution of a Controversy in Kansas Shows Why Scientists Must Defend the Search for Truth," *Chronicle of Higher Education*, Oct. 29, 1999, B7–8, for a response from the chancellor of the University of Kansas.

18. See Glenn, *Ambiguous Embrace*; and, from a different perspective, Jennifer S. Braden and Thomas L. Good, *The Great School Debate: Choice, Vouchers, and Charters* (Mahwah, N.J.: Lawrence Erlbaum Associates, 2000).

19. In *Agostini v. Felton* (1997), the Court allowed public school teachers to tutor private school students in their private schools, even if the schools were primarily religious in nature. In *Rosenberger v. University of Virginia* (1995), the Court ruled that a public university that pays printing costs for a number of student publications through the use of student activity fees cannot deny that benefit to a student-run religious publication. In *Zelman v. Simmons-Harris* (2002), the Court upheld the constitutionality of Cleveland's school-voucher program, which allows students to use public funds to attend private or parochial schools.

20. Roy S. Moore, "Putting God Back in the Public Square," *Imprimis*, Aug. 1999, 1–8, and Linda Greenhouse, "Cases Give Court Chances to Define Church and State," *New York Times*, Sept. 19, 1999, A1.

21. See the works of Carter, *Culture of Disbelief* and *Dissent of the Governed*; Warren Nord, *Religion and American Education: Rethinking a National Dilemma* (Chapel Hill: University of North Carolina Press, 1995); James H. Hutson, *Religion and the Founding of the American Republic* (Washington, D.C.: Library of Congress, 1998); Ellis Sandoz, *A Government of Laws: Political Theory, Religion, and the American Founding* (Baton Rouge: Louisiana State University Press, 1991); Gary L. Gregg II, ed., *Vital Remnants: America's Founding and the Western Tradition* (Wilmington, Del.: ISI Books, 1999); John Witte, *Religion and the American Constitutional Experiment: Essential Rights and Liberties* (Boulder, Colo.: Westview Press, 1999); Michael Novak, *On Two Wings: Humble Faith and Common Sense at the American Founding* (San Francisco: Encounter Books, 2001); and John Noonan, *The Lustre of Our Nation: The American Experience of Religious Freedom* (Berkeley: University of California Press, 1998).

22. Paul Marshall, *Their Blood Cries Out: The Untold Story of Persecution Against Christians in the Modern World* (Dallas: Word Books, 1997); Nina Shea, *In the Lion's Den: Persecuted Christians and What the Western Church Can Do About It* (Nashville: Broadman and Holman, 1997).

23. Church attendance, too, may understate the extent to which religious belief persists. See Hanna Rosin, "Believers in God, if Not Church," *Washington Post*, Jan. 18, 2000, A1.

24. *Washington Post*, Sept. 15, 2001, A13.

25. Karl Marx, "The Eighteenth Brumaire of Louis Napoleon," in *The Marx-Engels Reader*, 2d ed., ed. Robert C. Tucker (New York: Norton, 1978), 594–96: "And

just when they seem engaged in revolutionizing themselves and things, in creating something entirely new, precisely in such epochs of revolutionary crisis they anxiously conjure up the spirits of the past to their service and borrow from them names, battle slogans, and costumes in order to present the new scene of world history in this time-honored disguise and this borrowed language . . . the beginner who has learnt a new language always translates it back into his mother tongue."

26. Gertrude Himmelfarb's book *One Nation, Two Cultures* (New York: Knopf, 1999) argues not only that contemporary American culture is deeply divided, but also, perhaps more surprisingly, though plausibly, that it is the advocates of traditional values, morality, gender roles, and the like who comprise the "counterculture" in our time.

27. A good brief description of this coalescing outlook is provided in Robert P. George, "What Can We Reasonably Hope For?" *First Things*, Jan. 2000, 22–24. More detailed, more adventurous, and more controversial is Peter Kreeft, *Ecumenical Jihad: Ecumenism and the Culture War* (New York: Ignatius, 1996).

28. His religious commitments, and a general sympathy for religion, frequently surface in the work of *Washington Post* journalist E.J. Dionne Jr.; see, e.g., "A Shift Looms," *Washington Post*, Oct. 3, 1999, B1; and (with John J. DiIulio) *What's God Got to Do with the American Experiment?: Essays on Religion and Politics* (Washington, D.C.: Brookings Institution, 2000). Stephen Carter's work on this subject has already been mentioned. Robert Coles has written biographical studies of Dietrich Bonhoeffer, Dorothy Day, and Walker Percy, and has recently published *The Secular Mind* (Princeton, N.J.: Princeton University Press, 1999), calling into question the adequacy of the secular outlook of modernity. William E. Connolly's *Why I Am Not a Secularist* vigorously advances a new model of public life that more adequately addresses the deeper needs of human beings.

29. Also implicit in Eugene McCarraher, *Christian Critics: Religion and the Impasse in Modern American Social Thought* (Ithaca, N.Y.: Cornell University Press, 2000).

30. One can learn a great deal from observing the tenor of two major academic conferences held in the year 2000. The first one, held May 11–14 at the University of Minnesota's Interdisciplinary Center for the Study of Global Change, was titled "After Secularism/Religion: Interpretation, History, and Politics." This decidedly postmodernist undertaking, underwritten by the MacArthur Foundation, sought "to problematize the history by which religion and secularism are presented as polar oppositions," and, by "engaging with the assumptions about progress, pragmatism, and rationality that underpin the genealogy of secularism," to "generate new languages of interpretation that reveal both the partialities of secularism and the worldliness of religious belief." The second, a somewhat more mainstream undertaking supported by the Lilly Endowment, was titled "Congress 2000: The Future of the Study of Religion," and was held September 11–15 at Boston University and Harvard University. Yet there too, the conference announcement proclaims "the collapse of foundationalism," and the "frailty of the old secularization thesis," questions "the Enlightenment relegation of religion to the 'private' realm," doubts the possibility of "objective historical and ethnographic study"—and, for that matter, of any "normative and interpretative claims" at all.

31. See George A. Lindbeck, ed., *The Nature of Confession: Evangelicals and Post-Liberals in Conversation* (Downers Grove, Ill.: InterVarsity Press, 1996), and *The Nature of Doctrine: Religion and Theology in a Postliberal Age* (Louisville: Westminster/John Knox Press, 1984); Hans W. Frei, *The Eclipse of Biblical Narrative* (New

Haven, Conn.: Yale University Press, 1980); Stanley Hauerwas, ed., *Why Narrative? Readings in Narrative Theology* (Eugene, Ore.: Wipf and Stock, 1997); and John Milbank, Catherine Pickstock, and Graham Ward, eds., *Radical Orthodoxy: A New Theology* (New York: Routledge, 1999).

32. This view is well expressed in Jean Bethke Elshtain, *Democracy on Trial* (New York: Basic Books, 1995).

33. James Davison Hunter, *Before the Shooting Begins: Searching for Democracy in America's Culture Wars* (New York: Free Press, 1994), especially 45–82; and his earlier *Culture Wars: The Struggle to Define America* (New York: Basic Books, 1991).

34. Some of the dangers of overemphasizing the middle ground can be seen in Alan Wolfe, *One Nation After All: What Americans Really Think About God, Country, Family, Racism, Welfare, Immigration, Homosexuality, Work, The Right, The Left and Each Other* (New York: Viking, 1998).

35. Mary Ann Glendon, "Religious Freedom and Common Sense," *New York Times*, June 30, 1997; A25, and Glendon and Raul F. Yanes, "Structural Free Exercise," *Michigan Law Review* 90 (1991): 477–92.

36. See Michael Sandel, "The Political Theory of the Procedural Republic," in *Reinhold Niebuhr Today*, ed. Richard John Neuhaus (Grand Rapids, Mich.: Eerdmans, 1989), 19–32.

37. Stanley Fish, *The Trouble with Principle* (Cambridge, Mass.: Harvard University Press, 1999); and John Murray Cuddihy, *No Offense: Civil Religion and Protestant Taste* (New York: Seabury, 1978).

38. George M. Marsden, *The Soul of the American University: From Protestant Establishment to Established Unbelief* (New York: Oxford University Press, 1994).

39. It is perhaps for this very reason that some of the most interesting work on the concept of secularism is coming from South Asia. See, e.g., Rajeev Bhargava, *Secularism and Its Critics* (New York: Oxford University Press, 1998).

40. Alexis de Tocqueville, *Democracy in America*, trans. Phillips Bradley (New York: Vintage, 2000), especially 1: 303–14; Wilfred M. McClay, "The Judeo-Christian Tradition and the Liberal Tradition in the American Republic," in *Public Morality, Civic Virtue, and the Problem of Modern Liberalism*, ed. Gary Quinlivan (Grand Rapids, Mich.: Eerdmans, 2000).

41. This language comes from the Supreme Court's decision in *Planned Parenthood of Southeastern Pennsylvania v. Casey,* 505 U.S. 833 (1992): "At the heart of liberty is the right to define one's own concept of existence, of meaning, of the universe, and of the mystery of human life."

42. I did so completely unaware that the same title had already been used in a thoughtful essay by Leon Wieseltier, contained in *Isaiah Berlin: A Celebration*, Edna and Avishai Margalit, eds. (Chicago: University of Chicago Press, 1991), on which I stumbled in the process of revising this chapter for publication. I commend the essay to the reader's attention, although Wieseltier's distinction between "hard" and "soft" secularism is very different from my own distinction between negative and positive secularism.

43. Isaiah Berlin, "Two Concepts of Liberty," in *Four Essays on Liberty* (New York: Oxford University Press, 1969), 121.

44. Ibid., 127.

45. Ibid.

46. Ibid., 132–33.

47. Berlin, "Two Concepts," 142–43.

48. Ibid., 143.

49. Ibid., 133.

50. Ibid., 171.

51. Ibid., 171–72.

52. This is one of the central assertions put forward in Casanova, *Public Religions*.

53. See McClay, "Judeo-Christian Tradition."

54. Bernard Lewis, *What Went Wrong: Western Impact and Middle Eastern Response* (New York: Oxford University Press, 2001).

55. John Henry Cardinal Newman, *An Essay on the Development of Christian Doctrine* (Notre Dame, Ind.: University of Notre Dame Press, 1990).

56. Even this qualifier is itself qualified, however, by Christ's assurance (Matthew 6:33) that those who "seek first" God's Kingdom will also have their worldly needs recognized and cared for.

57. Berlin, "Two Concepts," 135–41.

58. Ken Myers, *Christianity, Culture, and Common Grace* (Charlottesville, Va.: Berea Publications, 1994), 62–63.

59. See the thoughtful essays in *Caesar's Coin Revisited: Christians and the Limits of Government*, ed. Michael Cromartie (Washington, D.C.: Ethics and Public Policy Center, 1996). See especially this remark of James V. Schall, 24. "The most revolutionary aspect of the Caesar's coin passage [in the Bible] is not the 'render unto God' part but the 'render to Caesar' part. Here we have the revelational tradition maintaining that there are indeed things of Caesar. And where do we acquire an understanding of those things? Not primarily from revelation. . . . The New Testament argues that if we want to find out what things belong to Caesar, we should go to those authors or experience wherein this matter can be directly and properly discussed. Revelation is not designed primarily to teach us what we can usually find out by ourselves, and this moderation on the part of revelation is part of its own claim to be true."

60. Peter D. Kramer, *Listening to Prozac* (New York: Penguin, 1993); and Walter Truett Anderson, *The Future of the Self: Inventing the Postmodern Person* (New York: Tarcher/Putnam, 1997).

61. See Isaiah Berlin and Ramin Jahanbegloo, *Conversations with Isaiah Berlin* (New York: Scribner's, 1991), 40–46.

3

The Religious Conscience and the State in U.S. Constitutional Law, 1789–2001

Charles J. Reid Jr.

When asked by Pontius Pilate, "Are you a king?" Jesus replied: "You say it. I am a king. This is why I was born, and why I have come into the world, to bear witness to the truth."[1] This declaration before Pilate came at the culmination of a public ministry that tested and taxed the religious and political establishments of Roman-governed Judea. Jesus drew both inspiration from the Jewish tradition of prophetic denunciations of failed rulers and bequeathed to following generations the idea that there is a fundamental dualism between church and state–one owes to Caesar that which is Caesar's, but one also owes to God that which is God's.

It is this dualism that is at the heart of Western ideas about religious freedom. Yet this Western tradition of religious liberty was only established with great difficulty, over a period of many years, and with much tribulation and many years of violent oppression and erroneous teaching. Following Saint Augustine's lead, who interpreted Matthew 22:1–14, the parable of the wedding guests, with its instruction "compel them to enter," *compelle entrare*, as authorizing the use of force against heretics, the West embarked upon a thousand-year experiment in enforced religious orthodoxy that included inquisitions, pogroms, and religious wars.[2]

This campaign did not cease immediately with the Protestant Reformation. Although the young Martin Luther preached religious toleration, the old Luther called for the death penalty for "blasphemy" and "sedition."[3] In England, Protestants and Catholics took turns executing their confessional rivals.[4] John Calvin's thought on religious liberty went through a trajectory that parallels Luther's move from greater to lesser tolerance, and the old Calvin saw to the execution of the anti-Trinitarian Michael Servetus.[5] It was only at the margin of the Reformation that ideas of religious tolerance took root and flourished—in the writings of the Silesian Anabaptist Caspar Schwenkfeld, the Lutheran preacher Valentine Weigel, and Menno Simons, the founder of the Mennonites.[6]

The history of religious freedom in the United States is explicable only in terms of this background. The idea of religious freedom, as it was articulated in the earliest years of American life, was the product of critical reflection on the failures of enforced orthodoxy as well the result of theologically grounded investigation into authentic Christian liberty. The subsequent history of religious freedom in this country, from its inception in the colonial era through the adoption of the Bill of Rights and its explication by succeeding generations of courts and policymakers, is not explained by clear axioms, though many would wish it were so. Rather, it is an ongoing process, an interaction of experience and principle over the course of two centuries. It has as its touchstone the belief that the conscience of the believer is sacred, and it is committed to the proposition that the religious and secular must find a means of coexisting in a way that maximizes religious freedom. Coercion of the believer by the secular state, on this view, is the great evil that must be guarded against.

In the Anglo-American tradition, Roger Williams occupies pride of place in the history of religious liberty.[7] It was he who first spoke of a "wall of separation between the garden of the church and the wilderness of this world."[8] In his *Bloudy Tenent of Persecution*, he argued that all persons were endowed with a conscience that must be free to decide for itself in matters of religion. Even "the most paganish, Jewish, Turkish, or antichristian consciences and worships [must] be granted to all men in all nations and countries."[9] Williams's stand on behalf of religious freedom was more total, and more radical, than the moderate toleration John Locke was willing to concede to dissenting Protestant groups in his *Letter Concerning Toleration*.[10]

Williams's radical commitment to religious liberty did not at once take hold in Britain's American colonies. The thirteen colonies, as much as the old world, conducted their own experiments in religious repression. Only in the eighteenth century, thanks to the insights of profound statesmen like James Madison, did conditions change.

The chapter is divided into five sections. The first section demonstrates that the constitutional principle of American religious freedom originated not in deistic skepticism of conventional religiosity, but in James Madison's vision that the principles of Christian faith demanded freedom in the ways we choose to know, love, and serve God. Madison thus gave shape to the language of the First Amendment's protection of religious liberty, but he failed in his attempt to apply the First Amendment to the states, with the result that at the state level establishments of various sorts continued to flourish for many years after the ratification of the Constitution. By the time one reaches the period of the Civil War, however, the most obvious aspects of state establishments had largely disappeared.

The second section covers the period of roughly 1879–1940, which witnessed in the Mormon polygamy cases the first sustained attempt by the U.S. Supreme Court to interpret and apply the First Amendment's religious liberty language. The distinction between constitutionally protected religious beliefs and unprotected overt acts drawn by the Court in the first of the polygamy cases (1879) proved ultimately unworkable, and the final cases (1890) make clear that the Court was willing to countenance even the suppression of belief. The Gilded Age Court that upheld government efforts to eradicate polygamy was itself predominantly progressive Protestant in its views, and it was suspicious of threats to social and moral improvement like the taking of multiple wives.

By the early twentieth century, the nationalism of the age led the Court to pronounce a series of decisions in favor of the near total subordination of religion to the necessities of state. A series of cases involving, on the one hand, pacifists seeking naturalization as citizens and, on the other, Jehovah's Witnesses objecting to the flag salute as the worship of a graven image stand in vivid reminder of this era, although simultaneously the Court was willing to take its first fledgling steps toward according robust constitutional protection to religious freedom.

The third section is concerned with the flowering of religious liberty in a series of judicial decisions between 1940 and 1990. Reacting to the violent suppression of religious belief and religious minorities in Nazi Europe, the Supreme Court breathed vitality into the First Amendment's guarantee of free exercise. In a series of cases, the Court struck down laws that tended to infringe religious practices, thus repudiating the old distinction between protected beliefs and unprotected acts. This development reached its high point in 1972, in a judicial decision that protected the Old Order Amish in their way of life by exempting Amish children from mandatory school-attendance laws.

Beginning in 1947, the Court distinguished between a "free exercise clause" and an "establishment clause" embedded within the First Amendment and applied the prohibition on establishments to the states through the Fourteenth Amendment to eradicate even the vestiges of government support for religion. The search for such vestiges has come to threaten religious freedom—for example, in the search for illicit religious motives behind particular pieces of legislation. It has led as well to incoherence in judicial reasoning on the subject of religious liberty.

The fifth section addresses the state of religious freedom in the United States since 1990.

At the end of the chapter, it should become apparent that the contemporary Supreme Court has erred in two fundamental respects in its treatment of religious liberty cases. First, with regard to free exercise, the Court has retreated from fifty years of according a high level of judicial scrutiny to religious liberty and is now in danger of returning to the era of the Mormon polygamy cases, where the attempt to distinguish between constitutionally protected beliefs and unprotected acts led ultimately to persecution of a religious movement for its beliefs. Second, the Court, in its analysis of religious "establishments," has lost sight of the dominant value at stake in the First Amendment's religion clause—freedom of religion—and has thus been led into a series of paradoxical decisions about what constitutes a religious establishment. A return to Roger Williams's admonition that even consciences we disagree with are worthy of respect seems much in order.

Pre-History

James Madison, who was responsible for introducing the amendment that ultimately guaranteed constitutional protection to the religious conscience, it has been established, acted out of a profound theological vision.[11] He was born into an Anglican family and educated at the Presbyterian College of New Jersey, where he studied under the supervision of John Witherspoon,[12] who saw it as his duty to inculcate his students in the basic truths of Christianity, as mediated by eighteenth-century Presbyterianism.[13]

Shortly after graduating, Madison admonished his friend, the future attorney general of the United States, William Bradford, to "keep the Ministry obliquely in view," and added: "I have sometimes thought there could not be a stronger testimony in favor of Religion or against temporal Enjoyments even the most rational and manly than for men who occupy the most honorable and gainful departments and are rising in reputation and wealth, publicly to declare their unsatisfactoriness by becoming fervent advocates in the cause of Christ."[14]

This background puts into context Madison's own theological argument on behalf of religious liberty found in his "Memorial and Remonstrance," which was drafted in 1785 in response to Patrick Henry's proposed Provision for the Teachers of Christian Religion. Madison began from the premise that "it is the duty of every man to render to the Creator such homage and such only as he believes to be acceptable to him. This duty is precedent, both in order of time and in degree of obligation, to the claims of Civil Society."[15] Madison argued that religious liberty was an "unalienable right" both because loyalty to God's commands was of higher priority than loyalty to the state and because the nature of humankind required such freedom.[16]

In 1787, Madison served as a delegate to the Convention assembled in Philadelphia for the purpose of preparing a Constitution for the newly independent states, a document that prohibited test oaths for governmental office,[17] but omitted any affirmative protection for the rights of conscience. Two years later, in February 1789, in a close race against James Monroe, Madison was elected to the new House of Representatives, in part on the strength of his pledge to the Baptists living in his district to support an amendment to the Constitution protecting "the Rights of Conscience."[18]

Madison took a leading role in the First Congress in drafting the text that would become the First Amendment's provision on religious freedom. In June 1789, Madison proposed for consideration an amendment to the Constitution providing that "the civil rights of none shall be abridged on account of religious belief or worship, nor shall any national religion be established, nor shall the full and equal rights of conscience be in any manner or pretext infringed."[19] In July of that year, Madison was nominated to the committee charged with preparing a bill of rights amending the new Constitution, and on July 28 three separate provisions were reported out of committee.[20] After much give and take between House and Senate versions, a conference of three senators and three representatives, including Madison, met in September 1789 and reported out the language that we know today as the First Amendment. "Congress," it was stated, "shall make no Law respecting an establishment of Religion, or prohibiting the free exercise thereof." John Noonan has observed:

> In two prepositional phrases (not clauses) the job was done. The first phrase assumed that establishments of religion existed as they did in fact exist in several of the states; the amendment restrained the power of Congress to affect them. The second phrase was absolute in its denial of federal legislative power to inhibit religious exercise. Succinct, the amendment referred to religion twice but used the term only once: no room to argue that the term changed its meaning in the second reference. Pleonastically the practice that could not be prohibited was denominated "free."[21]

The Madisonian vision of the religious conscience obliged to give priority to the dictates of God was echoed in early writing on the Constitution. Thus Joseph Story (1779–1845), believing Christian, Supreme Court justice, and a founding father of American law, wrote: "The rights of conscience are, indeed, beyond the just reach of any human power. They are given by God, and cannot be encroached upon by human authority, without a criminal disobedience of the precepts of natural, as well as revealed religion."[22]

But whereas the First Amendment's protection of free exercise prohibited Congress from infringing on the rights of conscience and thereby created a zone of protected liberty within which a believer was free to practice his faith, this provision was adopted against the backdrop of a society, and a legal profession, that was predominantly Christian and Protestant. Story, who had argued eloquently on behalf of freedom of conscience, answered charges by Thomas Jefferson that Christianity was not a part of the common law by demonstrating that, historically, Christianity was "a general principle of the English common law."[23] In his inaugural address as the Dane Professor of Law at Harvard University, Story elaborated on this claim: "One of the beautiful boasts of our municipal jurisprudence is, that Christianity is a part of the common law, from which it seeks the sanctions of its rights, and by which it endeavors to regulate its doctrines."[24] Subsequently, in the case of *Vidal v. Girard's Executors*, Justice Story judicially pronounced that Christianity was a part of the common law adopted by American courts, at least in the "qualified sense, that its divine origin and truth are admitted."[25]

Judicial decisions at the state level echoed Justice Story's sentiments. In a blasphemy case, Chancellor James Kent of New York asserted that

Christianity was the source "of all that moral discipline, and of those principles of virtue, which help to bind society together."[26] Early commentaries on the Constitution's treatment of religion, such as Jasper Adams's *Relation of Christianity to Civil Government* (1833), also asserted that U.S. law was rooted in Christian principles.[27]

Indeed, not only the principle of free exercise, but its corollary, the First Amendment's prohibition on national establishments,[28] must also be understood in light of the predominantly Christian outlook of society. In an important article, Daniel Conkle has noted a seeming anomaly:[29] Even though the First Amendment prohibited religious establishments at the national level, most of the states of the Union continued to retain religious establishments of some type at the local level. Conkle resolved the anomaly by demonstrating that the prohibition on establishments was supported by both "separationists" and supporters of state establishments because it was jurisdictional: Congress was not to legislate on the subject of establishments because this was a matter proper to the states.[30] Many of the state constitutions in force at the time of the ratification of the Bill of Rights, furthermore, provided, to a lesser or greater extent, for religious establishments.

The Madisonian vision was an expressly theological one, recognizing that loyalty to God must come ahead of loyalty to the state.[31] This is not to say, however, that there were not other elements to Madison's vision of free exercise. In addition to his theological arguments, he also argued on utilitarian grounds that a competition of sects would prevent any one of them from gaining preeminence over the others.[32]

As Madison originally conceived it, the principle of free exercise would have been binding on the states.[33] Congress, however, rejected this proposal, fearing the consequences for state autonomy if an amendment of this scope should be made binding upon the states. And in 1844, the Supreme Court specifically rejected the claim that the First Amendment's protection of religious liberty applied to state or local governments.[34]

At the level of the states, a wide diversity of practices flourished. Some states erected large and imposing establishments, whereas others enshrined basic principles of religious freedom. Gradually, by the 1840s and 1850s, formal religious establishments had largely disappeared, although for many years to come laws remained on the books, such as restrictions on officeholding, that continued to restrict civil rights on the basis of religious belief. For much of the nineteenth century, furthermore, a sometimes quite overt Christian, Protestant theological worldview continued to shape and support the development of U.S. law. Story could write with equal conviction about the inviolable rights of conscience and the Christian foundations of U.S. jurisprudence.

State Power and the Religious Conscience, 1879–1940

The Mormon Polygamy Cases

Joseph Smith, who was born in 1805 and was by his own account an adolescent intensely interested in religious matters, began to experience visions as early as the age of fourteen years.[35] In the middle and later 1820s, Smith was led by the angel Moroni, who came to him in a series of visions, to the Hill Cumorah outside Manchester, New York, where he discovered golden plates inscribed in a strange language.[36] Still only in his mid-twenties, Smith prepared a translation of the golden tablets and published these texts as the Book of Mormon.[37]

Smith, a charismatic figure, gathered around himself a deeply devoted group of followers, known as the Latter-Day Saints, who saw in his translations and claims of divine assistance the assurance that God's revelation had not stopped but continues to the present in the voices of the prophets of the church. Unconventional in its Christianity, the Latter-Day Saints aroused the hatred of their neighbors when they commenced the practice of plural marriage, which was publicly proclaimed a doctrine of the church in August 1852, although evidence suggests that Smith had begun to explore this option in the 1830s.[38] Because of their unshakable commitment to the teaching on plural marriage, Mormons were subjected to the violent hostility of their neighbors. Smith and his brother were murdered in 1844 after turning themselves in to the public authorities in Carthage, Illinois, and the Mormon faithful found it prudent to relocate to the Salt Lake Basin of Utah, perhaps the most remote corner of mid-nineteenth-century America.

Congress commenced its campaign against polygamy in 1862, with the passage of the Morrill Act declaring plural marriage a federal crime in U.S. territories punishable by fine or imprisonment.[39] In 1874, George Reynolds, secretary to Brigham Young, took a second wife partly at least to test the constitutionality of the statute.[40] Reynolds was convicted and appealed to the Supreme Court, arguing that polygamy was not *malum in se*—it was, after all, not forbidden by the Decalogue—and that its practice in Utah was carried out in furtherance of a religious mandate that ought to be respected by the civil authorities.[41]

Chief Justice Morrison Waite, writing for a unanimous Supreme Court, rejected Reynolds's claims.[42] Distinguishing between religious beliefs and overt acts motivated by religious belief, Waite asserted that "Congress was deprived of all legislative power over opinion, but was left free to reach actions which were in violation of social order or subversive of good order."[43] Polygamy, the Court continued, was a repugnant practice that Congress might quite properly outlaw in the territories.[44] Indeed, the health of society and even the future of constitutional governance depended on maintaining monogamy as the exclusive form of marital arrangement.[45]

The Latter-Day Saints greeted the outcome in *Reynolds v. United States* with massive resistance. The church leadership continued to teach that polygamous unions were celestial marriages of the sort the patriarchs of Israel enjoyed and that members of the church were duty-bound to follow their example.[46] Opposing the church's claims was an antipolygamy movement that itself took as a main taproot of vitality the sensibilities of progressive Protestantism.[47] Antipolygamy activists, whose belief in social improvement drew inspiration from abolitionists and Victorian moralists, often equated the patriarchal domination of Mormon men and Southern slaveholders.

The antipolygamy movement gathered force in the 1870s and 1880s, in the years just before and after the *Reynolds* decision. Even before *Reynolds*, in 1874, Congress passed the Poland Act, intended to restrict the right of Mormons to serve on juries considering polygamy cases by placing the selection process in the hands of federal officials.[48] With strong Republican backing, the Congress in 1882 passed the Edmunds Act, which strengthened the law against polygamy and also severely restricted Mormons' political rights by declaring vacant all "offices of every description in the Territory of Utah"[49] and by creating a five-member commission empowered to register voters in future elections and to disqualify all voters suspected of polygamous inclinations.[50]

Rudger Clawson, noted among Latter-Day Saints for his courage in facing down a lynch mob while on mission in Georgia,[51] argued on appeal in 1885 that the exclusion of Mormons from both grand and petit juries in his polygamy trial was improper.[52] In a decision that avoided constitutional issues, the Supreme Court ruled in favor of the Poland Act's exclusion of those Mormons who believed in plural marriage.[53] Also in 1885, the Court upheld a challenge to the Edmunds Act's denial of the franchise to polygamists and those who supported the doctrine, basing its decision on the paramount need to defend the sanctity of marriage.[54]

Still facing resistance, Congress in 1887 pronounced the corporate charter establishing the Mormon Church to be "dissolved" and "annulled"; decreed Mormon property, including "places of worship, parsonages connected therewith, and burial grounds . . . forfeited and escheated" to the United States; and authorized the appointment of a receiver "to wind up the affairs" of the church.[55]

In 1890, the Supreme Court affirmed the constitutionality of the legislative dissolution of the Mormon Church.[56] The power of Congress over the territories of the United States was plenary, the Court ruled, and this power included the right to suppress the Corporation of the Latter-Day Saints when that "sect or community . . . in defiance of the law [perseveres] in preaching, upholding, promoting and defending [polygamy]."[57] Mormon missionaries "are engaged in many countries in propagating this nefarious doctrine,"[58] the Court went on, and "[t]he existence of such a propaganda is a blot on our civilization."[59] The Church's claims to religious freedom were dismissed as representing backward practice, hostile to the march of civilization and no more worthy of constitutional protection than human sacrifice or the Hindu suttee.[60] The "enlightened sentiment of mankind" demanded no less than the eradication of this religious "pretence."[61]

The *Reynolds* case has become known to constitutional scholars for the low level of judicial scrutiny it afforded religious liberty claims.[62] Where a given law was "properly enacted" and of general applicability, the Supreme Court will enforce it irrespective of the religious motives of the defendant.[63] Religious beliefs, the Court conceded in *Reynolds*, might be protected by the First Amendment, but "overt acts" in violation of the law are to receive no protection. In practice, by 1890, even this distinction had been greatly eroded. Jurors and voters who merely favored polygamy might be disqualified. Mormon proselytizers who "propagate" the "nefarious doctrine" of polygamy were a "blot on civilization." In this way, both the action and beliefs of the Church of Jesus Christ of Latter-Day Saints came under attack in the latter half of the nineteenth century. It was the church that eventually capitulated.[64]

One Nation, Over God

The Spanish-American War, the subjugation of the Philippines, the circumnavigation of the globe by the Great White Fleet were visible expressions of a powerful new sense of nationalism that entered the American spirit in the years just before and just after 1900. This sense of nationalism persisted, and it is found in a series of Supreme Court cases of the 1920s or 1930s involving the relationship of religious belief to service in the armed forces or saluting the flag.

In 1917, in response to the U.S. entry into World War I, Congress enacted conscription legislation declaring all male citizens between twenty-one and thirty subject to duty in the armed forces of the United States and eligible to be called up.

It was the extent of the right of government to compel military service that was at stake in two post–World War I immigration cases that pitted conscientious objectors against the total demands of the state. A pacifist, Rosika Schwimmer, a forty-nine-year-old Hungarian woman of attenuated deistic views, sought to become a U.S. citizen. She "found the United States nearest her ideals of a democratic republic" and felt "that she could whole-heartedly take the oath of allegiance,"[65] but she refused to promise to take up arms in defense of the nation in time of necessity, finding it shocking that the government might even hypothetically demand military service of women. Taking the government's interests as paramount, the Court rejected Schwimmer's claim:

> Whatever tends to lessen the willingness of citizens to discharge their duty to bear arms in the country's defense detracts from the strength and safety of the Government. And their opinions and beliefs as well as their behavior indicating a disposition to hinder in the performance of that duty are subjects of inquiry. . . .[66]

The full logic of this position was tested two years later in *United States v. MacIntosh*.[67] Douglas MacIntosh was a Canadian national who had spent most of his life in the United States, earning an advanced degree at the University of Chicago and teaching at Yale Divinity School. Shortly after the outbreak of World War I, he enlisted in the Canadian Army as a chaplain and saw significant action. When asked during naturalization proceedings about his readiness to take up arms in defense of the United States, he responded affirmatively but added, "I should want to be free to judge of the necessity."[68] He stressed that his religiously formed conscience had to be the final arbiter on such an important matter.

In a 5–4 opinion authored by George Sutherland, the Court ruled in favor of the government. "From its very nature," Sutherland wrote, "the war power, when necessity calls for its exercise, tolerates no qualifications or limitations."[69] Constitutionally, MacIntosh had no protection. His only recourse was to Congress for legislative relief.[70]

In dissent, Chief Justice Charles Evans Hughes, joined by Louis Brandeis, Harlan Fiske Stone, and Oliver Wendell Holmes—the weightier if not greater part of the Court—avoided overt conflict between an all-powerful state and the religious conscience by distinguishing between two realms, "the domain of power" and the "forum of conscience."[71] The state is supreme in the domain of power, but "in the forum of conscience duty to a moral power has always been maintained."[72] Such a distinction, Hughes continued, reflects the nature of the religious liberty guaranteed by the First Amendment:

> One cannot speak of religious liberty, with proper appreciation of its essential and historical significance, without assuming the existence of a belief in supreme allegiance to the will of God. . . . [F]reedom of conscience itself implies respect for an innate conviction of paramount duty.[73]

Hughes went on to argue that the requirement of the oath violated liberty of conscience,[74] although he proposed the case be resolved on statutory, not constitutional grounds.[75]

Judicial recognition of the supremacy of the state over the demands of the religious conscience culminated in *Minersville School District v. Gobitis*, involving a school-district rule requiring all students to pledge allegiance to the flag.[76] Two students who were Jehovah's Witnesses refused to comply, having been taught "conscientiously to believe that such a gesture of respect for the flag was forbidden by command of Scripture."[77] The two students involved, Lillian and Billy Gobitas (not "Gobitis"), were moved to act as they did by the example of German Jehovah's Witnesses, who had refused to make the Hitler salute and were then being persecuted for their disloyalty to the Nazi regime.[78]

Felix Frankfurter, writing for a seven-justice majority, noted the importance of religious liberty to U.S. constitutionalism,[79] but simultaneously refused constitutional exemption from saluting the flag:

> Conscientious scruples have not, in the course of the long struggle for religious toleration, relieved the individual from obedience to a general law not aimed at the promotion or restriction of religious beliefs. The mere possession of religious convictions which contradict the relevant concerns of a political society does not relieve the citizen from the discharge of political responsibilities.[80]

Harlan Stone dissented. The law at issue, Stone argued, was coercive in its nature, requiring students outwardly to express a belief from which they inwardly dissented.[81] Stone maintained that the protection of liberty by the Constitution must necessarily require some limitations on governmental authority:

> The very fact that we have constitutional guaranties of civil liberties and the specificity of their command where freedom of . . . religion [is] concerned requires some accommodation of the powers which government normally exercises . . . to the constitutional demand that those liberties be protected against the action of government itself.[82]

Stone's argument failed to carry the day in *Gobitis*. Nevertheless, his vision of a robust First Amendment according substantial protection to the religious believer would sweep the field within months and would dominate constitutional analysis of religious liberty, at least until 1990.

First Steps toward Judicially Protected Religious Liberty

It would be a mistake to think that the courts were entirely unwilling to protect religious liberty in the period between 1879 and 1940. Such protection, however, usually occurred through recourse to other provisions of the Constitution. Thus, in *Meyer v. Nebraska*, the question at issue was the constitutionality of a statute that prohibited instructions in languages other than English to students who had not yet graduated from the eighth grade.[83] The statute was the product of anti-German sentiments in the aftermath of World War I and applied alike to private, denominational, parochial, and public schools.[84] It was a teacher in a religious school who challenged its constitutionality.[85] Relying on the due process clause of the Fourteenth Amendment, the Supreme Court struck down the statute, declaring:

> While this Court has not attempted to define with exactness the liberty . . . guaranteed [by the due process clause], the term has received much consideration. . . . Without doubt, it denotes not merely freedom from bodily restraint, but also the right of the individual to contract, to engage in any of the common occupations of life, to acquire a useful knowledge, to marry, establish a home and bring up children, to worship God according to the dictates of his own conscience, and generally to enjoy those privileges long recognized as common law as essential to the orderly pursuit of happiness by free men.[86]

At issue in *Pierce v. Society of Sisters* was an Oregon statute that required all parents in that state to send their children to public schools while those schools were in session, with the practical effect of closing the state's parochial schools.[87] Applying the due process clause as defined in *Meyer*, the Court held that the statute "unreasonably interferes with the liberty of parents and guardians to direct the upbringing and education of children under their control."[88]

In this way, the Court moved, by indirect and incremental steps, toward according religious freedom its own set of constitutional safeguards. The constitutional landscape would change decisively in 1940, when the Court chose to act directly and forthrightly to recognize religious freedom as an autonomous constitutional protection not dependent on speech or press or on prior conceptions of ordered liberty.

The Full Flower of Free Exercise, 1940–1990

Cantwell *and Its Offspring*

Constitutional adjudication in 1940 stood on the cusp of a revolution. The Court had acquired a new center of gravity. Harlan Fiske Stone had become "the intellectual leader of the Court," and he would be made chief justice the following year.[89] New Roosevelt appointees like William Orville Douglas and Hugo Black, furthermore, took an interest in the robust enforcement of the civil rights guarantees of the Bill of Rights, even against the states.[90] The vehicle the Court would employ to work this forthcoming transformation was the "incorporation doctrine"—the proposition that the Congress that ratified the Fourteenth Amendment had intended to incorporate into that text's due process clause the substantive guarantees of the Bill of Rights.[91] This doctrine, though criticized by conservative scholars for its historical anachronism,[92] has nevertheless remained the foundation of constitutional rights jurisprudence. In the spring of 1940, the Court stood ready to consider the constitutional status of religious liberty in the light of the incorporation doctrine.

Newton Cantwell and his two sons, Jesse and Russell, all of them Jehovah's Witnesses, were proselytizing on a street in New Haven, Connecticut, in a Catholic neighborhood.[93] They carried with them a phonograph and a recording entitled "Enemies," describing a book the Witnesses were selling that attacked Catholic beliefs.[94] The recording "incensed" two men, who had agreed to listen but were then "tempted to strike Cantwell unless he went away."[95] Cantwell and his sons were subsequently arrested and convicted of soliciting without a license, and Jesse Cantwell was also convicted of common-law breach of the peace.[96]

The Court, in a unanimous opinion by Justice Owen Roberts, vacated the convictions and thereby radically rearranged the landscape of religious liberty. As was noted above, following the rejection of James Madison's attempt to apply the principle of religious liberty to the states, the states were left free to regulate religion. The First Amendment's religion clause applied only to Congress and to U.S. territories, such as Utah before its admission to statehood. In *Cantwell v. Connecticut*, however, the Court read the doctrine of religious liberty into the Fourteenth Amendment's due process clause, thereby applying it to the states:

> The fundamental concept of liberty embodied in th[e] [Fourteenth] Amendment embraces the liberties guaranteed by the First Amendment. The First Amendment declares that Congress shall make no law respecting an establishment of religion or prohibiting the free exercise thereof. The Fourteenth Amendment has rendered the legislatures of the states as incompetent as Congress to enact such laws.[97]

In interpreting the First Amendment's guarantee of religious liberty, the Court rejected the old dichotomy between protected beliefs and unprotected acts drawn by *Reynolds v. United States*:

> The constitutional inhibition of legislation on the subject of religion has a double aspect. On the one hand, it forestalls compulsion by law of the acceptance of any creed or the practice of any form of worship. Freedom of conscience and freedom to adhere to such religious organization or form of worship as the individual may choose cannot be restricted by law. On the other hand, it safeguards the free exercise of the chosen form of religion. Thus the Amendment embraces two concepts—freedom to believe and freedom to act. The first is absolute but in the nature of things the second cannot be. Conduct remains subject to regulation for the protection of society. The freedom to act must have appropriate definition to preserve the enforcement of that protection. In every case the power to regulate must be so exercised as not, in attaining a permissible end, unduly to infringe that protected freedom.[98]

Thus religious belief was to be protected absolutely, whereas religious conduct would also receive constitutional protection, subject to constitutionally appropriate regulation.

Writing a quarter-century later, Mark deWolfe Howe explicated *Cantwell*, noting that the Court had set forth an intellectually satisfying unitary interpretation of the First Amendment's protection of religion:

> [W]e will have little difficulty in interpreting Justice Roberts' exegesis of the First Amendment's religion clauses. The non-establishment clause he read as nothing more complicated than an assurance of one brand of liberty—a guarantee that the government would not compel conformity in faith or ritual. The free exercise clause, also an assurance of liberty, forbade governmental interference with fulfilling acts of faith.[99]

Noonan has observed, regarding *Cantwell*, that it was a product of its times. The United States was on the verge of war with the Axis Powers, and Nazi Germany, the leader of the Axis, was engaged in efforts to eradicate religious minorities at home and in its conquered territory:

> With the beginning of World War II the Nazis' identification with religious persecution loomed large in America. Other religious persecutions had, of course, occurred earlier in the century—of Christian Armenians by Turks, of Catholics by anticlerical Mexicans and anticlerical Spaniards, of Christians and Orthodox Jews by the Soviet Union. But that Germany, a Western nation, known for its academic and artistic accomplishments, should stage pogroms, and that the now Nazified nation should be engaged in mortal struggle with a nation whose cause the United States had supported, was strong reason to assert the difference of America and to raise in particular the banner of religious freedom.[100]

Cantwell was quickly followed, in the 1940s and 1950s, by a rapid succession of cases outlining the boundaries of the religious freedom now protected by the Constitution. The most important of these early post-*Cantwell* cases was *West Virginia Board of Education v. Barnette*,[101] which presented to the Court an opportunity to reconsider the outcome in *Gobitis*. Relying on *Gobitis*, the West Virginia Board of Education had instructed local districts to make the flag salute "a regular part of the program of activities in the public schools," and to require all teachers and students to participate.[102] Students who failed to comply with the salute requirement were to be suspended or expelled from classes until such time as they actually complied and were to be treated as delinquent.[103]

Members of the Jehovah's Witnesses, who took literally the commandment of *Exodus* not to worship graven images, refused to comply. As a result, "[c]hildren of this faith have been expelled from school. . . . Officials threaten to send them to reformatories maintained for criminally inclined juveniles. Parents of such children have been prosecuted and are threatened with prosecutions for causing delinquency."[104]

In a 6–3 decision, authored by Justice Robert Jackson, the Court explicitly reversed the outcome in *Gobitis*.[105] Jackson took note of *Gobitis*'s teaching that "national unity is the basis of national security,"[106] but he stressed that national unity must be the product of persuasion and voluntary consent, not coerced participation in common ceremonies or rituals.[107] The freedoms guaranteed by the Bill of Rights—speech, press, assembly, and worship—must be conserved and "are susceptible of restriction only to prevent grave and immediate danger to interests which the State may lawfully protect."[108] Jackson concluded:

> If there is any fixed star in our constitutional constellation, it is that no official, high or petty, can prescribe what shall be orthodox in politics, nationalism, religion, or other matters of opinion, or force citizens to confess by word or act their faith therein. If there are any circumstances which permit an exception, they do not now occur to us.[109]

Compelling Government Interests and the Protection of Religious Liberty

In a development parallel to the decision in *Cantwell*, the Court proposed in *dicta*, in a case decided in 1938, that "[t]here may be narrower scope for operation of the presumption of constitutionality" when legislation appears to violate those parts of the Bill of Rights deemed applicable to the states through the Fourteenth Amendment.[110] Where statutes are directed at "particular religious . . . national . . . or racial minorities," the Court continued, "a correspondingly more searching judicial inquiry" may be necessary.[111]

This language gradually evolved into the judicial doctrine known as the "compelling government interests" or "strict scrutiny" standard. Application of this standard means that

> the Court raises the standard that legislation must meet under the due process guarantees if the law regulates or limits a fundamental liberty. Under the strict scrutiny standard the Court requires that the law be necessary to promote a compelling or overriding interest of government if it is to limit the fundamental rights of individual citizens.[112]

In 1963, the Court applied the strict scrutiny standard to claims of religious liberty under the First Amendment. *Sherbert v. Verner* involved a member of the Seventh-Day Adventists who was fired for refusing to work on Saturday, the Sabbath of her faith.[113] Her claim for unemployment compensation was rejected, however, because of her purported refusal to accept "suitable work when offered . . . by the employment office or the employer. . . ."[114]

The Court grounded its decision on the distinction *Cantwell* drew between religious belief and actions motivated by religious belief. Although the latter category is subject to legislative regulation, the Court, reviewing its prior decisions, determined that to pass constitutional muster the regulation must be directed at preventing "some substantial threat to public safety, peace or order."[115] The state's insistence that the appellant work on Saturdays, the Court continued, substantially burdened her religious practice and did not pose a threat to public safety or good order.[116] Having determined that Sherbert's religious faith was burdened by the denial of benefits, the Court applied the strict scrutiny test, thereby invalidating the decision by the unemployment service.[117]

This type of analysis was subsequently applied in a number of religious liberty cases.[118] In 1972, the Supreme Court decided perhaps the most important of the free exercise cases, *Wisconsin v. Yoder*.[119] The Old Order Amish, members of which were defendants in *Yoder*, originated in a split among the Mennonites of Alsace-Lorraine at the close of the sixteenth century over issues such as simplicity of dress and the proper distance to maintain from the world.[120] To escape persecution in Europe, many of the Amish made their way to the New World in the course of the seventeenth century.[121] Even today, the Amish maintain the doctrines of simplicity and separateness from the world, teaching that life lived in close-knit Amish fellowship is the path of salvation and holding that the "English" of the wider non-Amish world are destined for perdition.[122] The Amish, like their Anabaptist forebears, teach that one cannot be incorporated into the community until choosing adult baptism late in adolescence.[123]

In the late 1960s, the State of Wisconsin chose to enforce its school attendance rules, requiring students to remain in school until age sixteen, against Amish families who contended that the socialization policies of American high schools had the effect of destroying the Amish way of life. The Amish families responded by asserting the protection of the free exercise clause: adolescence was crucial to the formation of the next generation of Amish. "During this period, the children must acquire Amish attitudes favoring manual work and self-reliance and the specific skills needed to perform the adult role of an Amish farmer or housewife. . . . And, at this time in life, the Amish child must also grow in his faith and his relationship to the Amish community if he is to be prepared to accept the heavy obligations imposed by adult baptism."[124]

Reading its free exercise jurisprudence against a historical background that included older cases like *Pierce* and *Meyer v. Nebraska*, the Supreme Court first established that the state must show "a state interest of sufficient magnitude to override the interest claiming protection under the Free Exercise Clause,"[125] thus applying the strict scrutiny test. Citing *Sherbert*, the Court continued by declaring that the state's interest in education "is by no means absolute to the exclusion or subordination of all other interests."[126]

The Court then considered the gravity of the threat to the Amish way of life. Protection of a traditional way of life was insufficient to pass constitutional muster, the Court announced.[127] What was necessary was that the way of life "be rooted in religious belief,"[128] which in fact was the case. The state attempted to defend its compulsory attendance law by relying on the time-worn distinction between constitutionally protected belief and unprotected acts, but the Court rejected this proposition, relying on *Cantwell* for authority.[129] The Court similarly rejected the state's claim that the school attendance law was neutral on its face and therefore should be enforced even against the petitioners' religiously based objections. "A regulation neutral on its face" the Court opined, "may, in its application, nonetheless offend the constitutional requirement for governmental neutrality if it unduly burdens the free exercise of religion."[130]

Compelling Government Interests and the Overriding of Protected Religious Liberty

In the years 1940–90, the Supreme Court found the interest of government sufficiently compelling to override the interest of the individual in religious liberty in only a few narrowly drawn circumstances. In the area of national defense, the Court rejected the claim of a Catholic conscientious objector who invoked the traditional Catholic distinction between just and unjust wars to avoid service in the Vietnam War. Employing reasoning better understood as a statement of policy than constitutional analysis, the Court determined that selective conscientious objectors were protected neither by the First Amendment nor by the relevant provisions of the selective service law.[131] The Court has also ruled that an Orthodox Jew could not wear a yarmulke while on active military duty.[132] Military life, the Court noted, required "instinctive obedience, unity, commitment, and esprit de corps," and the enforcement of uniform standards of dress promoted these values.[133]

In the case of taxes, the Court also has deferred to governmental interests. In *United States v. Lee*, the Court rejected the claim of a member of the Old Order Amish to a constitutional exemption from Social Security tax.[134] And in *Bob Jones University v. United States*, the Court denied the university tax-exempt status on the basis of its policy of prohibiting interracial dating, holding that "the government has an overriding interest in eradicating racial discrimination in education. . . ."[135]

By the mid-1980s, therefore, it seemed as if a consensus had developed in the area of religious free exercise: Where such a claim was invoked, the strict scrutiny test would come into play. Only if governmental interests were demonstrably "compelling" could the individual's interest in religious liberty be overridden. In 1990, this consensus was abruptly swept aside. But before considering post-1990 developments, one must first consider a second aspect of the Court's treatment of religion: the effort, begun in 1947, to impart substantive life to the jurisdictional boundary that had been the First Amendment's prohibition on national establishments.

"Establishment Clause" Jurisprudence

The Establishment of the Doctrine

In 1947, there was presented to the Supreme Court the case of a New Jersey statute that permitted the parents of children attending parochial schools to be reimbursed for the expenses incurred using public transportation to travel to and from religious schools.[136] The Court chose this case to find in the First Amendment's prohibition on national establishments the foundation of a constitutional analysis that would come to be used as the main instrument by which public expressions of religious faith were to be regulated by government.

Although the outcome in *Everson v. Board of Education* was favorable to the religious students who were the beneficiaries of public transportation, the majority's analysis was decidedly hostile to their position. Hugo Black commenced his analysis of the statute with a history lesson: The Old World of Europe had seen, in "[t]he centuries immediately before and contemporaneous with the colonization of America," enormous "turmoil, civil strife, and persecutions generated in large part by established sects determined to maintain their absolute political and religious supremacy."[137] Many of the first settlers of the original thirteen colonies brought with them the Old World expectation that the state should support religion. But the factionalism that such support engendered ultimately led to sectarian strife and popular revulsion:[138] "These practices [public support of religion enforced by coercive laws] became so commonplace as to shock the freedom-loving colonials into a feeling of abhorrence."[139]

Black relied upon his reading of Madison and Jefferson as the principal guides to interpreting the First Amendment. Black made use of Madison's "Memorial and Remonstrance" to argue "that no person, either believer or non-believer, should be taxed to support a religious institution of any kind,"[140] and he subsequently quoted the Virginia Bill for Religious Liberty, written principally by Jefferson, for much the same proposition.[141] Severing the "establishment clause" from the "free exercise clause," Black then saw fit to impart a "broad interpretation to the 'establishment of religion' clause" and to apply that clause through the Fourteenth Amendment to the states:[142]

> The "establishment of religion" clause of the First Amendment means at least this: Neither a state nor the Federal Government can set up a church. Neither can pass laws which aid one religion, aid all religions, or prefer one religion over another. Neither can force nor influence a person to go to or to remain away from church against his will or force him to profess a belief or disbelief in any religion. No person can be punished for entertaining or professing religious beliefs or disbeliefs, for church attendance or non-attendance. No tax in any amount, large or small, can be levied to support any religious activities or institutions. . . . Neither a state nor the Federal Government can, openly or secretly, participate in the affairs of any religious organizations or groups and *vice versa*. In the words of Jefferson, the clause against establishment of religion by law was intended to erect a "wall of separation between church and State."[143]

Despite an analysis hostile to the claims of the Catholic schoolchildren, the Court, per Justice Black, ruled in their favor in a politicized decision.[144] After describing in vivid detail the horrors that followed from any use of tax money to support religious institutions, Black reasoned that expenditure of public funds on transportation was a form of public welfare expense akin to furnishing police or fire protection or other benefits provided neutrally to believers and nonbelievers alike.[145]

Two justices, Robert Jackson and Wiley Rutledge, wrote dissents, with Frankfurter joining Jackson's dissent and Frankfurter, Jackson, and Harold Burton joining Rutledge's. Jackson argued that Black was wrong in seeing the subsidy as a public welfare program and pointed to the direct benefits parents of parochial school children realized from the New Jersey statute. Citing the Catholic Code of Canon Law, Jackson concluded that the New Jersey scheme amounted to "compensat[ion] . . . for adherence to a creed."[146]

Rutledge's dissent explored the historical foundations of the First Amendment. Jefferson, and more especially Madison, and the efforts to enact the Bill for Establishing Religious Freedom in Virginia, in Rutledge's estimation, were the taproots of knowledge where the First Amendment is concerned.[147] Rutledge emphasized Madison's resolute opposition to the use of public funds to support religious activity: "In no phase was he more unrelentingly absolute than in opposing state support or aid by taxation. Not even 'three pence' contribution was thus to be exacted from any citizen for such a purpose."[148] "State aid," Rutledge opined, interpreting Madison, "was no less obnoxious or destructive to freedom and to religion itself than other forms of state interference."[149]

The prohibition on establishments, Rutledge asserted, was to be used affirmatively, if not aggressively, as a means of uprooting even the vestiges of governmental support for religion:

> The [First] Amendment's purpose was not to strike merely at the official establishment of a single sect, creed or religion, outlawing only a formal relation such as had prevailed in England and some of the colonies. Necessarily it was to uproot all such relationships. But the object was broader than separating church and state in this narrow sense. It was to create a complete and permanent separation of the spheres of religious activity and civil authority by comprehensively forbidding every form of public aid or support for religion.[150]

Rutledge proposed to read into the Constitution the claim—attributed to Madison—that "religion was a wholly private matter beyond the scope of civil power either to restrain or to support."[151] Rutledge concluded that the use of taxpayer funds "to aid or support any and all religious exercises" must be considered constitutionally infirm.[152]

Rutledge's reading of Madison, in particular, can be seen as a secularist's attempt to understand an essentially religious thinker.[153] Absent from

Rutledge's account is any recognition that the young Madison believed public servants should "keep the Ministry obliquely in view." Missing as well is any appreciation for the theological sophistication of the "Memorial and Remonstrance" or any sense of Madison's solicitude for the religious conscience as owing a loyalty to God and God's Word that is prior to and greater than any bond of statehood. Madison, on Rutledge's reading of history, has become the founder of the secular state.

The next year, the Supreme Court heard the case of *McCollum v. Board of Education*, involving the use of public school buildings by religious educators who gave weekly instructions to students who opted out of their secular classes.[154] The Court, in another opinion by Justice Black, ruled the arrangement unconstitutional. Relying on his own language in *Everson* and quoting Jefferson's endorsement of a "wall of separation" between church and state, Black declared the arrangements to be unconstitutional.[155] Frankfurter, concurring, stressed the need to maintain "[z]ealous watchfulness against fusion of secular and religious activities by Government itself. . . ."[156] Vigilance was particularly warranted where the public schools were concerned because "the public school [i]s a symbol of our secular unity."[157] "The public school is at once the symbol of our democracy," Frankfurter continued, "and the most pervasive means for promoting our common destiny."[158]

Stanley Reed, serving his first term on the Court, was the lone dissenter, arguing that the majority's definition of establishment was impermissibly expansive.[159] "The phrase 'an establishment of religion,'" he noted, "may have been intended by Congress to be aimed only at a state church."[160] Reed also asserted that a fair reading of Madison and Jefferson did not support either the opinions in *Everson* or in *McCollum*, and that historically the sort of religious activity struck down in *McCollum* had been generally upheld by the courts.[161]

Scholars were quick to criticize the opinions in *Everson* and *McCollum*. Edward Corwin, constitutional scholar and professor of jurisprudence at Princeton University, Madison's alma mater, challenged the Court's reading of First Amendment history, arguing that *McCollum*'s definition of establishment, borrowed from Rutledge's dissent in *Everson*, violated Madison's own definition of the establishment of religion.[162] Furthermore, Corwin continued, the Court erred in attempting to read Madison's "Memorial and Remonstrance" into the First Amendment. "Madison himself asserted repeatedly as to the Constitution as a whole that 'the legitimate meaning of the Instrument must be derived from the text itself.'"[163]

Corwin was equally critical of the Court's use of Jefferson. The reliance on Jefferson's Letter to the Danbury Baptists was a selective use of texts, Corwin contended, which ignored his later writings;[164] Jefferson, furthermore, was in Paris at the time the First Amendment was drafted and played no role in its composition.[165]

John Courtney Murray, Catholic theologian and expert on the relationship of church and state, also criticized the opinions, asserting that in its haste to erect rigid barriers between religion and public life, the Court ignored the whole dimension of religious freedom:

> One might have thought that a "civil rights Court" would have been sensitive on this neuralgic point of democratic theory; instead it is callous to the extreme of complete and utter insensibility. . . . [I]t does not lift a judicial finger to fortify against insidious attack a right that is the cornerstone of democracy in education—the parent's last rampart against the "unification" of his child with other children into a standardized "democratic" mass. It pursues, this time over the verge of quixotism, a hypersensitive concern for absoluteness of separation of church and state, with resultant legal damage to a human right that rests on the most absolute political and religious grounds, and is the foundation of a social freedom of the most indispensable sort.[166]

Everson and *McCollum* have continued to be the subject of criticism. Thomas Curry has confirmed Stanley Reed's assertion that the eighteenth-century meaning of "establishment" was decidedly narrower than the meaning adopted by *Everson* and *McCollum*.[167] Gerard Bradley has criticized the Court on historical and originalist grounds. Madison, in writing the "Memorial and Remonstrance," was concerned with a classic eighteenth-century question: "a separate, distinct tax, imposed and collected for the twin purposes of paying clergymen and for building and maintaining churches. The effect would have been to place a clergyman on the government payroll in his sacerdotal and ecclesiastical capacities and to fund the system by direct coercion of individuals."[168] Properly contextualized, "the general assessment has no modern analogue and thus cannot guide such a search for original intent."[169]

Furthermore, Bradley stresses, the Court failed to avail itself of important evidence. Records of congressional debates, the process of ratification of the First Amendment by the states, and newspapers and other sources of public opinion—all of which could have shed light on the understanding of the First Amendment that was shared by those who approved it—were never consulted by the Court.[170] Other commentators have maintained that the incorporation into the Fourteenth Amendment of the prohibition on establishments, a jurisdictional barrier, not a substantive right, has violated the federal structure of government established by the Constitution and has resulted in intellectual incoherence.[171]

Daniel Dreisbach, finally, in a careful study of the context of Jefferson's Letter to the Danbury Baptist Association, concluded that the Court in *Everson* and *McCollum* misunderstood Jefferson's view of church and state.[172] Jefferson's use of the word "church," rather than the more expansive term "religion," "emphasized that the constitutional separation was between ecclesiastical institutions and the civil state."[173] (Rutledge's dissent in *Everson* had subtly shifted Jefferson's metaphor from "church" to "religion.") Furthermore, Jefferson never repeated his use of the "wall" metaphor, even in contexts where its use would have been appropriate, suggesting that it occupied a relatively unimportant place in his mind.[174]

Despite this substantial body of criticism, no Court majority has ever repudiated the reasoning or results of *Everson* or *McCollum*. Indeed, an imposing edifice has been constructed on the brittle foundation of these two cases.

Expansion and Acceptance of the Doctrine

Energized by the charge "to uproot all . . . relationships" between religion and the state, the Supreme Court expanded its use of the prohibition of establishments in the early 1960s to school prayer. At issue in *Engel v. Vitale* was the New York Regents' Prayer, a nondenominational invocation to be recited daily by teachers in the public school system. Schoolchildren were free to choose whether or not to participate.[175] In yet another opinion by Hugo Black, the Court struck down the practice. Once again, Black relied upon a quick overview of colonial history to conclude that the use of governmentally sanctioned prayer created an impermissible establishment of religion.[176] Potter Stewart dissented, finding Black's history lesson "unenlightening" and the invocation of a "wall of separation" a misleading expression that appeared nowhere in the Constitution.[177] For Stewart, the freedom of schoolchildren to join in a voluntary prayer at the commencement of the school day was decisive: "[W]e deal here not with the establishment of a state church, which would, of course, be constitutionally impermissible, but with whether school children who want to begin their day by joining in prayer must be prohibited from doing so."[178]

School District of Abington Township v. Schempp, decided the following year, proved to be a far more comprehensive statement of the Court's views on school prayer.[179] The case was presented so as to highlight the violations of religious freedom that occurred when local schools sanctioned prayer. Unitarian complainants asserted that classroom Bible readings were "contrary to the religious beliefs which they held and to their familial teaching."[180] Solomon Grayzel, the great Jewish legal historian, testified that readings from the New Testament "were not only sectarian in nature but tended to bring Jews into ridicule or scorn."[181] Madalyn Murray, the famous atheist, challenged Bible readings on behalf of her son, alleging "that it threatens their religious liberty by placing a premium on belief as against non-belief."[182]

Applying the prohibition on establishments, in a decision authored by Tom Clark, the Court struck down the prayers as unconstitutional.[183] Developing a constitutional test that might be applied in future litigation, the Court proposed that legislation violates the establishment clause when either its purpose or its primary effect is demonstrated to violate the principle of neutrality:

> The test may be stated as follows: what are the purpose and primary effect of the enactment? If either is the advancement or inhibition of religion then the enactment exceeds the scope of legislative power as circumscribed by the Constitution. That is to say that to withstand the strictures of the Establishment Clause there must be a secular legislative purpose and a primary effect that neither advances nor inhibits religion.[184]

Concurring briefly, Arthur Goldberg asserted that both free exercise and establishment provisions must be read as a single clause supporting the principle of religious liberty.[185] It was, however, Potter Stewart, in dissent, who most fully appreciated the principle of religious freedom which the religion clause was intended to conserve. Noting that historically the prohibition on establishments was intended to prevent the creation of a national church, Stewart questioned but ultimately assented to its incorporation into the Fourteenth Amendment.[186] More compelling to Stewart, however, was religious freedom, the value protected by the First Amendment. At stake in the contested programs, he asserted, were competing claims of religious liberty. A truly neutral system, he further asserted, would accommodate the religious needs of all students—both those who wished and those who did not wish to pray.[187] Such accommodation, however, must avoid coercion,[188] and it must respect the free exercise rights of religious minorities.[189]

Subsequent case law refined the test set forth in *Abington* for determining "establishment clause" violations. In its final form, it has come to be known as the *Lemon* test, after *Lemon v. Kurtzman*, a 1971 case involving a statute authorizing state reimbursement to sectarian schools for secular educational services.[190] The *Lemon* test provided that:

> Every analysis in [establishment clause cases] must begin with consideration of the cumulative criteria developed by the Court over many years. First, the statute must have a secular legislative purpose; second, its principal or primary effect must be one that neither advances nor inhibits religion [citation omitted]; finally, the statute must not foster "an excessive entanglement with religion" [citation omitted].[191]

In recent years, the "purpose" clause of the *Lemon* test has been applied broadly, allowing, among other things, judicial inquiry into the religious motivations of legislators. *Wallace v. Jaffree* involved an Alabama statute allowing for a moment of silence at the beginning of the public school day "for 'meditation or voluntary prayer.'"[192] Basing its judgment on an uncontested statement by the legislation's sponsor that its purpose "was an 'effort to return voluntary prayer' to the public schools,"[193] a five-member majority of the Supreme Court declared the law unconstitutional. Two years later, in *Edwards v. Aguillard*, which struck down a Louisiana statute prohibiting the teaching of evolution except where accompanied by the teaching of "Creation Science," the Court reaffirmed that the religious motivations of legislators was a legitimate area of judicial inquiry in establishment cases.[194] The allegation that "[t]he preeminent purpose of the Louisiana Legislature was clearly to advance the religious viewpoint that a supernatural being created humankind" sufficed to show an improper legislative motive.[195]

In dissenting, Antonin Scalia criticized the expansion the religious purpose doctrine had undergone.[196] He noted that *Lemon*'s use of "religious purpose" language did not target the motivations of legislators, but rather legislation that explicitly advanced or promoted religion.[197] In the case of the act in question, the articulated legislative purpose was the need to provide a balanced account of the origins of life. The legislative record, Scalia observed, showed that the bill's sponsors were motivated not by religious concerns, but by the desire that students receive "a fair presentation of the scientific evidence" for and against evolution.[198] Legislative hearings stressed that creation science "is a collection of educationally valuable scientific data that has been censored from classrooms by an embarrassed scientific establishment."[199] By expanding purpose to cover the surmised religious motivation of individual legislators, especially where the legislative record lacked real evidence of such motivation, Scalia argued, the majority threatened the religious freedom of officeholders:

> Our cases in no way imply that the Establishment Clause forbids legislators merely to act upon their religious convictions. We surely would not strike down a law providing money to feed the hungry or shelter the homeless if it could be demonstrated that, but for the religious beliefs of the legislators, the funds would not have been approved. Also, political activism by the religiously motivated is part of our heritage.[200]

Scalia thus recommended that the Court abandon the *Lemon* test's whole emphasis on religious purpose.[201]

Despite Scalia's admonition, courts continue to scrutinize legislative actions for signs of impermissible religious motives. In *Coles v. Cleveland Board of Education*, the Sixth Circuit ruled unconstitutional the use of prayer by the school board to open its meetings on the ground that board members had been motivated by religious belief in reciting their prayers.[202] In *Metzl v. Leininger*, a three-judge panel of the Seventh Circuit ruled unconstitutional Illinois's observance of Good Friday as a school holiday, based in part on the religious motives expressed in a gubernatorial proclamation dating to 1942.[203] Three other courts, however—including a different three-judge panel of the Seventh Circuit—have sustained public Good Friday commemorations where a clear official religious motivation was absent.[204]

The courts have found themselves in this cul de sac because of a misplaced emphasis on the perceived need to search out and uproot the vestiges of establishments. An analysis that took account of religious freedom as the dominant concern and that sought to protect the free expression of religious belief from official coercion might reach many of the same results,[205] but it would achieve these results in a manner more respectful of the constitutional principles at stake in the religion clause.

Gathering Criticism

In the early 1990s, serious doubts emerged about the continued viability of the *Lemon* test. *Lee v. Weisman*, a case that ruled unconstitutional the recitation of ecumenical prayer at a middle school graduation, had avoided invoking the test as part of its analysis.[206] Two years later, concurring in judgment, Scalia objected to its use in *Lamb's Chapel v. Center Moriches Union Free School District*.[207] Its reappearance was akin to "some ghoul in a late-night horror movie that repeatedly sits up in its grave and shuffles about, after being repeatedly killed and buried. . . ."[208] "Over the years," Scalia observed, "no fewer than five of the current sitting Justices have, in their own opinions, personally driven pencils through the creature's heart. . . ."[209] In 1997, however, the *Lemon* test was once again reaffirmed,[210] albeit in somewhat modified form, although Scalia has continued to object.[211]

A second line of attack was opened in William Rehnquist's dissenting opinion in *Wallace v. Jaffree*.[212] Hearkening back to Stanley Reed's dissent in *McCollum*, Rehnquist stressed that Madison himself took a narrow view of what the religion clause was intended to accomplish.[213] Closely analyzing Madison's participation in its drafting, Rehnquist concluded that Madison "saw the Amendment as designed to prohibit the establishment of a national religion, and perhaps to prevent discrimination among sects. He did not see it as requiring neutrality on the part of government between religion and irreligion."[214] Early constitutional interpreters—Congress and the first presidents—understood the religion clause in this sense when the Northwest Ordinance's endorsement of the importance of "[r]eligion, morality, and knowledge"[215] was enacted into law, and when "Congress appropriated time and again public moneys in support of sectarian Indian education carried on by religious organizations."[216] Joseph Story was cited for the proposition that "[p]robably at the time of the adoption of the Constitution, and of . . . [the First Amendment], the general if not the universal sentiment in America was, that Christianity ought to receive encouragement from the State so far as was not incompatible with the private rights of conscience and the freedom of religious worship."[217]

Rehnquist's claims in *Jaffree* have come to be known as "nonpreferentialism," the theory that a proper understanding of constitutional history reveals that government might assist religious groups, as long as such aid is administered without preference to particular sects. Some leading scholars have endorsed this view, including some who wrote before 1985 and on whom Rehnquist relied.[218]

In the term ending in June 2000, a four-member plurality of the Court, while eschewing a nonpreferentialist account of the prohibition on establishments, made use of the concept of governmental neutrality to propose a broadly accommodationist view of the relationship of religion and the state.[219] "[I]f the government, seeking to further some legitimate secular purpose," wrote Clarence Thomas on behalf of the plurality, "offers aid on the same terms, without regard to religion, to all who adequately further that purpose, then it is fair to say that any aid going to the religious recipient has the effect of furthering that secular purpose."[220]

A further sign that the establishment clause jurisprudence of *Everson* and *McCollum* may now be facing serious challenge can be found in the Sixth Circuit case of *A.C.L.U. of Ohio v. Capitol Square Review Board.* In April 2000, a three-judge panel of the Sixth Circuit struck down as unconstitutional Ohio's motto "With God, all things are possible."[221] Tracing the origin of the expression to the Gospel of Matthew,[222] the judges applied the *Lemon* test to conclude that retention of the motto conferred "an unconstitutional preference to Christianity. The State of Ohio has effectively said to all who hear or see the words . . . that Christianity is a preferred religion to the people of Ohio."[223]

In March 2001, however, the entire Sixth Circuit, rehearing the case *en banc*, reversed this outcome.[224] Looking particularly to the early history of the Bill of Rights, the Court concluded that the original purpose of the First Amendment's prohibition on establishments "was to prevent any establishment by the national government of an official religion. . . ."[225] Relying on Joseph Story's exegesis of the meaning of religious freedom in United States, the Court then noted that the central principle protected by the First Amendment is freedom from "coercion."[226] Madison's "Memorial and Remonstrance" was read as further support for this position, as was Jefferson's *Bill for Establishing Religious Freedom.*[227] Applying this analysis to the case at hand, the Court concluded that the state motto was not coercive and so not unconstitutional:

> The motto involves no coercion. It does not purport to compel belief or acquiescence. It does not command participation in any form of religious exercise. It does not assert a preference for one religious denomination or sect over others, and it does not involve the state in the governance of any church. It imposes no tax or other impost for the support of any church or group of churches. Neither does it impose any religious test as a qualification for holding political office, voting in elections, teaching at a university, or exercising any other right or privilege. And, as far we can see, its adoption by the General Assembly does not represent a step calculated to lead to any of these prohibited ends.[228]

Free Exercise, 1990–2000: Return to *Reynolds* and *Gobitis*?

In his dissent in *Thomas v. Review Board*, Rehnquist argued that had the case been presented differently—had it involved an establishment clause challenge to a statute permitting those with religious scruples to collect unemployment benefits, instead of a free exercise claim to benefits—the whole scheme would have been ruled unconstitutional.[229] "By broadly construing both Clauses," Rehnquist observed, "the Court has constantly narrowed the channel between Scylla and Charybdis through which any state or federal action must pass in order to survive constitutional scrutiny."[230]

In 1990, the case was presented to the Court of two ex-employees of a private drug rehabilitation center who had used peyote in religious ceremonies.[231] The men, who had been fired from their positions, sought unemployment benefits, claiming their religious freedom had been violated.

Justice Scalia, writing for a five-member majority, rejected the free exercise claim and called into question fifty years of free exercise case law. Flying in the face of a half-century of history, he asserted: "We have never held that an individual's religious beliefs excuse him from compliance with an otherwise valid law prohibiting conduct that the State is free to regulate."[232] As authority for this proposition, he cited the majority opinion in *Gobitis*: "Conscientious scruples have not, in the course of the long struggle for religious toleration, relieved the individual from obedience to a general law not aimed at the promotion or restriction of religious beliefs."[233] No reference was made to *Barnette*'s explicit reversal of *Gobitis*.[234]

Scalia moved from *Gobitis* to revivify *Reynolds*. When *Cantwell* declared that religious acts as well as beliefs deserved some measure of constitutional protection, it indirectly questioned the viability of *Reynolds*. Scalia, however, cast doubt on *Cantwell* and its progeny by reference to *Reynolds*: "'Laws,' we said, 'are made for the government of actions, and while they cannot interfere with mere religious belief and opinions, they may with practices. . . . Can a man excuse his practices to the contrary because of his religious belief? To permit this would be to make the professed doctrines of religious belief superior to the law of the land, and in effect to permit every citizen to become a law unto himself.'"[235]

Scalia then confronted the embarrassing presence of cases that had reached contrary results. *Cantwell* and a number of the early cases, he declared, had involved more than simply religion; they involved as well the First Amendment's protection of free speech.[236] This reading of *Cantwell* ignored its explicit holding, which was premised on freedom of religion.[237] He attempted to distinguish *Pierce* and *Yoder* in a similar fashion, seeing in them not only the issue of free exercise but also the parental right to direct the education of offspring.[238] Here he ignored the reasoning of *Yoder*, which viewed *Pierce* as an early precedent for the growth of expansive free exercise protection and premised its holding on the compelling governmental interest test laid down by *Sherbert v. Verner*.[239] Finally, he confronted *Sherbert*, which, he concluded, should at most be confined to the unemployment compensation field.[240] Because the claims for First Amendment protection in *Employment Division v. Smith* involved not only unemployment compensation but actions that violated the criminal law, *Sherbert* should not be held to apply.[241]

Sandra Day O'Connor concurred in judgment, but she rejected Scalia's analysis.[242] She emphasized that what is at stake in the protection of free exercise is the exercise of one's religion—a concept that necessarily embraces actions and other outward observances.[243] Furthermore, "'[b]elief and action cannot be neatly confined in logic-tight compartments.'"[244] Scalia's resuscitation of *Gobitis* and *Reynolds*, she continued, was unsupportable in light of subsequent developments. "[I]n cases such as *Cantwell* and *Yoder* we have in fact interpreted the Free Exercise Clause to forbid application of a generally applicable prohibition to religiously motivated conduct." She noted that Scalia also erred in attempting to read *Cantwell* and *Yoder* as "hybrid" decisions: "Both cases expressly relied on the Free Exercise Clause. . . ."[245] She then explained what free exercise meant to her:

> In my view . . . the essence of a free exercise claim is relief from a burden imposed by government on religious practices or beliefs, whether the burden is imposed directly through laws that prohibit or compel specific religious practices, or indirectly through laws that, in effect, make abandonment of one's own religion or conformity to the religious beliefs of others the price of an equal place in the civil community.[246]

The compelling government interest test, O'Connor observed, was framed to measure the constitutionality of governmental intrusions on religious belief.[247] Applying that standard, she determined that the government had a compelling interest in combating drug abuse that overrode the claimants' interest in religious liberty.[248] Harry Blackmun, joined by William Brennan and Thurgood Marshall, dissented, maintaining that an exception should be made for the religious use of peyote.[249]

Scholars and policymakers alike reacted sharply to *Smith*. In an article that appeared the month after *Smith* was decided but that was substantially completed before the decision was handed down, Michael McConnell concluded, contrary to *Smith*, that exemptions from neutral laws of general applicability were a feature of religious liberty in the founding era and should thus be a part of contemporary constitutional law.[250] In such a way, the Madisonian concern with religious pluralism might be advanced.[251] In an article published in late 1990, responding explicitly to *Smith*, McConnell developed his arguments further. Exemptions from generally applicable law because of religious belief were a common feature of U.S. colonial experience and early constitutional law.[252] "The free exercise clause," he concluded, "by its very terms and read in the light of its historic purposes, guarantees that believers of every faith and not just the majority, are able to practice their religion without unnecessary interference from the government."[253]

In reply, Gerard Bradley and Philip Hamburger, in separate articles, questioned the soundness of McConnell's historical evidence. Reviewing case law from the early nineteenth century, Bradley rejected the proposition that protection of religiously motivated acts, known conveniently as a conduct exemption, was a feature of early constitutional thought.[254] Its source, rather, was in modern liberalism: "The conduct exemption . . . is bad constitutional law. It also is not, strictly speaking, a doctrine of religious liberty. It is one aspect of the post-World War II takeover of our civil liberties corpus by the political morality of liberal individualism."[255] Reviewing eighteenth-century sources, including state constitutions and records of the founding, Hamburger reached similar conclusions about the historicity of conduct exemptions.[256]

Noonan, for his part, made the point that *Smith* amounted to the restoration of the old order prior to 1940:

> Although there was a cosmetic attempt to save some of the previous decisions, the fundamental proposition of Justice Scalia's opinion undid the previous fifty years. On a fair reading of *Smith*, nothing remained of the major decisions of the past to the extent that they upheld the free exercise of religion against state action. To drive that point home, Justice Scalia took the extraordinary step of quoting Justice Frankfurter's opinion in the flag salute case. An opinion that had been heatedly condemned on all sides, and repudiated two years later by the Supreme Court, was now quoted by Justice Scalia as though it were good law, as though the new standards were the Frankfurter standards restored. He made no acknowledgement that *Barnette* had been the law since 1943.[257]

Policymakers responded to scholarly criticism and popular anger at the *Smith* decision in 1993 by enacting into law the Religious Freedom Restoration Act.[258] The constitutionality of this measure, insofar as it imposed on the states the burden of meeting the compelling government interest standard, was challenged in *City of Boerne v. Flores*.[259] The majority opinion, written by Anthony Kennedy, focused on the authority of Congress to impose constitutional standards that the judiciary was obliged to enforce. The act was premised on Congress's power under Section Five of the Fourteenth Amendment to protect the rights secured by that amendment. Free exercise having been incorporated into the Fourteenth Amendment, Congress sought to secure its protection against state infringement. Distinguishing the Religious Freedom Restoration Act from such constitutionally valid enforcement laws as the Voting Rights Act, the Court determined that its sweep was too broad to withstand scrutiny.[260] The act lacked "proportionality or congruence between the means adopted and the legitimate end to be achieved."[261] "Sweeping coverage ensured its intrusion at every level of government, displacing laws and prohibiting official actions of almost every description and regardless of subject matter."[262]

In dissenting, O'Connor maintained that *Smith* was wrongly decided, relying in large measure on the work of McConnell.[263] "Free exercise," she noted, appeared in colonial American legal documents as early as 1648, when the Crown pledged to Lord Baltimore that Maryland would remain a haven where Catholics might practice their faith.[264] Other colonies also guaranteed some measure of religious freedom: "[T]hese colonies appeared to recognize that government should interfere in religious matters only when necessary to protect the civil peace or to prevent 'licentiousness.' In other words, when religious belief conflicted with civil law, religion prevailed unless important state interests militated otherwise."[265] The same situation prevailed in the years after the Revolution. Numerous documents, O'Connor notes, demonstrate that "it was generally accepted that the right to 'free exercise' required, where possible, accommodation of religious practice."[266] Considering in particular exemptions enjoyed by believers in the areas of oaths, the draft, and religious assessments, she concluded that "if an individual's religious scruples prevented him from complying with a generally applicable law, the government should, if possible, excuse the person from the law's coverage."[267]

Although *Smith* abandoned the traditional case law that had imposed a heavy burden on government to justify burdens placed on religious believers by the operation of neutral, generally applicable laws, it did allow a narrow exception in which acts in furtherance of religious belief might still receive the protection of the courts. If a law was not neutral or of general applicability, but specifically targeted a religious practice, then believers were entitled to invoke the compelling government interest test.[268]

In *Church of Lukumi Babalu Aye, Inc. v. City of Hialeah*, the Supreme Court considered just such a situation.[269] Santeria, a religion practiced by Cubans of Yoruba descent, involves periodic animal sacrifice for important life stages, such as marriage, death, or the cure of the sick.[270] When the City of Hialeah, Florida, drafted animal protection ordinances with the express intention of eliminating Santeria practice within the municipality, the Court responded by invalidating the law. The ordinances, which outlawed the killing of animals in "sacrifices" and "rituals," were found to violate free exercise because they were drafted in a manner that ensured the Church would receive discriminatory treatment.[271]

Few cases, however, meet the stringent standard established in *Church of Lukumi Babalu*. Claims of religious freedom now routinely fail to gain judicial protection. Indeed, the reasoning of the *Smith* case has substantially chilled the filing of free exercise claims in the federal courts. Serious doubts cloud the future of the constitutional status of free exercise in the United States.[272]

Conclusion

In one of his draft revisions of the Virginia Declaration of Rights, Madison wrote:

> That religion, or the duty which we owe our Creator, and the manner of discharging it, can be directed only by reason and conviction, not by force or violence; and therefore, that all men are equally entitled to enjoy the free exercise of religion, according to the dictates of conscience, unpunished and unrestrained by the magistrate, Unless the preservation of equal liberty and the existence of the State are manifestly endangered; And that it is the mutual duty of all to practice Christian forbearance, love, and charity towards each other.[273]

Free exercise, "the manner of discharging" our duty to the Creator, is fundamental and is to be respected except where "the preservation of equal liberty and the existence of the State are manifestly endangered." Measured by this exalted standard, the history of the judicial treatment of the believing conscience has often fallen short. In the nineteenth century, a

Supreme Court dominated by Protestant progressives viewed with hostility the claim by Latter-Day Saints to divinely sanctioned polygamous relations. In the first forty years of the twentieth century, the demands of nationalism often took priority.

Cantwell and its progeny, in light of this history, might be aberration or harbinger. For a brief half-century in our constitutional history, it was recognized that the free exercise of religion enjoyed a claim to protection as worthy as free speech, or press freedom, or the other guarantees of the Bill of Rights. An impressive edifice of law—the compelling government interest standard, as articulated in *Sherbert*, *Yoder*, and other cases—was erected to shield the religious rights of Americans. Religious freedom was protected both in its individual and in its corporate forms of expressions. Free exercise was recognized as an individual right, but it was a right that religious groups, such as the Amish, might also successfully assert.

By the late 1940s, however, in the severance of the free exercise from the establishment "clauses," cracks appeared in the structure. Constitutional scholars and advocates of the strict separation of church and state—emboldened by a radical new vision of what the founders said and thought about the relationship of religion and the state—set a new goal for the courts: to search out the "vestiges" of the establishment of religion and to uproot them wherever found. On this reading of constitutional history, religion was to be privatized and religious freedom would come to mean freedom from religion. Although this separationist strain of constitutional thought has not always been dominant, it remains important even today.

After 1990, the Supreme Court turned decisively away from the Madisonian vision of free exercise as the ultimate right, to be safeguarded at all costs except where equality or the existence of the state itself is threatened. The language of the religion clause itself—exercise must mean acts, not simply beliefs—has been largely ignored. The Court has moved into a realm where an aggressive establishment-clause and timid free exercise jurisprudence threaten religious freedom from two directions.[274] The opinions of individual justices, furthermore, reveal incompatible viewpoints with the result that judicial outcomes are shaped by pragmatic alliances among the justices, rather than by principled or coherent constitutional theory. Indeed, it has been shown that the justices often speak in competing grammars, drawn from competing theological traditions within the American experience.[275]

A history of such complexity and the depth of contemporary disagreements, may, however, be inevitable and may point to a larger fact about the phenomenon of religious freedom, namely, the impossibility of achieving genuine neutrality. Protestant progressives in the late nineteenth century, nationalists in the first half of the twentieth century, and secularists in the second half of the twentieth century all necessarily imposed their vision on the First Amendment's command.

Although historical experience has been varied, the foundations of free exercise nevertheless have remained constant, even though ignored in much contemporary Supreme Court jurisprudence. When Madison wrote of religious freedom, he grounded the principle on a religious duty that transcended loyalty to state: the requirement of creatures freely to give obeisance to a sovereign God. His commitment to free exercise as the surest way of fulfilling our obligation to the Creator, enshrined in the organic law of the land, refutes contemporary efforts to root religious freedom in secular concepts, whether neutral principles or liberal notions of self-fulfillment.

The need to remain faithful to Madisonian foundations is compelling if we wish to fulfill the First Amendment's mandate. As Noonan has written: "For God must enter any account of religious bigotry and religious freedom. On that point you cannot be neutral. Religion is either the worship of a being distinct from the worshipers who is God for the worshipers, or God is the projection of personal and collective need. The latter alternative, the common humanistic interpretation of religious phenomena, affords no secure footing for religious freedom."[276]

Notes

1. See John 18:37.

2. See Saint Augustine, "The Correction of the Donatists" (Letter 185), excerpted in *The Believer and the Powers That Are: Cases, History, and Other Data Bearing on the Relation of Religion and Government*, ed. and trans. John T. Noonan Jr., (New York: Macmillan, 1987), 19–20.

3. See Roland H. Bainton, *The Travail of Religious Liberty* (New York: Harper & Brothers, 1958), 60–64. Cf. Steven Ozment, "Martin Luther on Religious Liberty," in *Religious Liberty in Western Thought*, ed. Noel B. Reynolds and W. Cole Durham Jr. (Atlanta: Scholars Press, 1996), 75–82.

4. See, most recently, Brad S. Gregory, *Salvation at Stake: Christian Martyrdom in Early Modern Europe* (Cambridge, Mass.: Harvard University Press, 1999), 162–96, 250–314.

5. See John Witte Jr., "Moderate Religious Liberty in the Theology of John Calvin," in *Religious Liberty in Western Thought*, 83–122.

6. See Joseph Lecler, *Toleration and the Reformation*, trans. T.L. Weslow (New York: Association Press, 1960), 176–85 (on Schwenkfeld); and 186–88 (on Weigel);

see also Noonan, *Believer*, pp. 62–64 (excerpting from Simons's basic tract on religious toleration).

7. On Roger Williams, see especially Timothy Hall, *Separating Church and State: Roger Williams and Religious Liberty* (Urbana: University of Illinois Press, 1998); and Edwin S. Gaustad, *Liberty of Conscience: Roger Williams in America* (Grand Rapids, Mich.: Eerdmans, 1991).

8. Roger Williams, "Letter to John Cotton," quoted in Noonan, *Believer*, 66.

9. Quoted in Noonan, *Believer*, 67.

10. For criticism of John Locke, see Charles J. Reid Jr., "The Fundamental Freedom: Judge John T. Noonan, Jr.s' Historiography of Religious Liberty," *Marquette Law Review* 83 (1999): 398–400.

11. See John T. Noonan Jr., *The Lustre of Our Country: The American Experience of Religious Freedom* (Berkeley: University of California Press, 1998), 61–91.

12. See Noonan, *Lustre of Our Country*, 65.

13. See Ralph L. Ketcham, "James Madison and Religion—A New Hypothesis," *Journal of Presbyterian History* 38 (1960): 65, 71.

14. See William T. Hutchinson and William M.E. Rachael, eds., *Papers of James Madison,* vol. 1 (Chicago: University of Chicago Press, 1962), 66, Cf. Noonan, *Lustre of Our Country,* supra note 1, pp. 65–66.

15. See James Madison, "Memorial and Remonstrance," in *Papers of James Madison*, vol. 8, ed. Robert A. Rutland and William M.E. Rachal (Chicago: University of Chicago Press, 1973), 299.

16. Ibid., 299.

17. On the relationship between the prohibition on religious tests and religious liberty, see Gerard V. Bradley, "The No Religious Test Clause and the Constitution of Religious Liberty: A Machine That Has Gone of Itself," *Case Western Reserve Law Review* 37 (1987): 674–747.

18. See Noonan, *Lustre of Our Country*, 78.

19. Quoted in John Witte Jr., *Religion and the American Constitutional Experiment: Essential Rights and Liberties* (Boulder, Colo.: Westview Press, 2000), 65.

20. The provisions included: (1) "No religion shall be established by law, nor shall the equal rights of conscience be infringed." (2) "No person religiously scrupulous shall be compelled to bear arms." (3) "No State shall infringe the equal rights of conscience, nor the freedom of speech or of the press, nor of the right of trial by jury in criminal cases." Quoted in Witte, *Religion*, 65.

21. See Noonan, *Lustre of Our Country*, 81.

22. See Joseph Story, *Commentaries on the Constitution of the United States*, vol. 3 (Cambridge, Mass.: Hilliard, Gray, and Co., 1833), sec. 1870, pp. 727–28.

23. See James McClellan, *Joseph Story and the American Constitution: A Study in Political and Legal Thought* (Norman: University of Oklahoma Press, 1971), 122. Cf. Joseph Story, "Christianity a Part of the Common Law," *American Jurist and Law Magazine* 9 (1833): 346; reprinted in William W. Story, *Life and Letters of Joseph Story*, vol. 1 (Freeport, N.Y.: Books for Libraries Press, 1971), 431–33.

24. See William W. Story, ed., *The Miscellaneous Writings of Joseph Story* (Boston: C.C. Little and J. Brown, 1852), 517.

25. See *Vidal v. Girard's Executors*, 43 U.S. (4 How. 127, 198 (1844). The *Vidal* Court was explicating the law of Pennsylvania and subsequently cited the Pennsylvania case of *Updegraff v. Commonwealth*, 11. Serg. & Rawle 394 (Pa., 1824).

26. See *People v. Ruggles* 8 Johns. 225 (1811).

27. See Daniel L. Dreisbach, ed., *Religion and Politics in the Early Republic: Jasper Adams and the Church-State Debate* (Lexington: University Press of Kentucky, 1996); cf. Daniel L. Dreisbach, "In Search of a Christian Commonwealth: An Examination of Selected Nineteenth-Century Commentaries on References to God and the Christian Religion in the United States Constitution," *Baylor Law Review* 48 (1996): 927, 965–67, 972–73.

28. Oral remarks of John T. Noonan Jr., Emory University School of Law, March 28, 2000 (terming the prohibition on establishments the "corollary" of the free exercise clause).

29. See Daniel O. Conkle, "Toward a General Theory of the Establishment Clause," *Northwestern Law Review* 82 (1998): 1113–94.

30. See Conkle, "Establishment Clause," 1133.

31. As Harold Berman has observed: "The covenant between God and man, Madison said, requires free exercise of religion, and that covenant takes precedence—both in order of time and degree of obligation—over the social contract." See Harold J. Berman, "Religion and Law: The First Amendment in Historical Perspective," *Emory Law Journal* 35 (1986): 777, 787.

32. See Noonan, *Lustre of Our Country*, 76–77, 83.

33. See Witte, *Religion*, 69.

34. See *Permoli v. First Municipality of the City of New Orleans*, 44 U.S. (3. How.) 589 (1844).

35. See Leonard J. Arrington and Davis Bitton, *The Mormon Experience: A History of the Latter Day Saints*, 2d ed. (Urbana: University of Illinois Press, 1992), 5–6.

36. Ibid., 8–10.

37. Ibid., 10–14.

38. See David J. Whitaker, "'The Bone in the Throat': Orson Pratt and the Public Announcement of Plural Marriage," *Western Historical Quarterly* 18 (1987): 293–314.

39. See 12 U.S. Stats. 501 (1862). The federal campaign against plural marriage has been the subject of much scholarship. Important works include Orma Linford, "The Mormons and the Law, Part I," *Utah Law Review* 9 (1964): 308–70, and "Part II," *Utah Law Review* 9 (1965): 543–91; and Sarah Barringer Gordon, "'The Twin Relic of Barbarism': A Legal History of Anti-Polygamy in Nineteenth-Century America" (Ph.D. diss., Princeton University, 1995).

40. See Linford, "Mormons and the Law, Part I," 332–33.

41. Ibid., 335–36.

42. See *Reynolds v. United States*, 98 U.S. 145 (1879).

43. Id., 64.

44. Id., 64.

45. Id., 165–66.

46. See B. Carmon Hardy, *Solemn Covenant: The Mormon Polygamous Passage* (Urbana: University of Illinois Press, 1992), 45; Richard S. Van Wagoner, *Mormon Polygamy: A History* (Salt Lake City: Signature Books, 1986), 118.

47. See Gordon, "'Twin Relic of Barbarism,'" 128–30.

48. See 18 U.S. Stats. 253 (1874).

49. 22 U.S. Stats. 30, 32 (1882).

50. Id., Cf. David L. Bigler, *Forgotten Kingdom: The Mormon Theocracy in the American West, 1847–1896* (Spokane: Arthur H. Clark Co., 1998), 317.

51. See Bigler, *Forgotten Kingdom*, 322.

52. Following his conviction, Clawson declared to the sentencing judge: "'I very much regret that the laws of my country should come in contact with the laws of God, but whenever they do I shall invariably choose the latter. If I did not so express myself I should feel unworthy of the cause I represent.'" Quoted in Bigler, *Forgotten Kingdom*, supra note 104, at 324. Cf. Orson F. Whitney, *History of Utah* (Salt Lake City: George Q. Cannon & Sons, Publishers, 1898), 293–324 (providing a detailed account of this case).

53. See *Clawson v. United States*, 114 U.S. 477 (1885).

54. *Murphy v. Ramsey*, 114 U.S. 15, 45 (1885).

55. See 24 U.S. Stats. 635, 637–638. Under sec. 26 of the act, the Court was empowered to appoint trustees who would manage the "houses of worship," "parsonages," and "burial grounds" for the use of the congregation, provided polygamy was suppressed. See 24 U.S. Stats. 641.

56. See *Late Corporation of the Church of Jesus Christ of Latter-Day Saints v. United States*, 136 U.S. 1 (1890).

57. Id., 49.

58. Id.

59. Id.

60. Id., 49–50.

61. Id., 50.

62. See Witte, *Religion*, supra note 19, pp. 122–23.

63. *Reynolds v. United States*, 164, 166.

64. Wilford Woodruff, who had succeeded John Taylor as president of the church, recorded in his journal that the decision in *Late Corporation of the Church of Jesus Christ of Latter-Day Saints* "is turning the Last that will seal the Condemnation of this Nation." See *Wilford Woodruff's Journal*, vol. 9 (Midvale, Utah: Signature Books, 1983–85), 94 (entry for May 19, 1890). I am grateful to Miss Krista Halverson for locating this publication for me. Federal authorities in Utah let it be known early in the summer of 1890 that Mormon temples in Logan, Saint George, and Manti were subject to confiscation. See Bigler, *Forgotten Kingdom*, 354. On Sept. 25, 1890, Woodruff issued a "Manifesto" in which he declared the church's readiness to submit to the law of the land, and the next day Charles Zane, chief federal judge in the Utah territory, pronounced himself satisfied at Woodruff's sincerity and suspended judicial proceedings against the Church. See Thomas G. Alexander, *Things in Heaven and Earth: The Life and Times of Wilford Woodruff, a Mormon Prophet* (Salt Lake City: Signature Books, 1993), 266–67.

65. *United States v. Schwimmer*, 279 U.S. 644, 647 (1929).

66. Id., 650–51.

67. *United States v. MacIntosh*, 283 U.S. 605 (1931).

68. See "Brief for Respondents," *United States v. MacIntosh*, 5.

69. See *United States v. MacIntosh*, 622.

70. Id., 623.

71. Id., 633 (C.J. Hughes dissenting).

72. Id.

73. Id., 634.

74. Id., 634.

75. Id., 630–31, 634–35.

76. See *Minersville School District v. Gobitis*, 310 U.S. 586 (1940).

77. Id., p. 592.

78. See Shawn Francis Peters, *Judging Jehovah's Witnesses: Religious Persecution and the Dawn of the Rights Revolution* (Lawrence: University Press of Kansas, 2000), 25–27.

79. See *Minersville School District*, 593.

80. Id., 594–95.

81. Id., 601 (J. Stone dissenting).

82. Id., 602 (J. Stone dissenting).

83. See *Meyer v. Nebraska*, 262 U.S. 390 (1923).

84. On the history of the *Meyer* case, see William G. Ross, *Forging New Freedoms: Nativism, Education, and the Constitution, 1917-1927* (Lincoln: University of Nebraska Press, 1994), 74–95; William G. Ross, "A Judicial Janus: *Meyer v. Nebraska* in Historical Perspective," *University of Cincinnati Law Review* 57 (1988): 125-204; Paul Finkelman, "German Victims and American Oppressors: The Cultural Background and Legacy of *Meyer v. Nebraska*," in *Law and the Great Plains: Essays on the Legal History of the Heartland*, ed. John R. Wunder (Westport, Conn.: Greenwood Press, 1996), 33-56; and Jack W. Rodgers, "The Foreign Language Issue in Nebraska, 1918-1923," *Nebraska History* 39 (1958): 1–22.

85. See *Meyer*, supra note 169, pp. 396–97.

86. Id., 399.

87. See *Pierce v. Society of Sisters*, 268 U.S. 510, 531–32, 534.

88. Id., 534–35.

89. See Bernard Schwartz, *A History of the Supreme Court* (Oxford: Oxford University Press, 1993), 247.

90. Ibid., 238–40.

91. See Elder Witt, *Guide to the U.S. Supreme Court*, 2d ed. (Washington, D.C.: CQ Press, 1990), 374–80.

92. See especially Raoul Berger, *Government by Judiciary: The Transformation of the Fourteenth Amendment*, 2d ed. (Indianapolis: Liberty Fund, 1997).

93. See *Cantwell v. Connecticut*, 310 U.S. 296, 300–1 (1940).

94. Id., 301.

95. Id., 303.

96. Id., 300–2.

97. Id., 302.

98. Id., 303–4.

99. See Mark de Wolfe Howe, *The Garden and the Wilderness: Religion and Government in American Constitutional History* (Chicago: University of Chicago Press, 1965), 107–8.

100. See Noonan, *Lustre of Our Country*, 33–34.

101. See *West Virginia State Board of Education v. Barnette*, 319 U.S. 624 (1943).

102. Id., 626.

103. Id., 629.

104. Id., 630.

105. Id., 642.

106. Id., 640.

107. "We set up government by consent of the governed, and the Bill of Rights denies those in power any legal opportunity to coerce that consent. Authority here is to be controlled by public opinion, not public opinion by authority"; id., 641.

108. Id., 639.

109. Id., 642.

110. See *United States v. Carolene Products Company*, 304 U.S. 144, 152, note 4 (1938).

111. Id., note 4, p. 153.

112. See Ronald D. Rotunda and John E. Nowak, *Treatise on Constitutional Law: Substance and Procedure*, vol. 2 (Saint Paul: West Publishing Co., 1992), 358.

113. See *Sherbert v. Verner*, 374 U.S. 398 (1963).

114. Id., 401.

115. Id., 403.

116. Id., 404.

117. Id., 406.

118. See, e.g., *Cruz v. Beto*, 405 U.S. 319 (1972) (per curiam) (holding that prison officials must accommodate the religious needs of a Buddhist inmate); *McDaniel v. Paty*, 435 U.S. 618 (1978) (striking down statute prohibiting "ministers of the Gospel" from holding public office); *Widmar v. Vincent*, 454 U.S. 263 (1981) (making use of free-speech clause to require universities which accommodate secular speech to accommodate religious speech as well); and *Thomas v. Review Board*, 450 U.S. 707 (1981) (reaffirming *Sherbert* in the context of a pacifist who declined work in an armaments factory).

119. See *Wisconsin v. Yoder*, 406 U.S. 205 (1972).

120. See John A. Hostetler, *Amish Society*, 4th ed. (Baltimore: Johns Hopkins University Press, 1993), 31–49.

121. Id., 50–65.

122. See Donald B. Kraybill, *The Riddle of Amish Culture* (Baltimore: Johns Hopkins University Press, 1989), 14–23.

123. "The typical age of baptism ranges from sixteen to twenty-one"; ibid., 100.

124. Id.

125. Id., 214.

126. Id., 215.

127. "A way of life, however virtuous and admirable, may not be interposed as a barrier to reasonable state regulation of education if it is based on purely secular considerations"; ibid.

128. Id.

129. Id., 220.

130. Id.

131. See *Negre v. Larsen*, 401 U.S. 437 (1971). Cf. Charles J. Reid Jr., "John T. Noonan, Jr., on the Catholic Conscience and War: *Negre v. Larsen*," *Notre Dame Law Review* 76 (2001): 881–959.

132. See *Goldman v. Weinberger*, 475 U.S. 503 (1986).

133. Id., 507.

134. See *United States v. Lee*, 455 U.S. 252 (1982).

135. See *Bob Jones University v. United States*, 461 U.S. 574, 604 (1983).

136. See *Everson v. Board of Education*, 330 U.S. 1 (1947).

137. Id., 8–9.

138. Id., 9–10.

139. Id., 11.

140. Id., 12.

141. Id., 12–13.

142. Id., 15.
143. Id., 15–16.
144. See Noonan, *Believer*, 374.
145. *Everson v. Board of Education*, 16–18.
146. Id., 25 (J. Jackson dissenting).
147. Id., 28–43 (J. Rutledge dissenting).
148. Id., p. 40 (J. Rutledge dissenting) (quoting "Memorial and Remonstrance," para. 3).
149. Id.
150. Id., 31–32.
151. Id., 39–40.
152. Id., 41.
153. "Rutledge, the son of a fundamentalist Baptist minister in Kentucky, had in later life become a modern Unitarian." See Noonan, *Believer*, 374.
154. See *McCollum v. Board of Education*, 333 U.S. 203 (1948).
155. Id., 210–12.
156. Id., 215 (J. Frankfurter concurring).
157. Id., 217.
158. Id., 231.
159. Id., 244 (J. Reed dissenting): "When the First Amendment was pending in Congress in substantially its present form, 'Mr. Madison said, he apprehended the meaning of the words to be, that Congress should not establish a religion, and enforce the legal observation of it by law, nor compel men to worship God in any manner contrary to their conscience.'" (quoting 1 *Annals of Congress* 730).
160. Id., 244.
161. Id., pp. 252–53 and note 24.
162. See Edward Corwin, "The Supreme Court as National School Board," *Law and Contemporary Problems* 14 (1949): 3, 10: "Madison's conception of an 'establishment of religion' . . . was . . . *a religion enjoying a preferred status*. The same conception, moreover, underlies the state constitutions of the day, when they deal with the subject.".
163. Id., 13 (quoting Madison).
164. Id., 13 (Corwin emphasizes that Jefferson wished religion to be a course of study at his own University of Virginia because of its great importance).
165. Id., 13.
166. See John Courtney Murray, "Law or Prepossessions?" *Law and Contemporary Problems* 14 (1949): 23, 37.
167. See Thomas J. Curry, *The First Freedoms: Church and State in America to the Passage of the First Amendment* (New York: Oxford University Press, 1986), 37, 210.
168. See Gerard V. Bradley, *Church-State Relationships in America* (Westport, Conn.: Greenwood Press, 1987), 12–13. Bradley also makes the point (on p. 12) that Madison himself never indicated that the First Amendment should be interpreted by reference to the "Memorial and Remonstrance."
169. Id., 12.
170. Id.
171. See Akhil Reed Amar, "The Bill of Rights as a Constitution," *Yale Law Journal* 100 (1991): 1131, 1157–58. Cf. "Note: Rethinking the Incorporation of the Establishment Clause: A Federalist View," *Harvard Law Review* 105 (1992): 1700–19.

172. See Daniel Dreisbach, "'Sowing Useful Truths and Principles:' The Danbury Baptists, Thomas Jefferson, and the 'Wall of Separation,'" *Journal of Church and State* 39 (1997): 455–501. Cf. James H. Hutson, "Thomas Jefferson's Letter to the Danbury Baptists: A Controversy Rejoined," *William and Mary Quarterly* 56 (3d ser., 1999): 775–90 (demonstrating, through an investigation of the preliminary drafts of the Jefferson letter, including some blotted out portions recovered through FBI Labratory testing, that "Jefferson's principal motive in writing the Danbury Baptist letter was to mount a political counterattack against his Federalist enemies"; p. 776). Cf. Daniel Dreisbach, "Thomas Jefferson and the Danbury Baptists Revisited," *William and Mary Quarterly* 56 (3d ser. 1999): 805–16 (defending Hutson's conclusions); and Daniel L. Dreisbach, "Thomas Jefferson and Bills Number 82-86 of the Revision of the Laws of Virginia, 1776-1786: New Light on the Jeffersonian Model of Church-State Relations," *North Carolina Law Review* 69 (1990): 159–211 (establishing that a review of Jefferson's complete contributions to the legislative history of religious freedom in Virginia reveals him to be more accommodationist than generally recognized).

173. See Dreisbach, "'Sowing Useful Truths and Principles,'" supra, 470–71, summarizing the work of Jon Butler, "Coercion, Miracle, Reason: Rethinking the American Religious Experience in the Revolutionary Age," in *Religion in a Revolutionary Age*, ed. Ronald Hoffman and Peter J. Albert (Charlottesville: University Press of Virginia, 1994), 29–30.

174. Dreisbach, "'Sowing Useful Truths and Principles,'" 471.

175. See *Engel v. Vitale*, 370 U.S. 421 (1962).

176. Id., 422–36.

177. Id., 445–46 (J. Stewart dissenting).

178. Id., 445.

179. *School District of Abington Township v. Schempp*, 374 U.S. 203 (1963). At issue were a Pennsylvania practice of daily Bible readings and prayers conducted over the school intercom system at the beginning of each day; and a Baltimore practice of daily Bible reading and recitation of the Lord's Prayer; id., 206–12.

180. Id., 208 (quoting trial testimony).

181. Id., 209 (quoting trial court).

182. Id., 212 (quoting the Murrays' petition).

183. Id., 225.

184. Id., 222.

185. Id., 305 (J. Goldberg concurring).

186. Id., 310 (J. Stewart dissenting).

187. Id., 313.

188. Id., 316.

189. Id., 319–20. A recent line of cases has sought to develop the principle of neutrality as applied to "establishment clause" cases. In *Witters v. Washington Department of Services for the Blind*, 474 U.S. 481 (1986), the Court upheld a state grant of funds to the petitioner, a blind man studying in a ministerial program, despite the pervasively religious character of his education. In *Zobrest v. Catalina Foothills School District*, 509 U.S. 1 (1993), the Court permitted a school district to provide a sign-language interpreter to a student in a Catholic school. And in *Rosenberger v. Rector and Visitors of the University of Virginia*, 515 U.S. 819 (1995), the Court permitted the use of state funds in providing for religious as well as secular speakers at a state university. Common to all these cases is the principle, perhaps articulated best in *Zobrest*, that where a "service . . . is part

of a general government program that distributes benefits neutrally" to all recipients, the beneficiaries may include religious as well as non-religious entities. See 509 U.S. at 10.

This quest for neutral principles has been criticized in some circles as essentially an impossible one. Thus: "The aspiration to neutrality can be understood as an effort to avoid or transcend the kind of theorizing that adopts or prefers in advance one of the competing religious or secular positions within a community and then allows other positions only as much freedom as the preferred position prescribes." See Steven D. Smith, *Foreordained Failure: The Quest for a Constitutional Principle of Religious Freedom* (New York: Oxford University Press, 1995), 77.

190. See *Lemon v. Kurtzman*, 403 U.S. 602 (1971).

191. Id., 612–13.

192. See *Wallace v. Jaffree*, 472 U.S. 38, 41 (quoting Alabama statute sec. 16-1-20).

193. Id., p. 57 and note 43.

194. See *Edwards v. Aguillard*, 482 U.S. 578 (1987).

195. Id., 591.

196. Id., 610–40 (J. Scalia dissenting).

197. Id., 614.

198. Id., 631.

199. Id., 611.

200. Id., 615.

201. "Given the many hazards involved in assessing the subjective intent of governmental decisionmakers, the first prong of *Lemon* is defensible, I think, only if the text of the Establishment Clause demands it. That is surely not the case"; id., 639.

202. See *Coles v. Cleveland Board of Education*, 171 F.2d 369 (6th Cir., 1999).

203. See *Metzl v. Leininger*, 57 F.3d 618 (7th Cir., 1995).

204. See *Bridenbaugh v. O'Bannion*, 185 F.3d 796 (7th Cir., 1999); *Granzeier v. Middleton*, 173 F.3d 568 (6th Cir., 1999); and *Cammack v. Waihee*, 932 F.2d 765 (9th Cir., 1991).

205. The facts in *Santa Fe Independent School District v. Jane Doe*, 68 U.S.L.W. 4525 (2000), brought by Mormon and Catholic parents, involved the student recitation of public prayer prior to each varsity football game, but also implicated significant coercion of religious minorities by members of the school district, including "several proselytizing practices, such as promoting attendance at a Baptist revival meeting, encouraging membership in religious clubs, chastising students who held minority religious beliefs, and distributing Gideon Bibles on school premises" (p. 4527). Cf. Dan Egan, *The Salt Lake City Tribune*, June 3, 2000, p. C1 (detailing further instances of coercive conduct by school district members). Rather than going through the steps of trying to determine whether the district "established" a religion, as did the majority in *Santa Fe*, a test focused on coercion would consider the implications of district policy and practice for the religious freedom of the affected students.

206. See *Lee v. Weisman*, 505 U.S. 577 (1991).

207. See *Lamb's Chapel v. Center Moriches Union Free School District*, 508 U.S. 384 (1993), 397–401 (J. Scalia concurring).

208. Id., 398.

209. Id.

210. See *Agostini v. Felton*, 521 U.S. 202 (1997). Cf. *Santa Fe*, p. 4532.

211. See *Tangipahoa Board of Education v. Freiler*, 68 U.S.L.W. 3771 (2000) (J. Scalia dissenting from denial of certiorari).

212. See *Wallace v. Jaffree*, 472 U.S. 38 (1985), 91–114. (J. Rehnguist dissenting).
213. Id., 95.
214. Id., 98.
215. Id., 100 (quoting 1 Stat. 50 (1789).
216. Id., 103.
217. Id., 104 (quoting Joseph Story).
218. See, e.g., Robert L. Cord, *Separation of Church and State: Historical Fact and Current Fiction* (New York: Lambeth Press, 1982); Michael J. Malbin, *Religion and Politics: The Intentions of the Authors of the First Amendment* (Washington, D.C.: American Enterprise Institute, 1978); Robert L. Cord, "Church-State Separation: Restoring the 'No Preference' Doctrine of the First Amendment," *Harvard Journal of Law and Public Policy* 9 (1986): 129–72. Cf. John Witte Jr., "The Theology and Politics of the First Amendment Religion Clauses: A Bicentennial History," *Emory Law Journal* 40 (1991): 489–507 (arguing that the First Amendment embodies both non-preferentialist and "separationist" strains); Douglas Laycock, "'Nonpreferential' Aid to Religion: A False Claim About Original Intent," *William and Mary Law Review* 27 (1986): 875–923 (arguing on behalf of separationism and against non-preferentialism); and Robert P. George, "Protecting Religious Liberty in the Next Millenium: Should We Amend the Religion Clauses of the Constitution?" *Loyola of Los Angeles Law Review* 32 (1998): 27, 38–48 (arguing that modern separationist and non-preferentialist claims represent anachronistic readings of the framing).
219. See *Mitchell v. Helms*, 68 U.S.L. W. 4668 (2000). The case involved a challenge to a federal statute that subsidized the use of library, media, and computer materials by nonsectarian and sectarian schools alike.
220. Id., 4672. Thomas added, "If the religious, irreligious, and a-religious are all alike eligible for governmental aid, no one would conclude that any indoctrination that any particular recipient conducts has been done at the behest of the government." Cf. *Jackson v. Benson*, 578 N.W. 2d 602, 218 Wis. 835 (1998) (employing the *Lemon* test to reach the accommodationist result of upholding the Milwaukee school vouchers program).
221. See *ACLU v. Capitol Square Review and Advisory Board*, 210 F.3d 703 (6th Cir., 2000).
222. See Matthew 19:26; cf. Mark 10:14–27 and Luke 18:15–27.
223. See *ACLU*, 727.
224. *A.C.L.U. of Ohio v. Capitol Square Review Board*, 243 F.2d 289 (6th Cir., 2001).
225. Id., 293.
226. Id., 294.
227. Id., 295.
228. Id.
229. See *Thomas v. Review Board*, 450 U.S. at pp. 724–25 (J. Rehnquist dissenting).
230. Id., 721.
231. See *Employment Division v. Smith*, 494 U.S. 872 (1990).
232. See *Smith*, 878–79.
233. Id., 879 (quoting *Minersville School District v. Gobitis*).
234. See *Barnette*, p. 642: "The decision of this Court in *Minersville School District v. Gobitis* . . . [is] overruled."
235. See *Smith*, 879 (Quoting *Reynolds v. United States*). *Smith* did accord protec-

tion to religious acts in certain narrowly drawn circumstances, such as assembling together for religious ceremonies or proselytizing. Scalia observed (p. 877): "It would be true, we think . . . that a State would be 'prohibiting the free exercise [of religion]' if it sought to ban such acts or abstentions only when they are engaged in for religious reasons, or only because of the religious belief that they display."

236. Id., 881.

237. See *Cantwell*, 303 ("We hold that the statute . . . deprives [the appellants] of their liberty without due process of law . . . . The First Amendment declares that Congress shall make no law respecting an establishment of religion or prohibiting the free exercise thereof").

238. Id. Scalia has recently asserted that the right to direct the development of one's offspring cannot be judicially enforced. See *Troxel v. Granville*, 68 U.S.L.W. 4458, 4467 (2000) (J. Scalia dissenting).

239. See *Yoder*, 213–314 (reading *Pierce* as involving the parental right to direct "the *religious* upbringing and education of . . . children . . . ") (emphasis added), 214–15, and 221–29.

240. *Smith*, 883–84.

241. Id., 884.

242. Id., 891–907 (J. O'Connor concurring).

243. Id., 893.

244. Id. (quoting *Wisconsin v. Yoder*).

245. Id., 896.

246. Id., 897.

247. Id., 899-903.

248. Id., 905–7.

249. Id., 909–10.

250. See Michael W. McConnell, "The Origins and Historical Understanding of Free Exercise of Religion," *Harvard Law Review* 103 (1990): 1409–1517.

251. Id., 1516.

252. See Michael W. McConnell, "Free Exercise Revisionism and the *Smith* Decision," *University of Chicago Law Review* 57 (1990): 1109–53.

253. Id., 1152. McConnell continues: "The clause is not concerned with facial neutrality or general applicability. It singles out a particular category of human activity for particular protection, a protection that is most often needed for practitioners of nonmainstream faiths who lack the ability to protect themselves in the political sphere."

254. See Gerard V. Bradley, "Beguiled: Free Exercise Exemptions and the Siren Song of Liberalism," *Hofstra Law Review* 20 (1991): 245–319.

255. Id., 248.

256. See Philip A. Hamburger, "A Constitutional Right of Religious Exemption: An Historical Perspective," *George Washington Law Review* 60 (1992): 915-48.

257. See John T. Noonan Jr., "The End of Free Exercise?" *De Paul Law Review* 42 (1992): 567, 577.

258. On the campaign to restore the compelling government interest standard after *Smith*, see Gustav Niebuhr, "Disparate Groups Unite behind Civil Rights Bill on Religious Freedom," *Washington Post*, Oct. 16, 1993, A7; Peter Steinfels, "Beliefs," *New York Times*, Feb. 29, 1992, sec. 1, p. 10; and Ruth Marcus, "Reins on Religious Freedom? Broad Coalition Protests Impact of High Court Ruling," *Washington Post*, March 9, 1991, A1. The Religious Freedom Restoration Act passed the United States Senate

on a 97-3 vote after passing the House on a voice vote. It was signed into law on Nov. 16, 1993. See Peter Steinfels, "Clinton Signs Law Protecting Religious Practices," *New York Times*, Nov. 17, 1993, sec. A, p. 18.

259. See *City of Boerne v. Flores*, 521 U.S. 507 (1997).

260. Id., 529–36.

261. Id., 533.

262. Id., 532.

263. Id., 544–65 (J. O'Connor dissenting). Concurring in the majority opinion, Scalia relied on Hamburger's article to challenge O'Connor's historiography (pp. 537–38) (J. Scalia concurring, in part).

264. Id., 551.

265. Id., 552. Drawing a contemporary conclusion, O'Connor continued: "Such notions parallel the ideas expressed in our pre-*Smith* cases—that government may not hinder believers from freely exercising their religion, unless necessary to further a significant state interest."

266. Id., 554.

267. Id., 567.

268. As *Smith* put it: "[I]t would doubtless be unconstitutional, for example, to ban the casting of 'statues that are to be used for worship purposes,' or to prohibit bowing down before a golden calf." See *Smith*, 877–78.

269. See *Church of Lukumi Babalu Aye v. City of Hialeah*, 508 U.S. 520 (1993).

270. Id., 525.

271. Id., 545.

272. John Noonan, however, cautions that there is more to free exercise than the doctrines of the courts: "[Free exercise] has been an experiment carried on for over two centuries chiefly by the men and women and the lawmakers of the country. Not very much of what has been tried has depended on the Supreme Court, a late-comer to the national conversation. The executive, the legislature, the citizenry are partners with the courts in the conduct of the experiment. The trajectory is not completed. May the movement toward the ideal, the free response in prayer and service to God, untrammeled by any law, resume and flourish." See John T. Noonan Jr., "Religious Liberty at the Stake," *Virginia Law Review* 84 (1998): 459, 475–76.

273. See *Papers of James Madison*, vol. 1, supra note 13, pp. 174–75.

274. See Mary Ann Glendon, "The Supreme Court, 1997: A Symposium," *First Things*, Oct. 1997, 30.

275. See Kathleen A. Brady, "Fostering Harmony among the Justices: How Contemporary Debates in Theology Can Help to Reconcile the Divisions on the Court Regarding Religious Expression by the State," *Notre Dame Law Review* 75 (1999): 433–578.

276. See Noonan, *Lustre of Our Country*, 1.

4

What Is a Public Religion?

José Casanova

To the seemingly straightforward question, "What is a public religion?" one could offer a seemingly simple answer: A public religion is one that has, assumes, or tries to assume a public character, function, or role. The complications begin the moment one tries to ascertain the diverse, often incongruous meanings of "public"; and it becomes even more complex if in talking about religion one distinguishes what Hugh Heclo has termed the *behavioral*, the *institutional*, and the *philosophical* levels of analysis—levels that correspond to what sociologists tend to call the interactional, the organizational, and the societal levels.[1]

Beginning with the various meanings of "public," one could use the analytical distinction between the three areas of the polity—the state, political society, and civil society—to distinguish three different types of public religion that correspond to these three areas.[2] Established state churches would be the paradigmatic example of public religion at the state level. Religions that mobilize their institutional resources for political competition through political parties, social movements, or lobbying agencies would be examples of public religion at the level of political society. Finally, public religions at the civil society level would be exemplified by those that enter the public square—that is, the undifferentiated public sphere of civil society—to participate in open public debates about the *res publica*—that is, about public issues, public affairs, public policy, and the common good or the commonwealth.

In the United States at least, there is a near unanimous consensus concerning the desirability of maintaining the separation of church and state. The voices advocating church establishment (i.e., public religions at the state level) are few and marginal. The contemporary debates in America, therefore, are not over disestablishment, which few people question, but over the structure of the wall of separation, that is, how impermeable or porous should this wall be and which kinds of religion should be allowed to enter the public sphere or to become publicly entangled. Concerning the kinds of religion that may enter the public sphere, I will briefly look at the less contested individual behavioral level of analysis before focusing on the more contested institutional and societal levels.

The Individual's Religion and the Public Sphere

The individual behavioral level is simultaneously the most fundamental level and the most elusive. It is fundamental because religion is unlikely to be of much public relevance unless it is relevant in the life of the individual citizen as a norm of conduct, as a motivational source of civic engagement, or as a discursive or normative resource for the citizen's public voice and public choices. Yet it is elusive because of the ideological bias toward the privatization of religion that is built into secularist readings of the "wall of separation" and into the "neutrality" principle of liberal theories of the public sphere. Secularist constitutional theories and liberal ideologies are not necessarily hostile to religion; they may even welcome it as a positive foundation for civic virtue, civic engagement, and the normative integration of the polity.

However, according to those theories, religion should remain private and implicit, rather than public and explicit. The positive liberal principle of "dialogic neutrality," which is meant to facilitate universal and equal access to the public sphere and to protect against discrimination based on religion, gender, race, or other ascriptive identities, is turned into an incapacitating "gag rule" the moment citizens are expected to relinquish their religious identities upon entering the "public square" and to exercise conversational self-restraint by banishing religious language from public discourse.[3] The model of the "unencumbered self" in this case turns into a hindrance.

Therein lies the paradox of the American experience. On the one hand, religion thrives in the private sphere; European observers since Alexis de Tocqueville have been struck by the widespread religiosity and by "the still impressively strong church-mindedness" (Max Weber) of the Americans;[4] and religious belonging has appeared almost as a condition for creditworthiness, at least in the past, and for political respectability and electability, even today. Yet it is religion in the abstract, not any particular religious doctrine or denominational allegiance, that is supposed to have a positive effect upon civic life. As President Dwight D. Eisenhower is reputed to have said, "I don't care which religion Americans have, as long as they have a religion."[5]

Tocqueville's analysis of the relevance of religion for the transcendence of individual egoism and privatist solipsism and, even more so, his analysis of the relevance of religious voluntarism and religious associations for civic associationism in general and, thus, for the vitality of civil society sounds as valid today as ever. Religious commitment continues to be a primary motivational source, a "habit of the heart," for involvement in social movements of all kinds and one of the keys to the shifting involvements between private interest and public action.[6] Moreover, even though praying alone, like "bowling alone," may be on the increase and according to Robert Putnam's computations American "social capital" may be diminishing, much of it still remains stored in religious associations.[7] Survey research and electoral polling keep tracking the changing relations among religious affiliation, shifting party alignments, and electoral choices, which in turn affect directly public policy.[8] But to examine the relationship between religion and the public sphere in more depth, one needs to go beyond the individual behavioral level of analysis.

Religious Institutions, the Secular State, and the Public Sphere

Karl Marx, of all people, articulated the unique paradox of American exceptionalism most succinctly in his essay "On the Jewish Question" when following Tocqueville he observed that America was both the model of "perfect disestablishment" and "the land of religiosity par excellence."[9] This unique paradox is constitutionally embedded in the dual clause of the First Amendment, which maintains a wall of separation between the state and any and all religions, while simultaneously guaranteeing the free exercise of religion, although the state through the courts reserves itself the right of determining what constitutes a religion and which religious activities deserve constitutional protection. It is the tension and the balance between these two interrelated principles that makes the American experience of religious freedom so different from the European one, "the lustre of our country," in John T. Noonan's words.[10] It is not necessarily the case that there has always been greater freedom of religion in the United States than in Europe.

Some European societies, most notably England, developed a pattern of religious freedom and toleration of religious minorities as early, if not earlier, and as lustrous as that of the United States. Yet in England this achievement was accompanied by the preservation of the formal establishment of the Anglican Church, which continues today. Other European countries, most notably France, after much struggle erected a wall of separation between church and state as strict as that of the United States. Yet in France disestablishment was accomplished by a laicist state that aggressively curtailed the free exercise of religion. Following Wilfred M. McClay's "two concepts of secularism," one could say that France evinces an extreme form of "positive secularism," whereas the United States has tended to display a more limited "negative" understanding of secularism.[11]

I repeat, the debates and the conflicts over secularism in America are usually not over the validity of disestablishment and strict separation, which few people question; nor are they usually based on a secularist Enlightenment-related bias, which viewing religion as an obstacle to progress, freedom, and reason, would like to curtail its free exercise.[12] The debates are over the right balance at any given time, mediated by the courts, between the establishment and the free exercise clauses—a balance that has proven hard to achieve, given what some constitutional scholars consider the inherent contradiction between the two clauses.[13] Put most simply, a fully consistent constitutional protection of the free exercise of religion would require the protection of nonconforming, even "deviant," religious practices, if necessary granting special legal exemptions to particular religious communities to accommodate their religious practices. But such a requirement would go not only against the principle of equality before the law, but also against the core principle of the establishment cause, which prohibits the government from providing any special aid or advantage to any particular religious community over another.

The areas of contestation, moreover, have shifted along with the changing relations among federal and state governments, public opinion, and religious majorities and minorities. Throughout the nineteenth century, under conditions of de facto Protestant hegemony in the public sphere of civil society, court decisions often reflected the religious sensibilities of the Protestant majority and served to protect establishmentarian Protestant norms. So-called church–state conflicts between the government and religious minorities, rather than being the expression of a "neutral" state zealously protecting no establishment, mostly reflected the confrontations between nonconforming religious minorities and the Protestant religious majority.

Through these confrontations and through litigation to protect the free exercise of their religion, nonconforming religious minorities have been instrumental in the constant expansion of the area of free exercise and in the institutionalization of more genuine religious pluralism.[14] Increasingly, however, during recent decades—as religious, cultural, and moral pluralism expanded and Protestantism lost progressively its majoritarian and establishmentarian character in religion, culture, and morality—the state (particularly the Supreme Court) has adopted a more "neutral" secular stance, which many critics view as a radical departure not only from established practice but from the Founders' intent. In the words of Charles J. Reid Jr., "the Court has moved into a realm where an aggressive establishment clause and timid free exercise jurisprudence threaten religious freedom."[15] This is arguably an overstatement, at least as regards the threats to religious freedom, but it is indicative nonetheless of the contemporary highly contested debates.[16]

The widespread perception, at least among many religious groups and sympathetic scholars, that the Court has moved too far in a "positive secularist" direction has led to a concerted effort from many sectors of society to move the pendulum back in the opposite direction. Indeed, there are clear signs that the correction towards the free exercise clause in two main areas of public policy, education and welfare, is well under way, as the debates over "school vouchers" and "faith-based charities" would seem to indicate.

Undoubtedly, when religious organizations become providers of public services with public funding, one may well speak of a particular form of public religion, if not of church-state entanglement. Throughout history in the United States as elsewhere, churches and religious groups have served as primary providers of social services—of education, health, and welfare. The increasing appropriation (and at times the monopolization) of these public services by states and government agencies, particularly during the past century, has been usually portrayed as a main indicator of the supposedly progressive process of secularization. Today, with the proliferation of schemes of privatization of public services and the renewed involvement of religious organizations in their provision, one can justifiably speak of a reversal of the process of secularization—yet another instance of what I have termed "the de-privatization of religion." In any case, it puts into question liberal and secularist claims that religion in the modern world is and ought to remain exclusively a private affair.

For peculiar historical reasons connected with the complex relations between the Protestant nativist majority and Catholic and Jewish immigrant religious minorities, entanglements in the area of public education are viewed most apprehensively by the courts and by secularist vigilantes as threats to the wall of separation. By contrast, religious advocates today tend to defend the same entanglements of religion in the provision of public services as legitimate expressions of the free exercise of religion. Although those might be the kinds of public religion that provoke much heated debate and litigation, they are not in my view the most analytically interesting or publicly relevant kinds. More interesting both analytically and practically are those instances in which religious groups or religious organizations enter the public sphere of political or civil society to participate either in political contestation or in public debate.

Elsewhere, I have used the public reemergence of Protestant Fundamentalism and the political mobilization of the Moral Majority into the New Christian Right as an example of public religion at the level of political society, whereas the public interventions of the Catholic bishops on issues such as the nuclear arms race, the U.S. economy, and abortion—especially once the bishops abandoned their initial strategy of electoral mobilization—are presented as instances of public religion in the public sphere of civil society.[17] Those are of course strictly speaking analytical distinctions, which are rarely present in such a clean clear-cut form in the messy reality out there. Nonetheless, it is important in my view to maintain the analytical distinction because of the actual repercussions that tend to follow from the different types of public religion.

Public Religions of Political Society

Public religions of political society may be conceptualized as the collective self-organization and mobilization of religious groups and their institutional resources as interest groups competing with other interest groups to advance their ideal and material interests in the political arena. This self-organization and mobilization can take three main forms. The first form is the mobilization of religious groups in single-issue social movements such as abolition, prohibition, civil rights, or the pro-life movement. This is the most typical form of public religion throughout American history.

The second form includes institutional lobbying by religious groups at the federal, state, and local levels. Strictly speaking, lobbying agencies are usually only quasi-public. They are public insofar as they are publicly registered. But most of their activities in trying to influence legislation and government policies take place in a secretive sphere outside of the public limelight. This form has become paramount in recent decades with the expansion of public policy and government intervention in all spheres of life, particularly after the New Deal.

The third form is the electoral mobilization of religious groups and their organization into political parties at the local, state, or federal level. Although the religious factor has been an important ingredient of American politics from the very origins of the U.S. party system and the fusion between party and denominational allegiance has generally been important, nonetheless the party system, at least at the federal level, has not been organized along strict denominational lines or secular–religious cleavages, as was the case in most European countries.[18] At the local level, however, given the frequent overlap of ethnic, religious, and class identities (working-class Irish Catholics being a case in point), the mobilization of religious resources and identities was a crucial ingredient in the organization of urban political machines.

The electoral mobilization of the New Christian Right may be viewed as a paradigmatic case of a public religion in political society. Mountains of books and articles, most of them polemical, have been written about the Christian Right. Here I can only quote from my own concluding remarks in my historical reconstruction of the transformation of Evangelical Protestantism from civil religion, to Fundamentalist sect, to New Christian Right:

> One might consider the basic dilemmas facing any religion, particularly a fundamentalist one, which wants to enter the competitive field of modern democratic politics and to score victories there. . . . Modern agonic electoral politics has certain rules of engagement which are inimical to fundamentalism. The name Moral Majority already signaled simultaneously the fundamentalist claim to hegemony, the choice of electoral mobilization as the road to power and public in-

> fluence, and an implicit willingness to submit the cognitive, practical, and moral validity claims of fundamentalism to the discretion of the ballot box and to the principle of majority rule. Mobilizational and electoral success, however, require not only strategic adjustment to the rules and dynamics of the organizational society and electoral politics but also ideological compromises, which tend to undermine fundamentalist principles and identities. A well-organized militant minority taking advantage of the element of surprise or using stealth methods can score early victories. But the successful mobilization of fundamentalism soon called forth the countermobilization of its opponents. Moreover, in order to join an electoral majority it became necessary to enter into electoral alliances and to fill a circumscribed and subordinated niche as a faction of a broad Republican party coalition. Soon it also became obvious that the very goal of legislating fundamentalist morality could hardly be reconciled with the kind of normative compromises and parliamentary horse trading that are usually required for legislative success.[19]

Public Religions of Civil Society

Public religions of civil society can be defined as those religions that enter the undifferentiated public sphere of civil society in order to participate in open public debates about the *res publica,* that is, about public affairs and the common good. The style of public Catholicism that emerged in the late 1960s after the Second Vatican Council may be considered a paradigmatic example. Using David O'Brien's characterization of the three different historical styles of Catholic involvement in American politics, which he terms "republican," "immigrant," and "public," will help to clarify what I mean by such a novel form of public religion.

"Republican" Catholicism

For O'Brien, the kind of "republican Catholicism" that emerged after the American Revolution was the natural style of a self-confident Catholic colonial elite which, well-versed in the "survival tactics" of Catholicism during years of suppression in England, had learned to keep their private piety and their public affairs strictly separate.[20] His characterization is very much akin Bernhard Groethuysen's masterful characterization of the eighteenth-century, self-made French Catholic "bourgeois." Both types represented the style of successful Catholic laypeople, faithful to the church but fully at home in the world, who had learned to segregate rigidly, in the liberal secular tradition, their political, economic, and religious roles. They urged the church to "stick to religion," while they "engaged in economic and political life with no direct and little indirect reference to religious faith."[21] John Carroll, the first Catholic bishop in the United States, reflected this liberal consensus when he noted: "I have observed that when ministers of religion leave the duties of their profession to take a busy part in political matters they generally fall into contempt."[22]

Bishop John England of Charleston still reflected this consensus when in his address to Congress on January 8, 1826, he concluded:

> We desire to see the Catholics as a religious body upon the ground of equality with all other religious societies. . . . We consider that any who would call upon them to stand aloof from their brethren in the politics of the country, as neither a friend to America nor a friend to Catholics. . . . We repeat our maxim: Let Catholics in religion stand isolated as a body, and upon as good ground as their brethren. Let Catholics, as citizens and politicians, not be distinguishable from their other brethren of the commonwealth.[23]

But John England's vision of the place of Catholicism in the American Republic and in the pluralist, denominational religious system would not be realized, at least not until the 1960s. The competing vision of a Christian America, zealously pursued by Evangelical Protestantism, and the system of Protestant denominationalism that ensued did not allow for the acceptance of Catholicism as just another American denomination. Moreover, the massive immigration of impoverished Irish Catholics made them clearly distinguishable, by class and ethnicity, from their fellow citizens and presented the Catholic hierarchy with radically new challenges. A very different type of Catholic church, the immigrant church, with a new type of episcopal leadership emerged in the 1840s.

"Immigrant" Catholicism

Most commentators have viewed Bishop John Hughes of New York as the most forceful and articulate representative of the new immigrant Catholic Church. Two incidents will serve as illustration. Bishop Hughes was appalled by the passivity and seeming impotence of Bishop Francis P. Kenrick of Philadelphia during the 1844 "Philadelphia riots." When plans for an anti-immigrant and anti-Catholic nativist rally at city hall in New York City were announced, Hughes demanded a meeting with Mayor Robert Morris to warn him that, "if a single Catholic church is burned in New York, the city will become a second Moscow." He added: "We can protect our own. . . . I come to warn you for your own good."[24] Thereafter, the Catholic bishop of New York—and bishops of other cities where Catholic immigrants would constitute a majority of the working class—would be a power to be reckoned with by politicians and elected officials.

The republican Catholic style had been based on the model of autonomous Catholic individuals, who entered the public sphere not as Catholics but as indistinguishable citizens, to participate in the advancement of the public good. The immigrant Catholic style, by contrast, was based on the premise of the collective organization and mobilization of Catholics as a group—distinguishable from other groups by religion, class and ethnicity—to advance their particular interests. The church, with the bishop as "church boss," became a vehicle for the protection, self-organization, and mobilization of Catholic immigrants. Once Irish Catholics began to control the urban political machines of many cities, the power of the local bishop became naturally enhanced. Although Bishop Hughes actually failed in his attempts to create a Catholic party under his control, nonetheless he taught the immigrants that a militant, politically united Catholic bloc, normally tied to the Democratic Party, could best defend their interests.

In 1841, Bishop Hughes had decided to enter a "Catholic ticket" in legislative elections, urging all Catholics to vote for it. At issue was the city's public schools, which in New York were funded with public monies but were operated by the Public School Society, a private, mainly Protestant organization, which promoted a nonsectarian, nondenominational religious education. Hughes objected to the use of the Protestant King James Version of the Bible in the public schools. When he failed in his efforts to get the Protestant Bible out of the public schools, he campaigned for state funding of Catholic schools, provoking in the process a Protestant nativist reaction.

When both major parties, Whigs and Democrats, refused to support his efforts, Bishop Hughes entered his own candidates, in support of state aid to Catholic schools. The Catholic ticket was defeated, but it obtained sufficient votes to persuade the New York state government to take over the administration of the city's public schools. If Hughes could not get state aid for Catholic education, at least he would remove Protestant education from the public schools. Moreover, a separate Catholic parochial school system now seemed more justified than ever, and Hughes became its most decisive champion. "To build the school-house first, and the church afterwards," became his famous dictum.

Many interpreters have seen the incident as a turning point in the history of American Catholicism. It certainly marked a turning away from John Carroll's and John England's vision of a fully integrated, equal American Catholicism. Having himself exacerbated anti-Catholic nativism with his abrasive and confrontational style, Hughes now viewed American society as hostile, and American culture as a threat from which it was necessary to protect the Catholic faithful. To keep the faith of the immigrants, protecting them from Protestant America, while helping them take their rightful place as a "separate but equal" ethnic and religious group in American society, became the central task of the immigrant church.

The repeated controversies surrounding public and parochial schools became the most evident signs of the different visions that Protestants and Catholics had of the United States and of religion's role in public life. The Protestant clergy active in the common school movement viewed the public school as a vehicle to Americanize, that is, Christianize religiously indifferent and immigrant Catholic alike, by teaching them personal morality and self-discipline, civic virtue, and true Christianity. With the creation of the parochial school system, the Catholic Church was serving notice that it had its own agenda of Americanization.

In 1884, at the Third Plenary Council of Baltimore, the American bishops promulgated a wide body of legislation that would set the direction of the Catholic Church in the United States for the next seventy years. Among the resolutions passed was a decree to establish a parochial school in each parish, commanding pastors to build them, the laity to finance them, and parents to send their children to them. Parochial schools soon multiplied.[25] In some cities, the Catholic school population became larger than that of the public schools. The combination of unique constitutional arrangements giving the Catholic Church unusual operational freedom and the Catholic perception that the public school system was an agent at first of Protestantification and then of secularization, led to the creation of a system of Catholic education unique and unparalleled in the entire Catholic world. The church and all its institutions would play a crucial function in the assimilation—Americanization—of Catholic immigrants, but it was done on Catholic terms. Out of the most varied national groups, there emerged one single Catholic religious body that stood distinctly apart from other religious bodies and from the dominant American culture.[26]

"Public" Catholicism

Until the 1950s, the process of Americanization had taken place within the safe haven of a quasi-segregated Catholic subculture built around the neighborhood ethnic parish. But World War II, the G.I. Bill, and the general economic boom set American Catholics on a new journey of emigration and geographical, educational, and occupational mobility—away from the working-class, urban, ethnic neighborhoods of the Northeast and Midwest and into higher education, higher income levels, and middle-class suburbs across the country.[27]

Paradoxically, after much resistance Catholics were fully incorporated into the national civil religion despite their separate school system. Will Herberg showed how by the mid-1950s, Protestant-Catholic-Jew had become the three denominational forms of a new American civil religion that had the Protestant ethic and faith in America's millennial role as its moral and doctrinal core.[28] The election of a Catholic president and the inaugural address of that president, John F. Kennedy, were viewed as confirmation of the thesis. Indeed, they were used by Robert Bellah to formulate the very thesis of an American civil religion.[29]

At last, after a long and unexpected detour, John England's liberal republican vision was being realized. American Catholics were joining the U.S. mainstream—indeed, they more than any other group were beginning to define middle America—and were entering public life not as Catholics, in defense of their particular group interests, but "as citizens and politicians" less and less distinguishable from other Americans. Whether intentionally or not, Kennedy's famous speech to Protestant ministers in Houston was almost a replica of John England's address to Congress.[30]

In his speech, Kennedy offered the classic liberal position of radical separation between the private religious and public secular spheres. Religious views are the individual's own affair and ought to be irrelevant in public affairs or in the exercise of public secular roles. Moreover, churches ought to stick to religion and not meddle in public matters. Actually, historical precedent, trends, and pressures in this direction were such that, had the Second Vatican Council and developments in global Catholicism not interfered, this liberal position probably would be today the de facto official position of the American Catholic Church. Instead, we witnessed in the late 1970s and 1980s a new style of "public Catholicism," which is clearly distinguishable from both the "liberal republican" and the "immigrant" styles.[31]

At the very moment when Catholicism had finally become American and the tension between Romanism and the Republic seemed to have been resolved (thanks in part to the anticommunist crusade of the Cold War), the Vatican's *aggiornamento* reopened again the old vexing question of the relationship between being Catholic and being American. Albeit for different reasons, Catholic liberals like Kennedy and conservative Catholics like Francis Cardinal Spellman of New York shared the conviction that there could be no conflict between the Catholic Church and the Republic. For Kennedy, this was because there was a wall of separation between private faith and the modern secular world. For Spellman, this was because Catholicism and American patriotism had become indistinguishably fused in the American civil religion.

These were the two minds of American Catholicism entering the Vatican Council. As the Roman *aggiornamento* reached U.S. shores, it became obvious that both types of Catholicism were being challenged by a new understanding of the relation between religion and world. Both the liberal wall of separation and the civil religion fusion were put into question. Private faith could no longer leave secular public matters alone. Nor could spiritual truths ignore the "signs of the times" or be immune to freedom of inquiry. A rediscovered eschatological dimension also warned not to identify any social order with God's Kingdom. A new tension, this time voluntary and purposeful, between Catholicism and Americanism emerged. For the first time, Catholic faith dared to challenge American public affairs.

Public Religion and *Res Publica*

It should be evident that the three styles of Catholicism presented here—republican or liberal, immigrant, and public—correspond to the three levels of analysis that (according to Heclo) one can use to examine the interrelations between religion and politics: the *behavioral*, the *institutional*, and the *philosophical*.[32] The behavioral refers to the ways in which private religion may affect, indirectly as it were, public affairs through the public choices and voices of the individual religious citizen. The institutional refers to the ways in which organized religions and religious groups may compete in the political arena to advance their ideal and material interests. The philosophical refers to "the intersections of religion and policymaking that involve ideas and modes of thought bearing on the fundamental ordering of a society's public life."[33]

At this philosophical level, one can distinguish two fundamentally different models of "republic" or *res publica* to which correspond two different models of civil public religion, "civil religion" proper and what I have termed public religions of civil society. The modern concept of civil religion, as elaborated by Bellah, goes back to Jean-Jacques Rousseau's discussion "Of Civil Religion" in *The Social Contract*.[34] According to Bellah, the American polity had been integrated normatively by a particular variant of a nondenominational civil religion that was made up of a peculiar combination of biblical–Puritan, republican–Enlightenment, and liberal–utilitarian religious–moral principles.[35]

The vision of "One Nation Under God" that had sustained the American civil religion was grounded in the nondenominational version of Evangelical Protestantism that grew out of the Second Great Awakening and became established as the hegemonic form of public religion in civil society throughout the nineteenth century. Progressively, however, throughout the twentieth century the model of a "Christian" nation was expanded into that of a "Judeo-Christian" one with the successful incorporation of the Catholic and Jewish minorities into the national covenant. It is this new national consensus that was described in Will Herberg's *Protestant-Catholic-Jew* and celebrated in Bellah's portrayal of the American civil religion.

But the celebration of the new national consensus of the 1950s and early 1960s did not last very long. In a few years, Bellah himself lamented that the national covenant that had sustained American civil religion had been "broken."[36] Moreover, it was not simply the case that due to the upheavals of the 1960s—the civil rights movement, the youth counterculture, feminism, and the Vietnam War—civil religion was in a "time of trial" from which it could easily recover through some kind of new great awakening. The welfare state and consumer capitalism itself fed the "cultural contradictions" that undermined the Protestant ethic irrevocably.[37] A third disestablishment of Protestantism, this time that of the Protestant ethic from the "American way of life," was under way.[38] From now on, the American way of life would be characterized by the plurality of ways of life, by a kind of moral denominationalism. Public morality was being secularized, leading to the emergence of a pluralistic system of norms and forms of life, which we have come to call "multiculturalism."

It is, moreover, fallacious to blame "secularism" and its imputed carriers—either professional public schoolteachers, or a Supreme Court that has gone too far in the direction of the establishment clause—for these developments. Public schoolteachers, or the school system as a whole, are not to blame for failing to transmit a moral consensus or a civil religion that does not exist anymore. In this respect, Charles Glenn's diagnosis is correct. A morally pluralistic society calls for a pluralistic educational system, and a civil society-, community-, and family-oriented strategy of diversification, responsive to the educational goals of parents, seems most appropriate.

The subsidiarity principle on which such a strategy should be based, however, would seem to require not only that schools become responsive to the local community and to parents, but that parents and the local community become responsible (i.e., accountable) for the local schools. Moreover, the parallel guiding principle of social justice would require that federal, state, and local governments still to ensure that every child receives equal access to a standard education. Without these guiding principles, school vouchers or similar privatization plans would amount to unsolidaristic strategies based on self- or group-interest and designed to enable citizens to abandon a sinking ship.

In my view, it is misleading to attribute the educational crisis to the triumph of secularist ideologies, which has resulted in "the eventual exclusion of all reference to contemporary religious belief from public schools," and thus to frame the issue as a case of free exercise of religion. Bringing school prayer or religion back will not solve the public school crisis. But neither will it endanger the establishment clause. Thus, it should be presented in less dramatic terms on both sides as a relevant yet mainly symbolic gesture. Nothing more, nothing less.

Indeed, to an outside observer like myself it seems ludicrous on the part of the courts or secularist vigilantes to keep using the public school as the last bulwark and juridical litmus test of the strict wall of separation between church and state, as *the* place, in the words of Justice Felix Frankfurter, where one ought to maintain "zealous watchfulness against fusion of secular and religious activities by Government itself, " since "the public school is a symbol of our secular unity," "at once the symbol of our democracy," and "the most pervasive means for promoting our common destiny."[39]

Today, when judges, presidents, and many of those who can afford it send their children to private rather than public schools, these solemn words sound hollow. They were uttered, however, at a high point of national moral consensus, at a time of general religious revival, when Baptists still acted as high guardians of the separation of church and state, and there reigned still a consensus among Protestant and secular elites that Catholicism, which after all was the target of these court rulings, represented the most serious threat to the separation of church and state and to U.S. religious freedoms.[40]

Indeed, to understand how the public school became not so much a "symbol of our secular unity" but "an island of secularity," one must take into account the peculiar historical dynamics between the Protestant religious majority and the Catholic and Jewish religious minorities in this country. The Protestant majority, or at least its elites, conceived the "common school" and the public school as instruments of Christianization and Americanization (for a long time both meant the same thing) of the immigrant "other."

The Catholic minority, or rather the primarily Irish church hierarchy, suspicious of this project of Christianization and of the "Protestant Bible," rejected this project and established its own system of separate Catholic schools precisely as an instrument of Americanization and Catholic homogenization, as a kind of Catholic ethnic "melting pot." Jews, the other significant religious minority, who were equally suspicious of the Protestant project of Christianization and of all the rhetoric about the Christian nation, chose the opposite strategy, embracing the public school as a vehicle of Americanization and social mobility, while using the establishment clause to divest the schools of any Christian remnants, symbolic or real.

Only this historic dynamic can explain why, as Glenn points out, "religion receives much more public recognition and support in Congress, in the military, in government-funded social and health services, in prisons, and in higher education than it does in public schools."[41] It is one of the peculiarities of American secularism that the schools remain the battleground over the wall of separation long after the successful Americanization of Catholics and Jews was accomplished and the dynamics of religious and moral pluralism in American society have changed radically, specially with the new wave of massive, mainly non-European, immigration from all over the globe.

Yet it is surprising that one hears few voices today calling for the public schools to play their traditional role of Americanization, that is, of incorporation and assimilation of the new immigrants. This may be due partly to the generalized perception of crisis in the public school system and partly to the realization that the meaning of assimilation has changed radically, as is illustrated by the debates concerning the "segmented assimilation" of the second generation.[42] Indeed, new immigrant families, Catholic and non-Catholic alike, as well as African-American families, are sending their children to Catholic schools in formerly Catholic neighborhoods in the inner cities, sometimes at significant costs given their low income, in the hope that they will receive the effective academic and moral education that they think their local public schools are failing to provide.[43]

It sounds ironic, however, given the history of the Catholic school system, to hear contemporary critics, many of them non-Catholic, offering the Catholic schools as a successful alternative to the allegedly failing public schools. No less ironic is the fact that such proposals promoting private religious schools (to be financed partly with public founds through vouchers) come at a time when the Catholic school system has entered a serious internal crisis. Insofar as this crisis is partly financial, public subsidies in whichever acceptable form, most likely indirect ones through tax deductions to skirt contested issues of church-state separation, would no doubt help to close the serious deficit gap that is forcing dioceses across the country to close parochial schools.

But the roots of the problems go much deeper. The crisis is primarily one of mission and identity, secondly one of an increasing shortage of the priests and religious brothers and sisters who have been the backbone of the system at a meager financial cost, and thirdly one of geographical dislocation of the existing parochial schools. The financial crisis itself is rooted in these three interconnected crises. Surely, the financial incentive of public subsidies could help in addressing those problems with greater confidence and determination. But the structural nature of the problems needs to be confronted directly and systematically.

Moreover, it is misleading to present such proposals foremost as an issue of the free exercise of religion. Surely, suburban middle-class Catholic families, which are now sending their children to public schools for which they pay local taxes, may consider (given the right financial incentive) sending their children again to parochial schools. But most Catholic families would not do it primarily for the sake of a Catholic religious education for their children, any more than non-Catholic families send their children to parochial schools for the sake of a Catholic "sectarian" education. They would do it if they thought that the local Catholic schools were comparatively better, academically and morally, than the local public schools.

By moral education, I do not mean particular Catholic moral teachings, but rather moral education in the broad Durkheimian sense of the term, comprising the three elements of "spirit of discipline," "attachment to social groups," and "autonomy or self-determination."[44] Durkheim expected public schools in France to provide the kind of secular moral education that he considered crucial for the inculcation of a shared moral consensus, a "collective conscience," which was necessary for the normative integration of modern societies, once the old common religious morality had been undermined by forces of secularization.

Durkheim's project of a secular moral education and his role in promoting its institutionalization in French public schools was similar to the one that Glenn attributes to John Dewey in the United States. The project worked in France, a relatively homogenized society, and to a large extent still works today, despite controversies over the Islamic veil and other similar issues of the free exercise of religion. And the project worked equally well in the United States, despite the existing religious pluralism, for as long as one could maintain the national myth of a civil religion that it was the task of the public school to inculcate and transmit.

In any case, the vision of a unitary morally homogeneous, covenanted nation grounded in moral consensus and of one national civil religion has given ground to the alternative vision of a morally, culturally, and religiously pluralistic society that must strive for common ground and a fragile working consensus through the public deliberation and contestation of normative guiding principles and through the democratic formulation of public policy. This is the situation in which we find ourselves today and the ultimate ground for the contemporary crisis of the public school.

"Multiculturalism," the code word for this situation according to Heclo, is one of the "brute facts" we are forced to confront. We may bemoan nostalgically the passing away of the American civil religion that sustained our national moral consensus, but only now can we also acknowledge honestly the hidden discriminations and the nonrecognition of silenced minorities that the old model entailed. Moreover, this brute fact of multiculturalism and the moral dilemmas it entails are only exacerbated by the other two brute facts of our contemporary situation so poignantly portrayed by Heclo:

> Begin with a vast political society that increasingly defines itself by self-consciously making collective decisions about what to do and not to do. Add a technological imperative that expands this society's policy agenda to raise ever more profound questions—the nature of life, brains, reproduction, death, and the sustainability of humankind's earthly existence. Together, policy-mindedeness and the technology trap would be challenge enough, but to these we must add the third feature: an increasingly fragmented sense of cultural

> identities among the self-governing people who are called upon to oversee these decisions. These three observations imply that the interaction of religion and public policy will be a growing challenge in the years ahead.[45]

The result is a continuous expansion of the *res publica* while the citizen's republic becomes ever more diverse and fragmented. That is, the increase in the number and the complexity of issues becoming open to public deliberation, moral contestation, and partisan policymaking coincides with the proliferation of diverse publics and interest groups, with a pluralism of moral positions often perceived as a dissolution of the prevailing moral consensus, and with competing visions of the common good that seem to lead to a fragmentation of the Republic.

As if this challenge were not serious enough, one must confront, moreover, yet another brute fact: globalization. This fashionable, controversial, much abused yet indispensable buzzword serves as shorthand for a complex multidimensional process that, though still only in its initial stages, is already challenging our very model of national public policy, civil society, and politics. The *res publica*—along with our markets, mass media, cultures, identities, and practically every social phenomenon that in the modern era had been circumscribed within the territorial boundaries of the nation-state—is becoming de-territorialized and is assuming increasingly transnational and even global dimensions.

National borders are becoming ever more porous, while the traditional distinctions and boundary lines between domestic and foreign issues and affairs are becoming ever more blurred and obsolescent. Foreign problems anywhere in the world—economic crises, environmental and natural disasters, epidemics and famines, civil wars and regional conflicts, ethnic cleansings and crimes against humanity, human rights violations and gender discriminations, migration and refugee flows—easily turn into domestic policy issues and concerns not only because of the traditional geopolitical interests of a superpower, but also because of the increasing perception of global interconnectedness made tangible by the electronic media and because of the mobilized engagement, ideal or material, of multiple American and transnational publics in those issues.

As a counterpart, U.S. domestic policy issues and public debates—on the economy, energy, environment, defense, immigration, abortion and reproductive health, civil or penal codes—soon become global concerns and the preoccupation of foreign publics. The shrinkage of the planet into a global village is accompanied by the expansion of the circles of human solidarity and by the transformation of the *res publica* into a world domestic policy arena.

Religion at all three levels of analysis—behavioral, institutional, and philosophical—is not only intrinsically affected by these brute facts and by the transformation of the *res publica* they entail. Religion is also one of the primary resources we possess in facing these new challenges. The penetration of all spheres of life, including the most private, by public policy; the expansion of scientific-technological frontiers giving humanity demiurgic powers of self-creation and self-destruction; the compression of the whole world into one single common home for all of humanity; and the moral relativism that seems inherent to multiculturalism—all these new transcendent issues engage religion and provoke religious responses. At the same time, the great world religions in particular, as the stored collective normative and moral memories of humanity, are bound to become a valuable resource for dealing with these issues. Thus, the interconnectedness of religion and public policy is only likely to increase in the future as we enter uncharted moral territory.

Public Religion and Contemporary Global Trends

Although this volume is meant as a retrospective look at the relations between religion and public policy in the twentieth century, I would like to conclude with a prospective, somewhat speculative look at what appear to be new global trends that are likely to affect the types and styles of public religion in the future. The style of public Catholicism that has emerged since the Second Vatican Council, which I view as paradigmatic of the kind of public religion called for by the new global condition, must be viewed in many ways as a new creative response to those trends.

A transnational religion like Catholicism, which for centuries had felt constrained by the straitjacket of the territorial nation-state, is being transformed and somewhat liberated by processes of globalization, and is regaining its "catholic" (i.e., universal or global) dimension and identity. Progressively, from the end of the nineteenth century to the present, one can witness the reconstruction, reemergence, or reinforcement of all those transnational characteristics of medieval Christendom that had nearly disappeared or been significantly weakened since the sixteenth century: papal supremacy and the centralization and internationalization of the church's government; the convocation of ecumenical councils; transnational religious cadres; missionary activity; transnational schools, centers of learning, and intellectual networks; shrines as centers of pilgrimage and international encounters; and transnational religious movements. The other world religions are undergoing their own particular transformations as a response to the same global processes.[46]

At issue is not anymore the old conflict between Romanism and the Republic, that is, the perceived threat that a foreign authoritarian power and potentially disloyal citizens presented to national sovereignty. What is at stake is the fact that all public issues are becoming "catholic," that is, normative issues of global concern to all of humanity. The engagement of the Catholic Church in public debates and moral contestation throughout the world—on abortion and sexual mores, on economic policies, social justice, and a fairer distribution of global resources, and on democracy, human rights, and world peace—is a manifestation of this transformation. Two recent interventions of Catholic leaders may serve to illustrate the self-conscious engagement and adaptation of the Catholic Church, at least of its leadership, to ongoing processes of globalization.

During his last visit to Mexico in 1999, Pope John Paul II gathered the bishops of all American countries, consecrated Our Lady of Guadalupe as the Virgin of all the Americas, and urged them to cease viewing themselves as separate national Catholic churches and to become one single Pan-American Catholic Church. Only a few decades ago, such a statement would have been unutterable and would have provoked vehement reactions and accusations of popish interference and Romanist threats to national sovereignty, both in the United States and in Mexico. But today such a statement can practically pass unnoticed in its normalcy, or it can be understood as a normal pastoral response to ongoing processes of continental integration spearheaded by the North American Free Trade Agreement and carried by the ongoing massive Latin American and Caribbean migration to the United States and Canada.

The Pope, in a way, is only responding to global structural developments that are making Southern borders and North–South boundaries ever more porous. Yet if his strategy of turning the Virgin of Guadalupe into a religious symbol unifying all the American Catholic churches into a single imagined community is in any way successful, it will open up a globalizing dynamic of its own that will further undermine the territorialization of national cultures.[47]

Latin American societies are being penetrated ever more by Anglo-American culture, but the reciprocal process of Latinization of North

American culture is taking place as well. The mutual penetration and reciprocal acculturation is taking place not only in the fields of popular music, sports, and culinary habits, but also in the sphere of religion. The Protestantification of Latin America and the Latin Americanization of U.S. Catholicism go hand in hand. Both may be viewed as instances of the deterritorialization of cultures associated with globalization.[48]

Francis Cardinal George of Chicago concluded his 2000 lecture at the Library of Congress, "Catholic Christianity and the Millennium: Frontiers of the Mind in the 21st Century," with an equally farsighted vision into the global future:

> In the next millennium, as the modern nation state is relativized and national sovereignty is displaced into societal arrangements still to be invented, it will be increasingly evident that the major faiths are carriers of culture and that it is more sectarian to be French, American or Russian than to be Christian or Muslim, Hindu or Buddhist. Inter-religious dialogue is more basic to the future of faith, therefore, than is Church-state dialogue, important though that remains. And among the dialogues, that between Christians and Muslims promises to be the most significant for the future of the human race. Islam did not undergo the Renaissance and Enlightenment and therefore enters the post-modern world as a fully universal faith without having gone through the experience of modernity which shaped European cultures and the Christian faith. The conversation between Christianity and Islam is not yet far advanced, but its outcome will determine what the globe will look like a century from now.[49]

To a certain extent, this conversation among all world religions is already taking place in the United States as a result of the new global migration flows. The United States has again become an immigrant society. During the past decade alone, approximately 1 million immigrants annually have entered the United States, the largest wave in the nation's history, even outnumbering the 9 million immigrants who came during the first decade of the twentieth century.

More important than the increase in numbers, however, are the changes in the origin and characteristics of immigrants. Whereas the "old" immigrants were almost exclusively European, the new immigrants are primarily non-European. The largest numbers are Asian, Latin American, and Caribbean in origin, but increasing numbers are also coming from Africa—indeed, from all regions of the world. This means not only a broader range of linguistic and ethnic diversity, but also an unprecedented representation of all the world's religions. For the first time in its history, the United States has large Buddhist, Hindu, and Muslim populations.

We have entered a new phase in the American experiment. The models of immigrant incorporation have been radically altered by expanding multiculturalism at home and by the proliferation of global transnational networks.[50] The increasing global immigration in turn leads to a spiraling acceleration of multiculturalism and religious pluralism, now encompassing all world religions. The United States is called to become not just the "first new nation" made up primarily of all the European nations. The traditional model of assimilation, turning European nationals into American "ethnics," can no longer serve as a model of assimilation now that immigration is literally worldwide.

The United States is bound to become the "first new global society" made up of all world religions and civilizations, at a time when religious and civilizational identities are regaining prominence in the global stage. At the same moment political scientists like Samuel Huntington are announcing the impending clash of civilizations in global politics, a new experiment in intercivilizational encounters and accommodation among all the world religions is taking place at home. American religious pluralism is expanding and incorporating all the world religions in the same way as it previously incorporated the religions of the old immigrants.

A complex process of mutual accommodation is taking place. Like Catholicism and Judaism before, other world religions—Buddhism, Hinduism, and Islam—are being "Americanized," and in the process they are transforming American religion. Moreover, the religious diasporas in the United States are simultaneously serving as catalysts for the transformation of the old religions in their civilizational homes, in the same way American Catholicism affected the transformation of world Catholicism.

Besides the relevance of the Christian-Muslim dialogue stressed by Cardinal George, of all the new immigrant religions Islam represents the most interesting testing ground and challenge to the pattern of immigrant incorporation, for three interrelated reasons. Th first is that, more than any other world religion, Islam is still represented frequently in the United States as "the other" and therefore as "un-American," due to geopolitical rationales and the common essentialist portrayal of Islam as a fundamentalist religion. Tragically, these debates have only exacerbated in the wake of the terrorist attacks of September 11, 2001, perpetrated as they were by Muslim militants, and the military response of the Western alliance in

Afghanistan against the Taliban regime and against Osama bin Laden's al Qaeda global network of terrorists.[51]

It is not surprising that many have viewed the terrorist attacks and the Western military and police responses as a dramatic confirmation of the civilizational clash between Islam and the West. Such an interpretation of the conflict appears to have found considerable resonance throughout the West as well as the Muslim world. The public denials of Western leaders that their interventions are not directed against Islam seem hardly credible when they are accompanied by the widespread and indiscriminate surveillance and detention of Arabs and Muslims in the United States and when those infringements of individual liberties go unchallenged by the courts and are condoned by public opinion, as if to confirm that Arabs and Muslims are collectively suspected of potential complicity with the terrorist perpetrators and presumed guilty by ethnic and religious association.

In turn, the public condemnations of the attacks by most Muslim political and religious leaders and their attempts to dissociate Islam from the illegitimate terrorist methods, if not from the legitimate anti-Western grievances that may have fueled them, are received in the West as ambiguous and inadequate responses to the U.S. categorical presidential ultimatum to be "with us or against us" in the global war against terrorism. Paradoxically, however, the events of September 11 and their aftermath are forcing not only a debate about the alleged civilizational conflict between Islam and the United States, but also a recognition that Islam has taken roots in America and is becoming a major American religion.

The second important reason that the incorporation of Islam in America may hold special relevance is because Islam has resisted perhaps better than any other world religion the modern colonial logic of racialization. Given the corrosive character of this logic of racialization so prominent in American society, the dynamics of religious identity formation among immigrants in the United States assume a doubly positive form. The affirmation of religious identities is enhanced among the new immigrants because of the established historical pattern of acceptance of religious pluralism and diversity.

But this positive affirmation is privileged even more by what appears to be a common defensive reaction by most immigrant groups against pervasive ascribed racialization, particularly against the stigma of racial darkness. Plural religious identities and plural ethnic or racial identities are likely to become, after all, the two main competing alternative forms of organization of American multiculturalism. The challenge confronting Islam in the United States is how to transform diverse immigrant groups from South Asia (which today constitute the largest and fastest growing group of Muslim immigrants), from Arab countries, and from West Africa into a single American Islamic community.

In this respect, the process of incorporation is not unlike that of the incorporation of different Catholic ethnic groups into a single American Catholic Church. The two options being debated today within Islamic communities across the United States—often put in terms of the Nation of Islam model vesus the model of an assertive and powerful Jewish minority—reiterate some of the debates in nineteenth-century American Catholicism. Indeed, structurally the position of Muslims in the United States today is in many respects similar to that of Catholic immigrants in the nineteenth century. At issue is whether Islam should be constructed as a segregated defensive subculture protecting itself from corrosive Americanization, or whether it should organize itself as a public self-assertive cultural option within competitive multiculturalism. The threat of Americanization of Islam this would entail would be balanced by the opportunity of the Islamization of America, which many Muslims view as an actualization of Islam's universalism.

The third reason that the incorporation of Islam is particularly relevant is because of the growing Islamization of the African-American community, in a process that African-American Muslims often depict not as conversion but rather as reversion to a preslavery African Islam. Indeed, the often contentious dialogue and dynamic interaction between African-American Muslims and immigrant Muslims is bound to have a dramatic impact upon the transformation of American culture.[52]

The process of the Americanization of Islam is already taking place, despite all the difficulties presented by internal pluralism and external nativist resistance.[53] Islam is becoming not just a fast-growing religion *in* the United States, but an American religion, one of the denominational alternatives of being religiously American. Moreover, Islam is destined to become, like Catholicism, an important public religion that is likely to play a relevant role in U.S. public debates in the future.

Notes

1. Cf. Hugh Heclo, "Religion and Public Policy: An Introduction," *Journal of Policy History* 13 (2001): 4–5 (a revised version of this essay appears as chapter 1 of this volume); and Niklas Luhmann, "Interaction, Organization, and Society," in *The Differentiation of Society* (New York: Columbia University Press, 1982), 69–89.

2. For a more systematic elaboration see José Casanova, *Public Religions in the Modern World* (Chicago: University of Chicago Press, 1994).

3. Cf. Richard John Neuhaus, *The Naked Public Square: Religion and Democracy in America* (Grand Rapids, Mich.: Eerdmans, 1984), and Seyla Benhabib's feminist critique of the liberal dialogic neutrality rule in "Models of Public Space: Hannah Arendt, the Liberal Tradition and Jürgen Habermas," in *Habermas and the Public Sphere*, ed. Craig Calhoun (Cambridge, Mass.: MIT Press, 1991).

4. Cf. Alexis de Tocqueville, *Democracy in America* (New York: Vintage, 1990); and Max Weber, "The Protestant Sects and the Spirit of Capitalism," in *From Max Weber*, ed. H. H. Gerth and C. W. Mills (New York: Oxford University Press, 1946), 303.

5. José Casanova, "The Politics of the Religious Revival," *Telos* 59, spring (1984): 8.

6. Robert Bellah et al., *Habits of the Heart: Individualism and Commitment in American Life* (Berkeley: University of California Press, 1985); Albert O. Hirshman, *Shifting Involvements: Private Interest and Public Action* (Princeton, N.J.: Princeton University Press, 1982).

7. Robert Putnam, *Bowling Alone: The Collapse and Revival of American Community* (New York: Simon & Schuster, 2000).

8. See chapter 6 of this volume.

9. Karl Marx, "On the Jewish Question," in *Early Writings* (New York: Vintage, 1975), 217ff.

10. John T. Noonan Jr., *The Lustre of Our Country: The American Experience of Religious Freedom* (Berkeley: University of California Press, 1998).

11. Wilfred M. McClay, "Two Concepts of Secularism," *Journal of Policy History* 13, no. 1 (2001): 47–72; a revised version of this essay appears as chapter 2 of this volume.

12. However, as Charles Glenn shows in his analysis of John Dewey's influential educational philosophy in chapter 10 of this volume, some of the same Enlightenment-based bias was operative in the transformation of the public school system in the twentieth century.

13. For a critical reconstruction of the Supreme Court's zigzagging between the two clauses, see chapter 3 of this volume. For different analyses of the inherent constitutional dilemma, cf. Jesse H. Choper, "The Religious Clauses of the First Amendment: Reconciling the Conflict," *University of Pittsburgh Law Review* 41 (1980): 673–701; and Leo Pfeffer, "Freedom and/or Separation: The Constitutional Dilemma of the First Amendment," *Minnesota Law Review* 64 (1980): 561–84.

14. Eric Michael Mazur, *The Americanization of Religious Minorities. Confronting the Constitutional Order*. (Baltimore: Johns Hopkins University Press, 1999).

15. See chapter 3 of this volume.

16. James Davidson Hunter, *Culture Wars: The Struggle to Define America* (New York: Basic Books, 1991); and Rhys H. Williams, ed., *Cultural Wars in American Politics: Critical Reviews of a Popular Myth* (New York: Aldine de Bruyter, 1997).

17. Casanova, *Public Religions*, chaps. 6–7.

18. Cf. Paul Kleppner, ed., *The Evolution of American Electoral Systems* (Westport, Conn.: Greenwood Press, 1981); Paul Lopatto, *Religion and the Presidential Election* (New York: Praeger, 1985); A. James Reichley, *Religion in American Public Life* (Washington, D.C.: Brookings Institution Press, 1985); M.P. Fogarty, *Christian Democracy in Western Europe, 1820–1953* (Notre Dame, Ind.: University of Notre

Dame Press, 1957); and Stein Rokkan, *Citizens, Elections, and Parties* (Oslo: Universitets Forlaget, 1970).

19. Casanova, *Public Religions*, 165–66.

20. David O'Brien, *Public Catholicism* (New York: Macmillan, 1989). See also Gerald Fogarty, S.J., "Public Patriotism and Private Piety: The Tradition of American Catholicism," *U.S. Catholic Historian* 4 (1982).

21. O'Brien, *Public Catholicism*, 5; Bernard Groethuysen, *The Bourgeois Catholicism vs. Capitalism in Eighteenth Century France* (New York: Holt, Rinehart, and Winston, 1968).

22. Quoted in James Hennesey, S.J., *American Catholics: A History of the Roman Catholic Community in the United States* (New York: Oxford University Press, 1981), 65.

23. Quoted in O'Brien, *Public Catholicism*, 30.

24. Quoted in Hennesey, *American Catholics*, 124.

25. At the time of the council, four of every ten Catholic parishes had primary schools. Following the council decree, and spurred by the dramatic increase in Catholic immigration in the following decades, the number of parochial schools grew from 2,246 in 1880 to 3,811 in 1900 and to 4,845 in 1910, while the number of students rose from 405,234 in 1880 to 854,523 in 1900 and to 1,237,251 in 1910. The figures are taken from Hennesey, *American Catholics,* 242–43.

26. Jay P. Dolan, *The American Catholic Experience: A History of the Roman Catholic Community in the United States* (New York: Oxford University Press, 1985), 262–93 and passim; and idem, *The Immigrant Church* (Baltimore: Johns Hopkins University Press, 1970).

27. Andrew Greeley, *The American Catholic: A Social Portrait* (New York: Basic Books, 1977).

28. Will Herberg, *Protestant-Catholic-Jew* (Garden City, N. Y.: Doubleday, 1955).

29. Robert Bellah, "Civil Religion in America," *Daedalus* 96 (1967): 1–21.

30. Andrew M. Greeley, *The Catholic Experience: An Interpretation of the History of American Catholicism* (Garden City, N.Y.: Doubleday, 1969), 283.

31. Casanova, *Public Religions*, chap. 7.

32. Heclo, "Religion and Public Policy," 4–5.

33. Ibid., 5.

34. Jean-Jacques Rousseau, *The Social Contract* (New York: Hafner, 1947).

35. Bellah, "Civil Religion."

36. Robert Bellah, *The Broken Covenant: Civil Religion in Time of Trial* (New York: Seabury Press, 1975).

37. Daniel Bell, *The Cultural Contradictions of Capitalism* (New York: Basic Books, 1976).

38. For an analysis of the three phases of the disestablishment of American Protestantism, see Casanova, *Public Religions*, chap. 6.

39. Quoted in Reid, "Religious Conscience," 76.

40. For a good analysis of the postwar religious scene, see Robert Wuthnow, *The Restructuring of American Religion. Society and Faith since World War II* (Princeton, N.J.: Princeton University Press, 1988). For a classic exponent of liberal anti-Catholic prejudices, see Paul Blanshard, *American Freedom and Catholic Power* (Boston: Beacon Press, 1958). For an exposure of lingering prejudices, see Andrew Greeley, *The Catholic Myth: The Behavior and Beliefs of American Catholics* (New York: Scribner's, 1990).

41. See chapter 10.

42. Cf. Alejandro Portes and Min Zhou, "The New Second Generation: Segmented Assimilation and Its Variants," *Annals of the American Academy of Political Science* 530 (1993): 74–96; Richard Alba and Victor Nee, "Assimilation Theory for a New Era," *International Migration Review* 31 (1997): 826–75; and Alejandro Portes and Rubén G. Rumbaut, *Legacies: The Story of the Immigrant Second Generation* (Berkeley: University of California Press, 2001).

43. This is one of the preliminary findings of a research project, "Religion and Immigrant Incorporation in New York," led by Aristide Zolberg and José Casanova at the International Center for Migration, Ethnicity, and Citizenship at New School University.

44. Emile Durkheim, *Moral Education. A Study in the Theory and Application of the Sociology of Education* (New York: Free Press, 1973).

45. Heclo, "Religion and Public Policy," 11.

46. José Casanova, "Globalizing Catholicism and the Return to a 'Universal' Church," in S.U. Rudolph and J. Piscatori, eds. *Transnational Religion and the Fading States* (Boulder, CO: Westview, 1997), 121–43. Martin E. Marty and R. Scott Appleby, eds., *The Fundamentalism Projects*, 5 vols. (University of Chicago Press, 1991–95); John Esposito and Michael Martin Watson, eds., *Religion and Global Order*. (Cardiff: University of Wales Press, 2000); Hans Küng, *A Global Ethic for Global Politics (*New York: Oxford University Press, 1998). Ernest Gellner, *Postmodernism, Reason and Religion* (New York: Routledge, 1992).

47. It is already having some visible effects in New York City. Four boroughs (Manhattan, the Bronx, Queens, and Staten Island) have already recognized officially the Feast of the Virgin of Guadalupe on Dec. 12 as a religious holiday. The festivity is solemnly celebrated at Saint Patrick's Cathedral by the cardinal with public representative participation of Mexican and other Latino immigrants as well as American Catholics from all over the city. More than forty Guadalupano committees have been established throughout the city, most of them linked to the Tepeyac Association, a religious-cultural organization of Mexican immigrants led by a Mexican Jesuit. By symbolically linking the sacred image of the Virgin of Guadalupe, Mexican national identity, and the self-organization of the Mexican community in New York around the human, civil, and labor rights of immigrants, in a few years the Tepeyac Association has already had significant effects on the incorporation of Mexicans, the most recent Latino immigrant community, into the U.S. Catholic Church and into the socio-political life of the city.

48. José Casanova, "Religion, the New Millennium, and Globalization," *Sociology of Religion* 60, no. 3 (2001): 415–41.

49. Francis Cardinal George, "Catholic Christianity and the Millennium: Frontiers of the Mind in the 21st Century (lecture presented at the Library of Congress, Washington, D.C., 2000), 13.

50. Cf. Alejandro Portes, "Introduction: The Debates and the Significance of Immigrant Transnationalism," and Peggy Levitt, "Transnational Migration: Taking Stock and Future Directions," in *Global Networks: A Journal of Transnational Affairs* 1, no 3 (2001), 181–217; and Peggy Levitt, *The Transnational Villagers* (Berkeley: University of California Press, 2001).

51. For a more systematic and critical discussion of Huntington's thesis and Islamic "fundamentalism," see José Casanova, "Civil Society and Religion: Retrospective Reflections on Catholicism and Prospective Reflections on Islam," *Social Research* 68, no. 4 (2001): 1041–80.

52. Cf. Aminah Beberly McCloud, *African American Islam* (New York: Routledge, 1995); and Jane I. Smith, *Islam in America* (New York: Columbia University Press, 1999).

53. The presence of a Muslim imam along with a Protestant minister, a Catholic priest, and a Jewish rabbi in the opening of public ceremonies is becoming routine. Among the symbolic milestones one could mention: The first commissioned Islamic chaplain in the U.S. Army was established in 1993, and in the U.S. Navy in 1996; a Muslim symbol was displayed on the White House Ellipse in 1997; the Pentagon hosted its first Ramadan meal for Muslims in 1998; on the first day of Ramadan in Nov. 2000 the New Jersey legislature opened its ceremony with a reading of the Qur'an by an imam. The Muslim public presence in official ceremonies and in interfaith encounters has become even more prominent after the terrorist attacks of Sept. 11, 2001.

Part II

Religion in Political Action

5

American Democracy and the Politics of Faith

Wilson Carey McWilliams

Belief was much in evidence during the 2000 U.S. presidential campaign. In the early days, George W. Bush declared that Jesus was his favorite "political philosopher," an affirmation variously imitated by many of his rivals; even after he had effectively won the Republican nomination, Governor Bush found time to declare June 10 to be "Jesus Day" in the State of Texas. Al Gore proclaimed himself a born-again Christian, and at the beginning of Joe Lieberman's campaign, almost no speech went by without some mention of his trust in the Master of the Universe. It seemed part of the pattern that Madonna could be found discussing the Cabala.[1] Some observers were sardonic, others alarmed, and almost everyone detected something different in the political air.

But appeals to religion are hardly unusual in U.S. political history. Lincoln, no orthodox believer, invoked God and the language of the Bible;

This essay is printed with the permission of the Eagleton Institute of Politics at Rutgers University, where it was originally given as a lecture.

Bryan likened the gold standard to the Crucifixion; Theodore Roosevelt saw Armageddon in the election of 1912; Franklin Roosevelt compared his opponents to the money-changers Jesus had driven from the temple, and stopped just short of declaring that God is a Democrat. "Divine justice," he told the Democratic Convention of 1936, "weighs the sins of the cold-blooded and the sins of the warm-hearted in different scales."[2] And religion furnished at least half the vocabulary—and more of the music—of the civil rights movement.

Of course, those voices spoke to a United States whose political culture was emphatically Christian, if not Protestant, and the critical reactions to 2000's religiosity partly reflect the greater diversity of our times. Yet it is also true that in the past, leaders largely sought to enlist religion on the side of policy, referring to religion as a definer of moral conduct and right public action.[3]

The 2000 candidates, however, were more apt to speak of "faith," sometimes with reference to personal life (he was led away from drinking, Bush said, when Jesus "touched my heart") but with only minimal, hedged reference to specific norms or policies.[4] A good deal of this, obviously, results from the calculation that the positions most associated with religion—opposition to abortion or homosexuality, for example, on the Right, or to consumerism on the Left—will play badly with the general public. Among religious conservatives, this is thunderously evident.

Religious conservatives—already frustrated by Republican inattention—were shaken by the failure of President Bill Clinton's impeachment and the recognition of their own marginality.[5] Some urged withdrawal from politics, at least for a time; a few, like Gary Bauer, raised the old flag; the most visible leaders, like Pat Robertson and Ralph Reed, accepted Bush, despite his evident urge to move to the political center, as a candidate likely to win. Yet John McCain's conservative credentials, notably in relation to abortion, are often better than Bush's, and though leaders like Robertson had pragmatic reasons for opposing McCain—campaign finance reform might lessen their movement's influence—they also distrusted him because he did not talk the talk.[6] To the religious right, Bush's reliance on the language of faith marked him, sufficiently, as one of their own.[7]

In the national campaign, only Pat Buchanan gave full-throated devotion to the moral causes of conservative religion. And Buchanan, who had been divisive in 1992 and nudged off the Republican stage in 1996, was reduced to federally funded irrelevance in the election of 2000.

All of this is apparent. It is less clear, however, that the visibility of religious faith in public life, and the partial eclipse of religious morals, points to a developing revolution in American political culture.

Religion and the Foundation of American Politics

Historically, Americans, by and large, have relied on religion as a source of moral unity.[8] Religion, so understood, upholds the fundamental modes and orders of society—notably, its distinctions of gender, age, family, and property—adding divine sanctions to laws and serving as a foundation able to withstand the strains and uncertainties of democratic political life.[9]

The U.S. Framers, however, rejected any effort at enforced religious uniformity, regarding attempts to dictate to the soul as violations of natural, unalienable rights. Liberty, James Madison asserted in *The Federalist* 10, is "essential to political life"—not merely republican politics, if we take Madison at his word, but politics of any legitimate sort.[10] Attempts to remove the "causes of faction" by directly controlling the soul, in this view, will be oppressive or ineffective or both, violations of liberty that are also likely to lead to disorder.[11]

The Constitution, consequently, confines itself to what human beings and governments *do*: It is silent on religion, and it also says nothing about natural rights, the basis of the Framers' civil creed. And in regulating conduct, the Framers relied on what they took to be morality in the natural sense: self-preservation and self-interest.[12]

The ordinary rule in public life, in the school of *The Federalist*, is that the great majority will be guided by immediate interests and passions.[13] Accordingly, the Framers set out to minimize the Republic's dependence on the virtue of citizens or statesmen, leaning instead on the "silent operation of the laws"—the rivalry of interests in a large and diverse Republic—to weaken attachments, moderate political passions, and promote a circumspect and ordered liberty.[14]

But the founding generation also recognized that republican politics demands more than a morality based on calculations of interest. They assumed a public schooled in the commandments against killing, stealing, sexual impropriety, and disrespect for parents, and they had no doubt of "the advantage of a religious Character among private persons" in shoring up the moral foundations of public life.[15]

In the first place, they regarded religion as a support for oaths and promises, and hence, given social contract theory, for society itself. Reason and interest argue for agreeing to whatever pledges are needed to escape the insecurities of the state of nature. But once society is established, the case for keeping those commitments is less compelling. I am tempted to set aside my general interest in order whenever the law thwarts my particular interests and desires.

Of course, if I break the rules, there is a risk that I will be found out and punished, and if I escape detection, my successful criminality may inspire distrust and imitation, eroding "social capital," as we would say nowadays, and edging society back toward precivil disorder.[16] These dangers may deter those who are likely to be noticed and who have much to lose, but if the stakes are great enough, they may seem worth the gamble. (As Clinton's missteps remind us, moreover, even the most public of persons can be reckless in pursuing trivialities.)

And the obscure, the poor, and the oppressed may easily conclude that they have little to lose. Without religion, John Locke thought, "promises, covenants and oaths" would be hopelessly insecure, leading him to reject toleration for atheists: "The taking away of God, though but even in thought, dissolves all."[17] The Framers stopped short of that position—although Jefferson came close, for a time—but they shared the view that it is invaluable for citizens to regard oaths and contracts as sacred.[18]

The founding generation also held that modern civilization—and especially, a modern Republic—presumes a benevolence and humanity, particularly a duty to the weak and helpless, most readily nurtured by religion and perhaps requiring it. In ancient civilizations, Locke observed, reason had been insufficient to establish that it is criminal to kill one's children by exposing them.

By prohibiting infanticide, revealed religion becomes consistent with reason, which indicates that we have some responsibility for what we beget, but reinforces that duty and extends it to a universal rule.[19] In the same spirit, Jefferson found the "peculiar superiority of the system of Jesus" in the fact that, gathering "all mankind into one family," it promotes "universal philanthropy."[20]

The Framers also knew that, in practice, preserving even unalienable rights requires something more than ordinary calculations of utility and interest. John Adams, in defending the British soldiers who had fired into a mob during the Boston Massacre, appealed to an absolute right of self-preservation: "That is a point I would not give up for my right hand,"

Adams declaimed, "nay for my life"—a moving peroration, probably, but not one that obviously follows from his argument.[21] Self-government presumes citizens who are prepared to sacrifice their interests and even their lives for the liberties of others.[22] Civic duty and the protection of liberty, in other words, call for a kind of nobility, most readily translated into republican politics through religion; heroism, John Witherspoon taught, is "not open to every man," but Christian magnanimity is accessible "to the very lowest stations."[23]

Yet although the Framers valued religion's contribution to morals, they distrusted faith, the transcendent dimension of religion, the yearning for the divine likely to express itself in prophecy, theology, or mysticism. Up to a point, all lawgivers must share that worry. *Theoria* takes us outside the familiar, calling customs and laws into question and suggesting that what passes for human knowledge is confined to signs and artifacts, that we "see through a glass, darkly."[24] In practice, faith may accept the fundamental orders of society, but it is also apt to deny that they are entitled to more than a subordinate, suspect obedience: "There is neither Jew nor Greek, bond or free, male or female, for all are one in Christ Jesus," Paul taught, denying ontological status to distinctions of nation, class, and gender.[25] To those who have glimpsed the glory of God, human things are apt to seem tawdry, and whether the result is a turning toward otherworldliness or an itch for messianic transformation, religion in this high sense is clearly dangerous to civil order.

Most societies have relied on an official teaching, the effort to school and discipline religious yearning, linking it, more or less compatibly, to the laws.[26] (Even Locke, after all, proposed a "reasonable" Christianity.) All established religion, in that sense, is intended to be civil religion, a public recognition of faith that also attempts to give it form. That the Framers ruled out official religious doctrine largely reflected their conviction that establishments infringe on liberty and threaten to create disorder rather than avoid it, especially given the plurality of sects and persuasions in the United States. But most of the great voices in the founding generation also had a fairly radical quarrel with faith as such.

In the first place, they associated religion with credulousness, indoctrination, and unreason, so that even the moral education it afforded was not much more than a primer. The belief in a "particular Providence," Franklin said, was suited only for "weak and ignorant Men and Women, and . . . inexperienced and inconsiderate Youth of both Sexes."[27] Religion, consequently, was not equal to the dignity of a public life dedicated to freedom and reasoned consent.

Saving the presumptively useful belief in an afterlife, the Framers were very likely to reduce any specifically religious argument, and virtually all the transcendent dimensions of faith, to folly or priestcraft.[28] Franklin, who regretted the time he had spent reading his father's books of "polemic divinity," disdained sermons that seemed concerned "to make us Presbyterians rather than good Citizens."[29] Similarly, Jefferson called traditional Christian doctrine a set of "artificial systems" deserving "euthanasia." In his letter to James Smith, he proclaimed the number of gods in whom a citizen believes to be a matter of civic indifference, as long as the religions in question "make honest men."[30] Though seeing a need for Christian morals—or, to be more precise, for so much of that morality as supports a liberal regime—the Framers rejected the public claims of Christian faith.[31]

Seeking to domesticate religion, the Constitution relies on America's multiplicity of confessions, which—on the familiar logic of *The Federalist* 10—makes it unlikely that any church can acquire enough strength to suppress the others.[32] Moreover, that religious diversity guarantees that any doctrine will be contested and subjected to challenge. And because the Constitution is prohibited from attempting to resolve such disputes—implicitly, because there is no answer or argument conclusive enough to be compelling in a public forum—the laws cast their vote for religious incertitude, or at least for open-mindedness. In this sense, the Constitution relies on, but also hopes to promote, a public opinion that moderates religious claims, rejecting or ridiculing enthusiasm, controlling faith without the intervention of government.[33]

At the same time, while the Framers left the nurturing of moral character largely to civil society—to families, churches, and local communities—they expected those institutions to be supported and regulated by public authority. In the first place, although many of the leading figures at Philadelphia in 1787 would have been happy with greater limits on state power, as a practical necessity the Constitution left the states with a relatively free hand in matters of morals and religion.

They could establish churches, until the Fourteenth Amendment was held to apply the First Amendment to the states, and though formal establishments disappeared early in the Republic's history, states continued to foster religious education (through practices like Bible reading and prayer in the schools), to aid the secular functions of religious institutions, and to provide civil advantages (e.g., tax breaks, and the authority to solemnize marriage) to churches and clergy.[34]

Perhaps more important, the founding generation held the Lockean position that it is proper for government to regulate conduct, even if associated with religious beliefs or observances, as long as it acts through general laws applicable to all citizens.[35] This allowed government to limit or forbid any religious practices thought to threaten civil order, as in the case of polygamy.[36] Of course, where public policy offended the convictions of any substantial body of citizens, government has often given ground, so law has tended to support the moral code of the religio-civil mainstream. Sometimes, minority religions have won victories in the courts. But to do so, they are compelled to make their case in civil terms; the constitutional rule is the subordination of religion to the laws.[37] Still, the Framers looked to something like a partnership with religion where morals are concerned, while they aimed to quiet, if not silence, the public claims of faith.

Religion and Individualism in Contemporary Life

That national frame is still intact but loosening, now visibly wobbly at the joins. Part of this is due simply to our greater variegation, the thinning of our religious commonalities, in morals as well as belief. In addition to the relatively familiar culture wars, more and more of American religiosity stands outside the biblical tradition, wholly or in part.[38]

It has been a long time since Salem: In 1998, Governor Paul Cellucci of Massachusetts found it necessary to offer apologies for a remark offensive to witches.[39] In polls, the overwhelming majority of Americans say they believe in God. But that finding obscures a shrinking of religious agreement. For almost one in eight of us, these professions reflect a belief in a "life force or spirit"—including astrology and extraterrestrial presences—rather than a personal Deity.[40]

The extent of this multiformity, however, is probably less significant than its broad acceptance by the general public. Most Americans still adhere to traditional moral precepts—or at least, a reasonable approximation of them—but they speak of those principles as essentially personal choices or preferences. The prevailing language of morals is individualism, utilitarian or expressive.[41]

In a sense, this is only the latest chapter in an old American story. Alexis de Tocqueville, who admired the American accommodation, expected the "spirit of religion" to lose ground, over the long term, to the "spirit of liberty" embodied in the laws.[42] A religion's first principles may remain inherent in its teaching, Tocqueville argued, but it must adapt its practice to circumstance and to the demands of civil society.[43] And though he considered it an advantage, on the whole, that religious freedom made churches dependent on the active commitment of members, he also recognized that it emphasized the need of churches to persuade, and hence their temptation to minimize or gloss over any demands that are troublesome or disabling in civil life.[44]

This contributed to the increasing ascendancy of individualism that Tocqueville noted in American speech. He observed that although Americans sometimes acted from generous or public-spirited motives, they explained their conduct by reference to the principle of "self-interest rightly understood," readier "to do honor to their philosophy than to themselves." The Framers' doctrine that human beings act from essentially private and self-interested motives, in other words, was preempting public speech and affecting self-understanding. And because the older virtues, rooted in custom, were being shaken by change, religion stood in danger of losing both its habits and its voice.[45] In this, as in so many things, Tocqueville speaks to our time.

Social and political discourse, especially among younger Americans, is notable for what Harvey Mansfield calls "creeping . . . libertarianism," a moral stance that condemns violence, psychological abuse, or intrusions on privacy out of respect for the other as an autonomous subject, but otherwise is content to leave individuals free to do as they please.[46] It is not that Americans are sanguine about the country's moral direction. Respondents regularly tell pollsters that they are worried about the decline of values; in a CNN–Gallup survey in 1999, a substantial majority (58 to 38 percent) ranked moral problems as more worrisome than economic ones.[47] Rather, it reflects the code of social liberalism, increasingly the language of civic morals. "Imposing" your convictions on the conduct of others is broadly held to be impermissible. In a recent *Washington Post* poll, 70 percent agreed that "we should be more tolerant of people who choose to live according to their own moral standards, even if we think they are wrong."[48]

In almost the only instance in which they cite Scripture, Americans who share this view are apt to quote "Judge not, that ye be not judged." Yet while Jesus, in that teaching, is asserting that we ought not to judge others by any measure we are unwilling to have applied to ourselves, his doctrine is not a tolerant indifference; he does not teach that we should leave a speck in our brother's eye, but that we should remove our own first.[49] The prevailing persuasion in the United States, though not disposed to harm others, is not inclined to do much to help them, either.[50]

It does not help that so many of the civil pillars of the Framers' moral design have been unsettled or pulled down. That states and local governments are now held to the same, essentially secular, standard as the federal regime would have pleased a good many of the Founders, even though the Supreme Court's insistence on the "wall of separation" goes far beyond their understanding or practice.[51] It would probably inspire greater concern, however, that the institutions of civil society have been so thoroughly penetrated, reshaped, or shattered by the market, technology, and the media.[52]

More and more, localities—and with them, a good many personal relationships—are exposed to mobility and change, regarded as transient connections to which we would be wise to limit our liability.[53] (This bothers a great many of us; 61 percent of respondents, in a recent *New York Times* poll, said things were better in the United States when attachment to place was stronger; an identical number felt that true love has become harder to find.[54])

Our relatively robust prosperity to the contrary, economics is also eroding our resources of trust and moral community. Inequality is escalating, whereas the vogue of downsizing and outsourcing makes jobs feel insecure, even in good times.[55] Employees, Kristin Downey Grimsley observes, are becoming less loyal to the firm or to their colleagues. So if the workplace is "leaner," it is also "definitely meaner."[56]

The dynamics and rewards of the market, moreover, tempt Americans to treat it as autonomous and irresistible, partly because doing so allows us a more or less guiltless pursuit of interests and enjoyments. But conceding sovereignty to the market leaves us with only the consumer's passive freedom to make choices, rather than having a say in defining what is worthy of choosing.[57]

In any case, all these tendencies help keep Americans from being more than hesitant or halfhearted about commitments, just as they encourage us to seek solace in short-term gratifications, an inclination recently visible even in high places. Yet all of these retreats diminish us, so that great numbers of Americans seem to be looking, sometimes furiously and sometimes wistfully, for what is missing.[58]

Regarded with hope, these are signs of transition to new, possibly better forms of social and moral order. Despite our uneasiness and posturing, after all, there have been real gains in the relations between the races and the genders, and many old abuses are subject to sanction. E.J. Dionne even sees a trend toward a new communitarian morality, though these signs are pretty faint.[59] Contemporary civic and political groups, at least as often as not, are fund-raising bureaucracies whose nominal members do not meet or deliberate. And though numbers of Americans do good works as volunteers, they do so at their convenience, in an episodic politics that falls short of persistent, reliable devotion.[60] (In fact, such voluntary participation is regularly in short supply; workers are overcommitted, and faith-based organizations are inadequate to public need.[61]) It is possible to value the direction of opinion. Alan Wolfe, for example, celebrates a new autonomy in which Americans increasingly decide which God suits their temperament best, which family structure works for them, and whether their country's government is worthy of trust.[62]

But this only underlines the fact that, as the practice of the time tends toward fragmentation, its moral idiom leans toward an easygoing self-concern.[63] There are evident signs of strain in what the Framers took to be the moral foundations of republican politics. Sacrifice for country does not appear to rank high among our imperatives: Americans of both Right and Left were strikingly unruffled when, during the 2000 campaign, vice presidential candidate Dick Cheney explained that he had avoided military service—even though he felt no moral objection to the Vietnam War—because he had "other priorities."

In relation to oaths and contracts, marriage—our most common sacred promise—is treated with remarkable casualness. And, as the impeachment crisis made clear, a substantial majority of Americans think it proper to lie or mislead, even under oath, to preserve one's privacy, especially in sexual matters.[64] We continue to forbid infanticide, but a considerable, and so far decisive, minority supports the right to choose a partial-birth abortion, which surely comes close. And the idea of human equality itself is subject to a fashionable critique from partisans of the "politics of difference."[65]

Similarly, though Americans cherish "family values," the definition of family in civil society is being opened to new and sometimes very complicated forms. Lawrence Tribe argues, for example, that efforts to forbid human cloning are not acceptable because, turning on the distinction between the natural and the unnatural, they may have a "chilling effect" on "experiment," and especially on alternative forms of romantic attachment, family life, "gestational mothering," and ways of experiencing the "joys and responsibilities of child-rearing."[66]

I find Tribe's willingness to give a preferred status to experiments by humans on humans chilling in another sense, but let that pass. On his own terms, is not Tribe claiming that child rearing *naturally* involves "joys and responsibilities"? Should he not be worried about inhibiting the freedom to experiment with joyless and irresponsible parenting? It is probably safer, however, not to ask those questions. Like Tocqueville's Americans, those who share Tribe's view might decide to honor their philosophy rather than themselves.

Whatever the merits of such ideas, it ought to be clear that, in the moral discourse of American civil society, religion finds itself an increasingly critical voice, less likely to uphold the prevailing pattern than to confront it prophetically.[67] This is pretty much true across the religious spectrum, albeit in differing ways and with different objects of criticism.[68] "Mainstream" religion, which is relatively sympathetic to social and moral change, is sharpest in censuring consumerism and its associated fantasies.[69]

Conservative religion, of course, is even more jaundiced about the direction of things. In November 1996, a symposium in *First Things* discussed whether American iniquity was great enough to justify active resistance, and Paul Weyrich has declared that the majority is no longer moral and that the culture wars are lost, at least for the moment.[70] Most important, the shrewdest among religious conservatives are questioning whether the dynamism and the relentless relativism of the capitalist market is not undermining the virtues and convictions they cherish.[71]

The media, so responsive to social trends, testify to—and amplify—this more adversarial relationship between religion and civil society. A half-century ago, religion was portrayed with a respect that bordered on the saccharine, on the model of Bing Crosby and Barry Fitzgerald in the film *Going My Way.* In dramas today, the clergy and serious believers are regularly presented as hypocritical or mad (and sometimes both). In the present mood, the film *The Apostle*, in which Robert Duvall plays a troubled evangelist who is guilty of homicide but a sincere believer who scorns racial distinctions, was generally regarded as benign.

Advertising sometimes follows the pattern. In a 1998 ad for the Website beyond.com, the residents at a "Spiritual Center" are depicted either as cranks eating unappetizing food or as poseurs; staring at her computer screen, a young woman remarks, "My tech fund just scored. I am *so* out of here." And on television news, clergy from mainstream denominations almost never appear (the most visible exception, Jesse Jackson, is obviously a peculiar case). Religious opinion is represented by leaders like Pat Robertson or Louis Farrakhan, who are popularly identified with extremism if not disruption.[72]

As a general rule, religion can be expected to seek at least a minimal accommodation with the prevailing morés. With time, even very militant churches tend to bend with the wind. But religion also has reasons to cherish a contentious role, not least among which is America's need to hear champions of the view that human life is not trivial and that human beings have both natural limits and high obligations.[73]

Religion and the Revitalizing of Democracy

Yet to the extent that religion ceases to be the basis of moral community, something almost taken for granted in public discourse, we can expect that faith will be more in evidence in public life and argument. This helps explain the stirrings within the electorate, in 2000 and since. Confronted with a time in which moral rules seem contested or uncertain, a great many voters have been looking for leaders with an inner moral center, something more than spin and sound bites—"people with definition and conviction," Randall Balmer observes, "even if it differs from their own."[74] Hence, David Leege writes, both George W. Bush, and the Democrats (in a somewhat softer way) have been aiming at voters "for whom religion is not a tight set of laws but a source of goodness."[75]

Although it invites hypocrisy from candidates and is all too likely to result in judgments that are vacuous or superficial, that inclination is not necessarily a bad thing, and even reflects a measure of sophistication. Ultimately, the political quality of that disposition will depend on the citizenry's ear for the language of faith.

In other words, in an era when religion and morals are less a matter of habits and givens, religious education is a critical part of civic education; secularity calls for schooling in the sacred. Even Jefferson thought so, at least late in life. The "study and investigation" of the relation between the human and the divine, he wrote in 1822, is a human imperative, and public authorities are not "precluded" from supporting instruction in "religious opinions and duties." In that spirit, he favored bringing "sectarian schools" into the university, integrating religious controversy into public higher education.[76] In contemporary America, the courts—and probably, even opinion—would rule out such support. That barrier, however, ought not to keep us from recognizing that religion's best gift to the Republic in these times will be faiths that are both informed by humility and disciplined by text and tradition.[77]

Tocqueville worried that secular society, caught up with the "interests of the world," would be blind to the needs of the soul and neglect its education. Yet because the demands of the soul are "constituent principles of human nature," they will make themselves felt, at times with great force. If the soul is left frustrated and untrained, Tocqueville noted, when it does break through it is likely to be "unrestrained, beyond the bounds of common sense."[78]

In the United States today, it is not hard to make a case in support of Tocqueville's argument. Religious literacy, after a long decline, is now socially marginal at best. In 1976, seeking to reassure Americans, and especially liberals, that he was not rigidly self-righteous, Jimmy Carter told *Playboy* that he lusted after women in his heart. Most people apparently took this to mean that Carter was what, in retrospect, we would probably call Clinton-like. Startlingly few seem to have recognized that Carter was referring to Matthew 5:28 and was suggesting that, informed by Christian teaching, he did not think his own decent conduct made him spiritually superior to sinners. Whatever their scriptural knowledge, Carter's successors have learned to keep their citations simple.[79]

Evidence of what Tocqueville termed "religious insanity" is also easily come by, and not just in cults and fringe groups. The position of more and more Americans is essentially paranoid, experienced as subject to forces that are overwhelming and baffling, half-visible powers pursuing shadowed ends.[80] In fiction, conspiracy theory is the stock-in-trade, but it is also a feature of a remarkable amount of what passes for nonfiction, on both Right and Left. The zeal for discovering and deciphering codes—sometimes intellectually serious, but often simply kooky—has taken on, as Edward Rothstein writes, an "urgency and passion that probably has not been seen since the seventeenth century."[81] In 1996, *Newsweek* reported that almost half of Americans believed that the government had been covering up evidence of unidentified flying objects, whereas nearly a third thought the government had made contact with extraterrestrials.[82]

It makes matters worse that Americans have little confidence in the direction of change: Think only of that epigraph on the television series the *X-Files* that read "Fight the Future." Trust in democratic institutions, moreover, is hitting record lows, despite our well-being. We worry that government may be increasingly irrelevant, an epiphenomenon shaped in the image of global economic and technological forces beyond its control.[83] Yet when it deals with us as individuals, government is fearsome, and we suspect that it may have been captured by great organizations and interests. At the same time, we have a good idea how much we depend on public institutions; on the *X-Files*, malign conspirators stalked the halls of power, but the heroes were also government agents. And there are hints, in popular culture, that we are tantalized by visions of leaders who take command of events, even if their messianic victories come at towering cost.[84]

In these circumstances, I am inclined to think that Jefferson was right, that public controversy between confessions that take their doctrines and heritages seriously could do a good deal to make our public life both livelier and saner. The growing recognition that it is our lot to be a country of plural faiths ought to make civil argument easier, especially given a crucial element of common ground.[85] Faith holds that the world, whatever its mystery and anguish, will ultimately prove to make sense. It supports our yearning for a truth that is "bedrock," not interpretation and image.[86] "It is faith," John Paul II recently declared, "which stirs reason to move beyond all isolation and willingly to run risks," serving as reason's "convinced and convincing advocate."[87] That faiths differ is an occasion for debate; faith itself assures them that they have something to debate *about*.

Of course, any suggestion that religions become more contentious is bound to raise fears, and not only in secular circles. The mainline churches especially, devoted to ecumenism and eager for friends and allies, have been inclined to play down their differences, muting their distinctive voices to avoid giving offense.[88] But the fraternity of faith is more agony than amiability. Its deepest likeness, the quest for the divine, is a rivalry that can turn fratricidal, as too much experience testifies, but one in which the other's best can also draw out one's own. In the United States today, the risks seem acceptably small; the laws have helped teach religions to observe the democratic civilities, and the public has little patience with zealots. And there are potential gains, because the great faiths have something to teach the Republic about the metaphysics of civic morality.

Among other things, the great religious teachings do not forget that human beings are dependent and subject to the limits of nature. They recognize, for example, the complex claims and moral dimensions of the body: Faith knows sin and shortcomings, but it is also aware of the potential dignity of the flesh and of the erotic, as in the Christian mystery in which the body is deemed worthy to receive the divine. Contemporary secular thinking often inclines to reduce sexuality to one more "choice," one desire among many, just as it is tempted to believe that community can be indefinitely expanded through technology.[89]

So far, however, experience with "virtual reality" suggests that it admits of a community that is inadequate at best, one that results, on the whole, in a "decline in feelings of connection."[90] Faith understands, by contrast, that short of divine intervention, communion in this world—as in the Christian ritual—is a matter of body and blood as well as spirit. It counsels us, consequently, not to expect from the Framers' extended Republic a warmer brotherhood than it can afford.

At the same time, the great traditions remind us that preoccupation with well-being and survival is at bottom enslaving, subjecting us to whoever and whatever can credibly threaten our comfort and safety. The pursuit of individual independence, in that sense, is a trap, just as it rests on an illusion. It is having obligations that make us willing to sacrifice life, liberty, or estate that frees us from dominations and powers, and from our own frailties.[91] American religion, in those terms, has been an old ally of the art of association.[92] In American practice, the passion for self-government has declined in favor of the desire for personal fulfillment.[93] Religion, however, still hears our whispered hope for dignity, and by affirming that, in secular life, human beings are capable of moral agency, responsible to God and to each other, faith may call us toward citizenship and self-rule.

The Framers warned us against religion's destructive power, and the headlines confirm the validity of that caution. But it is hard to avoid the conclusion that, facing a politics defined more and more by oligarchy and indifference, American democracy has worse things to fear than faith.

Notes

1. Laurie Goldstein, "White House Seekers Wear Faith on Sleeve and Stump," *New York Times*, Aug. 31, 1999, A1, and "The Religion Issue," *New York Times*, Aug. 6, 2000, 20.

2. Franklin D. Roosevelt, "Acceptance of Renomination for the Presidency," June 27, 1936, in *The Public Papers and Addresses of Franklin D. Roosevelt*, vol. 5, *The People Approve* (New York: Random House, 1938), 235.

3. "We do not see faith, hope and charity as unattainable ideals," Roosevelt said, "but we use them as stout supports of a Nation fighting the fight for freedom in a modern civilization"; ibid., 234–35.

4. Goldstein, "White House Seekers," A1, A16. Bush, of course, was speaking the language of what amounts to Evangelical political theory, the teaching that true reformation proceeds inwardly and one heart at a time.

5. Laurie Goldstein, "Religious Right, Frustrated, Trying New Tactic on G.O.P.," *New York Times*, March 23, 1998, A1 describes the pre-impeachment mood; for later sentiments, see Gustav Niebuhr and Richard L. Berke, "Unity Is Elusive as Religious Right Ponders 2000 Vote," *New York Times,* March 7, 1999, 11. Perhaps the best example of these feelings is William Bennett, *The Death of Outrage* (New York: Free Press, 1998).

6. David Firestone, "Republicans to Test the Religious Right's Strength in South Carolina," *New York Times*, Feb. 13, 2000, 34; Bill Kristol referred to the conservative Christian preference for Bush as a "surrender to the corporate interests in the party";

Hana Rosin and Dana Milbank, "The Excommunication of Gary Bauer," *Washington Post National Weekly*, April 3, 2000, 14. That Senator McCain was moved, in the heat of the moment, to refer to Pat Robertson et al. as an "evil influence" on the Republican Party is at least a fair indication that they read him correctly; David Barstow, "McCain, in Further Attack, Calls Leaders of Christian Right 'Evil,'" *New York Times*, March 1, 2000, A1.

7. Gustav Niebuhr, "Evangelicals Found a Believer in Bush," *New York Times*, Feb. 21, 2000, A13.

8. Americans, as John C. Green indicates, continue to expect religion to furnish a moral "grounding" for politics. Goldstein, "White House Seekers," A16.

9. "In the moral world everything is classified, systematized, foreseen and decided beforehand," Tocqueville wrote, "in the political world everything is agitated, disputed and uncertain. . . . Liberty . . . considers religion as the safeguard of morality, and morality as the best security of law and the surest pledge of the duration of freedom"; Alexis de Tocqueville, *Democracy in America* (New York: Knopf, 1980), vol. 1, 43–44.

10. *The Federalist*, ed. Jacob Cooke (Middletown, Conn.: Wesleyan University Press, 1961), 58.

11. The effort to impose religious unity, Madison wrote, had produced "torrents of blood"; *The Writings of James Madison*, ed. Gaillard Hunt (New York: Putnam, 1900–10), vol. 2, 189. The effect of such attempts, Jefferson asserted in *Notes on Virginia*, was to "make one half of the world fools, and the other half hypocrites"; *Life and Selected Writings of Thomas Jefferson*, ed. Adrienne Koch and William Peden (New York: Modern Library, 1944), 276.

12. Madison, *Writings*, vol. 4, 387; when our duties and interests appear to be at odds, Jefferson wrote, "we ought to suspect some fallacy in our reasonings"; *Life and Selected Writings*, 575.

13. *Federalist* 55, 374; and 72, 488.

14. Madison, *Writings*, vol. 6, 86; *Federalist* 51, 349.

15. Benjamin Franklin, *Benjamin Franklin: Writings*, ed. J.A. Lemay (New York: Library of America, 1987), 336.

16. The term "social capital," of course, refers to Robert Putnam, "Bowling Alone: America's Declining Social Capital," *Journal of Democracy* 6 (1995): 65–78.

17. John Locke, *A Letter Concerning Toleration* (Indianapolis: Bobbs Merrill, 1955), 52.

18. In *Notes on Virginia*, Jefferson questioned whether an atheist's testimony was reliable enough to be acceptable in a court of law; *Notes on the State of Virginia*, ed. William Peden (Chapel Hill: University of North Carolina Press, 1955), 159.

19. John Locke, *The Reasonableness of Christianity*, ed. I.T.Ramsey (Stanford, Calif.: Stanford University Press, 1958), 64.

20. Jefferson, *Life and Selected Writings*, 570.

21. *The Legal Papers of John Adams*, ed. L. Kinvin Wroth and Hillel B. Zobel (Cambridge, Mass.: Harvard University Press, 1965), vol. 3, 254.

22. The highest duty of citizens, Jefferson argued, reaches beyond written law to the commands "of necessity, of self-preservation, of saving our country when in danger"; *Life and Selected Writings*, 606–7. In Jefferson's Lockean formulation, it should be noticed that collective self-preservation rivals or takes precedence over *personal* self-preservation, presuming at least the subordination of the body to an extended idea of self.

23. John Witherspoon, *The Works of Reverend John Witherspoon* (Philadelphia: Woodward, 1802), vol. 3, 98–99.

24. 1 Corinthians 13:12.

25. Galatians 3:28. For a moment, Nietzsche argued, the Dionysia shattered "all the hostile, rigid walls which either necessity or despotism has erected between men," so that "the slave emerges as a freeman"; *The Birth of Tragedy and the Genealogy of Morals*, trans. Francis Golffing (Garden City, N.Y.: Doubleday, 1956), 23.

26. Peter L. Berger, *The Sacred Canopy* (Garden City, N.Y.: Doubleday, 1969).

27. *Benjamin Franklin: Writings*, 748.

28. In this, they reflected the "antitheological ire" that lies, as Leo Strauss argues, at the beginning of modern political thought. The logic of that position, Strauss observed, leads to a thoroughgoing rejection of transcendence and of the notion of eternity; *What Is Political Philosophy?* (Glencoe, Ill.: Free Press, 1959), 44, 51, 55.

29. *The Autobiography of Benjamin Franklin and Other Writings,* ed. Kenneth Silverman (New York: Penguin, 1986), 13, 90. On the subject of Presbyterians, Jefferson was more vehement than Franklin;. *Letters and Selected Writings*, 632, 697.

30. Jefferson, *Letters and Selected Writings*, 694, 704; personally, Jefferson was not at all indifferent about the question, telling Smith, with misplaced confidence, that he expected Unitarianism to become the "general religion of the United States" within the "present generation."

31. Wilfred McClay, "Mr. Emerson's Tombstone," *First Things*, May 1998, 16–22.

32. See Madison's Letter to Jefferson, Aug. 20, 1785, *Writings of James Madison*, vol. 2, 163–64.

33. Jefferson, *Life and Selected Writings*, 275; see also Jean Yarbrough, *American Virtues: Thomas Jefferson on the Character of a Free People* (Lawrence: University Press of Kansas, 1998), 190.

34. E.g., the "child benefit" test was applied to aid to the secular activities of schools until the last half century; *Cochran v. Louisiana Board of Education*, 281 U.S. 370, 1930, and *McCollum v. Board of Education*, 333 U.S. 203, 1948. Theodore Lowi, a critic of this aspect of American constitutionalism, describes its historic role in his *The End of the Republican Era* (Norman: University of Oklahoma Press, 1995), 28–30, 175–82.

35. Locke, *Letter Concerning Toleration*, 17; Thomas Jefferson, "Notes on Locke and Shaftesbury," in *Papers of Thomas Jefferson*, ed. Julian Boyd (Princeton, N.J.: Princeton University Press, 1954), vol. 1, 544–48. See *Employment Division v. Smith,* 494 U.S. 872 (1990) and *City of Boerne v. Flores*, 117 S.C. 2157 (1997); When the Court struck down an ordinance banning animal sacrifice, it did so because the law targeted religion; *Church of Lakumi Babalu v. Hialeah,* 113 S.C. 2217 (1993).

36. *U.S. v. Reynolds* 98 U.S. 145 (1879).

37. John West, *The Politics of Revelation and Reason* (Lawrence: University Press of Kansas, 1996); *Wisconsin v. Yoder* 406 U.S. 205 (1972), afforded the Old Order Amish exemption from compulsory school attendance on grounds of their law-abiding civil conduct, and a statute exempted them from Social Security taxes. But *U.S. v. Lee*, 455 U.S. 252 (1982) held that as employers, they must pay those taxes on their employees, religious beliefs to the contrary.

38. James Davison Hunter, *Culture Wars* (New York: Basic Books, 1991).

39. Gustav Niebuhr, "Salem Journal: Witches Appeal to a Political Spirit," *New York Times*, Oct. 31, 1998, A8.

40. Richard Morin, "Can We Believe in Polls About God?" *Washington Post National Weekly,* June 1, 1998, 30.

41 Robert Bellah et al., *The Habits of the Heart* (Berkeley: University of California Press, 1985); Alan Wolfe, *One Nation after All* (New York: Viking, 1998).

42. *Democracy in America,* vol. 1, 43; Sanford Kessler, *Tocqueville's Civil Religion* (Albany: State University of New York Press, 1994).

43. *Democracy in America,* vol. 2, 23–24.

44. As Peter Berger argues, there is a strong impulse in American religion to follow the "dynamics of consumer preference," hoping for a certain "product loyalty"; *Sacred Canopy,* 145–46.

45. *Democracy in America,* vol. 2, 122.

46. Harvey C. Mansfield, "Change and Bill Clinton," *Times Literary Supplement,* Nov. 13, 1992, 14.

47. Goldstein, "White House Seekers," A16.

48. Richard Morin and David Broder, "Worried about Morals but Reluctant to Judge," *Washington Post National Weekly,* Sept. 21, 1998, 10–11.

49. Matthew 7:1–5.

50. William Galston, "Home of the Tolerant," *Public Interest* 133 (1998), 119.

51. Michael Malbin, *Religion and Politics: The Intentions of the Authors of the First Amendment* (Washington, D.C.: American Enterprise Institute, 1978).

52. Allan Hertzke, *Echoes of Discontent* (Washington, D.C.: CQ Press, 1993); Robert D. Putnam, "Tuning In, Tuning Out: The Strange Death of Social Capital in America," *PS* 28 (1995): 671–81.

53. Lakis Polykarpou, "Littleton Isn't Anytown, It's Notown," *Washington Post National Weekly,* May 10, 1999, 23; Judith Wallerstein, Julia Lewis, and Sandy Blakeslee, *The Unexpected Legacy of Divorce* (New York: Hyperion, 2000).

54. *New York Times Magazine,* May 7, 2000, 66, 76.

55. Theodore Lowi refers to "domestic insecurity" as something close to a way of life; "Think Globally, Lose Locally," *Boston Review,* April–May 1998, 10.

56. Kristin Downey Grimsley, "Leaner—and Definitely Meaner," *Washington Post National Weekly,* July 20, 1998, 21.

57. Colin Campbell, "Consuming Goods and the Good of Consuming," *Critical Review* 8 (1994): 503–20.

58. *Democracy in America,* vol. 2, 98–99, 136–39.

59. E.J. Dionne Jr., "A New Wind Blowing," *Washington Post National Weekly,* Aug. 9, 1999, 27. Even the subtitle of Robert Putnam's new book refers to the "revival" of community: *Bowling Alone: The Collapse and Revival of American Community* (New York: Simon & Schuster, 2000).

60. Gilles Lipovetsky, "May '68, or The Rise of Transpolitical Individualism," trans. L. Maguire, in *New French Thought,* ed. Marc Lilla (Princeton, N.J.: Princeton University Press, 1994), 214, 218.

61. Polly Morrice, "It Takes More Than Faith to Save the Poor," *New York Times,* Aug. 29, 1999, WK15.

62. Alan Wolfe, "The Pursuit of Autonomy," *New York Times Magazine,* May 7, 2000, 54.

63. W. Lance Bennett describes contemporary political culture as pervaded by "socially dislocated individuals seeking social recognition and credible representation for

personal concerns"; "The Uncivil Culture: Communication, Identity and the Rise of Lifestyle Politics," *PS*, 31 (1998): 755.

64. Janny Scott, "Bright, Shining or Dark: The American Way of Lying," *New York Times*, Aug. 16, 1998, WK3; John R. Zaller, "Monica Lewinsky's Contribution to Political Science," *PS*, 31 (1998): 182–89.

65. See Rogers Smith's sympathetic critique of identity politics in his *Civic Ideals* (New Haven, Conn.: Yale University Press, 1997), 485–86. More generally, see Sheldon Wolin, "Democracy in the Discourse of Postmodernism," *Social Research*, 57 (1990): 5–30.

66. *New York Times*, Dec. 5, 1997, A31.

67. Stephen L. Carter, *The Culture of Disbelief: How American Law and Politics Trivialize Religious Devotion* (New York: Basic Books, 1993).

68. "Being a Catholic liberal or a Catholic conservative," E.J. Dionne writes, "inevitably means having a bad conscience about something"; "Courting the 'Catholic Vote,'" *Washington Post National Weekly*, June 26, 2000, 22.

69. William Sloane Coffin, "The Politics of Compassion," *Harvard Divinity Bulletin*, 28, no. 2–3 (1999): 11–12.

70. James Skillen, "Driving for Dominance, Fleeing for Purity," *Public Justice Report*, 22, no. 2 (1999): 1ff.

71. William Bennett is a notable example; Dionne, "Courting the 'Catholic Vote.'"

72. Ed Kilgore, " Holier Than Thou," *The New Democrat*, Sept.–Oct., 1998, 8.

73. Laurence Iannaccone observes that "strong" churches must balance between *distinctiveness* (and the community and sense of mission associated with it) and the social *costs* such differences impose on its members; "knowing when to give in" is important; a church that makes the price of membership too high will become a more or less marginal sect; "Why Strict Churches Are Strong," *American Journal of Sociology* 99(1994):1180–1212. Yet religion's noblest moments involve knowing when not to give in.

74. I cite Balmer from Gustav Niebuhr, "God and Man and the Presidency," *New York Times*, Dec. 19, 1999, WK7.

75. David Leege, "Divining the Electorate," *Commonweal*, Aug. 20, 2000, 19.

76. *The Complete Jefferson*, ed. Saul K. Padover (New York: Tudor, 1943), 957–58.

77. Peter L. Berger, "Protestantism and the Quest for Certainty," *Christian Century*, Aug. 26, 1998, 782ff.

78. *Democracy in America*, vol. 1, 310; vol. 2, 20–22, 25–26,134–35, 148.

79. Although it is notable that in the Oct. 18, 2000, episode of the hit television series *The West Wing*, President Josiah Bartlett routed a smugly rightist talk-show host by his command of Scripture.

80. Michael Paul Rogin, "JFK: The Movie," *American Historical Review* 97 (1992): 503–5.

81. Edward Rothstein, "Is Destiny Just a Divine Word Game?" *New York Times*, Aug. 12, 1997, C11.

82. *Newsweek*, July 8, 1996; Frank McConnell, "Expecting Visitors," *Commonweal*, Nov. 22, 1996, 21–22.

83. Bennett, "Uncivil Culture," 758.

84. Richard Rorty, *Achieving Our Country* (Cambridge, Mass.: Harvard University Press, 1998), 61.

85. James Skillen, *Capital Commentary*, Washington, D.C., Center for Public Justice, March 15, 1999.

86. The reference to "bedrock truth" is taken from Todd Gitlin, "On Being Sound-Bitten," *Boston Review*, Dec. 1991, 17.

87. *Fides et Ratio*, excerpted in the *New York Times*, Oct. 16, 1998, A10.

88. Randall Balmer, "United We Fall," *New York Times*, Aug. 28, 1999, A13. A caricatured version of this disposition is found in a growing fraction of the general public: a near plurality (42 as against 45 percent) in a recent *New York Times* poll agreed that the best religion "would be one that borrowed from all religions"; *New York Times Magazine,* May 7, 2000, 84.

89. Peter Steinfels, "Beliefs," *New York Times*, Aug. 22, 1998, A11.

90. Amy Harmon, "Sad, Lonely World Discovered in Cyberspace," *New York Times*, Aug. 30, 1998, 1.

91. Bertrand de Jouvenel, *Sovereignty: An Inquiry into the Political Good* (Indianapolis: Liberty Fund, 1997), 316–17.

92. Peter Berkowitz, "The Art of Association," *New Republic,* June 24, 1996, 44–49.

93. Robert Wiebe, *Self-Rule: A History of American Democracy* (Chicago: University of Chicago Press, 1995).

6

Faith in Politics

A. James Reichley

At the start of the new millennium, religion is a paramount concern for practitioners and analysts of American politics. During the campaign for the crucial 2000 presidential election, possibly shaping the balance of power in national politics for years to come, candidates and party leaders made religion a central factor in their strategies.[1]

Some commentators worry that the rising political salience of religion may create dangerous divisions in American society, as has often occurred in such places as the Balkans, India, the Middle East, and Northern Ireland. Some warn of threats to constitutional separation between church and state.[2]

Throughout most of American history, however, religion has played a potent, though varying, role in political life. Protestant clergy ardently supported the Revolution, and religious bodies enlisted on both sides in

The author particularly thanks Michael Cromarty, John Langan, S.J., David Walsh, Clyde Wilcox, and Robert Wuthnow for their help in preparing this chapter. Responsibility for facts and opinions is of course entirely mine.

the struggle over abolition of slavery that led to the Civil War. Religious groups played major parts in drives for women's suffrage and prohibition of alcohol early in the twentieth century, and provided vital support for passage of civil rights legislation in the 1960s. Catholicism was an issue with the presidential candidacies of Al Smith in 1928 and John Kennedy in 1960. The massive shift of white evangelicals from the Democratic to the Republican side in the 1980s deeply influenced the direction of national politics.

Whether mixing religion with politics in the current state of our culturally pluralist society is feasible or wise—and if so, to what extent and how—are questions that cannot fully be settled through knowledge of the past. But getting the historical record straight will be useful in considering these currently contentious issues.

In this chapter, I will trace the role of religion in American politics during the twentieth century and the decades leading up to it. After concluding this historical review, I will examine the current and likely future effects of religious faith on political behavior.

The Religious Factor

In the 1950s, Richard Scammon, premier master of election statistics, used to say that the two most important issues in every U.S. election, in terms of determining how votes were cast, were the Reformation and the Civil War. By this he meant that these two great seminal watersheds, at least one of which was religious, regularly aligned most Northern Protestants with the Republican Party, and most Catholics and white Southerners, who were mostly Protestants, with the Democrats.

The religious character of the Reformation is obvious. From about 1850 to 1960, the social divisions it defined in American life deeply affected electoral and legislative politics. After the massive waves of Catholic immigration to industrial and mining centers of the Northeast and Great Lakes states during the second half of the nineteenth century, most Protestants in these areas banded together in the Republican Party as a means for preserving the quasi-official, though not legally established, Protestant quality of American life. The United States had been the promised land of Protestantism—the place where, as Jonathan Edwards predicted in the eighteenth century, "the latter-day glory is probably to begin." Well into the twentieth century, a large majority of Americans regarded Protestant mores and values, to some extent secularized, as the underlying foundation of national culture.

Distrust of Catholicism among Protestants was not wholly based on theological differences or simple prejudice. ("What," a young staff member at one of the mainline Protestant Washington offices recently asked me, "was all *that* about?") Before the Second Vatican Council in the 1960s, the international Catholic Church held that, wherever politically feasible, Catholicism "ought to be, by constitutional law, the one religion of the state." As late as 1939, Pope Pius XII reaffirmed the traditional doctrine: "That which does not correspond to the truth and the norm of morality has, objectively, no right either to existence or to propaganda or to action." Such views were interpreted by many Protestants, and other non-Catholics, as challenges to religious freedom.[3]

Catholics, for religious and cultural as well as economic reasons, responded to Protestant alignment with the Republicans by giving their allegiance to the relatively more liberal Democrats. In urban and industrial regions of the Northeast and Midwest, Democratic machines, usually run by Irish Catholic politicians, commanded loyal followings among most Catholic voters.

Even in the late nineteenth century, there were exceptions, such as the Irish Catholic divisions of the Republican machines that controlled Philadelphia and Pittsburgh, and the so-called swallowtail faction of New York Protestant Democrats that supplied most of the Democratic candidates for president (including the only winner, Grover Cleveland) from the Civil War to 1896. But in general, Protestants in the urban areas of the Northeast and Great Lakes region were Republicans, and Catholics were Democrats. These allegiances were reinforced by the operations of patronage-based party organizations.

In the more rural regions of the Midwest, where Catholics were less numerous, and in much of the Far West, where religious observance tended to be more casual, denominational identification had fewer political effects, and other issues, often economic, were more likely to structure politics. Even in those areas of the non-South, however, the ties of pan-Protestantism helped maintain normal Republican dominance.

In the South, for the most part heavily Protestant, the effects of the Civil War and Reconstruction gathered most whites into the Democratic Party, in part because the Republicans were regarded as the party of the victorious and oppressive North, and even more after the end of Reconstruction in 1877 as a means for excluding African Americans from participation, including eventually the right to vote, in Southern politics. These ties were not themselves religious, but were reinforced by Southern Protestant churches, mostly Baptist and Methodist, joined by Presbyterians and Episcopalians at the upper rungs of society. Many of these denominations had split from their Northern counterparts on the slavery issue before the Civil War, and had loyally supported the Confederacy. (In a notable instance, Episcopal bishop Leonidas Polk of Louisiana had laid aside his clerical duties in 1861 to become a general in the Confederate Army.) Leaders of many of these religious bodies were integrated into state and local Democratic Party power structures.

In the North, the Union cause in the Civil War had been fed by religious passions, which had helped erase an earlier political divide between Protestant denominations. In the political battles of the early Republic, the more formal and austere Calvinist denominations, usually joined by the Episcopalians and Quakers, staunchly supported the succeeding relatively conservative Federalist and Whig parties, whereas the more evangelical Methodists and Baptists were enthusiastic Jeffersonians and Jacksonian Democrats. "I have waged an incessant warfare," declared the popular frontier evangelist Peter Cartwright, "against the world, the flesh, and the devil, and other enemies of the Democratic party."[4] This division, in part economic (evangelicals were generally poor and agrarian), was swept aside by common attachment to the party leading the war against slavery and Southern secession. In the last third of the nineteenth century, Northern Protestant pastors commonly urged their parishioners to "vote as we pray," supplementing Republican orators' appeal to "vote as you shot." German Lutherans, who earlier had often joined the Democrats as a refuge against sabbatarian and prohibitionist laws sponsored by reformist Whigs, were similarly drawn to the broad Republican coalition.[5]

African Americans, rising from slavery in the South and entering more actively into civil life in the North, were socially and politically organized through their Protestant churches, mostly Baptist and Methodist (which had broken away from parent denominations in response to racial discrimination by white majorities.) These, both in the South, until they were almost completely excluded from politics in the 1890s, and in the North, where they remained politically vibrant, were uniformly loyal to the party of Lincoln that had ended slavery and continued to be relatively liberal on civil rights issues.

Jews, who had maintained small communities in major Eastern cities since colonial times, began emigrating to the United States in substantial numbers toward the end of the nineteenth century. They seem in this period to have been mainly either Republicans or Socialists—the former following the leadership of influential bankers and merchants, and the latter preserving ideological inclinations developed in the ghettoes of Europe.

Religion and Reform

During the latter part of the nineteenth century and early twentieth, the Social Gospel movement achieved considerable force within American Protestantism. Building on the Whig reform tradition that earlier had given birth to abolitionism and prohibitionism, eloquent Social Gospel ministers such as Walter Rauschenbush, Josiah Strong, and Washington Gladden, and their feminist allies such as Susan B. Anthony and Frances Willard, applied moral values they found in the Bible to attack social, economic, and political ills associated with dynamically expanding industrial capitalism. The Social Gospelers aimed their rebukes not only at moral vices but also at systemic failures they concluded were inherent in unregulated market capitalism.

Both leaderships and laities in most Protestant denominations remained predominantly conservative in their political and economic attachments, basing their views on their own interpretations of the more austere and socially traditional side of Christianity as well as on their interests as part of the dominant social group. The Social Gospelers, however, made strong inroads in seminaries, among younger clergy, and even among some socially traditionalist laity, leading to what Martin Marty has called a Protestant "two-party system," pitting dominant conservatives against insurgent reformers.[6] Social Gospel militance was to some extent allied with the growth of rationalist liberalism, adapting biblical teachings to fit Darwinism and other findings of modern science, in what were later called the "mainline" Protestant denominations (Congregationalists, Episcopalians, some Lutheran bodies, Methodists, Presbyterians, and some smaller churches).

The Protestant two-party system was at first only indirectly linked to the competition between Republicans and Democrats in the larger polity. Most Social Gospelers, sharing the general Northern Protestant view of the Democrats as the party of "rum, Romanism, and rebellion," continued to work within the Republican Party or joined the new Prohibition Party. When a change in New York election law inadvertently permitted woman's suffrage in a single election, Susan B. Anthony proudly cast her ballot for "the straight Republican ticket." Within Republican ranks, Social Gospelers gave support to Progressive reformers such as Robert La Follette in Wisconsin, Hiram Johnson in California, George Norris in Nebraska, and Theodore Roosevelt in New York.

The deep economic depression of the 1890s sorely strained the Republican loyalties of many Northern Protestants, particularly in the rural Midwest. The new Populist Party that formed in the early 1890s gained support from many evangelical Protestant farmers. Populist publicists and politicians tied economic grievances to a vision of a "New Jerusalem" that went back at least to the Reformation. Positive proposals for economic and social reforms were mixed with rancorous sentiments of anti-Catholicism, ant-Semitism, and antiurbanism in general. When populist forces won control of the Democratic Party in 1896, William Jennings Bryan's "Cross of Gold" speech at the Democratic National Convention, urging coinage of silver on equal terms with gold, used religious imagery to convey social and cultural as well as economic discontents.

Bryan's candidacy for president on both Democratic and Populist tickets in 1896 attracted some backing among his fellow evangelical Protestants, helping him carry nine normally Republican Midwestern and Rocky Mountain states. But most church leaderships, Catholic as well as Protestant, alarmed by Bryan's perceived economic and social radicalism, gave open or tacit support to his victorious Republican opponent, William McKinley. Catholic archbishop John Ireland warned that the populists were "lighting torches which, borne in the hands of reckless men, may light up in our country the lurid fires of a commune." A leading Episcopal magazine declared that Bryan's election would cause "the ruin of national fiscal morality." On the Sunday before election, many Protestant pastors preached against Bryanism with the text, "Thou Shalt Not Steal." The Republicans more than made up losses in the farm states with increased support from Catholics and mainline Protestants in growing urban areas of the Northeast and Great Lakes region.[7]

Return of prosperity under McKinley and his Republican successor, Theodore Roosevelt, temporarily wilted the economic roots of populism. But the religious and cultural discontents that Bryan had also tapped continued to percolate. Some of these were channeled into the theological struggles that many evangelicals, particularly among Baptists, Methodists, and Presbyterians, were waging against liberal rationalism. Early in the twentieth century, the term "fundamentalism" was coined to designate those who insisted on the literal truth of the Bible in "every sentence, every word, every syllable, every letter," and rejected Darwinism and all other findings of modern science they held to be inconsistent with Scripture.

The next great wave of political reform came through the Progressive movement that grew during the late 1890s and early 1900s. Like populism,

Progressivism drew on religious enthusiasms, but more among middle-class Social Gospelers than agrarian evangelicals. When Roosevelt, deserting the Republicans, accepted the Progressive Party nomination for president in 1912, celebrating delegates at the Progressive convention, including some liberal Jews, sang rousing choruses of "Onward Christian Soldiers" and "The Battle Hymn of the Republic." "We stand at Armageddon," Roosevelt exhorted, "and we battle for the Lord." The Progressive platform, said the religiously inspired urban reformer Jane Addams, contained "everything I have been fighting for."[8]

After Roosevelt's defeat, some Progressives, including Social Gospelers, swung behind Woodrow Wilson's "New Freedom," which also embodied reform impulses. During Wilson's first term, considerable reform legislation was passed by the Democratic Congress, with help from the Progressives. By 1920, however, most of the old Progressives, having opposed the United States's entrance to World War I, and unpersuaded by Wilson's vision of a new international order, had rejoined the Republicans. In 1919, La Follette, Norris, and Johnson led the fight in the Senate against the United States joining Wilson's proposed League of Nations. Among the lasting achievements of Progressivism was enactment in 1920 of the Nineteenth Amendment to the Constitution establishing woman's suffrage, which was strongly supported by the Social Gospelers and other religious groups.

The Churches Come to Washington

Evangelical Protestantism won its greatest political victory in 1919 with passage of the Eighteenth Amendment prohibiting the manufacture or sale of intoxicating liquors. Prohibition seemed to work for a while, but it soon spawned a huge bootlegging industry that helped finance a teeming underworld culture and damaged respect for law among the general public. The failure of Prohibition, which was repealed in 1933, shook the political confidence of evangelicals. A further blow was struck when Bryan, coming out of retirement in 1925 to defend a Tennessee law prohibiting the teaching of evolution in the famous Scopes trial, was made a national laughingstock by Scopes's lawyer, the wily Clarence Darrow. Many evangelicals concluded that American society was hopelessly corrupt, and that a prudent Christian should avoid all participation in public life beyond paying taxes and voting.[9]

Catholic support for the Democratic Party, which had waned somewhat when the Democrats were led by Bryan and Wilson (particularly among

Irish and German Catholics during World War I), was renewed and reinforced by the party's nomination of Al Smith, the liberal Catholic governor of New York, for president in 1928. Smith went down to overwhelming defeat before Republican Herbert Hoover, after a campaign in which Smith's religion became an issue, particularly among normally Democratic Southern Protestants. But near solid Catholic support for Smith in Eastern and Midwestern cities provided a base for future Democratic successes. Jews, who had begun to regard the Democrats as the natural party of the excluded, also voted heavily for Smith.

The Great Depression that began in 1929 transformed U.S. politics. Franklin D. Roosevelt, elected president in 1932, ushered in a long period of dominance by his victorious New Deal coalition, which included the old Democratic bases among Catholics and Southern whites, plus secular liberals, many working-class and middle-class Protestants, most African Americans (after 1932) outside the South, and most Jews.

Leaderships of many mainline Protestant denominations reacted to the Depression with increased liberalism, even openness to socialism. The northern Presbyterian General Assembly resolved in 1932 that "nothing is more obvious than that the present economic order is now on probation." In 1934, the National Council of Methodist Youth endorsed socialism as "at present the most workable political expression of Christian social ideals." Except for 1936, when Roosevelt was reelected by a huge majority to a second term, however, substantial majorities of non-Southern Protestants, both clergy and laity, continued to support the Republicans.[10]

The flow of governmental authority to Washington under the New Deal and during World War II, which the United States entered in 1941, caused many religious groups to open or expand advocacy operations in the national capital. The Methodists had established an outpost on Capitol Hill early in the twentieth century to promote Prohibition. The stately Methodist Building (which still houses most mainline Washington offices), across from the Supreme Court, was completed in 1923. During World War I, the Roman Catholic bishops, leading what had become the nation's largest single denomination, authorized formation of the National Catholic War Council with an office in Washington. This body was transformed in 1919 into the National Catholic Welfare Council, charged with coordinating church activities that were national in scope. Until the mid-1940s, however, most denominations had no full-time representative dealing with the federal government.

In 1946, the northern Presbyterians assigned a part-time observer to Washington "for the purpose of securing information rather than the purpose of influencing legislation." Later that same year, the Baptist Joint Conference Committee opened a Washington office—mainly, according to one Baptist commentator, "to watch the Catholics." In 1948, the Methodist Women's Division appointed a full-time Washington representative to work on issues that went beyond the Methodists' traditional support for temperance. A study in 1951 found sixteen churches maintaining Washington offices, often, the study's author wrote, promoting "causes in which groups of church leaders are interested rather than the views of church members in general."[11]

Growing concentration by major elements of the religious community on Washington in part reflected centralization of both political and economic power in the larger society. But it also represented a tendency among some institutional leaderships—Catholic, Jewish, and Protestant—to find religious values dictating agreement with particular secular ideologies, usually liberal or socialist. As a student at the University of Pennsylvania in the early 1950s, I was startled to receive a publication from the Methodist campus fellowship linking Marx with Jesus. (In my upstate Pennsylvania hometown, almost all Methodists were Republicans.)

Roosevelt's leadership of the wartime alliance against Nazi Germany helped solidify Jewish alignment with the Democratic Party—though some Jews, particularly among intellectuals, criticized Roosevelt for not having done more to help Jews escape from Europe before the Holocaust. More than 90 percent of Jews voted for Roosevelt's election to a fourth term in 1944. Prompt recognition of Israel in 1948 by Harry Truman, Roosevelt's successor, reinforced Jewish loyalty to the Democrats.[12]

During the Republican administrations of Dwight D. Eisenhower in the 1950s, some Catholics were drawn by growing affluence and movement out of city ethnic neighborhoods to the suburbs, as well as fierce anticommunism, to political conservatism. Disapproval among Catholics of the divorced status of Adlai Stevenson, Eisenhower's Democratic opponent in 1952 and 1956, also contributed to a mild shift among Catholics to the Republicans. Most Catholics, however, remained normally Democratic, in part out of a kind of tribal identification that a good Catholic should be a loyal Democrat, and in part because Catholic communitarian values were consistent with the Democrats' support for a growing welfare state.

Rejection at the 1956 Democratic national convention of the vice presidential bid of the young Irish Catholic senator from Massachusetts John Kennedy helped sway some Catholic voters to Eisenhower in the fall election. When, four years later, the Democrats nominated Kennedy as their presidential candidate, Catholic defectors returned overwhelmingly to the Democratic ticket. Kennedy's election as the first Catholic president, the historian of American Catholicism James Hennesey writes, "loosened the psychological defensiveness that had historically marked the American Catholic."[13]

As they had against Al Smith in 1928, many Protestant clergy, mainline as well as evangelical, preached against Kennedy's election. During the fall of 1960, I attended a Sunday morning service at the Foundry Methodist Church in Washington (where President Bill Clinton and his family worshiped after 1993) at which I heard a fiery sermon on the theme that American democracy was founded in the cradle of the Reformation and might not survive if separated from it. Defections from Kennedy among some normally Democratic Protestants, particularly in the South, were not sufficient to prevent his victory over the Republican candidate Richard Nixon in a close election.

African-American Churches in Politics

Kennedy's assassination in the fall of 1963 was a dark foretaste of what turned out to be a prolonged period of political and social turmoil. The 1960s began, however, with enthusiastic collaboration among most religious groups—Catholic, Jewish, and Protestant—in support of historic civil rights legislation. Kennedy's successor Lyndon Johnson later said that the Civil Rights Act of 1964, and the Voting Rights Act of 1965 that followed, could not have been passed without the dedicated backing of churches and synagogues.

African-American churches, led by Martin Luther King Jr. and many other ministers, were in the forefront of the civil rights struggle. "The black church," Leonard Gadzepko writes, beside providing personnel and logistical support, "gave the movement an ideological framework through which passive attitudes were transformed into a collective consciousness supportive of collective action."[14]

Though African Americans had largely shifted to the Democrats in the 1930s, many of them, particularly in the South where most Democratic officeholders supported racial segregation, remained loyal to the Republicans. In 1956, Eisenhower received about 40 percent of the African-American vote, and in 1960 32 percent voted for Nixon. But when the Republicans in 1964 chose Barry Goldwater, who had opposed the Civil Rights Act, as their candidate for president, African Americans moved almost unanimously into the Democratic column.

There they have largely remained ever since. Though other sources of political leadership have developed, African-American ministers such as Jesse Jackson, Andrew Young, and William Grey have continued to be major political figures, and blacks are still more politically organized and represented through their churches than any other ethnic or religious group. African-American churches, Frederick C. Harris writes, have provided "African Americans with material resources and oppositional dispositions to challenge their marginality in the political system instead of exclusion from politics."[15]

Some African-American church leaders have come to feel that their interests would be better served if Republicans were attracted to offer more competition for black voters, or if the Democrats were challenged on the left by a new third party. But through the 1990s at least, most stuck to the strategy of increasing African-American turnout to produce Democratic victories in close national and state elections. In the 2000 presidential election, African Americans gave Democrat Al Gore 90 percent of their vote to less than 10 percent for Republican George W. Bush.[16]

A small but highly visible minority of blacks have converted to Islam, giving effective, though at times bitterly antagonistic, leadership to African-American militance.

The Divided Mainline

Among mainline Protestant leaderships, some of the enthusiasm generated by the civil rights struggle was carried over in the late 1960s and early 1970s into protest against the Vietnam War—though with much less united support among church laity. Mainline leaderships, through their national headquarters and Washington offices, moved increasingly to the Left. At their annual, biennial, or quadrennial national assemblies, mainline denominations regularly took highly liberal stands on a wide range of economic, social, cultural, and foreign policy issues. These pronouncements came to resemble political party platforms. During the Republican administrations of Ronald Reagan and George H.W. Bush in the 1980s and early 1990s, mainline offices in Washington kept up steady attacks on many executive branch policies.

The liberal shift of mainline leaderships received broad support from many of the clergy coming out of seminaries, themselves hotbeds of liberalism, after the late 1960s. Some social activists among mainline laities also took up liberal causes. For the most part, however, mainline laities remained moderate or conservative, and continued in most elections to vote Republican. Some mainline liberals argue that polling figures showing Republican majorities among their laities are misleading because these include many who are no more than nominal members. Surveys have shown, however, that active mainline Protestants tend to be *more* politically conservative than those who identify with their churches in name only. The political split between national leaderships and local laities gradually became divisive within mainline denominations such as Episcopalians, Methodists, and Presbyterians, and probably contributed to the sharp decline in mainline memberships, while evangelicals were growing, after the 1960s.[17]

There were several reasons for the leftward shift of mainline leaderships, seminaries, and many clergy. Some carried on the Social Gospel tradition, which found a mandate for political liberalism or socialism in the Old and New Testaments. "The Gospel is a political tract or it is nothing!" a young minister told me after a talk I gave to a church conference in the late 1980s. Opposition to the Vietnam War, which had brought many young people to seminaries in the first place, hardened political attitudes. The attraction of "liberation theology," which was first developed among Catholics in Latin America, provided ideological direction. Horror over the likely effects of nuclear war induced many liberal Protestants to promote accommodation with the Soviet Union and other communist countries. "Feminist theology" encouraged some of the many women entering mainline clergies, as well as male sympathizers, to reject much of traditional Protestantism, including much of the language of the Bible itself. "I never go to church," a young woman on the professional staff of a mainline Washington office whom I interviewed in the 1980s told me. "I can't stand all that Father-business and Son-business."

In promoting liberal causes, mainline activists often formed alliances with secular liberals. These sometimes led them to take positions to preserve political solidarity. A national mainline strategist told me that support by the churches for the Humphrey-Hawkins Full Employment bill in the 1970s, which many moderate as well as conservative economists criticized as inherently inflationary, came in response to pressure from trade union allies. Mainline liberals joined the attack on national celebration of the five hundredth anniversary of Columbus's discovery of America in 1992 to maintain solidarity with aggrieved American Indians and African Americans. On issues such as abortion, many mainline activists felt the need to keep proving their liberal credentials with secular feminists.

The development of genuine pluralism in American society, which Kennedy's election as the first Catholic president demonstrated, also may have been a factor in the liberal politicization of mainline leadership and clergy. Many of the old Social Gospelers had shared the widespread Protestant view of the United States as an essentially Protestant nation with free exercise rights constitutionally guaranteed to minorities. Mainline Protestant clergy, liberal as well as conservative, had often felt that they served as an unofficial moral conscience for the nation as a whole. After Kennedy's election, this view was harder to sustain. Pluralism, as Will Herberg's prescient 1955 book *Protestant-Catholic-Jew* announced, had arrived. No longer able to regard themselves as part of an informal establishment, some Protestant clergy were drawn to define themselves in opposition to the existing system.[18]

Beneath these social and cultural factors were intellectual and theological currents that had grown in liberal Protestantism since the early nineteenth century. Influential theologians had come to hold, often in opaque language, that foundational Christian beliefs, such as the immortality of individual souls, the divinity of Jesus Christ, and even the existence of a theistic God, all still devoutly if usually unreflectively maintained by most Protestants at the pew level, are metaphorical symbols, not to be taken literally, of some deeper metaphysical reality. The "God is dead" theology of the 1960s had a voguish impact in seminaries.

Some Protestant theologians, joined by a few Catholics, rejected the "uniqueness" of Christianity, and gave credence to the findings of the "Jesus Seminar" that regularly voted on which of the sayings of Jesus reported by the Gospels are "authentic." For these, Christianity was subsumed into a new super-religion, emphasizing a vague "spirituality" that would motivate good works in a multicultural society. Many mainline clergy were intellectually shaped by these tendencies. "The last thing they wanted was for their congregations to find out what they really believed," a younger Methodist theologian and historian recently told me. "So they stopped talking about doctrine." Among such clergy, and laity who shared their views, liberal social activism provided an outlet for spiritual and moral energies.

Evangelicals to the Right

While mainline leaderships and many clergy were moving to the left politically, many evangelicals, emphasizing personal salvation and the authority of scripture, were going in exactly the opposite direction. After the disappointments of the 1920s, most evangelicals had withdrawn from politics, even from civil life. The revivalist campaigns of the 1950s led by charismatic preachers such as Billy Graham had renewed evangelical morale and brought converts to evangelical churches. But this phase of evangelical awakening, despite Graham's highly publicized friendships with numerous presidents, was generally apolitical. To the extent that evangelicals were involved in politics, chiefly through voting, they remained mostly Democrats, in part because they were concentrated in the still one-party South.

In the late 1970s, all this changed. A new wave of television evangelists, including Jerry Falwell and Pat Robertson, helped guide evangelical laity toward increased political activity on the conservative and Republican side. The TV ministers were preaching to an audience already in ferment. Supreme Court decisions in the 1960s prohibiting prayer and Bible reading in the public schools had enraged evangelicals, along with many other Americans. The Court's decision in 1973 establishing a constitutional right to abortion further inflamed opinion (though abortion had not historically been a major issue with evangelicals.)

These judicial decisions, which many evangelicals associated with rising crime, spreading drug use, rising divorce, pervasive sex and violence on television and in the movies, and other forces of unwelcome social change, were traced to the influence of political liberalism. The racial desegregation of public schools in the South also helped turn many Southern whites against the liberal leadership of the Democratic Party. The message preached by Falwell (who had earlier argued against any involvement by Christians in politics), Robertson, and other conservative TV preachers thus fell on fertile soil.[19]

In the late 1970s, Right-wing political conservatives like Paul Weyrich and Howard Phillips spotted white evangelicals as the "sleeping giant" of American politics. In 1979, Weyrich persuaded Falwell to form the Moral Majority as a means for rallying evangelicals and fundamentalists behind conservative policies and candidates. The Religious Right was born.

The Moral Majority was never much more than a letterhead organization of evangelical preachers, fronted by Falwell. But its rise to national prominence, largely created by excited media critics, coincided with a sharp shift in political behavior by white evangelicals. (Most African Americans are evangelical in religious practice and belief but have followed a very different political course.) After supporting their fellow evangelical Jimmy Carter in 1976, white evangelicals, now making up more than 20 percent of the national electorate, voted by a two-to-one margin for Reagan, the conservative Republican candidate for president, against Carter in 1980. By 1984, Reagan's majority among white evangelicals rose to almost 80 percent. Four years later, only a slightly reduced majority of evangelicals backed Reagan's Republican successor, George H.W. Bush.[20]

The experience of the 1980s showed both the strengths and the weaknesses of the evangelicals' participation in politics. Their shift unquestionably contributed to the Republicans' growth of strength and the change of national politics in a more conservative direction. When in office, however, both Reagan and Bush concentrated more on economic and foreign policy goals than on the social changes, such as limitations on abortion and restoration of school prayer, particularly sought by evangelicals. Doctrinal differences between fundamentalists and pentecostalists, and personal rivalries among strong-willed preachers, undermined political unity. Robertson's candidacy for the Republican presidential nomination in 1988 failed to win the support of even a majority of evangelicals. In 1989, Falwell, facing falling membership and declining contributions, disbanded the Moral Majority.

Robertson soon launched the Christian Coalition to take its place. Under the management of a shrewd political operator, Ralph Reed, the Christian Coalition for a time seemed to be building a genuine national political organization, reaching beyond evangelicals to other conservative Christians. Liberals and the media again began to warn of a formidable Right-wing religious force. The 1990s would produce both further triumphs and disappointments for the Religious Right.

Catholics No Longer Monolithic

Catholics also underwent political change after the 1960s, though not as spectacular as that among white evangelicals. In 1972, faced with a choice for president between the incumbent Republican Nixon and his perceived radical Democratic opponent George McGovern, Catholics by a narrow majority for the first time in U.S. history supported the Republican candidate. After returning to the Democrats, in the wake of the Watergate scandals, to vote for Carter in 1976, Catholics gave majorities to Reagan in both 1980 and 1984, and split about evenly between Bush and the Democrat Michael Dukakis in 1988. In the 1990s, Catholics voted for Clinton in both 1992 and 1996, but by much smaller majorities than they usually gave to Democrats before the 1970s. A survey by the Pew Research Center in 1996 found white Catholics (which in Pew's definition does not include Hispanics) dividing about equally among Democrats, Republicans, and independents.[21]

The Supreme Court's ruling in 1973 establishing a constitutional right to abortion mobilized the institutional Catholic Church in a campaign to pass a constitutional amendment prohibiting abortion or at least to enact legislation limiting the right to have an abortion. This drive placed the church in diametric opposition to the Democratic Party, which in its national platforms again and again affirmed support for unlimited abortion rights. The Republican Party, in contrast, after 1980 firmly backed the right-to-life (antiabortion) position.

The effect of the abortion controversy on Catholic voters probably went beyond the small minority of committed right-to-lifers. Catholics who were liberal on economic and foreign policy issues continued to vote Democratic. But the growing number of Catholics with conservative economic and social inclinations, finding the church and the Democrats opposed on a basic moral issue, felt released from the old tribal bond of Catholics to the Democratic Party, and increasingly cast Republican ballots. Even many Catholics who were not particularly moved by the abortion issue were offended by the refusal of the 1992 Democratic National Convention to permit the Democratic Catholic governor of Pennsylvania Robert Casey to speak against the pro-choice plank in the party platform.

The institutional Catholic Church, through its annual fall conferences of bishops in Washington, was pulled in different directions on the conventional ideological scale by different issues. On abortion and some other social issues, as well as in support of the movement to provide state-financed vouchers to parents of children attending parochial or other private schools, the bishops were drawn to the conservative side. But on economic and many international issues, they remained predominantly liberal. The bishops' influential letter on nuclear arms policy in 1983 sharply criticized the Reagan administration's strategy of using the threat of nuclear weapons to intimidate the Soviet Union (a policy followed by every president since Truman.) Their letter on economic policy in 1986 called for extensive redistribution of wealth and increased government intervention in the market economy—with considerably less effect than the nuclear policy letter on Catholic or general public opinion.

By the end of the 1980s, the institutional Catholic Church itself was changing. Declining numbers of priests and nuns, as well as the reforms of the Second Vatican Council, were giving laity a growing role in church direction. Appointments by Pope John Paul II, an economic liberal but a theological and social conservative, were making the bishops a more conservative body. In background, the bishops, who formerly had been drawn mainly from working-class origins, were increasingly middle class, reflecting social change in the Catholic population. The bishops, nevertheless, continued to support "communitarian" values, in the sense of favoring a substantial role for government in shaping economic and social life.[22]

The Catholic share of national population continued to grow in the 1980s and 1990s, reaching almost 30 percent. This increase, however, was largely due to the huge influx of American Hispanic immigrants, mostly Catholics. Among European ethnic groups that had arrived earlier, Catholic affiliation somewhat declined. Church observance was sharply down from the 1960s, with only about 40 percent reporting weekly church attendance.[23]

Hispanic Catholics are not an ethnically or politically homogeneous group. In Florida, predominantly Cuban Hispanics, fleeing the Castro regime and largely middle class, have become a bulwark of Republicanism. In Texas, the Southwest, and California, however, much more numerous Latinos from Mexico and Central America, usually at lower levels of income and social status, have overwhelmingly supported the Democrats. Puerto Ricans in New York and other Northeastern states are also heavily Democratic. Conservative social attitudes among Hispanics (though mixed with relatively relaxed views on such matters as church attendance) have encouraged Republicans not to give up the pursuit of Hispanic voters (as they had until recently among African Americans).

Republican support for restrictions on immigration, widely interpreted by Hispanics, even Cubans, as "playing the nativist card," however actually reduced support for Republican candidates during the 1990s, particularly in the electorally crucial state of California.[24] Swimming against this tide, Republican governor George W. Bush in Texas, through earnest courtship of Mexican-American voters and stress on social solidarity, won about half the Hispanic vote in his 1998 reelection. In his run for president in 2000, Bush received about 30 percent of the Hispanic vote nationally—compared with only 20 percent for Republican Bob Dole in 1996.

A study of Catholic voters by Lawrence Kapp in the late 1990s found a continuing swing among "traditionalist" Catholics—those holding conservative social attitudes though often continuing to approve a large role for government in the economy—toward the Republicans. Catholics, however, are steadily less inclined to vote as members of a religious group.[25] In any case, the days of almost monolithic support among Catholics for the Democratic Party seem to be over.

Still Liberal Jews

Political behavior among Jews also changed somewhat after 1970, but remained much more consistent with earlier patterns. Though a small minority in the national population—about 2 percent—Jews since the 1930s have played an important part in national politics. Their influence has been magnified by their prowess as fund-raisers, enthusiastic participation in civil life, strong representation in the news and entertainment industries and academe, and concentration in electorally rich states like New York, California, and Florida. Though Jewish support for the Democrats receded from the extraordinary levels of the Roosevelt and Truman years, the great majority of Jews continued to vote Democratic.

In recent decades, active religious observance among Jews has been relatively low. Their group voice in politics has been expressed as much by secular Jewish organizations such as the American Jewish Committee and the Anti-Defamation League as by organized religious denominations. These secular agencies stay close to Jewish religious leaders, some of whom serve on their boards, and seek to represent "Jewish values," focused in recent years on "an amalgam of ethnic loyalty and political liberalism."[26]

In the 1970s, some Jews began to feel uneasy with traditional liberal allies. Growth of sympathy for the Palestinian cause in parts of the liberal community, particularly among mainline Protestants and some secular liberals, seemed antagonistic toward Israel. "To be 'liberal,'" Nathan Glazer wrote in 1972, "might mean . . . to support leftists who wished to see Israel destroyed, to oppose American aid to Israel."[27] More generally, many Jews became convinced that the defense of Israel, as well as resistance to the international challenge of the Soviet Union, required a militarily strong United States, and they grew impatient with pacifist doves in the liberal camp. Moving away from the McGovern brand of liberalism on military and foreign policy, some Jews also joined the conservative critique of big government liberalism on social and economic issues.

Jewish dissatisfaction with liberalism and the direction of the Democratic Party became most pronounced during the later phases of the Carter administration. In the 1980 election, only 45 percent of Jews voted for Carter's reelection, with 39 percent supporting Reagan, and 15 percent backing the independent candidate John Anderson.[28] Though Reagan stoutly supported Israel, most Jews soon became dissatisfied with his performance on domestic issues. The large role of the Religious Right in the Reagan coalition was particularly disturbing to many Jews. A report prepared for the American Jewish Congress in 1984 concluded: "Jews still stand to the left of where Americans as a whole are standing."[29]

The administration of George H.W. Bush that took office in 1989 seemed less supportive of Israel than Reagan had been and no less beholden to the Religious Right. By the end of the 1980s, many Jews had decided, as one of their leaders said, that Republican White Houses "do not look Jewish."

The band of "neoconservative" writers and intellectuals who in recent years have given much ideological direction and programmatic substance to the moderate wing of the Republican Party has included many Jews, such as Irving Kristol, William Kristol, Gertrude Himmelfarb, Norman Podhoretz, Martin Feldstein, and Elliott Abrams. These, however, have been a distinctly minority voice within the Jewish community.

Since 1980, Jews have generally given more than 70 percent of their vote to Democratic candidates, rising to 81 percent for Clinton in 1996. The Pew survey in 1996 found almost half of Jews identifying themselves as Democrats, but 37 percent as independents and 15 percent as Republicans.[30] Many Jews (like many other Americans) seem to long for a progressive national leader like the two Roosevelts, Theodore and Franklin, regardless of party affiliation.

Al Gore's selection of Joseph Lieberman as his vice presidential running mate in the 2000 election no doubt reinforced the loyalty of most Jews to the Democratic Party. Some liberal Jews, however, were critical of Lieberman's insistence on the role of religion in public discourse. In November, the Gore-Lieberman ticket received about 80 percent of the Jewish vote—about the same as for Clinton in 1992 and 1996.

A Changed Political Environment

In the 1990s, many religious groups, and their representatives in national political life, seemed to pull back from the extreme partisanship and bitter antagonism that had developed during the 1980s. In part, this change grew from disappointments and setbacks that most groups suffered at various times during the decade. It also may in part have reflected recognition of some shared values in the midst of rapidly rising secular materialism and moral dislocation.

Early in the decade, the Religious Right seemed to be riding high. Under Ralph Reed's operational direction, the Christian Coalition functioned with far more political sophistication and national organizational depth than was ever achieved by the Moral Majority. When the Republicans won control of both houses of Congress in 1994, for the first time in forty years, the media gave the disciplined legions of the Religious Right much of the credit. Clyde Wilcox, a leading scholarly observer of conservative religious political movements, predicted in 1996 that "the Christian Right will probably become institutionalized as a permanent fixture in American politics."[31]

Once in office, however, the new Republican majority in Congress, consistently outmaneuvered by Clinton, had trouble delivering on its promises. Conservative evangelicals decided, as they had with Reagan and George H.W. Bush, that their issues were given low priority. The Christian Coalition began to experience some of the same kind of infighting that had undermined the Moral Majority. Reed, his relationship with Robertson showing signs of strain, departed to take up a career as a political consultant. A survey of Washington insiders by *Fortune* magazine in the fall of 1999 found the Christian Coalition dropped in one year from seventh to thirty-fifth place in estimates of organizations with "political clout." By the end of 1999, Wilcox had concluded that the Christian Coalition had "fallen apart," with only about six viable state organizations remaining.[32]

Some analysts have detected a tendency among evangelicals to react to setbacks in the 1990s by returning to their former political passivity. *Blinded by Might*, a 1999 book by two former Falwell lieutenants, Cal Thomas and Ed Dobson, was widely interpreted to recommend retreat by evangelicals from politics. Read more closely, Thomas and Dobson argue that the church *as* church should stay out of political campaigns, but maintain that churches and other religious institutions should motivate their members to active participation in politics and other aspects of civic life.[33]

The decline of the Christian Coalition and some similar Religious Right organizations does not necessarily indicate a fall in either the participation or influence of evangelicals in national politics. The role of the less partisan and more moderate National Association of Evangelicals, which recently moved its national headquarters to Washington, D.C., seems actually to have increased. Wilcox has found evidence that the longer conservative Evangelical activists participate in politics, the more willing they are to compromise with others in the Republican Party to advance common electoral interests.[34] This may anger some among their more impassioned supporters, but may in the long run increase their political effectiveness. The fact is that the Republican Party cannot hope to win national elections without the strong backing it has received since 1980 from evangelicals. The problem for the Republicans has been that identification with a strident Religious Right frightens and turns off needed moderate supporters, most of whom are by no means hostile to religion. As evangelicals in politics become more pragmatic, they increase the possibility that a broad Republican coalition, in which they play a significant part, may win enduring political success.

Attacks by Senator John McCain during his race for the Republican presidential nomination in 2000 on Robertson and Falwell may have deepened the tension between evangelicals and other elements in the Republican coalition. In the short run, however, his attacks mobilized evangelicals to give overwhelming support to McCain's victorious opponent, George W. Bush.

Mainline Protestant offices in Washington have also found disappointments in and learned lessons from the events of the 1990s. The Republican takeover of Congress at the beginning of 1995 created a legislative atmosphere in which they had never before operated. (The last time the Republicans controlled both houses of Congress in the early 1950s, the mainline lobbies were not yet well off the ground.) They at first reacted by lining up firmly behind the Clinton administration. During the budget fight between Clinton and the Republican Congress in the fall of 1995, mainline church leaders took the unusual step of gathering in the Oval Office to place their hands on the president's shoulders in apparent endorsement of his cause. They also joined Clinton in opposing the Republican version of welfare reform.

Though Clinton easily won the budget battle, he later, as the 1996 election approached, disappointed mainline leaders by signing the Republican welfare reform bill passed by Congress. Mainline leaders generally opposed Clinton's impeachment in 1999, but, according to one familiar with their views, felt "betrayed and disillusioned by his unbelievably stupid behavior."

When Republican congressional majorities were maintained, though by reduced margins, in 1996 and 1998, the mainline Washington offices began reaching out not only to moderate Republicans in Congress, but also to conservatives, many of them active members of mainline churches. The drive in 1999 by mainline denominations, in cooperation with Catholic and Jewish groups, to substantially reduce the debt owed by poor countries to the United States—perhaps the most successful legislative effort by the combined religious community since the civil rights struggle of the 1960s—won support, not only from congressional liberals and moderates, but also from some conservative Republicans, such as House Majority Leader Richard Armey and Representative Spencer Bachus of Alabama. Mainline lobbyists found, somewhat to their surprise, that some conservatives were open to appeals on the basis of shared religious values.

The sociologist Robert Wuthnow, who since the 1980s has closely followed mainline Protestant behavior, observes that the mainline denominations in recent years have moved away from grand visions of social and economic restructuring and have concentrated more on incremental reforms. "There is less talk of major changes in the tax system, and more attention to issues like raising the earned income tax credit." In the foreign policy area, "liberation theology" has largely lost attraction, giving way to support for specific measures, such as debt relief for developing countries and international banning of landmines. Objective developments, as well as shifts in the political balance, may have influenced attitudes among mainline leaders. According to one veteran mainline social activist: "The way the Cold War turned out and the apparent success so far of welfare reform took some of the wind out of the liberals' sails."[35]

During all this time, majorities of most mainline Protestant denominations out in the country continued to register and vote Republican. A survey by the Presbyterian Church (USA), the largest Presbyterian denomination, in 2000, for example, found that 55 percent of Presbyterians nationally regard themselves as Republicans, 25 percent as Democrats, and 17 percent as independents.

Washington representatives of the Catholic Church also have learned to make their way in a changed political and legislative environment. In this process, the Catholic political scholar David Walsh points out, the more hierarchical structure of the Catholic Church provides operational advantages. According to John Carr, chief legislative strategist for the United States Catholic Conference, the church's policy is no longer "so much formed from the top down," and the bishops are "more open to influence from the grassroots."[36] Washington lawmakers, non-Catholic as well as Catholic, however, still regard Catholic lobbyists as speaking more than their Protestant counterparts for a united church. Catholic influence also has broadened through the rising representation of Catholics among Republicans in Congress: Of the 122 Catholics in the House of Representatives after the 1998 election, about two-fifths were Republicans.

Political Realignment

The electoral behavior of religious groups from 1992 to 2000 to some extent moved away from divisions along denominational lines, and toward divisions within denominations based on religious practice and belief. At the same time, at the policy level there has been some tendency toward convergence among religious groups, with liberals and conservatives at times joining forces on faith-related issues. These tendencies are to some extent in tension with each other.

At the electoral level, "traditionalists" across Protestant and Catholic denominations, who react to "social modernization and secularizing tendencies in American life" by "reemphasizing orthodox religious beliefs" and "stressing historic religious practices," have come together in the Republican Party, increasingly giving the Republicans some of the character of a European Christian Democratic party. A study of the 1996 election by the political scientists John Green, Lyman Kellstedt, James Guth, and Corwin Smidt found that 63 percent of traditionalist white Catholics (not including Hispanics), 72 percent of traditionalist white mainline Protestants, and 79 percent of traditionalist white Evangelical Protestants voted for Republican candidates for Congress. These were joined by Mormons, numerically small nationally but strongly represented in Utah and some other Western states, who voted 79 percent Republican.[37]

In opposition to these, "modernists" among Catholics and mainline Protestants, who react to social change and rising secularism by "revising historic religious beliefs" and "producing new rituals or practices," trended toward the Democrats. In 1996, by the measures used by Green and his colleagues, 63 percent of modernist white Catholics and 54 percent of modernist white mainline Protestants (but only 40 percent of modernist evangelicals) voted for Democrats for Congress. These were joined by 68 percent of Jews, 86 percent of African Americans, 82 percent of Catholic Hispanics, 67 percent of the growing body of "seculars" who claim no religious affiliation (13 percent of the total), and 61 percent of those whom Green and his colleagues found to be only "nominally religious."[38] Traditionalists outnumbered modernists among white Catholics and evangelicals, and modernists were slightly more numerous than traditionalists among mainline Protestants.

In the closely contested 2000 presidential election, the cleavage between the religiously observant and the nonreligious turned out to be a major source of political division. Among the 42 percent of all voters who told exit pollsters they usually participate in religious services at least once a week, 58 percent voted for George W. Bush and 40 percent for Al Gore—a spread 50 percent greater than the famous gender gap. Among the 14 percent who said they never attend religious services, 61 percent voted for Gore and only 32 percent for Bush.[39]

A study by John Green and his colleagues found that in 2000 traditional differences in party alignment by denomination had by no means disappeared; but that within all major denominational categories, regular churchgoers were much more likely to be for Bush. Among "observant" (attend church services at least once a week) mainline Protestants, 65 percent voted for Bush to 35 percent for Gore; 84 percent of observant Evangelical Protestants for Bush to 16 percent for Gore; and 57 percent of observant Catholics for Bush to 43 percent for Gore. Among "less observant" (attend church less than once a week) mainline Protestants, 57 percent voted for Bush to 43 percent for Gore; 55 percent of less observant evangelicals for Bush to 45 percent for Gore; and 41 percent of less observant Catholics for Bush to 59 percent for Gore.[40]

A study by William Martin (published as chapter 11 of this volume), which has potentially major significance for the political future, found that in 2000 Moslems, now about as numerous as Jews and rapidly increasing, after voting heavily for Clinton in 1996 changed course in 2000 and overwhelmingly supported Bush. In Florida alone, Bush's majority among Moslems seems to have been at least 20,000 votes—far more than his overall majority in the state that gave him the presidency.[41]

After the terrorist attacks of September 11, 2001, President Bush visited a mosque in downtown Washington. Speaking to a large gathering, he emphasized that the United States was not at war against Islam but against a group of fanatical terrorists who he said had "hijacked" the name of the Islamic religion. Whether the war against terrorists who identify themselves as "Islamists" will undermine the new ties of American Moslems to the Republicans remains to be seen. Involvement by the Bush administration in the murderous struggle between Israelis and Palestinians in the Middle East may place even greater strains on relations between Bush and American Moslems.

Policy Convergence?

At the social policy level, a kind of convergence on some issues among religious groups seems to be taking place, complicating the political effects of religion. Most major religious groups have recently worked together at the national level on a number of critical, though not necessarily headline-grabbing, issues. Probably the most important of these was the successful drive in 1999 for debt relief for poor and developing nations. "It would not have happened," said John Carr, "without the leadership of the religious community." Jay Lintner, interim director of the Washington office of the National Council of Churches, agreed: "Working together, we achieved far more than we at first thought was possible." Learning that Pat Robertson supported debt relief, Tom Hart, director of the Capitol Hill Episcopal office, called the Religious Right leader and succeeded in adding him to the coalition.[42]

Ad hoc coalitions have formed on other issues. Rabbi David Saperstein, director for more than twenty years of the Washington office of Reform Judaism, and a harsh critic of the Religious Right, found himself in the late 1990s working with conservative evangelicals, as well as with Catholics and mainline Protestants, on such causes as the defense of religious freedom abroad, crime prevention, and campaigns against international exploitation of women and children.[43] Catholics, evangelicals, and most mainline denominations, after some initial skepticism, have explored the potentialities of the charitable choice provision of the 1996 welfare reform act, which facilitates cooperation between government and faith-based organizations to improve delivery of social services to the poor and disabled. President Bush's proposal in 2001 to go beyond charitable choice to a more extensive "faith-based initiative" linking government to religious institutions in combating social ills received positive interest among most religious groups, although civil liberties groups and some mainline Protestants and Jews warned of dangers of church–state entanglement, and some evangelical groups expressed fears that government support might undermine the spiritual aspects of church social programs.

The extent of issue-focused collaboration among religious groups should not be exaggerated. Plenty of differences still exist. The Catholic Church, many evangelicals, and most Orthodox Jews seek state-funded vouchers for parents of children attending church-related schools, which most mainline Protestant and non-Orthodox Jewish groups oppose. Evangelicals and Catholics campaign vigorously against abortion, whereas Jewish and mainline Protestant leaderships are generally pro-choice. Catholics and conservative evangelicals part company on some welfare state issues. After an initially united drive to restore religious liberties restricted by the Supreme Court's 1991 decision expanding state authority to regulate religious practices, several mainline Protestant and Jewish organizations pulled out in 1999 under pressure from civil liberties, civil rights, and gay rights groups. These groups argued that restoration of religious liberties might be interpreted to permit racial or gender discrimination—even though, Lintner said, opponents could not produce "a single instance of real discrimination."

Nevertheless, most religious groups are finding more common ground on social policy than would have seemed possible in the 1980s or early 1990s through their shared concerns over such continuing problems as family breakdown, failing education, persistent poverty, and continued repression of human rights abroad.

September 11, 2001

The ultimate social, political, and indeed moral and spiritual effects of the horrendous atrocities committed by terrorists claiming inspiration by Islam against the American people on September 11, 2001, remain unclear as this is written in the spring of 2002. The immediate response among most Americans was, in addition to personal shock and grief, strong group expressions of patriotic emotion and community solidarity. These expressions were usually accompanied by religious devotion. The deaths of almost 3,000 Americans (at first thought to be many more) were commemorated and the struggle against terrorism affirmed in a joint service including representatives from many faiths at the National Cathedral in Washington, stirringly addressed by President Bush.

Most major faith communities approved the use of some kind of force to bring the perpetrators of the attacks to justice and to build safeguards against future terrorism. Some religious activists who had come to regard themselves as pacifists found themselves convinced that acts so heinous justified a carefully calibrated military response.

Most religious groups cautioned that military action, if needed, should be carried out, not in a spirit of vengeance, but to restore peace and uphold justice. Many called upon Americans and their government to search for the causes of bitterness against the United States and the West that had helped motivate the attacks. Some doubted that all-out war was the appropriate remedy.

The United States Catholic Conference issued a pastoral message declaring: "Every military response must be in accord with sound moral principles, notably such norms of the just war tradition as noncombatant immunity, proportionality, right intention, and probability of success." The Executive Council of the Episcopal Church praised Bush "for his leadership in these difficult days" but cautioned that "the United States need not be at war while pursuing the full force of justice against those who committed these crimes against humanity." [44]

The United Methodist Board of Church and Society, after a heated meeting covering several days in Washington, affirmed "resolve to bring terrorists to justice" but called for exploration of alternatives to military action on the conviction that "war is not an appropriate means of responding to criminal acts against humanity." On October 11, after the United States began bombing Afghanistan, the stated clerk of the Presbyterian Church (USA) released a letter to Bush acknowledging that "our theological tradition as Presbyterians supports the limited use of force to protect the weak and to restrain evil," but he warned that force "has always been understood as a means of last resort, which can never be more than a temporary solution to conflict."[45] Most Jewish groups, finding models for the assaults on the World Trade Center and the Pentagon in atrocities being committed in Israel and even the Holocaust, gave unequivocal support to Bush's leadership in the war against terrorism.[46]

Some liberal critics of American foreign policy and economic globalization in the mainline churches traced terrorist acts by al Qaeda and its allies at least in part to U.S. and Western imperialism. Writing in the Presbyterian publication *Church & Society*, Vernon S. Bayles III, associate director for social justice with the National Ministries Division, while condemning terrorism, reproved "the 'Christian West' whose values are forced on the world by an economic and military hegemony." The perpetrators of the attacks on September 11, he maintained, were motivated by "a determination to redress their grievances through the calculated actions of a guerilla force that sees itself engaged in a 'war' with us and our minions."[47]

At the other end of the political spectrum, Jerry Falwell, appearing on Pat Robertson's *700 Club*, declared that the terrorist attacks were "probably what we deserve" as God's judgment on "all the pagans, and the abortionists, and the gays and the lesbians" active in American society. Robertson agreed. Faced with a storm of protest from within the Religious Right itself as well as from the general public, Falwell apologized and Robertson conceded that the remarks had been "inappropriate." A few weeks later, Robertson resigned as president of the Christian Coalition, announcing that he would devote himself to more spiritual pursuits.

Among most Americans, the general response to the challenge of terrorism was not only overwhelming support for the administration's war strategy, but also renewal of confidence in the nation's underlying moral fiber. For many years, polls regularly showed a large majority of Americans believing that the country's "moral climate" was "on the wrong track." In contrast, a Fox News poll in December 2001 found 59 percent convinced that the nation was headed morally "in the right direction," and only 29 percent the other way. Other national polls produced similar results. Later polls showed some reduction, but normal confidence remained substantially higher than before the September attacks.[48]

This sense of restored moral confidence was widely tied to religion. The Gallup Poll in December 2001 found belief that religion is increasing its influence in American life, rising from a steady level of about 40 percent to 71 percent. A national survey by the Pew Research Center in March 2002 found 58 percent agreeing that "the strength of American society is based on the religious faith of its people." President Bush consistently cast the war against terrorism in religious and moral terms. "As we struggle to defeat the forces of evil," he said early in 2002, "the God of the universe struggles with us."[49]

For a time at least, Americans appear to have rediscovered the deep rootedness of national character in religious faith. How this new spirit, if it continues, will play out politically remains uncertain. In the short run, it benefited Bush and the Republicans, who are regarded by large majorities among the public as stronger on moral values as well as on national defense. Polls taken early in 2002 found the Republicans with about a 5-percentage-point advantage in party identification over the Democrats-the first time in more than seventy years that the Republicans have held a definite, though small, edge among party identifiers. Among the groups swinging toward the Republicans were suburban women. By spring, the balance between the parties had to be returned to near parity.[50]

How these factors will mix with the effects of economic turbulence and the growing social and religious pluralism of American society remains to be seen. But it seems possible that we may be approaching a major turning point in U.S. political history.

A Religious People

The recently restored consciousness among many Americans of the religious foundations of national life holds distinct perils. As was shown by the behavior of the Taliban in Afghanistan—as well as by countless conflicts and repressive movements arising from the institutional mingling of religion with government and politics all throughout history—religious zealotry can threaten human rights and social harmony. These dangers are particularly acute in a society as diverse as the contemporary United States—though diversity itself is probably a partial safeguard against their getting out of hand.

As the U.S. Founders foresaw, political life pervaded by religious rivalry or bigotry will undermine civil society and will in the long run be harmful to religion itself. But the principal Founders, including some like Thomas Jefferson and Benjamin Franklin who were not conventionally religious, also believed that moral values coming from religion are essential sources for democracy and republican government. Can "the liberties of a nation be thought secure," Jefferson wrote in 1781, "when we have removed their only firm basis, a conviction in the minds of the people that these liberties are the gift of God?"[51] There seems, to me at least, no reason why moral principles derived from religious faith should not play a continuing role in political discourse, as they have throughout most of American history.

Notes

1. Albert R. Hunt, "Americans Still Split on Religion in Politics," *Wall Street Journal*, March 9, 2000; Ceci Connolly, "Taking the Spirit to the Stump," *Washington Post,* Aug. 28, 2000; "God and the Democrats," *Wall Street Journal*, Oct. 25, 2000.

2. Gustav Niebuhr, "God and Man and the Presidency," *New York Times*, Dec. 19, 1999; E.J. Dionne Jr., "Religion and Politics," *Washington Post,* Dec. 28, 1999; "Religion Rhetoric Moratorium Urged," *Washington Post,* Jan. 12, 2000; Jeffrey Rosen, "Is Nothing Secular?" *New York Times*, Jan. 30, 2000.

3. John Courtney Murray, *The Problem of Religious Freedom* (Newman Press, 1935), 13–14.

4. Robert V. Remini, *Andrew Jackson and the Course of American Democracy, 1833–1845* (New York: Harper & Row, 1985), 74; Ronald P. Formisano, *The Birth of Mass Political Parties* (Princeton, N.J.: Princeton University Press, 1971), 137–64; Nathan O. Hatch, *The Democratization of American Christianity* (New Haven, Conn.: Yale University Press, 1989), 30–34; Daniel Walker Howe, *The Political Culture of the American Whigs* (Chicago: University of Chicago Press, 1979), 210.

5. Paul Kleppner, *The Cross of Culture* (New York: Free Press, 1970.)

6. Martin Marty, *Righteous Empire: The Protestant Experience in America* (New York: Dial, 1970), 177–79.

7. Richard Jensen, *The Winning of the Midwest* (Chicago: University Chicago Press, 1971), 283–85.

8. Gabriel Kolko, *The Triumph of Conservatism* (New York: Free Press, 1963), 195–200.

9. Christian Smith, *American Evangelicalism: Embattled and Thriving* (Chicago: University of Chicago Press, 1998), 6–9.

10. Robert N. Miller, *American Protestantism and Social Issues, 1919–1939* (Chapel Hill: University of North Carolina Press, 1958), 68–75, 118–25.

11. Luke Eugene Ebersole, *Church Lobbying in the Nation's Capital* (New York: Macmillan, 1951), 97–100.

12. Ira N. Forman, "The Politics of Minority Consciousness," in *Jews in American Politics*, ed. L. Sandy Maisel (Lanham, Md.: Rowman & Littlefield, 2001), 155.

13. James Hennesey, *American Catholics* (New York: Oxford University Press, 1981), 308.

14. Leonard Gadzepko, "The Black Church, the Civil Rights Movement, and the Future," *Journal of Religious Though* 54 (1997), 103.

15. Frederick C. Harris, *Something Within: Religion in African American Political Activism* (Oxford: Oxford University Press, 1999), 40.

16. Interview with Cain Hope Felder, Howard University School of Divinity, Dec. 2, 1999.

17. Robert Wuthnow, *The Restructuring of American Religion* (Princeton, N.J.: Princeton University Press, 1988), 215–40; Jay Lintner, "Representing God in Washington," *The Turner Lectures* (Washington, D.C.: Office for Church in Society, United Church of Christ, 1996), 18–19; Ted G. Jelen, *The Political Mobilization of Religious Beliefs* (New York: Praeger, 1991), 26; Christopher P. Gilbert, *The Impact of Churches on Political Behavior* (Westport, Conn.: Greenwood Press, 1993), 47, 74–77; *America at the Polls 1996* (Storrs, Conn.: Roper Center for Public Opinion Research, 1997), 97.

18. Will Herberg, *Protestant-Catholic-Jew* (New York: Anchor, 1955).

19. Clyde Wilcox, *Onward Christian Soldiers? The Religious Right in American Politics* (Boulder, Colo.: Westview, 1996), 35–38; Wuthnow, *The Struggle for America's Soul* (Grand Rapids, Mich.: Eerdmans, 1989), 119–22.

20. *American National Election Study*, University of Michigan, Ann Arbor, various years.

21. Ibid.; Pew Research Center for the People and the Press, *The Diminishing Divide . . . American Churches, American Politics* (Washington, D.C.: Pew Research Center for the People and the Press, 1996), 19.

22. Timothy A. Byrnes, *Catholic Bishops in American Politics* (Princeton, N.J.: Princeton University Press, 1991); Thomas J. Reese, *A Flock of Shepherds: The National Conference of Catholic Bishops* (Kansas City: Sheed & Ward, 1992).

23. Pew Research Center, *Diminishing Divide*, 12.

24. Peter Skerry, *Mexican Americans: The Ambivalent Minority* (New York: Free Press, 1993), 233–34.

25. Lawrence Knapp, "The Political Values and Voting Behavior of American Catholics: Changes and Continuities since 1984" (Ph.D. diss., Catholic University, 1999).

26. Nathan Glazer, *American Judaism* (Chicago: University of Chicago Press, 1972), 178.

27. Ibid., 178–83.

28. Forman, "Politics of Minority Consciousness," 153.

29. Donald Feldstein, *The American Jewish Community in the 21st Century* (New York: American Jewish Congress, 1984), 27.

30. Pew Research Center, *Diminishing Divide*, 16.

31. Wilcox, *Onward Christian Soldiers?* 25.

32. "Fortune Cookie," *Washington Post,* Nov. 25, 1999; interview with Wilcox, Nov. 18, 1999.

33. Cal Thomas and Ed Dobson, *Blinded by Might: Can the Religious Right Save America?* (Grand Rapids, Mich.: Zondervan, 1999.)

34. Wilcox, *Onward Christian Soldiers?* 110.

35. Interviews with Robert Wuthnow, Oct. 28, 1999; Lon Dring, retired director of Community Ministry of Montgomery County, Md., Oct. 21, 1999; Tom Hart, Episcopal Church Washington Office, Nov. 2, 1999; Melissa Rogers, Baptist Joint Committee on Public Affairs, Nov. 2, 1999; Mary Cooper, National Council of Churches, Nov. 23, 1999; and Walter Owensby, Presbyterian Washington Office, Nov. 23, 1999.

36. Interviews with David Walsh, Dec. 16, 1999; John Carr, Dec. 16, 1999.

37. John Green, Lyman Kellstedt, James Guth, Corwin Smidt, "Who Elected Clinton: A Collision of Values," *First Things*, Aug.–Sept. 1997, 37.

38. Ibid. For the origins of transdenominational realignment in the 1980s, see Wuthnow, *Restructuring*, 132–72.

39. Exit polls, ABC News, Dec. 11, 2000.

40. John C. Green, "Born-Again Ballots: The Christian Right and the 2000 Presidential Election," paper presented at the James A. Baker III Institute for Public Policy at Rice University, Houston, Feb. 1, 2001.

41. William Martin, "Muslims—A New Force in American Politics?" paper presented at the James A. Baker III Institute for Public Policy at Rice University, Houston, Feb. 1, 2001.

42. Interviews with Jay Lintner, Dec. 17, 1999; Hart, Jan. 25, 2002.

43. Interview with David Sapperstein, Nov. 4, 1999.

44. United States Conference of Catholic Bishops, *Living with Faith and Hope after September 11* (Washington, D.C.: United States Conference of Catholic Bishops, 2001); interview with Carr, Jan. 25, 2002; statement by the Executive Council of the Episcopal Church in the United States, Jacksonville, Fla., Oct. 17, 2001.

45. Statement by the United Methodist Board of Church and Society, Washington, Oct. 13, 2001; letter from Clifton Kirkpatrick, state clerk, Presbyterian Church (USA) to President George W. Bush, Louisville, Oct. 11, 2001. Interviews with staff of church offices on Capitol Hill, Washington, Jan. 2002.

46. Interview with David Bernstein, director, American Jewish Committee, Washington, Jan. 25, 2002.

47. Vernon S. Bayles III, *Church & Society*, Sept. 15, 2001.

48. Robert J. Samuelson, "2001: A Lesson in Living," *Washington Post*, Dec. 28, 2001; "America's Struggle with Religion's Role at Home and Abroad," (Washington, D.C.: Pew Research Center, March 20, 2002).

49. Robert L. Bartley, "Christmas in Terror's Wake," *Wall Street Journal*, Dec. 24, 2001; E.J. Dionne, "Conservatism Recast," *Washington Post*, Jan. 27, 2002.

50. Thomas B. Edsall, "GOP Gains Advantage on Key Issues," *Washington Post*, Jan. 27, 2002; "Public Images of the Two Parties," *New York Times*, Jan. 27, 2002.

51. Anson Phelps Stokes, *Church and State in the United States* (New York: Harper, 1950), vol. 1, 339.

7

Mainstream Protestantism, "Conservative" Religion, and Civil Society

D.G. Hart

Just fifty-five years ago, the idea of a front-running presidential candidate from either the Democratic or Republican parties campaigning at Bob Jones University was unthinkable. After all, Bob Jones was on the cultural periphery, owing to its Fundamentalist reputation.[1] Having lost the battles in the mainline Protestant denominations and having suffered the ignominy of the Scopes Trial, Fundamentalists like those who sent their children to Bob Jones in the 1940s were so busy trying to recover from these defeats that the thought of deciding a presidential election would have been delusional.[2]

Carl F.H. Henry spoke volumes for the movement when, in his important little book *The Uneasy Conscience of Fundamentalism* (1947), he lamented that for "the first protracted period in its history," the Evangelical faith of Fundamentalists stood "divorced from the great social reform movements."[3] Henry, who was emerging as an influential leader of a new generation of Fundamentalists, or Neo-Evangelicals as they would call themselves, wrote this book as a protest against Fundamentalism's self-chosen social and political isolation.[4] In other words, the task for Evangelical leaders at midcentury was to prod Fundamentalists back into public life. And this is what makes George W. Bush's appearance at Bob Jones during the weeks leading up to the 2000 South Carolina Republican primary truly remarkable. It reveals a seismic shift among conservative Protestants.[5] Within a brief period, Evangelicals went from denouncing politics as a form of worldliness to demanding a place at the table.

In fact, only thirty years after Henry's book came out, *Newsweek* magazine dubbed 1976 "the year of the evangelicals."[6] The reason for this appellation stemmed directly from the recently discovered political strength of conservative Protestants in the presidential contest between Jimmy Carter and Gerald Ford. Evangelicals differed in their preferences for Carter and Ford, each of whom played up his religious identity. But by 1979, with growing dissatisfaction over Carter, a Gallup Poll indicating that born-again Christians made up 40 percent of the population, and conservative political strategists courting Fundamentalist Protestants, Evangelicalism entered the political mainstream as a definite segment of political conservatism.[7]

Since then, the Religious Right has been a permanent fixture in U.S. electoral politics, first with Jerry Falwell's formation of the Moral Majority and later with Pat Robertson's and Ralph Reed's engineering of the Christian Coalition.[8] Although its legislative success has been marginal, the Religious Right has been a factor in presidential, senatorial, and congressional races since 1980 and shows no signs of becoming less so. But the reality of these developments during the past two decades should not minimize how fantastic the political presence of Evangelicalism today looks from the vantage of 1945. Not only was secularization supposed to have ended religiously inspired politics, but before 1970 most observers regarded Fundamentalism as part of a lost world that could never be recovered.[9]

The most common way of accounting for this phenomenal reversal is to trace the ideology and activities of Fundamentalist political leaders since the 1920s. In this rendering, the Religious Right emerges as the most recent stage of Protestant Right-wing politics to appear periodically throughout the twentieth century. The first stage surfaced during the 1920s, when Fundamentalists participated actively in campaigns against alcohol, Catholicism, and evolution. In the aftermath of the Fundamentalist controversy and in opposition to the New Deal, some conservative Protestants became virulently anticommunist, picking up the strains of fascism and anti-Semitism that afflicted twentieth-century conservatism. By the 1940s,

Fundamentalist politics lost some of its extremism but retained its animosity to communism and socialism. During the Cold War, the second wave of Fundamentalist politics crested, this time led by such well-known anticommunist preachers as Carl McIntire, Billy James Hargis, and Edgar C. Bundy. When anticommunism lost credibility thanks to Senator Joseph McCarthy's tactics and after political conservatism more generally suffered through the defeat of Barry Goldwater in 1964, who ran as the Republican presidential nominee, Fundamentalists assumed their default location of political isolation.

But just as Ronald Reagan in 1980 reinvigorated American conservatism, so Fundamentalists achieved greater political respectability in their third and more recent phase of notoriety through broadly based, well-organized groups designed to eliminate various social evils, such as abortion and pornography, and to counter the dominance of secularism in public life, especially in public education. The Religious Right, according to this perspective, is the latest manifestation of a variety of twentieth-century political conservatism known as the Christian Right.[10]

As helpful as this way of viewing the Religious Right may be, it neglects a longer and arguably more obvious context, namely, Anglo-American Protestant involvement in public life. What follows is an effort to trace the premises and instincts of the Religious Right back to important religious, cultural, and political developments in the middle decades of the nineteenth century. During the 1840s and 1850s, the religious style of Evangelicalism combined with new political alignments to give Anglo-American Protestantism a specific cultural outlook that would have important repercussions for liberal Protestants during the progressive era and for Evangelicals later in the twentieth century.

Rather than regarding the Religious Right as another variety of the Christian Far Right, the argument here is that the recent Evangelical engagement with public life reflects religious and cultural habits that Anglo-American Protestants, both liberal or Evangelical, learned when threatened by Americans of different religious and ethnic backgrounds. Although such an understanding of the Religious Right lessens some of its unsavory associations with Right-wing politics, this perspective nonetheless raises deeper and perhaps more troubling questions about the legitimacy of religion in public life. Despite the difficulties surrounding religion and politics, the history of American Protestantism provides an alternative to the Religious Right, also addressed in what follows, that is every bit as conservative religiously but better suited to contribute to civil society in the United States.

Whiggery and Revivalism

Most scholars locate the origins of the Religious Right in the late 1960s and early 1970s. The chief catalysts for Evangelical politics were a series of developments that threatened the family, such as the sexual revolution, feminism, and abortion. Closely related were national debates that changed the character of public schools, at least in the Religious Right's mind, such as busing to achieve racial integration and banning prayer and Bible reading. Finally, disputes over U.S. involvement in Vietnam nurtured a sour estimate of the country that did not sit well with many Protestants who regarded the United States as at the very least a generically Protestant nation that had been mightily blessed with divine favor.[11] Historians, political scientists, and sociologists may differ on how profound these changes were for American society, but the estimate of Sydney Ahlstrom, long-time historian of American religion and civilization at Yale University, seems particularly apt for understanding the rise of the Religious Right:

> The exploration and settlement of those parts of the New World in which the United States took its rise were profoundly shaped by the Reformation and Puritan impulse, and . . . this impulse, through its successive transmutations, remained the dominant element in the ideology of most Protestant Americans. To that tradition, moreover, all other elements among the American people—Catholic, Orthodox, Lutheran, Jewish, infidel, red, yellow, and black—had in some way, negatively or positively, to relate themselves. Or at least they did so *until the 1960s*, when the age of the WASP, the age of the melting pot, drew to a close.[12]

This is another way of saying that the fortunes of Protestantism reversed drastically at the same time that the Religious Right was waking from its political slumbers.

The challenges to Protestant hegemony that the United States witnessed in the 1960s caught the mainline denominations off guard. Those churches had worked diligently during the middle decades of the twentieth-century to shore up their stature as the Protestant establishment by making liberal democracy and domesticated free markets virtually synonymous with the message of Christianity. These efforts were particularly apparent during World War II and the Cold War, when it became a Christian duty to defend the American way of life against totalitarianism on the Left and the

Right.[13] But after the social and political adjustments of the late 1960s and early 1970s, the blessings of Protestantism for the United States were not altogether obvious. In fact, in the minds of at the least the most vocal African Americans, women and college students, Protestantism was a liability, if not actually a curse.

Consequently, at the same time that the Religious Right was assembling to march on the public square in defense of Protestant mores, mainline Protestants were taking out old notes on Modernist theology, in search of another way to adjust the Gospel to modern culture, this time a post-Puritan one. In other words, the collective leadership of the National Council of Churches, the ecumenical arm of the mainline Protestant denominations, was leaning decisively to the political and cultural Left in the name of Christ just about the same time that Jerry Falwell and Pat Robertson were searching their Bibles and audiences for support of the Right.[14]

The recent political cleavage between liberal and Evangelical Protestants makes it hard to remember that before the 1960s conservative Protestant politics were virtually indistinguishable from those of mainline Protestants, except, perhaps, for differences owing to class. It might even be appropriate, even if confusing, to say that mainline Protestant political reflection generally bears the imprint of Evangelical ways of understanding government and the destiny of the United States. The reason for putting it this way is that from the middle of the nineteenth century until today, most Protestants of Anglo-Saxon stock have identified politically with the Whig-Republican tradition. This close identification between Protestants of British descent and capital "R" Republicanism stems from political realignments during the middle decades of the nineteenth century that reflected the influence of piety as much as political philosophy.

The crucial link between revivalist Protestantism and Whiggery was individual commitment to Christ, manifested first in the conscious decision of a person to convert, and second in a concerted effort to live a disciplined (read: holy) life. This understanding of Christian devotion differed in important ways from older corporate forms that looked to infant Baptism as the beginning of the Christian life and took sustenance from family and church for spiritual nurture. The revivalist emphasis on individual responsibility and self-denial was a crucial ingredient in the Whig outlook, which promoted "rational order over irrational spontaneity" and "self-control over self-expression."[15] What is more, it fed naturally the demands of the expanding market economy that Whigs and Republicans favored, and it hatched any number of social reforms that were designed to Christianize

America (a revivalist desire) and achieve cultural uniformity (a Whig goal).[16]

Revivalist Protestants gave the Whig and Republican parties a particular religious stamp after the arrival in the 1840s of large numbers of Catholic immigrants who identified with the Democratic Party. To be sure, some of these differences were explicitly political. But they also stemmed from divergent convictions about Christian faith and practice. Unlike Democrats, who believed in a limited, populist government that did not legislate social behavior but rather gave room for the expression of self-interest and local autonomy, Republicans trusted government to enact laws based on eternal truths that would nurture virtuous citizens and a righteous society.[17]

By the late nineteenth century, the Democrats had also begun to incorporate reformist and moralistic perspectives, as evidenced by the Evangelical politician, William Jennings Bryan, and his less Evangelical colleague, Woodrow Wilson, both of whom were Presbyterian and who represented regional constituencies of Anglo-American Protestants that would not countenance voting for the party of Lincoln. Despite the traces of Evangelicals in both parties at the turn of the twentieth century, revivalist Protestants were still indistinguishable from liberal Protestants of British descent. In a good summary of Anglo-American Protestant politics in the Bryan era, Mark A. Noll writes:

> Protestants in the progressive era relied instinctively on the Bible to provide their ideals of justice. They believed in the power of Christ to expand the Kingdom of God through the efforts of faithful believers. They were reformists at home and missionaries abroad who felt that cooperation among Protestants signaled the advance of civilization. They were thoroughly and uncritically patriotic. On more specific issues, they continued to suspect Catholics as being anti-American, they promoted the public schools as agents of a broad form of Christianization, and they were overwhelmingly united behind prohibition as the key step toward a renewed society.[18]

Rare would be the white Protestant today who could not agree with this progressive Protestant view of American politics (minus some of the hostility to Catholics, and minus some of the confidence in public schools).[19]

The tricky period in American Protestant history for showing broad political agreement among Evangelical and liberal Protestants is the era after Bryan's death. This is, of course, the time when two parties in Anglo-American Protestantism are clearly visible, when the terms "mainline" and

"Evangelical," or "liberal" and "Fundamentalist," as used today, begin to make sense. What makes the time from 1925 to 1965 especially difficult for understanding Evangelical politics is the effect that Fundamentalist understandings of the end of history had on Evangelical notions about public life. Fundamentalists believed that the United States was hurling precipitously toward moral degeneracy and religious apostasy. This downward turn in American history, they also believed, corresponded with the end of history prophesied in the Bible. Fundamentalist eschatology, consequently, undermined political involvement by making the reform of society pointless.[20]

Many historians have concluded that after 1925 and the humiliation that Fundamentalists received at the Scopes Trial, they withdrew from public life, formed their own ghettolike culture held together by a variety of religious organizations, and abandoned hopes for constructing a Christian America.[21] Nevertheless, the United States in which Fundamentalists lived was not overly threatening to conservative Protestant ways of life. To be sure, they did not worship alongside mainline Protestants. But Fundamentalists did benefit from the Christian culture that the Protestant establishment labored to keep patched together, no matter how generically Christian it was. The schools included prayer and Bible reading, abortion was illegal, federal officials were not threatening to transport young children to school in another neighborhood, and women were still models of domesticity. Even liberal Protestant weeklies like the *Christian Century* rated and reviewed the products of Hollywood according to the good taste of the Protestant home.

All in all, the Protestant establishment maintained exactly what the Religious Right today desires—standards of public decency. So even if mid-twentieth-century Evangelicals were not politically active, they did not need to be. The United States from 1925 to 1965 was generally friendly to white Anglo-Saxon Protestants (WASPs) whether they were members of either First Presbyterian Church or Calvary Baptist Church across town.[22]

If the culture of the United States before 1970 was generally decent according to Anglo-American Protestant conceptions, then the reason for the Religious Right's emergence in the 1970s is clear. Evangelicals only took to the political arena once their culture was threatened—a culture that may be described in ethnic categories as WASP. Before 1970, they did not need to be active politically because most of their social and cultural concerns, which revolved around the sanctity of the home and the ability of parents to reproduce their ways, were safe in the hands of the Protestant establishment.[23]

In other words, after the 1920s, the Right wing of Anglo-American Protestantism benefitted from the cultural hegemony of their liberal Protestant rivals.

This would be an ironic outcome to the Fundamentalist-Modernist controversy if that conflict were merely theological. And this has been the primary way of accounting for differences between Evangelical and liberal Protestants, even if it yields a caricature. On the one side, accordingly, are Fundamentalists (and later Evangelicals), who were chiefly concerned with right doctrine because of their interest in the salvation of souls (i.e., an individual Gospel). On the other were their opponents, the Modernists (and later the mainline), who refashioned the message of Christianity for the sake of saving society (i.e., the Social Gospel).

But this perspective on the 1920s obscures the culture wars of that decade, which, instead of pitting orthodox against heterodox Protestants, actually caused Fundamentalists and Modernists to join hands politically. As Martin E. Marty described it, taking his cue from André Siegfried's opening question in *America Comes of Age*, "Will America Remain Protestant and Anglo-Saxon," by the late 1920s "original-stock Protestant could still credibly dream of keeping their cultural dominance."[24] And Anglo-American Protestants decisively asserted that dominance in response to the 1928 presidential candidacy of Al Smith, governor of New York, who ran for the highest office on the Democratic ticket. The results of this election proved what the politics of Prohibition had already demonstrated, namely, that when it came to maintaining a Christian society, the deity of Christ, the vicarious atonement, and the Virgin Birth did not really matter. In 1928, practically all low church Southern Protestants abandoned the one candidate who could have likely affirmed the five points of Fundamentalism—the Roman Catholic, Smith—to vote with New York's businessmen for Hoover, whose Quaker upbringing shored up liberal Protestant support.[25]

From a longer historical perspective, however, Evangelical indebtedness to the Protestant establishment from the 1920s to the 1960s looks much less ironic. Perhaps in textbook treatments of American religion Evangelical and mainline Protestants are enemies. But the ethno-cultural interpretation of American politics teaches that they are siblings whose parents are revivalist Protestantism and Whig-Republican ideology. In the nineteenth century, the Protestant establishment harmonized reform and evangelism. In the twentieth century, Anglo-American Protestants had greater difficulty executing that harmonization. But even if liberals and

Evangelicals circa 1950 found themselves in different denominations, both sides were hard-pressed to choose between reform and evangelism. And this is because Anglo-American Protestantism's understanding of the Christian life has been inherently activist and reform-minded; it creates virtuous individuals who pursue an equally virtuous society. In sum, the heirs of revivalism and the Whig tradition, both Evangelicals and liberals, believe in reforms aimed at maintaining a Christian social order, though the techniques of implementing this order may differ. In which case, today's Religious Right is merely following in a path already well trod by nineteenth-century Evangelical social reformers and liberal Protestant Social Gospelers.

The Religious Right and Secularization

If the goals of the today's politically engaged Evangelicals are not essentially different from earlier generations of Anglo-American Protestants, then the Religious Right should have had an easier time justifying their concerns. After all, the United States has a long history of religious involvement in public life. Why, then, should the Religious Right appear so threatening to the non-Evangelical segment of the U.S. population?[26]

This question clearly haunted Richard John Neuhaus, one of the first public intellectuals to defend the Religious Right. In a 1985 essay for *Commentary*, he compared the resurgence of Evangelicals in politics to that of "country cousins" who had "shown up in force at the family picnic." "They want a few rules changed right away," he explained." "Other than that they promise to behave."[27] This way of explaining the rise of the Religious Right had a disarming character about it. But it also suggested unease. As much as Neuhaus sympathized with the Religious Right, a sense lingered that something was amiss.

One reason for this suspicion was that the Religious Right contradicted much of the social scientific literature on religion and modern society. For instance, Neuhaus objected to the sociological convention that linked secularization (i.e., the disappearance of religion from public life) to modernity. He cited the updated survey of Middletown that gave evidence of the American people, contrary to the logic of secularization, becoming even more religious, with 86 percent of Muncie's residents affirming the deity of Christ and 97 percent believing the Bible to be inspired.[28] Those statistics made Evangelicals look normal. If so many Americans believed the way they did, and if the United States is some form of democracy, then what was wrong or unusual about Evangelicals giving political expression to their beliefs? By citing evidence of how mainstream the Religious Right's beliefs were, Neuhaus was trying to show that its political agenda—prayer and Bible reading in public school, a pro-life amendment, restrictions on pornography, fewer regulations on Christian schools, opposition to gay and feminist legislation, increased defense spending, and terminating social welfare programs—were really moderate.[29]

Still, the explicitly Evangelical character of the Religious Right made many wonder if religion and politics could mix in such an open way, or if the norms of liberal democracy required a different kind of public religion. Since 1980, the sociological literature on religion and politics has exploded.[30] But two recent studies by sociologists, both of which question the convincingness of the secularization thesis, are helpful for considering the propriety of the Religious Right's appeal to Evangelical Protestantism for specific political initiatives.

The first comes from José Casanova, whose perspective on the Religious Right is generally favorable. The heart of his book *Public Religions in the Modern World* has less to do with the Religious Right than with the problem that the secularization thesis has posed for understanding religiously inspired political endeavors such as those of American Evangelicals. According to Casanova, the dominant sociological perspectives on religion and modernity are mainly useless when trying to explain the recent phenomena of public religion in such diverse settings as Brazil, Poland, Spain, and the United States. He describes this trend as the "deprivatization" of religion, that is, "the process whereby religion abandons its assigned place in the private sphere and enters the undifferentiated public sphere of civil society."[31]

Although Casanova's case studies come from recent events, his argument has more of a theoretical quality to it. His aim is to articulate an understanding of religion in the modern world that not only accounts for these particular examples of public religion but also recognizes and accommodates the essentially public dimension of religion in modern society. Instead of dismissing public religion as either duplicitous ("an instrumental mobilization of available religious resources for non-religious purposes") or extremist ("fundamentalist antimodern reactions of hierocratic institutions unwilling to give up their privileges"), he regards modern efforts to politicize religion as "new types of immanent normative critiques of specific forms of institutionalization of modernity which presuppose precisely the acceptance of the validity of the fundamental values and principles of modernity."[32] The Religious Right, then, may represent an instance of the valuable contribution religion makes to public life.

Yet despite the elegance and nuance of Casanova's theory of de-privatization and his masterful grasp of sociological theory, the Religious Right leaves several difficulties unresolved. On the one hand, as Casanova observes, leaders in the world of the Religious Right use words such as "restore" and "reestablish" when talking about Christianity and public life. What they want to resurrect is not entirely clear, but, as he admits, the theocratic impulse in some of this language is out of step with modern politics.[33] On the other hand, the Religious Right sometimes speaks of another Great Awakening that will contribute to a moral renewal of the United States. This may take either a national form, one where Americans turn to religion as they did in the 1950s, or a local form where Evangelical institutions gain new recruits and energy. The ambiguity of the Religious Right on what Evangelical resurgence means leads him to conclude that "Protestant fundamentalism has not made up its mind which public identity it should assume" and that its effects on American public life are unclear.[34]

Perhaps because Anglo-American Protestantism has yet to articulate a satisfying conception of religion in public life, Steve Bruce, another sociologist who has written several books on the Religious Right, takes a different view. Unlike Casanova, Bruce is less concerned with general theories of religion and modernity, even though he is equally critical of many of the assumptions driving the secularization thesis. Still, in his 1998 book, *Conservative Protestant Politics*, a case study of Protestant public religion in Ulster, South Africa, Scotland, the United States, Canada, Australia, and New Zealand, he begins with a theoretical chapter that explains his skepticism about the Religious Right. Instead of using the concept of secularization, he relies instead on the idea of modernization and starts with the premise that this process fundamentally undermines religion. As sociologists are wont to do, he employs four "unfortunately inelegant" neologisms to put flesh on this premise. First, modernization involves social differentiation—that is, the separation of the pragmatic and instrumental public sphere from the expressive and emotional private domain.

Second, along with social differentiation comes, societalization, or the displacement of small-scale communities with large-scale bureaucracies. The third feature of modernization is rationalization, which describes the way that people in a modern society think about the world without reference to God. (Bruce acknowledges that the origins of this aspect of modernization are religious or at least have strong affinities to Judaism and Protestantism.) Fourth, modernization yields cultural diversity, which leads to a more and more neutral state, and terminates a social ethos that makes a particular religion plausible. Bruce concludes that these developments in modern, Western societies automatically produce secularization "except where religion finds or retains work to do other than relating individuals to the supernatural."[35]

From the perspective of modernization, the Religious Right is for Bruce less an instance of the contribution that Evangelical Protestantism may make to public life than a recurring manifestation of "ethnic interests," in which religion provides the language of dissent.[36] According to Bruce, religious beliefs have been the principle means, at least among the Protestants he studies, of negotiating the onslaught of modernity. On the one hand, religious institutions, especially in the late nineteenth and early twentieth centuries, helped immigrants assimilate to American society by perpetuating the older ways of the homeland and providing stability during difficult periods of adjustment. On the other hand, religion throughout the twentieth century functioned as a catalyst for native born Americans to defend a national, local, or ethnic pattern of living.

For Bruce, the Religious Right fits neatly in the latter category—religion as a mechanism of cultural defense. No matter how much the older depictions of Fundamentalism as Southern and rural relied upon a caricature, the Southern and provincial qualities of today's Religious Right are hard to miss. Jerry Falwell and Pat Robertson, to date the Religious Right's most prominent spokesmen, hail from the South while speaking for many Americans who lament the recent decline of Protestant norms in national culture. Bruce observes, furthermore, that the Religious Right has not been successful in courting other ethnic groups, such as African Americans, Catholics, and Jews, many of whom (especially African Americans) share its concerns about public decency and family values. No matter what the polling data suggest about the extent of the Religious Right's appeal or what religious historians argue about the diversity of Evangelicalism, Bruce is convinced that contemporary Evangelical politics is best explained as "a 'nativist' defence of the culture of native-born Anglo-Saxon Protestants."[37]

By putting the matter this way, Bruce identifies a significant dilemma that confronts any religious group or tradition that seeks to shape public policy from explicitly religious ideals. The problem is not the Religious Right's alone. But as the most vocal religious community to assert itself in recent decades, Evangelical Protestants offer a good example of the dangers that attend public religion.[38]

One way to illustrate these dangers is to consider the remarks of Carl F.H. Henry at a 1990 Ethics and Public Policy conference devoted to Evangelicals and politics. Henry, not only called upon Fundamentalists in the 1940s to leave their ghettos and enter the fray of mainstream society, but he later would become the leading Evangelical theologian, writing shelves of highly acclaimed books, in addition to serving as the founding editor of *Christianity Today*. What is more, he knew almost firsthand the dilemmas confronting believers who serve in public office because his son, the late Paul Henry, held office in Congress for close to a decade.

Still, Henry made the mistake that even the less gifted Falwell or Robertson would commit when he praised the Religious Right for reentering "the cultural arena to press the claims of the biblical world-and-life view comprehensively upon modern society."[39] It would be one thing to have said something like the Religious Right deserved credit for taking underappreciated stands based on their religious convictions in the give and take of the democratic process. But Henry did not say that. To be sure, he disavowed the theocratic implications of pressing the claims of the Bible on modern society when he identified Christian Reconstructionists as an extreme wing of Evangelicalism.[40] Nonetheless, he complimented Evangelicals for furthering "the public relevance of both morality and religion."[41]

The point here is not that the Religious Right has been explicitly theocratic in desiring a religious presence in public life. Most, if not all, of the public figures in the Religious Right have admitted that they do not want Christianity to become the official religion of the United States and so affirm the value of America's separation of church and state. Still, the ideal of applying the Bible to politics is what makes many people uncomfortable with the aims of the Religious Right. The Bible, according to Evangelical beliefs, is an absolute standard of faith and life and is relevant to every sphere of human conduct.[42] Making the Bible a standard for public morality while also protecting religious liberty is an exceedingly complex feat. Neuhaus put it well when he wrote:

> The religious new right . . . wants to enter the political arena making claims on the basis of private truths. The integrity of politics itself requires that such a proposal be resisted. Public decisions must be made by arguments that are public in character. . . . Fundamentalist morality, which is derived from beliefs that cannot be submitted to

examination by public reason, is essentially a private morality. If enough people who share that morality are mobilized, it can score victories in the public arena. But every such victory is a setback in the search for a public ethic."[43]

The reason that Evangelicals even of Henry's intellectual caliber have not seen this tension may be the legacy of mainstream Protestantism. The United States used to welcome appeals to the Bible in public life, so why should matters be different now? The answer, for Bruce, is that only since the 1960s has the United States begun to reckon with the Enlightenment ideals that provided at least part of the inspiration for the American polity. And part of this reckoning involved the disestablishment of public Protestantism. But in Bruce's estimate, the process of secularization is not inherently hostile to the church and Christianity. Instead, it is the inevitable result of the United States's demographics and political ideals. The illegitimacy of religion in public life, he writes, is the natural outcome of "a modern democratic society which happens to be culturally heterogeneous and which places great stress on individualism."[44] Bruce adds:

> Our societies permit (and in some places even encourage) the maintenance of distinctive religious world-views and thus encourage socio-moral contests, but they also create a structure (the division of the life world into public and private spheres) and a culture (universalism and tolerance) which of necessity restrain such contests and require that they be fought on general universalistic ethical and public-policy principles. In modern democratic culturally plural societies, no socio-moral interest group can plausibly promote its case on the grounds that "the Bible (or the Koran or the Book of Mormon) says so." Instead it must argue that equity or reason or the public good says so. [45]

His conclusion is that the Religious Right has yet to embrace the "cultural pluralism" that results in "a democratic industrial democracy" such as the United States.

Casanova reaches a similar estimation, even if his argument is more sympathetic to the Religious Right. Like Bruce, Casanova is cautious about the chances of biblically informed public policy proposals succeeding in a modern democracy. In fact, his case for de-privatization is grounded on the premise that the cases of public religion he has surveyed assume "a modern normative perspective." He concludes, "only a religious tradition which reformulates its relationship to modernity" by incorporating the Enlightenment critique of religion while also upholding the "sacred" values of modernity, namely, human life and freedom, "may contribute to the revitalization of the modern public sphere."[46] If Casanova and Bruce are correct, then it need not be only secularists who have felt uneasy about the recent return of Evangelicals to U.S. politics.

Piety and Politics

If sociologists have turned up many of the social factors that make the Religious Right look out of place in recent U.S. politics, political historians have unearthed patterns of personal piety that are equally important for understanding the peculiar character of Evangelical approaches to public life. But here, as above, the unique features of Evangelicalism should not be isolated from the larger context of Anglo-American Protestant piety or from considerations of how this conception of the Christian life nurtured a specific approach to politics.

Of the many parallels between Evangelical and mainline Protestants, the this-worldly character of Evangelical devotion is among the more striking. The conventional wisdom about Protestantism in the United States is that Evangelicals maintain an expression of Christianity that is fundamentally otherworldly or directed toward the end of time, the salvation of souls, and the rewards of heaven. In contrast, liberal Protestants are supposed to be oriented chiefly toward the affairs of this world, either because they have diminished historic Christian teaching about the afterlife, or because of their conviction that the Kingdom of God is being realized on earth.[47] Yet, despite this common way of regarding liberal and Evangelical Protestants, most observers of Evangelicalism are struck by the movement's pragmatic knowhow and activist spirit. Robert Wuthnow put this irony well when he wrote, "It is, of course, peculiar to say that the Religious Right includes a this-worldly orientation, for many of its constituents are fundamentalists."[48]

Wuthnow attributes this feature of the Religious Right to the general cast of American religion, which he concludes is absorbed with the present life. But linking such religious activism to the generally pragmatic quality of the American character is not as useful as showing the connection between Evangelicalism's this-worldly piety and revivalist Protestantism. Here the contrast between revivalism as it took shape in nineteenth century and its Protestant rival, liturgicalism, is helpful for seeing the connection between piety and politics.

As alluded to above, Evangelical low church Protestants differed from another set of the Reformation's heirs, namely, Episcopalians, Lutherans, German Reformed, and some Presbyterians (politically, this group included Catholics). These churchly Protestants held to a organic conception of religious life, that was corporate in its piety in contrast to Evangelicalism's individualism, sacramental as opposed to conversionist, and sober about human progress in contrast to revivalism's optimistic millennialism. Political historians have made the most of these distinctions, perhaps to the discredit of religious historians. In fact, the liturgical-pietist continuum developed in the works of Lee Benson, Richard Jenson, Paul Kleppner, Robert Kelley, Robert P. Swierenga, and others, which refers to these differences between more traditional forms of Protestantism and the novel variety of Anglo-American revivalism, may turn out to be more useful than the liberal-Evangelical dichotomy for analyzing the public role of American Protestants.[49]

One obvious difference between liturgical and pietistic Protestants is the other-worldly character of the former's devotion. The best way of illustrating this is to consider the nature of the church's ministry. In contrast to Evangelical piety, which was individualistic and experiential, liturgical spirituality was churchly and sacramental. The church, they believed, was a place for assisting members in their pilgrimage from birth, confirmation, marriage, child rearing, and vocation to death. Clergy ministered chiefly through the means of grace, namely, word and sacraments, and these rites strengthened the faith of members as they looked for the world to come. In other words, the church was not an agency for social reform or nation building, nor was faith a means for making good workers. Instead, the church was a spiritual institution with sacramental means for otherworldly ends. In today's vernacular, liturgical Protestantism was a private religion; revivalistic Protestantism was its public rival.[50]

The formal similarities between liturgical Protestantism and Roman Catholicism are obvious but no less real. My suspicion is that in Anglo-American Protestant circles the similarities between Protestantism and Catholicism became unbearable once Roman Catholics after 1840 began to threaten Protestant dominance. At that point, Protestants began to stress their low church piety to set themselves off from Catholicism's churchliness.[51]

The funny thing about most interpretations of American religious history is that scholars typically regard Evangelicalism as *the* conservative expression of Protestantism.[52] What makes this line of analysis odd is that Evangelical Protestantism is largely indifferent to those churchly and liturgical practices that have been part of historic Christianity, whether Eastern Orthodox, Catholic, or Protestant. Instead of identifying devout Christians by their involvement in such acts of devotion as Baptism, church attendance, receiving the Eucharist, or daily prayer, scholars of American religion identify conservative Protestants according to the behavioral norms and minimalist doctrinal affirmations characteristic of the Religious Right's Evangelical faith.[53] Conventional wisdom about American Protestantism, then, ignores large portions of traditional Christian belief and practice. What is more, the liberal-Evangelical dichotomy virtually disregards liturgical Protestants, whose interaction with public life may offer a better alternative for engaging modern secular society than the Religious Right.

On the surface, the otherworldly devotion of liturgical Protestantism would appear to be unfertile soil for political reflection or civic involvement. If someone thinks this world is not her home, she would seem to be guilty of doing exactly what Jean Bethke Elshtain thinks is impossible for any serious believer. Keeping his religion to himself, she writes, is "precisely what a devout person cannot do for religious faith isn't a private matter; it is constitutive of membership in a particular body."[54] But, in fact, liturgical Protestant piety came to terms with public life in the secular, modern, religiously diverse United States in ways that tried to do justice to both parts of their dual identity as believers and citizens.

First, liturgical Protestantism's beliefs about the Kingdom of God were especially fruitful for negotiating American political realities. According to Robert P. Swierenga, liturgical Protestants believed that "God's kingdom was other-worldly, and human programs of conversion or social reform could not usher in the millennium."[55] Lutherans arrived at this conviction through the doctrine of the two kingdoms, Presbyterians via teaching about the spirituality of the church.[56] Both views emphasized that God's Kingdom could not be identified with any earthly power. This teaching nurtured skepticism about political life that made liturgical members wary of pinning their hopes on the United States or thinking that the United States had a special place in God's redemptive plan. The church, not the state, was the Kingdom of God, and efforts to make the state conform to the church always confused the ends of the church and politics.

But such skepticism did not prompt liturgical Protestants to withdraw from public life. Instead, in the nineteenth century many joined the Democratic Party which, in contrast to the Republicans, worked toward a limited, populist government and opposed using state power to legislate social behavior. The Democrats, in effect, provided liturgical church members with the greatest insurance that the state would not encroach on their churches, parochial schools, or the lives of their members.[57] Liturgical Protestant estimates of the state were not simply negative, however. The Bible clearly taught submission to political rulers. What is more, the doctrines of creation and providence assured liturgical members that political involvement was beneficial. If God really had created the world good, and if God actually used secondary means to achieve divine ends, then participating in public life was not illegitimate or even a waste of time. To be sure, the goodness of government was not of an ultimate sort. Nor could its accomplishments achieve eternal significance. But being wary of politics did not require withdrawal.[58]

In addition, liturgical Protestants tended to steer clear of the biblicistic moralism that informed so much of Evangelical Protestantism's political philosophy. Because the Kingdom of God was different from the human kingdom, the Bible was not a rule for political life. God's special revelation, from the liturgical perspective, was for the church. The norm for the state came from patterns revealed in creation and human nature, that is, general revelation. Indeed, because liturgical churches recognized the revelatory character of creation and providence, they could accept arguments for the common good drawn from the wisdom and observations available to all people. In other words, while Evangelicals looked to the Bible for standards of public decency and patterns of just rule (an outlook that invites making Old Testament Israel the model for good government), liturgical Protestants believed that the ideals for politics were not so specific or explicitly Christian. Consequently, while Evangelicals sought a Christian America, liturgical believers desired an America where Christians could practice their faith, a position that made them willing to accept religious diversity.[59]

Liturgical Protestant piety, accordingly, appears to have been well suited to adapt to the changes that accompanied the secularization and modernization of the United States. The reason is that liturgical forms of devotion presumed a different, older understanding of the secular. Most discussions of secularization, like those drawn from Casanova and Bruce above, follow sociological conventions in explaining the displacement of religion in the modern society. According to this conception, the "secular" vies against the "religious," public against private, church against state. But for liturgical Protestantism, the actual contrast to the secular is the eternal. From this perspective, secular government is not irreligious because all legitimate authority comes from God. Rather, what makes government secular is its temporary and provisional character—it rules during this age but not for eternity.[60]

Obviously, such an understanding of secular politics fits well with otherworldly liturgical Protestant piety. The goal of history is the age to come, and in the new heavens and new earth government will no longer be needed to restrain evil and supply order. This understanding of the end of history allows liturgical believers to accept the kind of differentiation that accompanies modernization as part of the provisional character of life on earth. Put simply, for liturgical Protestants secularization is not a threat; it is simply a way of ordering the world until the second advent.

But whatever the relationship between liturgical Protestantism and secularism, the contrast drawn here between liturgical church members and Evangelicals is important for seeing the Religious Right in a different light. On the one hand, the conservative religious credentials of contemporary Evangelicals look less authentic when compared with those of churchly and liturgical Protestants, thanks to the Evangelicalism's low church impulses. On the other hand, the contrast between liturgical and pietist Protestantism demonstrates how much more flexible a churchly religiosity may be for engaging in modern politics.

Genuinely conservative Protestantism (accepting for the sake of argument that liturgical Protestantism qualifies as such) need not oppose secular modernity. Instead, secularism of the kind witnessed throughout U.S. history—where church and state are separate, where religion is primarily private, and where public expressions of religion are out of place—is the kind of arrangement that suits liturgical Protestantism's understanding of this world, the purpose of history, and the nature of the Bible. By no means did liturgical Protestantism resolve the dilemmas that attend religious disestablishment. But by following a course similar to that of the early church before Constantine, when Christianity was a private faith, liturgical Protestants offered a strategy for engaging in public life that was both consistent with their beliefs and compatible with the rules of U.S. government.

Learning from Liturgical Protestants

If liturgical Protestants actually represent a viable way for conservative believers to participate in public life, they may also provide an escape from the impasse that has bedeviled recent discussions about the relationship between religion and civil society.[61] Ever since 1980, when the Religious

Right emerged as factor in electoral politics, the typical approach to religion and public life assumed a bipolar perspective. Either the public square welcomes or excludes religion; either religious convictions are private or they legitimately inform the aspirations that guide public life.[62] In other words, no middle ground exists. If Evangelicals are going to participate meaningfully in public life, the wall between church and state has to come down. Or at least some gates have to be added to allow for passage back and forth. In this way of looking at the problem, the Religious Right and secularists are made for each other. As much as Evangelicals try to say all areas of life belong to God and so religion should not be excluded from public affairs, secularists see that such divine possession can likely end up dispossessing those who do not believe in the deity of Evangelical Protestantism.[63]

Of course, this is not the first time such an impasse has arisen. The bipolar character of most discussions about religion and public life is the legacy of Anglo-American Protestantism's political philosophy. Ever since the heady days of the American republic's birth, when the United States tried to live without the older authorities of monarchy and established church, Evangelicals have operated according to a simple political formula—if it is divine it is trustworthy, if it is human it is suspect.[64] Though responsibilities as presidents, chemists, parents, and umpires have forced Evangelicals to modify this formula, it still lurks within the Evangelical soul and plays havoc with Protestant efforts to relate their religious convictions to nonreligious walks of life.[65]

Liturgical Protestantism offers a way around this impasse. A different way of putting it is to say that liturgical Protestantism represents a way for Protestant believers to support the wall between church and state. By looking for religious significance not in this world but in the world to come, liturgical Protestantism lowers the stakes for public life while still affirming politics' divinely ordained purpose. The public square loses some of its importance but retains its dignity. It is neither ultimately good nor inherently evil; politics becomes merely a divinely appointed means for restraining evil while the church as an institution goes about its holy calling.[66] For some Evangelicals, the liturgical Protestant approach to public life is not a solution but rather a sellout.[67] Religious convictions demand unswerving allegiance in all spheres. In fact, the moral absolutes of Christianity require the same kind of conduct at home and city hall. To admit otherwise is inconsistent and leads inevitably to moral relativism.

But if Daniel Bell is right about the nature of modern society, liturgical Protestantism may very well be the best approach for Protestants. In his

1978 foreword to *The Cultural Contradictions of Capitalism*, Bell described himself as a socialist in economics, a liberal in politics, and a conservative in culture. "Many persons might find this statement puzzling," he explained, "assuming that if a person is radical in one realm, he is a radical in all others; and, conversely, if he is a conservative in one realm, then he must be conservative in the others as well." But modern capitalistic society does not permit such ideological consistency. According to Bell, "Such an assumption misreads, both sociologically and morally, the nature of these realms."[68]

In the end, the most important lesson the Religious Right could learn from liturgical Protestantism is not how to negotiate public life but how to prevent a legitimate concern for politics from distorting the faith. Here the Religious Right could well take a page from one of their neglected heros, J. Gresham Machen. Machen was a Presbyterian Fundamentalist who almost single-handedly fought liberalism within the northern Presbyterian Church during the 1920s until he was suspended from the ministry and started a new Presbyterian denomination.[69] What is more, he was particularly active in fighting legislation that undermined, in his view, family life and the legitimate authority of parents.

In other words, Machen would appear to meet the Religious Right's theological and political litmus tests. But he was keenly aware that religious liberty in the United States prohibited Christianity from providing the norms for public life. In fact, he ridiculed the hypocrisy of liberal Protestant churches that took pride in theological diversity while also supporting legislation aimed at achieving Anglo-American cultural homogeneity. Mainline Protestants were guilty of such duplicity precisely when they argued that religion was beneficial for community or public life.

For example, Machen wrote, "there is the problem of the immigrants; great populations have found a place in our country; they do not speak our language or know our customs; and we do not know what to do with them." So religion is "called in to help." It is "thought to be necessary for a healthy community." And in the process, Protestants "proceed against the immigrants now with a Bible in one hand and a club in the other offering them the blessings of liberty," or what some called "Christian Americanization."[70] For Machen, the norms of America and the churches were necessarily distinct, and to conflate them violated religious liberty.

But Machen was even more concerned about what politicizing religion did to Christianity. In order to make religion relevant to public life, he argued, Protestants had turned to the Bible only for its ethics while ignoring almost completely its ultimate message about sin and grace. This was one of the reasons he opposed prayer and Bible reading in public schools. Aside from questions surrounding the separation of church and state, even more alarming was what this practice did to the Gospel. "What could be more terrible," he asked, "from the Christian point of view, than the reading of the Lord's Prayer to non-Christian children as though they could use it without becoming Christians?" In effect, a politicized Christianity ends up being little more than moralism. "When any hope is held out to lost humanity from the so-called ethical portions of the Bible apart from its great redemptive core," then, Machen concluded, "the Bible is represented as saying the direct opposite of what it really says."[71]

Curiously enough, H.L Mencken, who admired Machen while abhorring the Fundamentalist's Presbyterian colleague, William Jennings Bryan, the leader of the Religious Right in the 1920s, agreed with Machen's assessment. Mencken wrote:

> It is my belief, as a friendly neutral in all such high and ghostly matters, that the body of doctrine known as Modernism is completely incompatible, not only with anything rationally describable as Christianity, but also with anything deserving to pass as religion in general. Religion, if it is to retain any genuine significance, can never be reduced to a series of sweet attitudes, possible to anyone not actually in jail for felony. . . . That, it seems to me, is what the Modernists have done, no doubt with the best intentions in the world. They have tried to get rid of all the logical difficulties of religion, and yet, preserve a generally pious cast of mind. It is a vain enterprise.[72]

Mencken did not think one needed to be a partisan to see what politics was doing to the Christian religion. For him, as for Machen, the logic was simple. Anytime religion is forced to perform a function it cannot do, it necessarily becomes something different.

The lesson for the Religious Right should be obvious. The effort to bring religious values to bear on public life is similar to what Protestant Modernists did seventy years ago when they advocated prayer and Bible reading in public schools, Prohibition, and a rating system for Hollywood's movies. And like the Protestant establishment during the middle decades of the twentieth century, today's advocates of public religion could presumably add greater dignity and decency to American society.

But at what cost? What will happen to the non-Evangelical citizens of the United States if they do not comply with Evangelicalism's moral code?

Even more important, what will happen to the faith once delivered to the saints that Evangelicals are so eager to share? As difficult as it may be to find a common ethical platform for public life without the foundation of revealed religion, the difficulties on the other side are just as great, if not greater.

To be sure, the desire to make Christianity relevant for public life does not automatically force someone to deny the Virgin Birth or the Resurrection of Christ. Neither is it immediately obvious, however, what these articles of belief have to do with limited government, free markets, or family values. And so, a comprehensive biblical program for American society and politics turns out to be little more than the second table of the Ten Commandments, the ones having to do with love of neighbor. Loving neighbors is a good thing. But historic Christianity involves much more. The irony is that by reducing Christianity to its ethical teaching the Religious Right and its defenders could be making one of the greatest concessions to modern secular life imaginable. For that reason it may be better to scrap altogether the project of public or civil religion.[73] In the case of Anglo-American Protestantism, such efforts have not worked out well for either the Republic or the churches.

Notes

1. On Bob Jones University and Fundamentalism in the 1940s, see Mark Taylor Dalhouse, *An Island in the Lake of Fire: Bob Jones University, Fundamentalism, and the Separatist Movement* (Athens: University of Georgia Press, 1996); Daniel L. Turner, *Standing without Apology: The History of Bob Jones University* (Greenville, S.C.: Bob Jones University Press, 1997); and Sean Michael Lucas, "Fundamentalisms Revived and Still Standing: A Review Essay," *Westminster Theological Journal* 60 (1998): 327–37.

2. The best book for understanding what the Fundamentalist controversy means to Evangelical Protestantism in the United States remains George M. Marsden, *Fundamentalism and American Culture: The Shaping of Twentieth-Century Evangelicalism, 1875–1925* (New York: Oxford University Press, 1980).

3. Carl F.H. Henry, *The Uneasy Conscience of Modern Fundamentalism* (Grand Rapids, Mich.: Eerdmans, 1947), 36.

4. On Neo-Evangelicalism, see Joel A. Carpenter, *Revive Us Again: The Reawakening of American Fundamentalism* (New York: Oxford University Press, 1997).

5. In this chapter the words, "Fundamentalist," and, "Evangelical," are used interchangeably because the differences between the two are not great in the arena of politics. In fact, the point of this chapter is that the religious style of Evangelicals and Fundamentalists, namely, pietism, has specific consequences for political engagement and reflection that turns whatever religious differences Evangelicals and Fundamentalists have into sociopolitical commonalities.

6. Kenneth L. Woodward, "The Year of the Evangelicals," *Newsweek* , Oct. 25, 1976, 68.

7. On the emergence of the Religious Right, see Robert Booth Fowler, *A New Engagement: Christian Evangelical Political Thought, 1966–1976* (Grand Rapids, Mich.: Eerdmans, 1982); Michael Lienesch, *Redeeming America: Piety & Politics in the New Christian Right* (Chapel Hill: University of North Carolina Press, 1993), 1–4; George M. Marsden, "Preachers of Paradox: Fundamentalist Politics in Historical Perspective," in *Understanding Fundamentalism and Evangelicalism* (Grand Rapids, Mich.: Eerdmans, 1991), 104–9.

8. The term, "Religious Right," as I will be using it, covers more than simply the Moral Majority or Christian Coalition. For the purpose of this chapter, Religious Right means the constellation of Evangelical Protestants engaged in politics whose leadership includes Paul Weyrich, Ralph Reed, Cal Thomas, Jerry Falwell, Don Eberly, James Dobson, and Charles Colson, along with the organizations that the oversee and publications for which they write. This list, though debatable, was the one that editors of *Christianity Today*, Evangelicalism's magazine of record, made in their feature, "Is the Religious Right Finished? An Insiders' Conversation," *Christianity Today*, Sept. 6, 1999, 43–59. As will become apparent throughout this chapter, the particular style of Evangelical politics, that is, of looking to the Bible for social and political solutions, can also be found among Evangelicals on the so-called Left, individuals such as Ron Sider and Jim Wallis. But to avoid confusion, I will use "Religious Right" only in connection with those people and institutions identified by *Christianity Today*.

9. On the largely unfavorable depiction of Fundamentalism in the historiography before 1970, see Stewart G. Cole, *The History of Fundamentalism* (New York: Richard R. Smith, 1931); Norman Furniss, *The Fundamentalist Controversy, 1918–1931* (New Haven, Conn.: Yale University Press, 1954); Ray Ginger, *Six Days or Forever? Tennessee v. John Thomas Scopes* (Chicago: Quadrangle Books, 1968); and Richard Hofstadter, *Anti-Intellectualism in American Life* (New York: Vintage Books, 1962). This negative estimate only changes with Paul A. Carter, "The Fundamentalist Defense of the Faith," in *Change and Continuity in Twentieth-Century America: The 1920s*, ed. John Braeman, Robert Bremmer, and David Brody (Columbus: Ohio State University Press, 1968), 179–214.

10. See, e.g., Clyde Wilcox, *God's Warriors: The Christian Right in Twentieth-Century America* (Baltimore: Johns Hopkins University Press, 1992), 1–20; Lienesch, *Redeeming America*, 4–9; Marsden, "Preachers of Paradox"; and Leo P. Ribuffo, "God and Contemporary Politics," *Journal of American History* 79 (1993): 1515–33.

11. On the origins and rise of the Religious Right, see Lienesch, *Redeeming America*; Steve Bruce, *The Rise and Fall of the New Christian Right: Conservative Protestant Politics in America, 1978–1988* (New York: Oxford University Press, 1988); William C. Martin, *With God On Our Side: The Rise of the Religious Right in America* (New York: Broadway Books, 1996); and Wilcox, *God's Warriors*.

12. Sydney E. Ahlstrom, *A Religious History of the American People* (New Haven, Conn.: Yale University Press, 1972), 1079; emphasis his.

13. See, e.g., Martin E. Marty, *Modern American Religion, Volume 3: Under God, Indivisible, 1941–1961* (Chicago: University of Chicago Press, 1996); William R. Hutchison, ed., *Between the Times: The Travail of the Protestant Establishment in American, 1900–1960* (New York: Cambridge University Press, 1989); and Heather A. Warren, *Theologians of a New World Order: Reinhold Niebuhr and the Christian Realists, 1920–1948* (New York: Oxford University Press, 1997).

14. See Leonard I. Sweet, "The 1960s: The Crises of Liberal Christianity and the Public Emergence of Evangelicalism," in *Evangelicalism and Modern America*, ed. George Marsden (Grand Rapids, Mich.: Eerdmans, 1984), 29–45; Douglas Sloan, *Faith & Knowledge: Mainline Protestantism and American Higher Education* (Louisville: Westminster/John Knox Press, 1994); and Lloyd Billingsley, *From Mainline to Sideline: The Social Witness of the National Council of Churches* (Lanham, Md.: Ethics and Public Policy Center, 1990).

15. Daniel Walker Howe, "Religion and Politics in the Antebellum North," in *Religion and American Politics: From the Colonial Period to the 1980s*, ed. Mark A. Noll (New York: Oxford University Press, 1990), 124.

16. On this point, see ibid., 121–45; Robert P. Swierenga, "Ethnoreligious Political Behavior in the Mid-Nineteenth Century: Voting, Values, Culture," in *Religion and American Politics*, 146–71; George Marsden, "The Religious Right: A Historical Overview," in *No Longer Exiles: The Religious New Right in American Politics*, ed. Michael Cromartie (Washington, D.C.: Ethics and Public Policy Center, 1992), 1–16; and Allen C. Guelzo, *Abraham Lincoln: Redeemer President* (Grand Rapids, Mich.: Eerdmans, 1999), chap. 1.

17. Swierenga, "Ethnoreligious Political Behavior," 152–53. See Lyman A. Kellstedt et al. "It's the Culture Stupid! 1992 and Our Political Future," *First Things*, April 1994, 28–33, for evidence of these differences between Republicans and Democrats even after the 1930s.

18. Mark A. Noll, "The Scandal of Evangelical Political Reflection," in *Being Christian Today: An American Conversation*, ed. Richard John Neuhaus and George Weigel (Washington, D.C.: Ethics and Public Policy Center, 1992), 73.

19. On contemporary Evangelical attitudes toward American society, see Christian Smith, *American Evangelicalism: Embattled and Thriving* (Chicago: University of Chicago Press, 1998); idem, *Christian America: What Evangelicals Really Want* (Berkeley: University of California Press, 2000); and James Davison Hunter, *Culture Wars: The Struggle to Define America* (New York: Basic Books, 1991).

20. For the influence of premillennialism on Evangelical politics, see Noll, "Scandal of Evangelical Political Reflection," 74–82; and Marsden, *Fundamentalism and American Culture*, chaps. 22 and 23.

21. A popular book that faulted Evangelical quietism during the Nixon era is David O. Moberg, *The Great Reversal: Evangelism versus Social Concern* (Philadelphia: Lippincott, 1972). Timothy L. Smith, *Revivalism and Social Reform: American Protestantism on the Eve of the Civil War* (Baltimore: Johns Hopkins University Press, 1980), made a similar argument about a reversal among Evangelicals, without Moberg's practical application. See also, Marsden, *Fundamentalism and American Culture*; and Carpenter, *Revive Us Again*. Though this argument makes sense for much of the Fundamentalist movement, it does not account for real political involvement by such Fundamentalists as Gerald Winrod, William Bell Riley, J. Frank Norris, or Carl McIntire during the precise decades when Evangelical quietism was supposed to be at its zenith. On Fundamentalist politics, see Leo Ribuffo, *The Christian Right: The Protestant Far Right from the Great Depression to the Cold War* (Philadelphia: Temple University Press, 1983); Glen Jeansonne, *Gerald L. K. Smith: Minister of Hate* (Baton Rouge: Louisiana State University Press, 1997); William Vance Trollinger Jr., *God's Empire: William Bell Riley and Midwestern Fundamentalism* (Madison: University of Wisconsin Press, 1990); and Barry Hankins, *J. Frank Norris*

and the Beginnings of Southern Fundamentalism (Lexington: University of Kentucky Press, 1996).

22. See James Hudnut-Beumler, *Looking for God in the Suburbs: The Religion of the American Dream and Its Critics, 1945–1965*; and Paul A. Carter, *Another Part of the Fifties* (New York: Columbia University Press, 1983).

23. On mid-twentieth-century Evangelical concerns, see David Harrington Watt, *A Transforming Faith: Explorations of Twentieth-Century American Evangelicalism* (New Brunswick, N.J.: Rutgers University Press, 1991). The moral and familial concerns may also help to explain how the Religious Right differs from the Christian Far Right. Although both groups opposed communism and the centralizing efforts of the state, the Religious Right's opposition to government control is less ideological. In other words, the Religious Right tends to be more concerned with politics as they relate to the family, and less interested in a consistently conservative set of political principles.

24. Martin E. Marty, *Modern American Religion, Volume 2: The Noise of Conflict, 1919–1941* (Chicago: University of Chicago Press, 1991), 63.

25. On the cultural significance of 1920s politics, see Allan J. Lichtman, *Prejudice and the Old Politics: The Presidential Election of 1928* (Chapel Hill: University of North Carolina Press, 1979); and Lynn Dumenil, "'The Insatiable Maw of Bureaucracy': Antistatism and Education Reform in the 1920s," *Journal of American History* 77 (1990): 499–524. The reason for claiming that Al Smith might have been able to affirm the five points of Fundamentalism (i.e., biblical inerrancy, the Virgin Birth, vicarious atonement, the Resurrection, and Christ's miracles) is that the Roman Catholic Church affirmed all of these doctrines and in 1899 condemned Modernism as a heresy.

26. Only a decade ago, pollsters discovered that 34 percent of Americans perceived Evangelicals as a menace to civil society, compared with only 14 percent who had similar perceptions of the Ku Klux Klan. See Os Guiness, "Tribes People, Idiots or Citizens? Evangelicals, Religious Liberty and Public Philosophy for the Public Square," in *Evangelical Affirmations*, ed. Kenneth S. Kantzer and Carl F. H. Henry (Grand Rapids, Mich.: Academie Books, 1990), 461.

27. Richard John Neuhaus, "What the Fundamentalists Want," originally published in *Commentary* (1985) and reprinted in *Piety and Politics: Evangelicals and Fundamentalists Confront the World*, ed. Richard John Neuhaus and Michael Cromartie (Washington, D.C.: Ethics and Public Policy Center), 18.

28. See Theodore Caplow, Howard M. Bahr, Bruce A. Chadwick, and Dwight W. Hoover, *All Faithful People: Change and Continuity in Middletown's Religion* (Minneapolis: University of Minnesota Press, 1983).

29. Neuhaus, "What the Fundamentalists Want," 16.

30. See, e.g., John C. Green et al, *Religion and the Culture Wars: Dispatches from the Front* (Lanham, Md.: Rowman & Littlefield, 1996); Martin E. Marty and R. Scott Appleby, eds., *Fundamentalisms and Society: Reclaiming the Sciences, the Family, and Education* (Chicago: University of Chicago Press, 1993); Robert Wuthnow, *The Restructuring of American Religion: Society and Faith since World War II* (Princeton, N.J.: Princeton University Press, 1988); James L. Guth, *The Bully Pulpit: The Politics of Protestant Clergy* (Lawrence: University of Kansas Press, 1997); Roger Finke and Rodney Stark, *The Churching of American: Winners and Losers in Our Religious Economy* (New Brunswick, N.J.: Rutgers University Press, 1992); Nancy T. Ammerman,

Bible Believers: Fundamentalists in the Modern World (New Brunswick, N.J.: Rutgers University Press, 1987); Stephen R. Warner, *New Wine in Old Wineskins: Evangelicals and Liberals in a Small-Town Church* (Berkeley: University of California Press, 1988); David Stoll, *Is Latin America Turning Protestant? The Politics of Evangelical Growth* (Berkeley: University of California Press, 1990); David Martin, *Tongues of Fire: The Explosion of Protestantism in Latin America* (Cambridge, Mass.: Blackwell, 1990); and Steve Bruce, *Religion in the Modern World: From Cathedrals to Cults* (New York: Oxford University Press, 1996).

31. José Casanova, *Public Religions in the Modern World* (Chicago: University of Chicago Press, 1994), 65–66.

32. Ibid., 215, 221–22.

33. Ibid., 158–61.

34. Ibid., 161–65; the quotation is on 157.

35. Steve Bruce, *Conservative Protestant Politics* (Oxford: Oxford University Press, 1998), 12–16; the quotation is on 19.

36. Ibid., 219.

37. Ibid., 19, 21. Arguably the best recent estimate of Evangelicalism's scope is Smith, *American Evangelicalism.* The classic statement of Evangelicalism's variety is Timothy L. Smith, "The Evangelical Kaleidoscope and the Call to Christian Unity," *Christian Scholar's Review* 15 (1986): 125–40.

38. It is my conviction that this is true for all Christian traditions, not just Protestants. Still, the Catholic experience in the United States teaches that Christian involvement in public life is not inevitably geared toward establishing a Christian America. My sense is that the pronouncements of the Catholic bishops have been directed more toward policies that protect Catholics from the state rather than trying to make the state conform to Catholic views and practices.

39. Carl F.H. Henry, "Response," in *No Longer Exiles: The Religious New Right in American Politics*, ed. Michael Cromartie (Washington, D.C.: Ethics and Public Policy Center, 1992), 75.

40. This is a group of Protestant theonomists, whose leaders include Rousas J. Rushdoony and Gary North. They believe that biblical law should be the norm for modern society. For an introduction, see Gary North, *Christian Reconconstruction: What It Is, What It Isn't* (Tyler, Tex.: Institute for Christian Economics, 1991).

41. Henry, "Response," 77, 75.

42. This statement might sound patently obvious. But Evangelicals are different from other Christians in thinking that Bible speaks to all of life. Other Christian traditions would speak instead of the Bible teaching all things necessary for salvation, meaning that Scripture does not speak to numerous areas of life that are not directly related to salvation. In those areas, wisdom applies. For one expression of the Bible's applicability to all of life, see John M. Frame, "In Defense of Something Close to Biblicism: Reflections on Sola Scriptura and History in Theological Method," *Westminster Theological Journal* 59 (1997): 269–91.

43. Richard John Neuhaus, *The Naked Public Square: Religion and Democracy in America* (Grand Rapids, Mich.: Eerdmans, 1984), 36–37, quoted in Casanova, *Public Religions*, 165.

44. Bruce, *Conservative Protestant Politics*, 185.

45. Ibid., 188, 189.

46. Casanova, *Public Religions*, 214, 230, 233.

47. This distinction finds support from the two best books on Fundamentalism and liberalism: Marsden, *Fundamentalism and American Culture*; and William R. Hutchison, *The Modernist Impulse in American Protestantism* (Cambridge, Mass.: Harvard University Press, 1976).

48. Robert Wuthnow, "The Future of the Religious Right," in *No Longer Exiles*, 30. What David N. Livingstone writes of the Fundamentalist psyche—"the passion to hammer down history, to tough the transcendental, to earth the supernatural in the mundane"—is an equally fitting description of Evangelicalism more generally. See David N. Livingstone, "Introduction: Placing Evangelical Encounters with Science," in *Evangelicals and Science in Historical Perspective*, ed. David N. Livingstone, D.G. Hart, and Mark A. Noll (New York: Oxford University Press, 1999), 9.

49. For some of the contributions to the ethno-cultural interpretation of nineteenth-century American politics, see Paul Kleppner, *The Cross of Culture: A Social Analysis of Midwestern Politics, 1850–1900* (New York: Free Press, 1970); idem, *The Third Electoral System, 1853–1892: Parties, Voters, and Political Cultures* (Chapel Hill: University of North Carolina Press, 1979); Ronald P. Formisano, *The Birth of Mass Political Parties: Michigan, 1827–1861* (Princeton, N.J.: Princeton University Press, 1971); idem, *The Transformation of Political Culture: Massachusetts Parties, 1790s–1840s* (New York: Oxford University Press, 1983); Robert Kelley, *The Cultural Pattern in American Politics: The First Century* (New York: Knopf, 1979); and Robert P. Swierenga, ed., *Beyond the Civil War Synthesis: Political Essays of the Civil War Era* (Westport, Conn.: Greenwood, 1975). For the importance of ethnicity to Anglo-American Protestantism, see John Higham, "Ethnicity and American Protestants: Collective Identity in the Mainstream," in *New Directions in American Religious History*, ed. Harry Stout and D. G. Hart (New York: Oxford University Press, 1997), 239–59.

50. Two books that show how liturgical Protestantism evolved through conflict with revivalistic Protestantism are David A. Gustafson, *Lutherans in Crisis: The Question of Identity in the American Republic* (Minneapolis: Fortress Press, 1993); and Allen C. Guelzo, *For the Sake of Evangelical Christendom: The Irony of Reformed Episcopalians* (University Park: Pennsylvania State University Press, 1994). Another important figure in liturgical Protestantism is John Williamson Nevin, who grew up in Scotch-Irish Presbyterianism, moved into the German Reformed church, and penned what is arguably the best critique of revivalism written in the nineteenth century, *The Anxious Bench* (Chambersburg, Pa.: *Weekly Messenger*, 1843). On Nevin's place in nineteenth-century Protestantism, see Theodore Appel, *The Life and Work of John Williamson Nevin* (1889; New York: Arno Press, 1969).

51. For the effects of anti-Catholicism on Anglo-American Protestantism, see John Wolffe, "Anti-Catholicism and Evangelical Identity in Britain and the United States, 1830–1860," in *Evangelicalism: Comparative Studies of Popular Protestantism in North America, the British Isles, and Beyond, 1700–1990*, ed. Mark A. Noll, David W. Bebbington, and George A. Rawlyk (New York: Oxford University Press, 1994), 179–97.

52. See, e.g., Douglas Jacobsen and William Vance Trollinger Jr., "Historiography of American Protestantism: The Two-Party Paradigm," *Fides et Historia* 25 (1993): 4–15, which shows implicitly that religious historians have ignored liturgicalism, identifying Evangelicalism as the Right wing of American Protestantism.

53. For historiographical examples of this tendency, see Christine Heyrman, *Southern Cross: The Beginnings of the Bible Belt* (New York: Knopf, 1997); Paul K. Conkin, *Uneasy Center: Reformed Christianity in Antebellum America* (Chapel Hill: University

of North Carolina Press, 1995); and Willliam R. Sutton, *Journeyman for Jesus: Evangelical Artisans Confront Capitalism in Jacksonian Baltimore* (University Park: Pennsylvania State University Press, 1998), all of whom dissolve denominational differences into revivalist Protestantism. For examples from the social sciences that make the same mistake, see Liniesch, *Redeeming America*; Robert Wuthnow, *The Struggle for America's Soul: Evangelicals, Liberals, and Secularism* (Grand Rapids, Mich.: Eerdmans, 1989); and Hunter, *Culture Wars*.

54. Jean Bethke Elshtain, "The Bright Line: Liberalism & Religion," *New Criterion* 17 (1999): 10. The distinction between public and private religion is not very helpful. The reason is that "public" may be applied to churchly and political aspects of human society. Public worship, for instance, would technically fall on the private side of Elshtain's dichotomy. It is public in the sense that, in most Christian traditions, it is open to everyone in the community. But to hold a public worship service in the public square, thereby implying the endorsement of the civil authority, would violate American canons of propriety. The words, "civil" and "churchly," as modifiers of "religion," then, would seem to work much better than public and private. But few of today's advocates of public religion would want to take up the cause of civil religion because of that phrase's association with the older Protestant establishment.

55. Swierenga, "Ethnoreligious Political Behavior," 152.

56. On the Lutheran doctrine of two kingdoms, see Lutheran Church–Missouri Synod, Commission on Theology and Church Relations, *Render unto Caesar . . . and unto God: A Lutheran View of Church and State* (Saint Louis: Lutheran Church–Missouri Synod, 1995); and Mark A. Noll, *One Nation Under God? Christian Faith and Political Action in America* (San Francisco: Harper & Row, 1988), chap. 2. On the Presbyterian notion of the spirituality of the church, see D.G. Hart, "The Spirituality of the Church, the Westminster Standards, and Nineteenth-Century American Presbyterianism," in *The Westminster Confession in Current Thought: Colloquium in Calvin Studies VIII*, ed. John H. Leith (privately published, 1996), 106–18.

57. Guelzo, *Abraham Lincoln*, chap. 1, shows with great effect the differences between the social outlook of Republicans and the Jeffersonian tradition inherited by Democrats.

58. The literature on liturgical Protestantism and its political significance is generally confined to nineteenth-century developments. On the twentieth century, see Lichtman, *Prejudice and the Old Politics*; Dumenil, "'Insatiable Maw of Bureaucracy'"; James D. Bratt, "Protestant Immigrants and the Protestant Mainstream," in *Minority Faiths and the American Protestant Experience*, ed. Jonathan D. Sarna (Urbana: University of Illinois Press, 1997), 110–35; and Mark Granquist, "Lutherans in the United States, 1930–1960: Searching for the 'Center,'" in *Re-Forming the Center: American Protestantism, 1900 to the Present*, ed. Douglas Jacobsen and William Vance Trollinger Jr. (Grand Rapids, Mich.: Eerdmans, 1998), 234–51.

59. Of course, liturgical Protestants could be drawn into the mainstream of American civil religion. But ethnic differences along with theological depth prevented total submersion. For one example of these tensions within Dutch-American Calvinism, see James D. Bratt, *Dutch Calvinism in America* (Grand Rapids, Mich.: Eerdmans, 1984), 40-66.

60. For this conception of the secular, see Oliver O'Donovan, *The Desire of the Nations: Rediscovering the Roots of Political Theology* (New York: Cambridge University Press, 1996).

61. See, e.g., Neuhaus, *Naked Public Square*; Stephen L. Carter, *The Culture of Disbelief: How American Law and Politics Trivialize Religious Devotion* (New York: Basic Books, 1993); Michael J. Sandel, *Democracy's Discontent: America in Search of a Public Philosophy* (Cambridge, Mass.: Belknap Press, 1996); Kent Greenawalt, *Religious Convictions and Political Choice* (New York: Oxford University Press, 1987); Richard P. McBrien, *Caesar's Coin: Religion and Politics in America* (New York: Macmillan, 1987); Max L. Stackhouse, *Public Theology and Political Economy* (Grand Rapids, Mich.: Eerdmans, 1987); Garry Wills, *Under God: Religion and American Politics* (New York: Simon & Schuster, 1990); Hunter, *Culture Wars*; Don E. Eberly, *Restoring the Good Society: A New Vision for Politics and Culture* (Grand Rapids, Mich.: Hourglass Books, 1994); Ronald F. Thiemann, *Religion in Public Life: A Dilemma for Democracy* (Washington, D.C.: Georgetown University Press, 1996); Glenn E. Tinder, *The Political Meaning of Christianity: An Interpretation* (Baton Rouge: Louisiana State University Press, 1989); and Isaac Kramnick and R. Laurence Moore, *The Godless Constitution: The Case against Religious Correctness* (New York: Norton, 1996).

62. In the words of the Yale philosopher Nicholas Wolterstorff, who is by no means a member of the Religious Right but echoes Evangelicals' sentiments, "To suppress the religious voice in the public arena would be to suppress the most powerful force available to us for the cause of justice and human flourishing"; Wolterstorff, "Inner Voices," *Civilization*, Aug.–Sept 1999, 67.

63. The bipolar character of these matters applies as much to Evangelicals on the political Left as it does to the Religious Right. Although James Dobson, the voice of Focus on the Family, and Jim Wallis, the editor of *Sojourners*, disagree about any number of policies, both agree that Evangelicalism is relevant to public life and that Evangelicals need to be active politically. In which case, the tension between religion and politics automatically ensues, because the claim that religion is good and necessary for public life does not address the rules that apparently forbid mixing religion and politics. Compare, e.g., *Christianity Today*'s recent coverage of the Religious Right and their Evangelical peers on the Left: "Is the Religious Right Finished? An Insiders' Conversation," *Christianity Today*, Sept. 6, 1999, 43–59; Tim Stafford, "The Criminologist Who Discovered Churches," *Christianity Today*, June 14, 1999, 35–39; John Wilson, "Mr. Wallis Goes to Washington," *Christianity Today*, June 14, 1999, 41–43; and Michael G. Maudlin, "God's Contractor," *Christianity Today*, June 14, 1999, 45–47. See also Charles W. Colson, with Nancy Pearcey, *How Now Shall We Live?* (Wheaton, Ill.: Tyndale House, 1999), a book that appeals directly to the public relevance of Evangelical Protestantism.

64. This is the point well made in Nathan O. Hatch, *The Democratization of American Christianity* (New Haven, Conn.: Yale University Press, 1989).

65. This is a point developed more fully in Mark A. Noll, *The Scandal of the Evangelical Mind* (Grand Rapids, Mich.: Eerdmans, 1994). For other episodes illustrating the way Protestantism polarized public debates on public schooling, see Charles L. Glenn Jr., *The Myth of the Common School* (Amherst: University of Massachusetts Press, 1987); on church and state matters during the Progressive Era, see Robert T. Handy, *Undermined Establishment: Church–State Relations in America, 1880–1920* (Princeton, N.J.: Princeton University Press, 1991); and on Protestants and higher education, see D.G. Hart, *The University Gets Religion: Religious Studies and American Higher Education* (Baltimore: Johns Hopkins University Press, 1999).

66. For a good brief recent statement of this view, see Kenneth A. Myers, "Biblical Obedience and Political Thought: Reflections on Theological Method," in *The Bible, Politics, and Democracy*, ed. Richard John Neuhaus (Grand Rapids, Mich.: Eerdmans, 1987), 19–31. A fuller and older expression is Stuart Robinson, *The Church of God as an Essential Element of the Gospel* (Philadelphia: J.M. Wilson, 1858).

67. Part of the problem, of course, is that the public and private spheres overlap more and more, thanks to the growing interdependence of local and national institutions. But this is a political problem, one that may call for greater limits on government. It is not something to be solved by adding more religion to public life.

68. Daniel Bell, *The Cultural Contradictions of Capitalism* (New York: Basic Books, 1996), xii.

69. On Machen, see D.G. Hart, *Defending the Faith: J. Gresham Machen and the Crisis of Conservative Protestantism in Modern America* (Baltimore: Johns Hopkins University Press, 1994).

70. J. Gresham Machen, *Christianity and Liberalism* (New York: Macmillan, 1923), 149, 151.

71. J. Gresham Machen, "The Necessity of the Christian School," in *What Is Christianity? and Other Essays*, ed. Ned B. Stonehouse (Grand Rapids, Mich.: Eerdmans, 1951), 299.

72. H.L. Mencken, "Doctor Fundamentalis," *Baltimore Evening Sun*, Jan. 18, 1937.

73. Other scholars to make this point include Peter L. Berger, "Different Gospels: The Social Sources of Apostasy," *This World* 17 (spring 1987): 6–17; Ted G. Jelen, "In Defense of Religious Minimalism," in *A Wall of Separation? Debating the Public Role of Religion*, ed. Mary C. Segers and Ted G. Jelen (Lanham, Md.: Rowman & Littlefield, 1998), 3–51; and Vigen Guroian, "The Struggle for the Soul of the Church: American Reflections," in *Ethics After Christendom: Toward an Ecclesial Christian Ethic* (Grand Rapids, Mich.: Eerdmans, 1994), 83–101.

Part III

Policy Applications

8

American Catholicism, Catholic Charities USA, and Welfare Reform

John A. Coleman, S.J.

This chapter seeks to give at least a thumbnail sense of American Catholicism's background assumptions, policy contours, and vehicles for engaging in public policy discussions. To do this, it will eventually concentrate on one major recent public policy discussion in the United States: the debates on welfare reform that led up to—and continue vigorously even after—the passage of the Personal Responsibility and Work Opportunity Reconciliation Act of 1996.

The chapter focuses on the welfare reform debates because American Catholic institutions, including the United States Catholic Conference and Catholic Charities USA, played a crucial and continuous role in the debates.[1] Indeed, New York's Senator Daniel P. Moynihan, a vigorous opponent of the proposed welfare reform bill, in excoriating his fellow liberals for signing on to the bill, could lift up the example of the Catholic bishops' lobbying and exclaim: "The bishops admittedly have an easier time with matters of this sort. When principles are at stake, they simply look them up. Too many liberals, alas, make them up!"[2] This particular debate (which is not, by any means, over) also helps to show some of the unique assumptions behind proposals found in Catholic interventions in the policy sector. In what follows, I briefly develop four subthemes for the chapter:

1. Catholic social thought: five background assumptions for policy: human dignity, the common good, solidarity, subsidiarity, and justice;
2. the move from background assumptions to policy;
3. Catholic policy proposals: their style and instrumentalities; and
4. Catholicism and welfare policy.

To be sure, Catholics have significantly engaged in any number of diverse policy discussions for many years. The scope covers issues of foreign policy (ranging from concern in the 1930s about the Spanish Civil War, to later support for a policy of anticommunism, to disputes with the Ronald Reagan and George H.W. Bush administrations about El Salvador and Nicaragua); interpretations of the First Amendment; abortion, euthanasia, and policies concerning sexual orientation and marriage; immigration policy; health care issues; vouchers or government funding for programs in parochial schools; U.S. nuclear policy; and family policy issues.[3] But perhaps nowhere else can one better see certain Catholic strengths and weaknesses in the policy arena than by taking a fresh look at the Catholic role in the welfare reform debates. Moreover, at least since the latter part of the nineteenth century, American Catholics have been rather continuously involved in the salient shifts in U.S. welfare policy.[4] No other policy issue has such a long history of Catholic engagement.

Catholic forays into public policy remain a puzzle to many, both inside and outside the church. On some issues (e.g., abortion), Catholics seem closely aligned with segments of the conservative Evangelical community. On others (e.g., opposition to capital punishment), they are more likely to build coalitions with the American Civil Liberties Union. On still others, they are in close contact with welfare professionals. The so-called Catholic Consistent Ethic of Life does not fit neatly into any of the more secular or religious ideological divisions.[5] On nuclear and military policy, Catholic policy stands with the doves. On abortion, it stands with the pro-life lobby. On welfare, it takes a position at the left end of the spectrum.

Moreover, different units and levels of the national Catholic Church—the bishops' conference; the thirty state conferences that serve statewide groups of bishops; diocesan bishops and their peace and justice or public policy committees; separately incorporated groups, such as Catholic Charities

USA; Network, a lobbying group concerned with poverty founded by Roman Catholic sisters; the National Catholic Educational Association; and the Catholic Health Association—engage in public policy discussions and proposals and lobbying. They do not all always sing from the same songbook.

Peter McDonough and Josephina Figueira-McDonough—focusing their research mainly on Catholic family policy—comment on some anomalies in Catholic public policy behavior:

> Catholic family policy is an amalgam of morally conservative and socially progressive tenets, with an eclectic middle-ground driven by trial and error, professional norms and improvisation—Catholic family policy is part dogma, part pragmatism, part social critique, and part ethos. The family has been the nexus binding together Catholic social and political thought as it ranges over a variety of topics. The family has been to Catholic social order what class has been to social conflicts in Marxism, and what the individual has been to the capitalist market, and the voluntary association to democratic theory.[6]

Catholic Social Thought: Five Background Assumptions for Policy

Catholic social thought constitutes the essential intellectual armory to which the Catholic Church and its major institutions (networks of schools, hospitals, and welfare agencies) have recourse when thinking about and generating public policy proposals.[7] To be sure, like any other institution, Catholic institutions also draw upon a more naked self-interest. Thus, some American Catholic policy proposals may stem, primarily, from institutional self-interest (e.g., vouchers for parochial schools, religious exemptions from taxation or from federal labor union regulations, the charitable choice option).

No one should do a purely altruistic reading of institutional churches' engagement in policy formation. Like any organization, much of the church's behavior is interest driven. But only a cynical reading of the practice of Catholicism in the arena of policy would reduce its policy proposals to *mere* or *only* institutional interests. A long tradition exists in Catholicism of periodically promulgating papal and episcopal documents whose purpose is to "provide moral wisdom to assist in the formation of conscience" and political and civil behavior in the light of new economic, cultural, or technological developments.[8] This tradition of Catholic social thought addresses political, cultural, economic, religious, and family issues. It exhibits a unique set of presuppositions and assumptions about the human person and the social order.

Human Dignity and the Common Good

The concept of human dignity and the core notion of "a common good" represent two of the key components in the Catholic intellectual tradition. Human dignity is grounded in both biblical warrants which see the person as the *imago Dei* and in rational natural law assumptions about the person as a rational and voluntary moral agent, endowed with inalienability and rights. To speak of the human dignity of the person is to appeal to his or her "sacred" worth or value as a concrete existing human being. Dignity asserts that human beings have a value or a worth qualitatively different from that of anything else in the world, that this dignity is inalienable, and that it is never permissible to use a human being merely as a means toward some ulterior aim or purpose. Human dignity evokes corollary concepts of human responsibility, moral agency, and freedom. To root its meaning concretely, Catholic social thought anchors it in appeals to the concepts of both *human rights* and *human needs.*[9]

In his 1963 encyclical *Pacem in Terris*, Pope John XXIII, basing his argument on both the philosophy of natural law and biblical theology, defined the scope and range of human rights in a most extensive way. He was clearly veering his text closely toward the human rights demands that have been formulated in the United Nations Declaration of Human Rights (in the development of which Declaration European Catholics, including the Pontiff, contributed). Thus, the Catholic theory of human rights—much like the U.N. Declaration—contains both a liberal or personalist and a social dimension. In Catholic social thought, according to the pope, there is no unbridgeable chasm between personal rights and civil, social, or subsistence rights.

Among the individual human rights demands, John XXIII lays emphasis on the right to life and to freedom from bodily harm as well as on the right to those commodities necessary for an appropriate standard of living (food, clothing, a home, education, health care, unemployment aid, and help in old age) that are consonant with human dignity. Rights flow from needs as much as from human moral agency and freedom. *Pacem in Terris* also stresses both the right to freedom of religion and conscience, freedom of opinion and information, freedom of migration, and freedom to choose one's profession or life partner in marriage and also the right to an impartial legal guarantee and juridical protection for these freedoms. In referring to political participation, the pope stresses freedom of assembly and freedom of association. The pope sees the right to private property as derived from the nature of humankind—although he urges that consideration be given to the social obligations of holding any property.[10]

Many disputes in public policy stem from debates about the legitimacy of any extension of the rights to freedom seen as rights of defense against state intervention in certain areas of private life (*negative* freedoms) to further claims to social rights to a minimum provision of commodities (a decent floor of subsistence) that permit any genuine participation in the life of society and, thus, *effective* freedom (*positive* rights). Catholic social thought embraces both and adds a third right to participatory access to political and cultural life (i.e., rights to take genuine part in the process of work and the formation of political opinion). With others, Catholicism argues that the guarantee of elementary social rights (based on need) anchor, as the indispensable condition, any individual possibility to develop true moral agency and freedom.[11]

The question of how social claims to certain rights can be adequately met—given the differing economic capability of countries—is of course much more complex than simply guaranteeing negative rights to freedom. But this by no means detracts, in the Catholic view, from the fundamental human rights character of such claims. Rather, it demonstrates the need to change those economic conditions, if possible and need be, toward more just divisions of wealth and to change the conditions governing opportunity, access, and competition operating in the world market. Finally, the Catholic demand for a democratic constitutional order with basic rights, guaranteed independent of political party interests, is based on the claimed right of the individual (as a rational being who is essentially called to be a moral agent) to be heard in matters that affect him or her and thus to participate, in some real sense, in the political decisionmaking process.

The Catholic notion of a common good reflects its belief about the essentially communitarian character of human existence. Persons flourish only in community and the good of each person is bound up with the good of community. "The common good is a social reality in which all persons should share through their participation in it. It is not simply the arithmetic aggregate of individual goods suggested by the utilitarian formula 'the greatest good for the greatest number.'"[12] Recent Catholic formulations anchor the common good in structural terms: "the sum total of conditions of social living whereby persons are enabled more fully and readily to achieve their own perfection."[13] In *Pacem in Terris*, the common good is linked closely to human rights. Human rights, *Pacem in Terris* claims, specify the *minimum* standard for any society that is "well ordered and productive" and in which the dignity of each person is realized.[14] Promoting the common good, in this view, entails the duty to protect the human rights of all.

Commitment to the common good rejects individualistic presuppositions in some forms of modern liberal thought with their one-sided emphasis on human autonomy. It skews Catholic policy thinking in directions that diverge from a consensus among many political liberals who follow John Stuart Mill when he asserts that "the only freedom which deserves the name is that of pursuing our own good in our own way, so long as we do not attempt to deprive others of theirs or impede their efforts to obtain it."[15] Catholic social thought assumes, against Isaiah Berlin and John Rawls, that we *can* meaningfully deliberate together about the essentially public goods we must share in common and about the substantive goods we *will* pursue in common. The common good is not imposed nor read off of a preexisting blueprint.[16] Unlike Rawls and Berlin (but in consort with some liberal thinkers, such as William Galston), Catholicism desires a thicker and more substantive (not merely procedural) notion of the human and social good.[17] The common good , with its concomitant notion of a deliberative democracy, impels Catholics in society to cooperate with all men and women of goodwill. Catholic social documents, in the past forty or so years, typically address themselves not only to believers but to all fellow citizens engaged in deliberative democracy. They also, typically, mix genres by including references to biblical warrants and expressions couched in nonrevelatory human, rational argument.

Catholics argue that the common good, as sociologist Philip Selznick has insisted, "is the state of the system, not an attribute of individuals."[18] The common good is an *institutional* reality. It looks to creating the societal conditions to enhance and justly distribute common or public goods. The common good is the institutional face and indispensable font of a society's commitment to distributive and social justice. Even the good of individuals and small groups depends on the societal flourishing of the common good. Although the common good is not the mere additive sum of individual properties, it looks, nonetheless, to the dignity and well-being of individuals. The common good is *personalistic* inasmuch as it redounds back on persons. Selznick captures this same sense when he asks us to think of the common good as profoundly *systemic*—"not reducible to individual attributes or interests, yet *testable* by its contribution to personal well being":

> The common good is served . . . by institutions that provide collective goods, such as education or public safety. The strength or weakness of these institutions is a communal attribute, not an individual one. Furthermore, it is not necessarily in every individual's interest to support such institutions. They may be better off, as individuals, if they can avoid paying taxes for schools or other services they do not use but which are important to society as a whole.
>
> Similarly, a major collective good is social integration. When social integration is measured, the measure will take into account, at least indirectly, individual attitudes, behaviors, opportunities and affiliations. And a connection is likely between personal and social integration. People can live more coherent lives and have more coherent personalities when they belong to coherent social worlds.[19]

As Jacques Maritain argued, the common good is an analogical notion. It is also pluralist in intent. In Maritain's view, humans are always persons in relationship. The *full* common good, in the Catholic theological vision, exists supremely in the communion of all persons with God and with each other in God. Catholic social thought thus rejects any theory that makes the good of a state or nation the highest good or that grants absolute sovereignty to the state.[20] This analogical notion of the common good is antitotalitarian without being antistatist. Human beings are destined to a good that is beyond both civil society and the state. Both civil society and the state have an obligation to respect the person and his or her transcendence. But because the freedom and dignity of persons are achieved in communal relationship with other persons, not in isolation, respect for their freedom and dignity demands support for the many forms of relationship in which personhood is realized: friendships, families, voluntary associations, civil society, politics, and the state. Each has a role to play.

The state, to be sure, has a proper and indispensable role in both defining and enacting the common good. It does not, however, have any monopoly on either definition or enactment. David Hollenbach speaks to this limited yet absolutely indispensable and active role of the state in the furtherance of the common good:

> Government has a limited but nonetheless indispensable role in the pursuit of the common good. Subsidiarity does not mean that a government that governs least governs best. It calls for as much government intervention as necessary to enable the other parts of civil society to contribute to the common good. Government, therefore, does not

> have the responsibility for promoting the full common good of the people, for doing so would lead to massive intervention in spheres such as family life, the arts, education and religion. Each of these sectors of civil society has its own proper contribution to make to the common good, and government must respect and encourage these contributions. But government is responsible for the achievement of that part of the common good that enables society to function as a community of fellow citizens.[21]

Solidarity, Justice, and Subsidiarity

Hollenbach has evoked for us the concept of subsidiarity. It and two other concepts round out the salient background assumptions and essential social lexicon that Catholics tend to bring to social debates about policy: solidarity, justice, and subsidiarity. Subsidiarity is relatively easy to define. It flows from the analogical character of the differing relationships that make for the human flourishing of the person-in-relationship.

The principle of subsidiarity states that the more extensive or larger forms of community such as political society should not replace or absorb those that are smaller but rather should provide help (*subsidium*) to them when they are unable or unwilling to make their own proper contribution to the common good. The government, in these cases, directs, coordinates, restrains, and partially regulates the activities of these other voluntary associations or smaller units "as occasion requires and necessity demands" to make sure that they do contribute to the common good rather than undermine it.[22] It is interesting that this quintessentially Catholic concept of subsidiarity has begun to shed its sectarian provenance as it becomes a "secular" slogan for policies of devolution in the European Union and is adopted more and more by American Evangelical groups active in politics that champion, somewhat one-sidedly, its emphasis on decentralization (while neglecting the crucial role the principle gives to the state in Catholic thought).

Each of the three elements of the triad of subsidiarity, solidarity, and justice is given comparable prominence in the tradition. They are evoked again and again, and they stand at the center of almost all of the standard expositions of Catholic social thought. Even when the main emphases are on the primary concepts of "person" and "the common good," ideas related to justice, subsidiarity, and solidarity almost always find their way back into the heart of the conversation.

It can be argued that solidarity is a key concept that redefines Catholic notions of rights and justice in ways that differ from seemingly cognate notions found elsewhere. Solidarity (a concept much cited in the social documents of Pope John Paul II) is both a moral and a theological virtue. Morally, solidarity is a habitual disposition of mind and heart by which the interdependence of human beings is recognized as both an empirical fact and as a moral demand. Solidarity places on us duties to build up the bonds of relationship and mutuality. The good of persons is attained when they are able to participate in the rich diversity of communal relationships, ranging from those as small as the family to those as large as the nation-state and global interaction. Solidarity, John Paul II says in one place, "is not a feeling of vague compassion or shallow distress at the misfortunes of so many people, both near and far. On the contrary, it is a firm and persevering determination to commit oneself to the common good."[23]

The dominant secular liberal ideologies consign solidarity to an exile or to some Cinderella status. But in Catholic social thought, it plays a crucial theological, moral, and affective role. Theologically, solidarity, though distinct from and less exalted than "love," nevertheless opens us in the direction of love. Solidarity includes the many pale approximations to "love" (*agape*, God's love of solidarity with the created universe; and *caritas*, the love by which we love God in return and love his creation as he does), which are seen as *vestigiae trinitatis* (Saint Augustine's evocation of vestiges of the Trinity). These can be found in relationships of community, sociability, civility and civic friendship, social consciousness, and public spirit. Family, locality, workplace, and random encounters—all serve as testing grounds of solidarity. So also do civic life, politics, and international encounters. Jonathan Boswell reflects on the way solidarity colors almost every other Catholic social concept:

> It is important to realise that complex solidarity in Catholic social thought goes further than a first order descriptive acceptance of humanity as "socially constituted" (as stated almost tritely by some communitarian thinkers). Rather, it is a para-norm for personal life and society. It plainly goes much wider than the "given," "tight," often parochial or conservative groupings of blood, place, memory, religion. As for reading solidarity as simple homogeneity or identity, there lies perhaps the greatest travesty, for its essence is to be unity in diversity, difference not flattened but bridged or mutualized. At almost every turn solidarity in social Catholic terms imparts to these

other values a distinctive character, to the extent that it is not too much to say that without it an understanding of the values of justice, human rights, freedom, subsidiarity etc. in Catholic thought is impossible. Torn away from solidarity, a plausible similarity, perhaps even a superficial equivalence, may exist with understandings of the same terms in other traditions; impelled and contoured by it, however, they take a quite different turn.

> Take the Catholic social interpretations of "freedom," "power-sharing," "subsidiarity" and related ideas. They are emphatically not individualistic. The freedoms to which every person is entitled are to guarantee human dignity, to protect against slavery, above all to make room for growth through responsibilities and relationships. Indefinite "rights-ism" is off bounds. Degrees of freedom are to attach also to associations of the varied forms of sociality, needed for people's development. It was not for nothing that Christian movements worked hard to get this incorporated into some post-war European constitutions. Power is to be diffused, spreading out both vertically (from citizen, through locality or region, to nation state, and supranationally) and horizontally (in terms of a plurality of political, cultural and economic forms). The term "subsidiarity" seeks to capture this idea of power-sharing.[24]

Michael Schuck, similarly, raises up solidarity to stress that even quite divergent views within Catholic social thought (progressive, liberal, neoconservative, and radical) tend to endorse a communitarian perspective:

> In their own ways, each has accented the socially embedded character of human existence, each has insisted that humans are defined by the totality of their relations with other selves. Thus, Catholic conservatives, liberals and radicals have again been joined: none of them has reduced the human person to an unencumbered chooser of autonomous ends. If this communitarian impulse is correct, it explains why Catholic social thinkers, as a whole, have retained a distinct understanding of freedom, equality, rights and justice in the modern world.[25]

The dominant American view attaches a premium to individual liberty while maintaining deep misgivings about any social welfare initiatives.[26] Catholic teaching stresses the reverse combination, giving greater weight to communal bonds. In practice, communitarianism has often been bound up with repressive regimes and can impose conformity on members of the community.[27] From this perspective, institutional Catholicism is often suspect in U.S. policy discussions. But as the McDonoughs point out, at the grassroots level, Catholic communitarianism is less an ideological position than a concern for reinforcing the fabric of social relations and a commitment to ingenuity in problem solving and community participation: "Catholic communitarianism is not a philosophical system but a tacit mutuality articulated."[28]

The Move from Background Assumptions to Policy

There are both prerequisites and obstacles toward turning these five background assumptions into accessible principles for social policy. Policy generation has not, in the past, been the main strong suit of Catholic social thought. "Catholic social thought mainly suffers . . . in contingent thinking about policy."[29] Hollenbach echoes this point: "The strategic moral priorities of the Catholic rights theory are less developed than are its ultimate foundations."[30] Moreover, its relation to policy has been, historically, primarily reactive. This is perhaps best described in the terms chosen by the McDonoughs: "The Catholic church as an interest group appears to have had almost no impact on the formulation of Great Society programs. But it has played an enormous role in the management and evaluation of such programs."[31]

Obstacles to the Move toward Policy

The two principal obstacles to the move toward policy are that (1) the intellectual complexity of the tradition makes easy integration or accessible simplification of its many elements difficult to achieve; and (2) Catholic social thought largely emanates from or gains legitimacy under the sponsorship of the hierarchy. The bishops are, naturally, loathe to move from more universal and perennial principles (the high moral ground) toward contingent and prudential discernments about the "better and concretely feasible" directions and reforms that drive most of secular social policy. Moreover, the bishops are chary about bringing the kinds of political controversies, which are ingredients in struggles over competing policy proposals, into the heart of the church. Let us look for a moment at each of these two obstacles.

With regard to the first obstacle, the complexity of the intellectual tradition: The five background assumptions and other closely cognate notions such as the "preferential option for the poor" and "work as a vocation and participatory way of entering culture and society" remain somewhat abstract, general, quasi-metaphysical, airy.[32] The preferential option for the poor is, arguably, a subset of solidarity and a conclusion flowing from a lexical ordering of human rights that privileges subsistence rights as having a priority as the very preconditions for an effective exercise of moral agency and freedom. But the preferential option also rests on distinctively biblical visions of God's care for the poor and the Christian criteria for undergoing the last judgement as found in Matthew 25. In the end, when it is invoked in Catholic policy documents such as the U.S. bishops' letter on the economy, it is given a secular-sounding rhetorical ring, such as the formulation former New York governor Mario Cuomo used to employ: "The litmus test for the health of any society is the way it treats its poor."

Each of these core and cognate notions is, however, sometimes dense, thick, and diffusely multivalent. Frequently, they are grounded in both theological and secular warrants (which complicates their easy understanding). As a consequence, they lend themselves readily to very divergent interpretations. Subsidiarity, for example, looks in two directions. One emphasis stresses the conservative protection of existing intermediate associations and urges the restriction of governmental intrusion on their life. Another emphasizes the essential and indispensable role of government to help coordinate, regulate, stimulate, and if need be subsidize these associations. The policy implications of each emphasis diverge widely. In part, the second emphasis links subsidiarity to a wider solidarity (called socialization in the social thought of John XXIII) and to the Catholic basic need strategy in its theory of rights. Thus, the American bishops, in their appeals to subsidiarity, come to quite different conclusions about policies for the economy or nuclear weapons than do Michael Novak and his lay Catholic associates, who wrote their own alternate letters of both topics.[33]

A second example flows from the Catholic theory of private property. On the one hand, property ownership is seen as a fundamental human right. On the other, this right is hedged by a social mortgage on property based on the original commonality of all earthly goods in creation. Depending on which face is emphasized, the Catholic doctrine of property has more conservative and more progressive applications. In fact, Catholic social thought has spawned in the past (and probably continues to generate) more reactionary, neoconservative, moderate reformist, liberal, and radical variants.[34]

With regard to the second obstacle, the allergy of the hierarchy to bringing secular conflicts into the heart of the church: Three things are crucial for overcoming the penchant of bishops to remain at the level of appealing generalities and general principles of the moral high road. First is a renewed emphasis on the prophetic mission of the church. This theme has grown in salience since the Second Vatican Council, leading to what some may find as an oxymoron—language among the American bishops about the essentially prophetic role of the episcopacy!

Second, Catholic institutional networks of educators, social workers, service providers, and health care professionals frequently push the bishops to address policy options that affect their clientele and their own social work. Here, one can never underestimate the role of the networks of schools, hospitals, and Catholic charity agencies in impelling the Catholic move toward policy. In these networks, church workers know firsthand the impact that government policy decisions have on their work.

Third, the bishops can find ways to distinguish between the levels of moral authority inherent in firmly grounded theological and relatively perennial moral principles, on the one hand, and the authority that accrues to prudential and specific applications of Catholic moral principles to concrete cases and policy, on the other. The American bishops followed this road in their episcopal letters on nuclear weapons policy and their letter on the U.S. economy:

> We believe that the recommendations [e.g., for a full employment policy, for welfare policy, for measures to halt the loss of family farms, etc.] are reasonable and balanced. In analyzing the economy, we reject ideological extremes and start from the fact that ours is a "mixed economy," the product of a long reform and adjustment. We know that some of our specific recommendations are controversial. As bishops *we do not claim to make these prudential judgments with the same kind of authority that marks our declarations of principle.* But we feel obliged to teach by example how Christians can undertake concrete analysis and make specific judgments on economic issues. *The church's teaching cannot be left at the level of appealing generalities.* [emphasis mine][35]

The bishops hedge any morally binding claims when they move toward policy. In so doing, they try to diffuse extreme controversy as a result of their turn toward policy. They claim for it only contingent and prudential warrants. Elsewhere in the letter, they eschew utopian visions and come closer to an American ethos of policy discussion: "It is in the spirit of the American pragmatic tradition of reform that we seek to continue the search for a more just economy."[36]

Two Prerequisites for Turning Catholic Social Teaching into Policy

Two prerequisites also seem necessary to turn the background assumptions into policy. The first is a church that argues—in modern terms—for its right and competence to speak to policy issues and sees itself as compelled—even by theological considerations—to care about the quality of the structures of society. The Catholic set of institutional arenas, willy-nilly, force the church to deal with issues of social policy and enable it to gain experience and even expertise in the issues of policy. Catholics are very strong in arguing for the need to appeal to mediating principles to translate the biblical vision into a more secular notion of the common good. They can derive these mediating principles, among other sources, from lived experience in church institutions that deal with education, health care, social welfare, housing, and the like. The second prerequisite is a rationale for the turn to policy that suggests the tradition can both enrich and be enriched by this turn. Let us look at each of these.

A Theological Rationale for Addressing Social Policy. Recent Catholic thought has been quite explicit about seeing itself as a legitimate actor in the public arena. Indeed, as Bryan Hehir has argued, since the nineteenth century the church has claimed the right and competence to annunciate its vision for the social order in public debate and discussions in pluralistic societies.[37] At the Second Vatican Council, two documents especially address this issue. The Pastoral Constitution, *The Church in the Modern World* (*Gaudium et Spes*) forthrightly declared that the most eloquent proof of the church's solidarity as a fellow journeyer through history with the entire human family consists in its engaging the world in conversation about the "anxious" questions about current trends in the world.[38] *The Declaration on Religious Freedom* (*Dignitatis Humanae*) makes it a very element of religious liberty that church members can engage (not as proselytizers or as those who can command assent or obedience but as conversation partners in civil society) in public explanations of their church's social teaching and its implications for policy:

> In addition, it comes within the meaning of religious freedom that religious bodies should not be prohibited from freely undertaking to show the special value of their doctrine in what concerns the organization of society and the inspiration of the whole of human activity. Finally, the social nature of man and the very nature of religion afford the right of men freely to hold meetings and to establish

> educational, cultural, charitable and social organizations, under the impulse of their religious sense.[39]

For the Catholic self-understanding, the issues involved in policy discussions contain, irretrievably, a moral, often at times, a religious dimension. Justice movements, discussions and legislation to further justice are not seen as purely secular. They are linked to the church's prophetic mission to announce and enable the Kingdom of God. As the Synod of Bishops of 1971 famously put it: "Action on behalf of justice and participation in the transformation of the world fully appear to us *as a constitutive dimension of the preaching of the gospel*, or, in other words, of the church's mission for the redemption of the human race and its liberation from every oppressive situation."[40] This position contains a strong animus against any attempts to segregate the church from participation in the formulation of the moral aspects of political and social questions and to be relegated to the sacristy.

Here it is important to note the evolution of Catholicism toward a public role of the church during the late nineteenth and early twentieth centuries. In the nineteenth century, besieged in Europe by liberal yet anticlerical governments, the church stood its ground against civil liberties and did not, in any sense, privilege democracy as a form of government. Until the eve of the World War II, Catholic social thought still espoused a version of what it then called "a third way" between socialism and capitalism that envisioned a "corporatist" order. Often, this earlier variant of social Catholicism was seen to have some affinities with fascism. Since World War II, however, the church has shifted ground dramatically. Because the church itself was a major actor in debates about human rights in the United Nations in the aftermath of the war, the Catholic position came to favor forms of social democracy, premised no longer on any especial confessional claims, but on a more "universalistic" appeal, beyond confessional warrants, to modern democratic theory. It appeals to a notion of "civil society" and links its public claims less to direct power moves and more to a cooperative stance within civil society for a public good.[41]

In a similar way, in the American setting, the church underwent massive changes in its view of its role in society (and its view of the world as an arena for churchly action) during the twentieth century. The immigrants who built up American Catholicism came to a setting where anti-Catholicism was coin of the realm. Catholics reacted in two disparate ways. One strand sought to build a separated enclave of Catholic institutions that would act as a buffer, a kind of ghetto, against the values of a more liberal, pluralist (but prejudiced against Catholics, for all its vaunted liberalism!) society.

Another strand (most represented by the so-called Americanists at the time of the turn of the century who sought to accommodate Catholicism to the best values of American democracy) sought to enter fully into public debates about American society and take their place—not with any appeal to sectarian special status or confessionally based arguments, relying on papal authority or biblical text—but by an appeal to "the common good." To be sure, Catholic Americanists attempted to show the affinities between their more "secular" (or, perhaps, better universalistic) positions and Catholic theology. They could appeal to a kind of "worldly" autonomy in God's designs, to doctrines of a dyadic relation between church and state, where the state included its own rightful authority. Often accused of not being "truly American," these more modernist American Catholics often struggled to prove they were more American than any white Anglo-Saxon Protestant. They could not do so by an appeal to the Protestant evangelical language, alien to their own typical language. Instead, they linked up to a more universalistic heritage of human rights: the dignity of the person. The very anti-Catholic biases, so strong in the United States in the nineteenth and early twentieth centuries, forced the church to make its appeals to public policy in a public rather than a sectarian language. Otherwise, it would not gain a hearing.[42]

There is a sense in which the Catholic position on public policy now becomes more paradigmatic for many other religious groups, including Protestant, Jewish, and other groups. Religious voices have legitimacy in policy debates, but only if they can make their case—at least in the public arena—in language that is not sectarian, that does not depend for its authority solely on the Bible or papal pronouncements. Modern Catholicism sees itself, very much, as José Casanova describes it, as a public religion in the modern world.[43] It is *public* inasmuch as it claims its rightful voice and place in debates in civil society. It resists moves to force the sheer privatization of the religious voice or denude it of its citizenlike rights to speak. It is *modern* inasmuch as, with *The Declaration of Religious Freedom*, it fully supports separation of church and state and desanctifies the state as such.

According to *The Declaration*, the proper religious role of the state vis-à-vis religion is not to promote any substantive religion or set of religious ideas (which would hamper human freedom and conscience and which lie beyond the competency of the state to adjudicate) but to promote the kind of religious liberty found in the First Amendment. The freedom asserted in *The Declaration* as a limit on state power is more than just the freedom of the church or individual religious conscience. The document joins its case for religious freedom to the rightful freedom of mediating corporate groups in civil society. There is a juridical as well as moral and theological premise behind *The Declaration*: "The demand is also made that constitutional limits be set to the powers of government in order that there be no encroachment on the rightful freedom of the person and of association."[44]

The church pitches its tent and bets its fortunes on its place in a rightfully constituted sphere of civil society. From that sphere, it claims the same rights and responsibilities as any responsible citizen or group in a pluralist, democratic polity. In that same sphere, it constructs its network of institutions where it rubs shoulders with issues involving education, health care, welfare, and so on and thus gains experience and competence to address these topics. Thus, the will and desire to engage in public policy are present in contemporary Catholicism. But its will and desire are less to impose a separate sectarian vision on a common policy than to demand the right to be one other voice in pluralist debates about the morally and socially good society. As the United States ceases to be a Protestant (or a Christian) society, the new pluralism would seem to call *all* public religions to become modern in this Catholic sense, to find ways to couch their arguments (however much, in original provenance, they stem from a Christian moral vision) in more neutral, more universalist languages and metaphors.

What I have here described is, without much doubt, the normative contemporary Catholic position on Christian engagement in the social order. No theocracy is envisioned. No special privileges are asked. No assumed authority to the church's position is expected. Naturally, like any institution, as a bearer of interests, representatives of the church from time to time "cheat" in the public arena and fall back on earlier and more authoritarian stances. Because these have become, generally, counterproductive in a pluralist democracy, however, such "slips back" are rarer and rarer. In any event, they now lack any intrinsic Catholic ideological justification. The latter rests almost entirely on a view of society as an arena of possible moral good and as a desanctified zone of contestation among groups in civil society working to forge public policy. The church no longer claims to stand above but places itself squarely within civil society—hitching its own privileges to more universal claims for associational life.

A Rationale for the Tradition to Enrich Policy and Be Enriched by It. The bishops suggested in their economic pastoral that the church's teaching can not be left at the level of appealing generalities. In an earlier period,

Catholic moral theory got tested in case studies (casuistry). Concrete cases helped the tradition to sort out conflicting moral claims and to sift through—if not the trade-offs—the hard cases to uncover the crucial priorities or lexical orderings among moral principles. In his book on Catholic human rights theory, Hollenbach notes how Catholic social thought now needs to engage what he calls "a strategic morality"—that is, a synthesis of historical interpretation and basic value commitments.[45] He decries how efforts of the Catholic social theory to somehow stand "above ideology" or "beyond any social system" led to a loss of explicit strategic direction.

Hollenbach's appeal to a "strategic morality" that engages in priority principles for policy forces Catholics into alliances, beyond the church, in seeking the common good. It also assumes that truth, at least for the social order, is not only "ahistorical" or "revelational" but grows out of tested experience and the wisdom of practice. Hence, he is making the case that Catholic social thought not only has something to offer to policy but itself can profit from engagement in more concrete discernments of the possible, the morally good, the better that is achievable. The distinctively Catholic background vision gets concretely mediated not by theology nor revelation nor appeals to the Bible. It gets mediated into policy by political prudence that is widely shared by nonbelievers and forces believers to a certain humility about the deep authoritative nature of their own concrete policy proposals. Like the bishops, they have to make moral distinctions between the binding character of their universal principles and concrete applications of those principles to policy that are decidedly more fallible.

Catholic Policy Proposals: Their Style and Instrumentalities

Almost all of the organizations that generate Catholic public policy initiatives are closely aligned with the hierarchy. Only one American Catholic university, Georgetown, has a specialized program in public policy. Catholicism does not sponsor policy think tanks akin to the Brookings Institution, Cato Institute, American Enterprise Institute, or Heritage Foundation. A few Catholics in more secular policy-formation settings, such as the University of Pennsylvania's John DiIulio, Harvard University's Gary Ornfield, the University of California at Los Angeles's David Hayes-Bautista, and Michael Novak of the American Enterprise Institute seem to draw genuine inspiration or directionality for their policy work from the Catholic social tradition. Yet the lack of a richer ongoing institutional grounding for Catholic public policy dooms it to mainly reactive stances. It largely joins an already constituted "secular" policy conversation more often than it initiates one.

The organizations that make up the relatively finite universe for Catholic generation of policy fall into five categories. The first category includes the National Conference of Catholic Bishops (NCCB) and the United States Catholic Conference (USCC). The USCC serves as a kind of service bureaucracy for the NCCB and, in some departments, specializes in church–world relationships.

The second category includes about thirty state Catholic conferences of bishops that, like the national organization, maintain public policy outreach and lobbying to state governments and legislatures. Several of the state conferences (e.g., those in California, Illinois, Minnesota, New York, and Texas) are important actors in engaging public policy in their state settings. The Arizona Catholic Conference, for example, led a coalition of nonprofits to oppose, successfully, turning over of Arizona's welfare-to-work programs to the for-profit Lockheed-Martin Corporation.[46]

The third category includes nearly a hundred peace and justice offices that are maintained in some dioceses. These offices engage, broadly, in policy and lobbying, although most restrict themselves to educational or activist thrusts.

The fourth category includes lobby and policy arms that serve as modest subunits of national federations of Catholic institutions such as the National Catholic Educational Association, the Catholic Health Association, and Catholic Charities USA. Although legally separately incorporated from dioceses or the USCC, these federations keep in close touch with the USCC. Sometimes, as with Catholic Charities USA with issues of welfare policy or the Catholic Health Association on questions of health care reforms, these federations may take the national lead from the USCC on a given policy issue.

The fifth category includes unofficial lobbies associated with the Catholic community but not connected to the episcopacy. These include Network, which lobbies in Washington, D.C., on issues of welfare, housing, human rights, and global development; the Catholic Campaign for America, whose lobbying focuses on abortion, euthanasia, and educational reform (the Catholic Campaign does not advocate on other issues); and the Catholic League for Civil Rights, which serves as a kind of Catholic equivalent of the Jewish Anti-Defamation League. Other unofficial organizations, such as Pax Christi USA, a Catholic peace group, occasionally lobby on peace and military issues. Pax Christi has been in the forefront of

Catholic lobby efforts to have the United States sign a treaty outlawing soldiers younger than eighteen years old.

By any standards, it is a small universe. Moreover, most of these organizations maintain relatively small staffs, especially in their departments that involve actual lobbying. Almost all are incorporated with 501(c)(3) status as tax-exempt religious or charitable organizations. Congressional restrictions place severe limits on these organizations' lobbying outreach. By law, they may not endorse candidates, be aligned closely to any political party, or devote a "substantial" amount of their resources to lobbying. The legal definition of "substantial" (is it a dollar amount or a proportion of the annual budget?) remains in contention.

The National Conference of Catholic Bishops and United States Catholic Conference

The USCC maintains a Government Liaison Office, with four lobbyists and a director. This office is commissioned to monitor legislation that might affect the financial and legal welfare of the NCBB and the Catholic institutional networks. It also watches closely federal legislation that affects issues of importance for Catholic social teaching. The liaison office looks at forthcoming legislation touching taxes, welfare, immigration (the church's membership includes a very significant new immigration population of Asians and Hispanics), civil rights, education, labor, pro-life concerns, and health.[47]

The smallish Government Liaison Office does not have to do all of its own background research. It can rely on other larger USCC departments—such as the Department of Domestic Social Development, the Pro-Life Department, the Department of International Justice and Peace, the Department of Migration and Refugee Services, and the Department of Education—for ideas and suggestions about both pending legislation and policy directives. No USCC department, however, can sign off on a policy initiative without the explicit approval of the bishops (usually through their Administrative Committee). In that sense, the bishops are, ultimately, responsible for the policy directions taken by the USCC (although they often defer to their service experts). A decided attempt is made in proposals from the USCC staff to the bishops to link their positions on concrete pieces of legislation or debated policy initiatives to elements from the Catholic social teaching. The USCC—unlike some other denominational or religious lobbies—is not an arena for pure policy thinkers with few links to the theological tradition on social thought.[48] Catholic social teaching may remain "our best kept secret" for people in the pews, but it can be no secret for USCC policy professionals who must know it well.

The USCC staff sets out a set of policy priorities each year. Any proposed action must be seen as involving something "substantively important" to the Catholic organizational interests or the social Catholic vision. Over the years, the USCC has stated positions or testified before Congress on a range of issues including abortion, civil rights, communications policy, criminal law, family policy, welfare reform, farm policy, labor legislation (e.g., in strong support of minimum wage legislation), military issues, and foreign policy. Since 1976, every four years, in the year before the presidential elections so as not to seem to be partisan, the NCCB issues a pastoral letter on political responsibility, outlining the range of its concerns pertinent to the upcoming presidential campaign and debates.

Direct lobbying takes many forms. It can involve (1) issuing a position statement, a kind of "white paper," from the conference on an issue (e.g., welfare reform, health care, or immigration policy), which is published and disseminated to congressional staff and governmental officials and through the Catholic network; (2) testifying before congressional committees; and (3) sending letters to government officials (whether in the executive branch or Congress). Such letters to congressional committees can be quite specific in proposing the revised wording or amendments to a bill, to cover a salient Catholic concern.

The USCC's main "strengths" as a policy and lobbying organization lie in its moral authority and the sense that any position taken by it has the backing of the collective bishops. "They know we speak for the bishops," the USCC's John Carr told one scholar.[49] Some other Washington-based religious lobbies lack this tight link to denominational officers. It is not clear for whom they speak. The USCC's strength also lies in the quality of its presentations in position papers, testimony, and letters. The USCC has a long procedural process in place before it comes to any decided position that will gain the backing of the bishops. As a result, its presentations tend to have been hashed out, carefully crafted, and well documented. Another strength is the access many of the USCC staff have (whether directly or through a bishop they call upon) to influential legislators in both political parties.

The main weaknesses of the USCC as a lobbying unit is its relative failure to engage grassroots support for its positions, to mobilize local Catholic groups to write Congress. The NCCB is chary of trying any tactic that might suggest that Catholics represent a single voting bloc. Bishops are quick to deny that they expect the Catholic population to be or become a bloc.[50] By contrast, Jewish or Evangelical lobby groups are often much better at delivering grassroots reaction and the vote.

Secular social science observers tend to give the USCC high marks for its lobbying efforts. Stephen Johnson and Joseph Tamney, in their book *The Political Role of Religion in the United States*, could claim: "The U.S. Catholic Church is the most effective political force advocating the liberal agenda."[51] Conversely, the USCC is also a potent force on some issues not considered part of the liberal agenda (e.g., pro-life issues and family policy). On these and some related issues, the Catholic Church is not perceived by liberals as an ally.

In his study of religious lobby groups in Washington, *Representing God in Washington*, Allen Hertzke gave the USCC high marks for its adeptness at gaining access to congressional offices because of the quality of information provided by its staff:

> This fact, combined with the focused agenda of the Conference, has earned it the envy of both liberal and conservative church groups. One conservative congressional aide, who said he wanted the fundamentalists to be more effective, observed that: "They should take a lesson from the Catholic Conference. For example, on fetal experimentation their staff assistant got in touch with moral theologians and medical scientists to put out a position. They had been thinking about it." On the liberal side, while the bishops joined a number of Protestant lobbies in opposing the MX missile, they were able to argue that their opposition flowed out of their "carefully delineated" position in the Peace Pastoral on nuclear arms. Moreover, none of the liberal church groups has produced a document of comparable length and complexity to the bishops' draft letter on the U.S. economy and it is widely used by liberal Protestants.[52]

U.S. Catholicism is also a major provider of services. Its social message is embodied not just in pastorals or lobbying positions but in the schools and hospitals it runs, the food pantries and homeless shelters it provides, and in its outreach to immigrants and refugees. So another major actor in developing Catholic social policy is Catholic Charities USA, especially in the arena of welfare policy, where historically its influence has been quite strong.

Catholic Charities USA

Catholic Charities USA was founded in 1910 (thus predating the USCC's formation by a decade) and is far and away the largest single nongovernmental provider of social services in the United States. With an annual budget of $2.5 billion, Catholic Charities serves 10.6 million clients a year through emergency services (e.g., food pantries, shelter, and housing assistance); counseling; family, youth, and elderly services (including residential facilities); job training; refugee and immigration assistance; disaster relief; community development; child care; adoption; and prison outreach.

At the national and diocesan levels, Catholic Charities' agencies are separately incorporated as public charitable trusts (not explicitly as religious institutions). They have an organizational autonomy from the USCC and the dioceses. Two-thirds of the Charities budget comes from governmental funds from outsourcing for welfare programs, including municipal, county, state, and federal funds. As a public charitable trust, Charities is bound to a nondiscrimination policy in hiring, staffing, and serving clientele. Seventy percent of its clients are non-Catholic poor people. Since the 1960s, it has opened its doors to all in need from all religions (and none).

Catholic Charities sees its nonproselytizing service to those in need (regardless of creed) as an outgrowth of its own religious mission. The primary way Charities identifies itself as Catholic is through its adherence to the Catholic social tradition, in which it inculcates its staff. Its president, Fred Kammer, has written a widely read book on Catholic social teaching.[53] Charities sees itself, then, not as the whole church but as the social service and advocacy outreach of the church in a pluralist, democratic society. This focus on the church "in the world" "differentiates [and brackets?] the objectives of the church as servant and healer in the world from its full mission of teaching, evangelizing, sanctifying and governing a bonded-faith community."[54]

With a paid staff of 47,532 and a cadre of volunteers and board members numbering 262,622, Catholic Charities reaches out through 1,400 agencies to deliver social services. It commits itself to a threefold mission: direct service to those in need, public policy and advocacy, and the convening of like groups and community organizations. The national service bureaucracy for the Charities' federation, which is located in Alexandria, Virginia, engages in policy formulation, advocacy, and lobbying. With a lobbying staff of 6, it uses its limited resources to focus on priority policy areas. For example, in 2000 its highest priorities (which involved "a leadership in Washington, pressing and proactive, involving research, testimony and active lobbying") focused on the following issues: child care; child welfare; housing, homelessness, and housing counseling; the minimum wage; and the restoration of funding for the Social Services Block Grant. Its secondary priorities (which involved policy formulations and some proactive coalition building and lobbying) focused on children's health insurance, juvenile justice, the Older Americans Act, and the Violence Against Women Act. Its other priorities included attention to an increase for the food stamps program and the development of proposals to continue benefits for the working poor.

The welfare reform act of 1996 involved a wide devolution of federal welfare programs, through block granting, back to the states. The individual states now become an important arena for welfare policy and decisions. Hence, there is a new importance for the network of state Catholic conferences (almost all of which target welfare reform measures for their advocacy efforts). Catholic Charities plays a key role at the state conference level. Its own evolution has moved it to statewide coordination and federation of the separately incorporated diocesan agencies as it competes with other nonprofits and for-profits for outsourced programs and projects (and of course funds!). At the same time, Charities frequently serves as the umbrella organization for other nonprofits in both funding and convening.

Moreover, diocesan Charities agencies often maintain a staff position on public policy. One diocese, Oakland, has an annual breakfast for local political figures focused on the relevance of Catholic social thought for policy. So throughout the Catholic Charities network, there exists a broader band of Catholic policy experts than is found, typically, in the USCC or on a diocesan bishop's staff. At the annual convention of Catholic Charities, a long—several days—open hearing addresses legislative policy across the spectrum of welfare issues. Out of this hearing, national priorities emerge and models of policy initiatives are disseminated. Charities also maintains a weekly Adfax service, which alerts members to legislation pertinent to welfare providers.

Throughout its long history, Catholic Charities USA has been engaged at the municipal, state, and federal levels with the articulation of welfare policy. More than the USCC, it is closely in touch with grassroots groups. A recent, well-received history of the organization and movement could claim: "Catholics have played a critical but largely undocumented role in the evolution of American welfare."[55] As a movement, Catholic Charities began in this country as an attempt by Catholics to care for their own poor and needy (in orphanages, foundling homes, etc.) and then to leverage this position as a service provider to win a voice in local, state, and national policymaking, including gaining access to public funding for its programs. Very soon, officers of Catholic Charities joined local federations of charities (which became, in time, the United Way) and served prominently on city and state welfare boards. By 1909, Catholic social service agencies served as co-organizers of the White House Conference on the Care of Dependent Children and have played analogous roles for all such White House Conferences on family, child care, and welfare issues ever since.

Catholic Charities was a key supporter of the New Deal legislation, especially the provisions for aid to dependent children (ADC) and child welfare services. A Catholic social worker, Jane Hoey (who rose out of the Charities ranks) came to administer the ADC program through its first two decades. Charities actually had much more influence on shaping the Social Security Act of 1934 than did the USCC. It was probably not by chance that the roster of keynote speakers at the 1933 National Charities Convention included President Franklin D. Roosevelt; Frances Perkins, his secretary of labor; Harry Hopkins, his executive assistant; U.S. Postmaster General James Farley; and New York's Senator Robert Wagner.

In the context of the War on Poverty of the 1960s (inspired in part by the former Catholic Worker member Michael Harrington's book *The Other America*), Catholic Charities agencies took major steps to reconfigure themselves as "justice" workers, committed to advocacy as well as service to the poor, irrespective of race or creed.[56] But as early as its 1912 meeting, the National Conference on Catholic Charities was pressing the importance of preventing poverty, as against only giving relief.[57] Poverty, not welfare, was the primary problem. Charities' slice of the nonprofit welfare sector increased dramatically during those years, especially after federal regulations in 1969 strongly encouraged state welfare agencies to purchase services for ADC families from private nonprofits such as Catholic Charities. When a further move toward outsourcing of government social service programs took place in the 1980s, Catholic agencies once again expanded their budgets and programs. And they moved into new areas, such as low-cost housing.

Throughout its history, Catholic Charities USA (mirroring the Catholic theory of subsidiarity) has also always championed a public–private partnership that stresses the role of private agencies as intermediaries (providing human contact, room for flexibility and experimentation, and community building) between the resources of the state and the distress of the poor. Yet it also stresses the public obligation to care for those in true need and the government's inalienable role to contribute to the common good. Charities finds itself with the dilemma of both opposing the total secularization of charity and its simultaneous and deliberate accommodation to the emergence of the modern welfare state.

We can now turn to a brief rehearsal of the Catholic policy efforts before and after the passage of the Personal Responsibility and Work Opportunity Reconciliation Act of 1996. My main concern is to show (1) what moves the USCC and Catholic Charities USA took to contest, amend the legislation, or provide alternative policy proposals for the 1996 act; (2) how these moves can be seen as policy consequences of the background view of the human person and society in Catholic social thought; and (3) how, in its monitoring of welfare reform, Catholic social thought returns to the table with an agenda based on its distinctive tradition of social thought.

Catholicism and Welfare Policy: Through the Lens of Welfare Reform

In a sense, Catholics already began to engage the welfare reform debate in a new way in 1986 in the bishops' economic pastoral letter, *Economic Justice for All*. Paragraphs 186–214 of that document dealt with guidelines to treat the problem of structural poverty. Note that the bishops define the underlining problem as one of *poverty* rather than one of *welfare dependency*. The seventh and final guideline in that section of the pastoral called for "a thorough reform of the nation's welfare and income support programs." In the brief discursus on welfare reform in the document, the bishops suggest two major changes: (1) They call for national eligibility standards and uniform minimum benefit levels for recipients of Aid to Families with Dependent Children (AFDC), in order to eliminate state-by-state disparities, unrelated to the level of real need in low-income families; and (2) the bishops call for a redesigning of public assistance programs to "assist recipients, wherever possible, to become self-sufficient through gainful employment."[58]

Under the rubric of welfare reform, the 1986 pastoral letter gives several caveats. A work strategy to overcome dependency would need a serious job-creation program when work was lacking and also need to provide services for job training, counseling, and child care. It would also have to address the so-called notch effects such that entering the workforce actually penalized those who had been on assistance. "Under current rules, people who give up welfare benefits to work in low-paying jobs, soon lose their Medicare benefits."[59] In a throwaway line of great common sense, the bishops note: "Individuals should not be worse off economically when they get jobs than when they rely on public assistance."[60] Not every recourse to work, the bishops suggest, addresses the root problems of structural or personal poverty.

Between 1988 and 1992, when President Bill Clinton famously promised "to end welfare as we know it," the welfare policy debate focused more and more on issues-of-family values (e.g., does welfare discourage intact families and reward out-of-wedlock pregnancies?); welfare dependency; the need for a work obligation and not just an incentive to work; and issues of teen and welfare pregnancies. In 1994, the new Republican Congress moved toward its equally famous Contract with America, which put welfare reform at the top of the agenda. To the bishops and Catholic policymakers, some of the voices in the welfare policy debate seemed reductionist in their appeal to punitive measures as a prod for "rational actor" responses.

In tying welfare dependence entirely to the economic incentives and arguing that taking those incentives away would lead to work responsibility for all welfare dependents, these voices seemed to Catholic Charities' caseworkers to oversimplify the issue. Some seemed too willing to sacrifice innocent children and other needy people, in the short run, to gain a long-term breaking of the cycle of dependency and poverty. There was a kind of utilitarian argument fueling the debate that stood in opposition to Catholic core notions of dignity and rights. Rigid time limits seemed to offer little flexibility or attention to the different kinds of people who depend on welfare. Nor was enough attention being given by many of the welfare reform proponents to the commitment of new resources for job preparation for those who would be running up against newly imposed time limits. Some provisions being suggested (e.g., a family cap on assistance, refusal to provide welfare for children of teen age mothers or of legal immigrants) struck many Catholic policymakers as incentives to abortion or just downright punitive.

In what almost amounted to a barrage, Catholic voices were among the first to join the welfare reform debate. Merely to list the documents and actions generated in a two-year flurry period tells part of the story. Catholic Charities USA published its eighteen-page white paper, *Transforming the Welfare System* on January 24, 1994, five months before President Clinton unfurled his own welfare reform proposals of 1994.[61] In December 1994, the bishops of Connecticut wrote a short piece, "Welfare Reform and Basic Human Needs," in which they conceded the need for welfare reform but insisted that "the end result must not harm the vulnerable." The Connecticut bishops insisted on the legitimacy of need as a moral claim to support. They also stressed the government's proper role in furthering the common good. Concern for the common good could not be left only to the churches and private charities.[62]

In early January 1995, Bishop John Ricard of Baltimore, in his capacity as chair of the NCCB's Domestic Policy Committee, sent a letter to the House Ways and Means Committee, Senate Finance Committee, and Department of Health and Human Services expressing his objections to the Personal Responsibility Act, then being discussed in Congress. Many of the salient Catholic themes in the welfare policy debate emerge with this early testimony of Ricard. He appeals to the credibility of the Catholic experience "as the largest non-public provider of human services to poor families." He stated the nub of the debate as he saw it:

> We are not defenders of the welfare *status quo* which too often relies on bureaucratic approaches, discourages work and breaks up families. However, we oppose abandonment of the federal government's role in helping families overcome poverty and meet their children's basic needs. Genuine welfare reform should rely on incentives more than harsh penalties, for example, denying needed benefits to children born to mothers on welfare can hurt the children and pressure their mothers toward abortion.[63]

In his statement of the aims of welfare reform—a formula that soon became a kind of slogan throughout the Catholic network—Ricard says that the Catholic Church sought the following aims in welfare reform. It sought a welfare reform that supports family life, encourages and rewards work, preserves a safety net for the vulnerable, builds public–private partnership to overcome poverty, and invests in human dignity. The policy target, argued Ricard, "ought to be poverty, not poor families."

Another refrain in Ricard's testimony echoes again and again in the Catholic policy papers. It responds to proponents of welfare reform who would take government entirely out of welfare and relegate welfare to the nonprofit and religious sectors: "Private and religious efforts to serve those in need are being severely stretched. They cannot and should not be seen as a substitute that promotes effective public–private partnerships in overcoming poverty and dependency."

Ricard opposed rigid time limits and called for a targeted, flexible policy in place of attempts to get a policy where "one size fits all." He supported a move toward responsibility and work but cautioned that what must be sought is "work with wages and benefits that permit a family to live in dignity." Finally, he attacked the punitive approach of some welfare reformers. "We cannot support punitive approaches that target immigrants and propose to take away the minimal benefits they now receive, such as emergency medical care and nutrition programs, especially those targeted to pregnant women."

In February of 1995, the bishops of Florida, in their turn, wrote a letter, "Promoting Meaningful Welfare Reform," addressed to state and federal officials.[64] In March 1995, the USCC published a nine-page bishops' statement, "Moral Principles and Policy Priorities for Welfare Reform," which mainly re-echoed the points in Ricard's testimony and took over his formulation of the aims of reform. "Moral Principles and Policy Priorities" links these aims to the Catholic principles of subsidiarity, solidarity, the option for the poor, human dignity and the common good, and the value of work. Again, in this document the refrain was heard: "as the largest nonpublic provider of human services to poor families."[65]

Throughout 1995, Catholic voices continued to engage in the welfare debate. Catholic Charities USA president Kammer testified before the House Ways and Means Committee with an echo of Ricard: "Proposals which hurt the children without necessarily changing the behavior of parents cannot gain Catholic support." The family cap, he suggested, hurts children and encourages abortion. Private charity could not and should not replace the government's rightful role. Subsidiarity does not mean that the government steps out of care for the common good. "We cannot support proposals that would deny aid to parents for whom there are no jobs."[66]

Meanwhile, welfare reform measures were also moving forward at the state level. Boston's Bernard Cardinal Law reproached Massachusetts governor William Weld's proposal to eliminate any benefits to teenage mothers. In a pastoral response addressing the Catholic Alliance (a wholly owned subsidiary of the Christian Coalition, seen as a kind of cognate Catholic branch), Law faulted attempts to turn Catholics into a visible voting bloc. He also noted that Catholics needed to avoid this group because the Christian Coalition held positions on welfare reform at deep variance with Catholic social teaching.[67] At the state level, Catholic Charities agencies began to work toward increases from the states in supplemental state programs for food stamps and aid to immigrant children and to block more narrowly construed welfare options in the federal bill.

The two major documents that seem to have guided most of the Catholic voices in the policy debate are the Catholic Charities paper

Transforming the Welfare System and the USCC's statement "Moral Principles and Policy Priorities for Welfare Reform." I have found it helpful, in reading through this material, to make a list from these disparate documents of what the Catholic voices were *for* in the welfare debates; what they were *against*, and what *alternatives* they offered to the bill. In the next subsections, I briefly give the positions I found in the documents and policy papers from Catholic sources on these three points.

What Catholic Voices Were For in the Welfare Reform Bill

Catholic voices wanted to see six things come out of the welfare reform bill. First, in general, they were for welfare reform that called for more responsibility on the part of welfare recipients and that reduced waste, corruption, and fraud.

Second, they were for an emphasis on work, with the caveat that work must "be judged by standards of justice in wages, fair expectations and support for family life." As the USCC's "Moral Principles and Policy Priorities" put it: "Those who can work ought to work. Employment is the expected means to support a family and make a contribution to the common good."[68]

Third, they advocated a new kind of language that called for responsibility and accountability. But as the Catholic Charities white paper put it: "We must be willing to build into our welfare system responsibility and accountability on the part of *both* the recipient *and* the giver of public assistance."[69] Fourth, they were for policies that promised to reduce welfare dependency and move people into productive participation both in work and in civil society.

Fifth, they favored new flexibility in the welfare system. They were, at least, not in principle against all forms of devolution schemes to move welfare back to the states, provided federal responsibilities for a safety net were maintained and some federal oversight continued.

Sixth, they favored the new openness to partnership with churches and nonprofits, as long as this was not seen as an unrealistic move to ask them to shoulder a burden of welfare they could not sustain. They were in favor of tax benefits for charitable choice for charities that work with the poor. As Kammer put it in his testimony to Congress: "The religious groups and non-profits that shoulder the bulk of charity and services to the poor have all indicated that the magnitude of cuts contemplated in the Personal Responsibility Act would bankrupt their institutions."[70]

What the Catholic Voices Were Against in the Welfare Reform Bill

Catholic voices were against seven matters regarding the Personal Responsibility Act. First, they were against couching the debate as primarily an issue of welfare rather than a larger context of often structural poverty. "Targeting poverty and not just welfare dependency," a slogan taken from the USCC's "Moral Principles and Policy Priorities," was much bandied about.

Second, they were decidedly against sacrificing innocents (especially children) in the short term, for any long-term hopes of achieving an antidependency, work-based strategy. On the issues of family caps and teenage mother exclusions (which the new welfare law allows states to adopt), the bishops were adamant in their opposition. They cited the potential harm these measures might cause to innocent children, both those who might be aborted and those who would be deprived of human necessities because of the policy innovations. "No attempt to justify them in terms of long-term social benefits (such as fighting the root cause of dependency by changing the social landscape of behavioral expectations) could ever over-ride those moral objections to the short-term human impact of such policies."[71] "Do no harm to children or other innocent humans" was the moral maxim. "Society has a responsibility to meet the needs of those who cannot care for themselves, especially young children."[72] It may be that religious voices have a major role in policy debates (usually fueled by a utilitarian cost–benefit calculus) to bring us back to deontological principles. There are some absolute moral prohibitions, even in politics. In the Catholic case, the roots for the prohibition of experimenting with the welfare children is the Catholic theory of human dignity as linked to subsistence rights and its preferential option for the poor.

Third, they were against a one-sided employment strategy, not balanced by an income maintenance strategy. "Maintaining a social safety net" was the slogan. As the Catholic Charities' white paper explained in detail, AFDC recipients could be divided into recognizable groups, one of which consists of the approximately "30 percent who are chronic or persistent users. Many of these long-term drug and alcohol users have severe learning disabilities or serious health problems. Policies or programs of intervention must take into account the differences."[73] To be blunt, some welfare recipients were very unlikely candidates (at least in the short run) for the workforce. Work is a legitimate criterion for a welfare policy, but genuine human need has its legitimate moral claim as well. Indeed, the bishops seemed outraged that, for the first time since American welfare policy evolved in the post–Civil War period, need had no persistent legitimate moral claim.[74]

Fourth, they were against rigid work requirements (which might penalize, for example, education as a route out of welfare) and rigid time requirements as a "one size fits all category." Here the Catholics were resonating with research done by Mary Jo Bane before she became an assistant secretary of health and human services in the Clinton cabinet. Her research showed a cycle by which welfare recipients were not all simply "long termers" or "short termers." Many single mothers try to make "work exits," only to find themselves back onto the rolls. Research data showed how hard it is to make work exits stick. She argued that it is not realistic to expect labor markets entirely to replace government programs as reliable sources of income for all single mothers with children.[75] Bane, a Catholic, resigned from the Clinton administration the day Clinton signed the Personality Responsibility and Work Opportunity Act of 1996 into law.

Fifth, they were against family caps. Indeed, they succeeded in having them removed as mandates from the final bill.

Sixth, they fought (successfully it turns out) provisions of the original bill that would have block granted nutrition dollars from the Women and Infant Children (WIC) nutrition program for pregnant and recent mothers and babies or which would have removed Medicaid coverage from families forced off AFDC (or, as it is now called in its time-capped form, temporary assistance to needy families, TANF). Seventh, they were against penalizing those who sought work and, for structural reasons, could not find it.

Alternatives for Welfare Reform Suggested by Catholic Policymakers

Catholic policymakers suggested four alternatives to welfare reform proposals. First, Kammer, in his testimony before the House Ways and Means Committee, expressed surprise at the lack of child care support, which would seem necessary to get welfare mothers into the workforce. The bishops sought increased child care funding. The final bill reflected this consensus, which Catholics shared with a broad range of nonprofit groups.

Second, they suggested that real welfare reform would demand educational resources, job skill training, and transitional help. The Catholic Charities white paper called for "tailored investments in families," which would include a series of initiatives, including better child care support and an expanded earned-income tax credit so that work really does pay. Both the USCC and the Charities documents evoke the Catholic notion of community and solidarity and propose that we think of welfare as part of a "social contract" in which government, as well as the private sector (including industry), become "partners" with recipients.

Third, they suggested—in opposing amendments to the contrary—that welfare-to-work clients be paid the same minimum wage the law enacts for other employment. They wanted to avoid a situation whereby people in transition from welfare to work brought unfair wage competition to the already working poor. Indeed, they suggested increasing the minimum wage.

Fourth, they suggested the need for direct inter personal contacts (beyond bureaucratic paternalistic schemes) and mentoring of welfare recipients. As "Moral Principles and Policy Priorities" put it: "Increased accountability and incentives should be tailored to a particular family's needs and circumstances, not one size fits all requirements. Top down reform with rigid national rules cannot meet the needs of a population as diverse as poor families.[76]

After the Welfare Bill Passed

The welfare reform debate did not simply go away after the 1996 bill passed. The Catholic Charities network, especially, and state Catholic conferences went to state legislatures and county and municipal governments to provide a "softer welfare landing" by extending deadlines, choosing more generous options offered to them by the federal legislation, and offering vouchers and noncash assistance for needy families. At the state level, Catholic Charities worked for the following options:

1. *Time limits*: Federal law allows recipients to receive assistance for up to sixty months of their lifetimes, but states may set shorter limits. Catholic Charities agencies urged states to adopt the maximum time limit and to set aside state money to aid families in need of long-term help. Thirty-seven states have adopted the more permissive sixty-month limit.
2. *Work requirements*: Federal law requires ablebodied welfare recipients to work at least part time within two years. Catholic Charities urged states to allow hours spent in training to fulfill work requirements.
3. *Child care*: States that continue their previous investment in child care provision are eligible for full federal subsidies. Charities urged states to provide child care subsidies to families for the allowable two years after employment.

4. *Waivers*: Charities recommended that states request waivers of time limits in areas with an unemployment rate above 10 percent.

Among the lobbying efforts at state levels undertaken by Catholic Charities or state Catholic conferences was a bill (drafted by Catholic Charities of Maine) passed by the Maine legislature that enables the Department of Human Services in Maine to provide TANF benefits, using state money, after the five-year federal time limit has passed. Catholic Charities conferences in Maryland and Kansas were successful in lobbying for state versions of the earned-income tax credit. In Maryland, Catholic Charities was also instrumental in passage of a bill requiring the state to reinvest all its welfare savings back into the TANF program. In California, the Charities agencies did a welfare reform monitoring project in five metropolitan areas to track the increased populations coming to food pantries and soup kitchens after the passage of the welfare reform. Through strategic press conferences announcing the results and lobbying efforts, they gained passage of a California supplemental food stamp program.[77]

Any visitor to the Websites of state Catholic conferences, local Catholic Charities agencies, and Catholic Charities USA will find page after page of welfare reform initiatives aimed at restoring, minimizing, or finding alternatives for the 1996 welfare reform bill. Charities sponsors a national welfare monitoring project that tracks, through member agencies, the increases in clientele for emergency services and its relation to being removed from the welfare rolls. As they continue to use their voices in the welfare debate, the USCC and Catholic Charities can be expected to root policy proposals in the background assumptions of Catholic social thought: human dignity; human rights and subsistence as a right; the common good and the government's indispensable role in defining, enabling, and producing it; subsidiarity and its impact on the sense of public-private partnerships in working for the common good; and the preferential option for the poor. The Catholic agencies link these background assumptions to policy principles that can be translated into a larger discussion in a pluralistic society.

In his book *Catholic Social Teaching and United States Welfare Reform*, Thomas Massaro links the Catholic policy initiatives to the Catholic theological anthropology of the human and society. He suggests that policy principles, originally rooted in the Catholic social tradition, can indeed (if not without remainder, at least substantively) be translated into more secular warrants that might garner a broader overlapping consensus between Catholics and other citizens. He suggests the following "secularly" translated Catholic principles or maxims for welfare policy:

1. Focus on the struggle against poverty itself, not merely against welfare dependency.
2. Acknowledge insuperable barriers to employment where they exist and compensate for them by some form of a safety net or job-creation program.
3. Respect some absolute moral prohibitions for politics—especially, do no harm to the innocent poor, whether children or those who are victims of structural unemployment.
4. Recognize both "carrots" and "sticks" (incentives and obligations), without subscribing to a reductionist view of the human person as simply a rational actor maximizing economic rewards.
5. Avoid fostering the demonization or marginalization of recipients of public assistance (i.e., respect their human dignity and call them to justice as participation in work and civic life).
6. Social policy cannot be successful in ushering people to self-sufficiency unless it commits adequate resources to empowering low-income citizens to move into work on reasonable terms. An underlying principal must be that welfare reform is not primarily punitive or principally a cost-saving devise but a sincere effort to move from welfare dependency to sustainable work.
7. The well-being of family life deserves special policy attention because children represent the future of the nation.
8. There is no practical substitute for the federal government in serving as the primary conduit of social assistance to low-income families.[78]

As long as Catholic Charities USA remains the "largest, non-governmental provider of social services" in the United States, some variant of these policy principles will continue to be urged at federal, state, county, and municipal levels. Whether Catholics will succeed in injecting a more communitarian ethos into the U.S. policy discussion, of course, remains to be seen. But it strikes me that more than their success or failure in working for any given policy issue is at stake. Catholic public policy formation presents an important case of a relatively conservative religious group that (despite some anomalies) has found a way to operate as a public-citizen church in the modern world.

Notes

1. Thomas Massaro, *Catholic Social Teaching and United States Welfare Reform* (Collegeville, Minn.: Liturgical Press, 1998).

2. Cited in R.W. Apple, "His Battle Now Lost: Moynihan Still Cries Out," *New York Times*, Aug. 2, 1996, A16.

3. This list can be found in Thomas Reese, *A Flock of Shepherds: The National Conference of Catholic Bishops* (Kansas City: Sheed & Ward, 1992), 187–88.

4. For the history, Dorothy Brown and Elizabeth McKeowun, *The Poor Belong to Us: Catholic Charities and American Welfare* (Cambridge, Mass.: Harvard University Press, 1997).

5. Joseph Cardinal Bernadin, *Consistent Ethic of Life* (Kansas City: Sheed & Ward, 1988).

6. Peter McDonough and Josephina Figueira-McDonough, "The Evolution of Catholic Family Policy," unpub. research proposal, Arizona State University, Department of Political Science, 35.

7. For several reliable introductions to Catholic social thought, see David Hollenbach, *Claims in Conflict* (New York: Paulist Press, 1979); Jean Calvez, *The Church and Social Justice* (Chicago: Regnery, 1961); Donal Dorr, *Option for the Poor* (Maryknoll, N.Y.: Orbis, 1992); Michael J. Schuck, *That They Be One: The Social Teaching of the Papal Encyclicals* (Washington, D.C.: Georgetown University Press, 1991).

8. For the citation from John Paul II's *On Social Concerns* 41, cf. *Catholic Social Thought: The Documentary Heritage*, ed. David O'Brien and Thomas Shannon (Maryknoll, N.Y.: Orbis, 1992).

9. Thomas Hoppe, "Human Rights," in *A New Dictionary of Catholic Social Thought*, ed. Judith Dwyer (Collegeville, Minn.: Liturgical Press, 1994). The concept of a Catholic appeal to needs is developed in William O'Neil, "Commonweal or Woe? The Ethics of Welfare Reform," *Notre Dame Journal of Law, Ethics, and Public Policy* 11, no. 2 (1997): 487–505.

10. *Pacem in Terris*, in *Catholic Social Thought*, 137–57.

11. For a more "secular" public policy argument, cognate to the Catholic case, to subsistence needs as grounding rights, see Henry Shue, *Basic Rights: Subsistence, Affluence and U.S. Foreign Policy* (Princeton, N.J.: Princeton University Press, 1996.

12. David Hollenbach, "The Common Good," in *New Dictionary of Catholic Social Thought,* 193.

13. Mater et Magistra 60, "Christianity and Social Progress," in *Catholic Social Thought*, 146.

14. *Pacem in Terris*, in *Catholic Social Thought*, 141.

15. John Stuart Mill, *On Liberty*, ed. John Gray (New York: Oxford University Press, 1991), 72.

16. Isaiah Berlin, "Two Concepts of Liberty," in *Four Essays on Liberty* (New York: Oxford University Press, 1969), 118, 122; John Rawls, *Political Liberalism* (New York: Columbia University Press, 1993), 99–107.

17. William Galston, *Liberal Purposes: Goods, Virtues, and Diversity in the Liberal State* (New York: Cambridge University Press, 1991).

18. Philip Selznick, *The Moral Commonwealth* (Berkeley: University of California Press, 1992), 537.

19. Selznick, *Moral Commonwealth*, 537; cf. John A. Coleman, S.J., "A Common Good Primer," *Dialog* 34 (1995): 249–54.

20. For a denial of the sovereignty of the state, cf. Jacques Maritain, *Man and the State* (Chicago: University of Chicago Press, 1951), 194–95.

21. Hollenbach, "Common Good," 195–96.

22. The citation from *Quadragesimo Anno*, "Forty Years Afterwards," no. 80 in *Catholic Social Thought*, 60.

23. John Paul II, *Sollicitudo Rei Socialis*, "On Social Concern," no. 40 in *Catholic Social Thought*, 421.

24. Jonathan Boswell, "Catholic Social Thinking: Is It Underdeveloped?" unpub. ms. for Cambridge University Conference on the Future of Catholic Social Teaching, 9–10.

25. Michael Schuck, "Modern Catholic Social Thought," in *New Dictionary of Catholic Social Thought*, 630–31.

26. Cf. Hugh Heclo, "General Welfare and Two American Traditions," *Political Science Quarterly* 101 (1986): 179–96.

27. Herbert McClosky and John Zaller, *The American Ethos: Public Attitudes Toward Capitalism and Democracy* (Cambridge, Mass.: Harvard University Press, 1984).

28. McDonough and Figueira-McDonough, "Evolution of Catholic Family Policy," 12.

29. Boswell, "Catholic Social Thinking," 8.

30. Hollenbach, *Claims in Conflict*, 187.

31. McDonough and Figueira-McDonough, "Evolution of Catholic Family Policy," 7.

32. For the preferential option for the poor, see Donal Dorr, *Option for the Poor*, 1–7, 193–95; 376–77. On Catholic concepts of work as a vocation, cf. William May, "The Theology of Work" in *New Dictionary of Catholic Thought*, 991–1002, and John Paul II's encyclical "On Human Work" in *Catholic Social Thought*, 352–92.

33. The American bishops' letters on nuclear weapons and economic justice are in *Catholic Social Thought*, 492–571, 572–680; Michael Novak, *Moral Clarity in the Nuclear Age* (Nashville: Nelson, 1983; Michael Novak, *Freedom with Justice: Catholic Social Thought and Liberal Institutions* (San Francisco: Harper & Row, 1984).

34. I treat some of this range in my "Neither Liberal nor Socialist," in *One Hundred Years of Catholic Social Thought*, ed. John Coleman (Maryknoll, N.Y.: Orbis, 1991), 25–42.

35. "Economic Justice for All," no. 20 in *Catholic Social Thought*, 576.

36. "Economic Justice for All," no. 131 in *Catholic Social Thought*, 609.

37. Bryan Hehir, "The Right and Competence of the Church in the American Case," in *One Hundred Years of Catholic Social Thought*, 55–71.

38. *Gaudium et Spes*, no. 3 in *Catholic Social Thought,* 167.

39. *Dignitatis Humanae*, in *Renewing the Earth*, ed. David O'Brien and Thomas Shannon (Garden City, New York: Doubleday, 1977, p. 295.

40. *Renewing the Earth*, p. 391.

41. I treat this evolution in my "Neither Liberal nor Socialist."

42. For the evolution in American Catholicism in attitudes toward the state and public policy, cf. David O'Brien, *Public Catholicism* (New York: Macmillan, 1989).

43. José Casanova, *Public Religions in the Modern World* (Chicago: University of Chicago Press, 1994).

44. *Renewing the Earth*, 297.

45. Hollenbach, *Claims in Conflict*, 189.

46. For the new competition (or threat?) to religious and nonreligious, nonprofit welfare providers by for-profit providers, cf. William P. Ryan, "The New Landscape for Nonprofits," *Harvard Business Review*, Jan.–Feb. 1999, 127–36.

47. For a treatment of the USCC and policy, cf. Reese, *Flock of Shepherds*, 187–224.

48. For a complaint about theologically untutored policy workers driving some Protestant denominational policy in the United Methodist Church, cf. Robert Bellah, et.al., *The Good Society* (New York: Knopf, 1991), 196.

49. Reese, *Flock of Shepherds*, 210.

50. A rejection of trying to make Catholics into a voting block is found in Bernard Cardinal Law, "Christian Coalition's Catholic Alliance," *Origins* 25, no. 35 (1996): 574–77.

51. Stephen Johnson and Joseph Tamney, eds., *The Political Role of Religion in the United States* (Boulder, Colo.: Westview Press, 1986), 223.

52. Allan Hertzke, *Representing God in Washington: The Role of Religious Lobbies in the American Polity* (Knoxville: University of Tennessee Press, 1988), 81.

53. Fred Kammer, *Salted with Fire* (New York: Paulist Press, 1995).

54. Melanie diPietro, "Organizational Overview," in *Catholic Charities USA: Who Do You Say We Are?—Perspectives on Catholic Identity in Catholic Charities* (Alexandria, Va.: Catholic Charities USA, 1998), 29.

55. The well-being of family life deserves special policy attention because children represent the future of the nation.

56. Brown and McKeown, *Poor Belong to Us*, 11.

57. Edward Ryle, "Catholic Charities: The American Experience," *Catholic Charities USA,* Jan.–Feb., 1987, 14 (the whole two-part article, pp. 8–24, is a good overview of the history and organizational development of Catholic Charities USA).

58. Cited in Brown and McKeown, *Poor Belong to Us*, 197.

59. "Economic Justice for All," no. 210 in *Catholic Social Thought*, 625.

60. "Economic Justice for All," no. 211 in *Catholic Social Thought*, 626.

61. *Transforming the Welfare System* (Alexandria, Va.: Catholic Charities USA, 1994).

62. "Connecticut Bishops' Welfare Reform and Basic Human Needs," *Origins* 24, no. 26 (1994): 435.

63. Bishop John Ricard, "The Factors of Genuine Welfare Reform," *Origins* 24, no. 24 (1995): 564.

64. Bishops of Florida, "Promoting Meaningful Welfare Reform," *Origins* 24, no. 27 (1995): 610–12.

65. "Moral Principles and Policy Priorities for Welfare Reform," *Origins* 24, no. 34 (1995): 673–77.

66. Fred Kammer, "Why Some Welfare Reform Proposals Can Backfire," *Origins* 24, no. 34 (1995): 565–70.

67. Bernard Cardinal Law, "Christian Coalition's Catholic Alliance," *Origins* 24, no. 34 (1995): 574.

68. "Moral Principles and Policy Priorities," 6–7.

69. *Transforming the Welfare System*, 12.

70. Kammer, "Why Some Welfare Reform Proposals Can Backfire," 567.

71. Massaro, *Catholic Social Teaching and United States Welfare Reform*, 59.

72. "Moral Principles and Policy Priorities," 5.

73. *Transforming the Welfare System*, 7.

74. For the history of U.S. welfare policy and its earlier recognition of need as a moral claim, cf. Theda Scocpol, *Protecting Soldiers and Mothers: The Political Ori-*

gins of Social Policy in the United States (Cambridge, Mass.: Harvard University Press, 1992).

75. Mary Jo Bane and David Ellwood, *Welfare Realities: From Rhetoric to Reform* (Cambridge, Mass.: Harvard University Press, 1994); Mary Jo Bane, "Poverty, Welfare and the Role of the Churches," *America*, Dec. 4, 1999, 8–11.

76. "Moral Principles and Policy Priorities," 4.

77. See *Responding to Welfare Reform: A Report from Catholic Charities USA* (Alexandria, Va.: Catholic Charities USA, 1998).

78. For these principles, see Massaro, *Catholic Social Teaching and United States Welfare Reform*, 181–88.

9

Charitable Choice: Bringing Religion Back into American Welfare

Stanley W. Carlson-Thies

According to the most influential metanarratives in American social policy history, religion was virtually irrelevant to the development of American welfare in the twentieth century. In crude terms, the main story line is that public welfare replaced religion—for good. The chief alternative story agrees that religion was replaced—but for bad. More carefully, the mainstream story portrays a "quasi-welfare state" supplanting the fragmentary assistance offered by local sectarian, voluntary, and municipal programs, and measures welfare progress by the growth of government provision at the expense of private and religious action.[1] The competing interpretation regards the creation of the government welfare system to constitute, in Marvin Olasky's terms, "the tragedy of American compassion," because effective, personal, and spiritual assistance was replaced by bureaucratic programs unable to address the deepest needs of the poor.[2] Although the two stories evaluate the outcome differently, they agree about the disappearance or irrelevance of religion to American public welfare.

But religion did not vanish. Care for the poor in twentieth-century America cannot rightly be understood without taking into account many roles of religion: providing a wide range of services outside the government welfare system, delivering government-funded services, advocating for changes in welfare policy, and raising questions about how much and what kind of assistance is offered. Yet the metanarratives are right to this extent: As the U.S. welfare state was constructed during the century, religion was marginalized, privatized; it became "boxed-in,"[3] sidelined. It did not disappear, but it was no longer a major player.

However, by the end of the century, a prominent role for religion was being revived. If in the early decades the growth of government involvement was applauded as a way to overcome the localism, moralism, and discretionary nature of sectarian and private welfare, by the last decade many were welcoming an expanded role for religion precisely to reintroduce a personal, tailored, and value-centered approach. In its new role, though, religion would not be an alternative to government welfare but rather a supplement and even a partner. Federal welfare reform legislation included a specific measure, the Charitable Choice provision, designed to make faith-based programs part of the mix of services offered by the public sector to families in need. Religion was being de-privatized, becoming explicitly part of the nation's public welfare system.[4] It is this more complicated story of religion and American welfare that I sketch here.

The Trajectory of Twentieth Century American Welfare

Notwithstanding the rhetoric of some latter-day politicians and policy thinkers, there never was a period in American history in which all care for the poor was provided by the churches. From the early days of European settlement, government played a role; indeed, in the colonial era local government was the main actor in the Poor Law system of assistance carried over from England. However, lacking a sharp division between church and state, even within this system religion was important; in the South, for instance, Anglican clergy administered public relief.[5] And as the new American nation took form after the Revolution and then matured, religious figures and organizations, along with other nongovernmental actors, assumed a major role in providing assistance.

Before the New Deal, arrangements in the new nation for care of the poor were fragmentary, locally diverse, and continually changing. After the Civil War, the federal government provided pensions to veterans and their dependents; in the early twentieth century, state governments began to operate workers' compensation programs and to offer mothers' pensions. The main foundation of support throughout, however, was local government. But private and religious charities became essential resources: Care for the needy was a prime example of that flowering of associational activity that so captured Alexis de Tocqueville's attention as characteristically American.

The flood of orphans produced by a midcentury cholera epidemic, for instance, prompted Protestant churches to organize the Chicago Orphan Asylum. Evangelical Christians burdened to rescue bodies as well as souls founded rescue missions in big-city slums to provide shelter, sustenance, counseling, and jobs, along with a Gospel message. The Salvation Army, brought over from England in 1880, is the best-known example. Olasky notes a wide range of efforts, such as New York City's Female Domestic Missionary Society for the Poor, started in 1816 to supply schooling as well as Bibles; the industrial school, "Working Girl's Society," and kitchen to prepare food for invalids that sprang from Grace (Episcopal) Church in Chicago; and the sewing schools, child-care facilities, and employment services organized by women from New York City synagogues.

Catholics, to ensure that their needy received care compatible with their faith, or sometimes care at all, in the last quarter of the nineteenth century developed an extensive network of programs and facilities.[6] Some of these Catholic programs, as also some of the facilities and services organized by other religious groups, operated in conjunction with government, were funded in part by government, and served as elements of the local welfare delivery systems.[7] African Americans after the Civil War, freed from slavery but excluded from the mainstream, started churches that were the center of community life and of self-help and charitable activity.[8] Settlement houses and Charity Organization Societies, efforts in the latter part of the century to make assistance more professional, themselves had religious roots.[9]

This dynamic and independent religious role dwindled, however, as a determined government welfare effort was launched in the 1930s. Indeed, the conventional story of welfare from the New Deal on hardly includes religion at all. In part, this is simply a mistake: In fact, organizations such as Jewish Vocational Services, Catholic Charities, and the Salvation Army became essential elements of the welfare delivery system, and congregations and other religious organizations provided vital help to the needy outside of public welfare. Religion disappeared only from observers with secularist blinders.[10] Yet in a profound sense, the conventional story is correct, for the growth of government welfare spelled the marginalization of religion in welfare.

President Franklin D. Roosevelt's social legislation has been called the "big bang" of American public welfare.[11] His New Deal was a crisis response to the Great Depression and the overwhelming of private charity and state and local government assistance, to be sure. And yet it was also the catalyst and pattern, setting in motion the development of a new arrangement of social assistance that was then fleshed out in the postwar years and in the Great Society's War on Poverty in the 1960s. Religion was marginalized because of the way that pattern was woven, because of the particular path of American welfare development.

Two changes were key. The first was the shift to a government-centered system of help, a change from a mix of local organizations, many of them connected with religion, to an arrangement of assistance in which the dominant element was a complex of secular government-operated and government-funded programs. Significantly, the very first regulation promulgated by the Federal Emergency Relief Administration, established in 1933 to funnel federal relief through state and local agencies, demanded the displacement of nongovernmental organizations. The regulation noted that state and local authorities depended on hundreds of private organizations to deliver welfare assistance but insisted that public funds henceforth could be spent only by public agencies. Personnel from private agencies would have to be made public agents if they were to handle government money.[12] This regulation initiated "the reversal of a tradition whereby voluntary agencies shaped the contribution of public agencies to social welfare." Enactment of the Social Security Act, two years later, "furthered the process and established the dominance of public welfare."[13]

Government had not been absent before, and nongovernmental assistance did not now vanish. But the center of gravity had radically shifted. The major provider of services became government; direction and dynamism now came from government. And not just government; it would be the federal government that dominated as the senior partner even when programs had a joint federal–state structure. The content of welfare, the substance of society's care for the poor, would no longer be in large measure what local associations, religious as well as secular, devised. The major part of assistance became government assistance. And, given what the U.S. Constitution requires of government programs, government welfare meant secular welfare.

And welfare was government and secular even though, thanks to new federal rules in the late 1960s and early 1970s, the system increasingly came to depend on nonprofit organizations to actually deliver the services.[14] Such organizations were regarded as vendors, chosen to do what government specified, not as allies that naturally and legitimately would engage in the joint cause in their own way.[15] And though religious organizations could become vendors, what government sought and would accept from them was secular services. In principle, and to a significant degree in practice, religious organizations that decided to work with government welfare had to set aside their religion.[16]

The second key change was the trend to redefine welfare as nondirective assistance. For the "friendly visitors" of both religious and secular charities in the nineteenth century, and even for settlement house workers and early social workers, who were also concerned about structural impediments, effective help for poor persons and families was understood in normative terms and dealt with choices and behavior. A growing preoccupation with disputes over "method"—social reform versus casework—and the professionalization of social work delegitimated such moral or normative concerns.[17] The New Deal welfare system, which had been created in response to the economic crisis of the Great Depression in which the new poverty was obviously not the fault of the poor, and designed by activists more attuned to structural than behavioral causes,[18] gradually came to focus on income maintenance, not changes in life direction, despite recurrent reforms emphasizing job training and employment.[19]

Thus, by the early 1990s, as welfare advisers to Democratic President Bill Clinton ruefully noted, the symbol of public welfare had become the public assistance office that devoted its effort not to helping families regain their footing but rather to determining the size of the government check to which they were entitled.[20] This was a style of assistance very different from the transformative and personal approach favored by earlier religious (and secular!) social activists—and by many current faith-based programs that operate outside the government system. The New Deal–Great Society welfare structure systematized and expanded care for the poor, but in a way that had little room either for the religious organizations that had been so prominent before or for some of their distinctive normative concerns.

The marginalization of religion in welfare was aided by trends in America's majority Protestant religion, which in the early part of the twentieth century was divided and weakened by the modernist–Fundamentalist controversy over the relationship between the Bible and modern values.[21]

Seeking spiritual purity, the Evangelical or conservative current, in what one observer has labeled "the great reversal," abandoned its earlier commitment to social involvement,[22] and for much of the century also largely withdrew from cultural and political involvement in general.

The mainline or liberal Protestant churches, in contrast, became even more involved in society and politics, but on a changed basis. In the nineteenth century, they crusaded to get their fellow citizens to adopt new ways so that the United States might become a Christian nation. Now the key concern seemed to be not so much the direction of the path as the pace of progress; in the Social Gospel movement, as Robert Handy suggests, "the priorities had subtly been reversed" and Christian mission had become inspiration rather than the source of the goals.[23] As the government took over welfare, the mainline churches turned to urging it to assume ever greater responsibilities for the poor on behalf of society. In this new perspective, the role of religious institutions was subordinated to the government effort; thus the Presbyterian Church (USA) declared in 1989 that religious organizations collaborating with government ought to provide the services "in a way that does not support or advance religion."[24]

Most generally, the marginalization of religion in welfare was a signal instance of the sweeping redefinition in nineteenth- and twentieth-century America of the relationship between church and state, between religion and public life. What the U.S. Constitution requires, of course, is religious liberty and no established church—dual requirements originally thought compatible with the easy expression of religion in public life. As long as the vast majority was in some fashion Protestant, the resulting "informal and voluntary" establishment of Protestantism[25] troubled few. But it became problematic as the nation became more and more heterogeneous in religious convictions. Catholics could see, for instance, that the supposedly common faith of the common school and purportedly superior moral upbringing offered to needy Catholic children in New York institutions were in fact Protestant creations that would displace Catholic beliefs.[26] Jews, a small minority with a long history of persecution, were always on guard against signs of official favoritism toward Christianity. In a nation of many faiths, the dominance of one, even if not officially established, could not continue.

The U.S. Supreme Court's solution to the problem, promulgated in a series of decisions after World War II, was no-aid separationism; roughly, the government would support no religion and nothing government supported could be religious. The response to multiple faiths was for government to exclude all religion from those things it touched. This was not a workable doctrine for public policy, however. In the very case in which the Court announced that not a single dollar could go to religion, it authorized the State of New Jersey to pay to transport students to parochial schools (*Everson v. Board of Education*, 1947). Succeeding decisions are widely acknowledged also to lack consistency, and the justices have proposed various substitute interpretive schemes. Furthermore, the actual focus of the Court's no-aid decisions was elementary and high schools and not the wide range of government policy.[27] But no-aid separationism became the taken-for-granted meaning of the Constitution's church–state requirements, adopted without thinking even by some private foundations and corporations as if it also prevented them from aiding religious programs and organizations.

No-aid separationism obligated government's own welfare programs to be free of religion. It required also that the services government procured from nongovernmental providers had to be devoid of religion; one Supreme Court case thus held that "pervasively sectarian" organizations—thoroughly religious agencies—could not be government-funded providers because they would be unable to keep religion out of the services they would offer.[28] Such extreme fastidiousness about religion was more at the level of doctrine or aspiration than practice, to be sure. In fact, the various levels of government collaborated with organizations and programs that included significant religious practices. But the no-aid doctrine always put such collaborations at risk. At any time, lightning might strike and an official or a court might declare the arrangement illegal or unconstitutional.[29]

Inside the government welfare system—which grew out of the New Deal's emergency response to the great economic crisis that overwhelmed the religious, private, and local-government programs that had constituted the nation's safety net—a variety of organizations of religious provenance were important players. But they were under great pressure to set aside their religious components. The rule of the government welfare system was this: no religion in government welfare and no religion in the services government buys from private providers. Religious organizations unwilling or unable to downplay the faith elements still did provide essential services as private parts of the nation's safety net; by one estimate, in 1997 their services were worth as much as $34 billion.[30] But such faith-based or pervasively sectarian organizations were outside the government system, outside the public welfare effort.

For people of faith, for whom caring for needy neighbors is a core religious requirement, the intentions of the New Deal–Great Society public welfare system, if not the practice, would have to be applauded. The system acknowledged that external or systemic causes of poverty could not be ignored and that families in need, whatever the cause, required and should receive assistance, even if local authorities and private charities were unable or unwilling to respond. And the rules excluding religion from public welfare were an attempt to preserve the rights and dignity of the poor, who, as most people of faith would readily acknowledge, should not be coerced into religious belief nor treated as if need were the simple product of the absence of faith. Yet people of faith might legitimately wonder whether these gains had to be achieved in a way that so marginalized religion. Some faith communities—most Jews, the Catholic Church, and mainline Protestants—willingly set aside "sectarianism" when they obtained government funds and were driven by their faith to advocate for improved government welfare. Nevertheless their programs had a distinct religious flavor, often including voluntary religious activities, religious symbols, and a readiness to discuss faith matters with clients.[31] How could they not? But such practices conflicted with the stated requirements of the system. Was such a welfare system the best way to assist those neighbors in need?

Reforming Welfare

American public welfare seems to be always the target of critique and reform, not so much with the aim of refinement but rather as an object of persistent battles about extent and value. Concerns about dependency—that is, in colloquial terms, whether programs are functioning as a "hand up" or only as a "handout"—have been particularly insistent. At the outset, President Franklin D. Roosevelt warned against the "dole" and sought to provide work opportunities wherever possible. In the 1960s, renewed concern brought the introduction of modest work requirements for some welfare recipients. In 1988, continued concern about dependency led to the Family Support Act, combining a conservative demand for work requirements with a liberal demand for better government programs to prepare people for employment.[32] Yet these reforms made only marginal changes in the actual operations and outcomes of public welfare.

In the mid-1990s, radical welfare change arrived. Preceded by state experiments with various parts of the system under waivers from the federal government, in 1996 Congress and the president agreed to far-reaching changes designed to "end welfare as we know it," in President Clinton's words. The changes affected most of the federal welfare system, and especially the core program, Aid to Families with Dependent Children, which was transformed into Temporary Assistance for Needy Families (TANF). The reforms on paper this time almost immediately began to be translated into changed practices on the ground.[33] Most significant of all, the 1996 reforms overturned the New Deal–Great Society design for public welfare, including its marginalization of religion. The 1996 federal welfare reform law reversed the trajectory of six decades of American welfare development.

Three trends set the stage for this dramatic change. The first powerful factor was the growing belief by many, not only in the general public but also in government and academia, that much of the government welfare effort and expenditure had done little good and sometimes even did real harm to the poor. This was more than a revival of conservative animus against welfare and the federal government; if it took a libertarian like Charles Murray to propose as a "thought experiment" the abolition of welfare as the best way to help the poor, it was equally striking that progressive welfare scholar David Ellwood would chose the double-entendre title "Poor Support" for his book proposing fundamental changes to welfare on behalf of the needy.[34]

Second, a renewed appreciation that poverty can have behavioral as well as economic roots was also important. No doubt people are often poor because of a lack of opportunity, racism, or other external factors. But scholars pointed out that sometimes persons and families were poor because of choices they themselves made: rejecting opportunities, falling into negative habits, responding to external challenges by giving up rather than redoubling their efforts.[35] If so, then to provide only income support or even job training without addressing problems of motivation or of mental preparedness to advance was to relegate people to a life outside the mainstream of society.

The third vital trend was the upsurge of interest in civil society and volunteerism. Activists in communist-dominated Eastern Europe had turned to civil society as the social space for free action and thought to unmask and topple their totalitarian governments. In the United States, interest in civil society represented a renewal of that cultural instinct celebrated by Alexis de Tocqueville for Americans to turn to voluntary associations and personal activism, not first to government, to address social problems. Some conjured up a "nanny state" that had robbed civil society of its functions; the more general concern was whether, in building the government welfare system, the desire and capacity of people directly to help their neighbors had been allowed to wane and the appropriate place of nongovernmental assistance had been neglected.[36]

The 1996 federal welfare reform law, the Personal Responsibility and Work Opportunity Reconciliation Act, responded to these trends by changing the direction of welfare in three ways.[37] First, increasing federal dominance was replaced by increased state and local design and control of welfare. There is no longer a federal welfare system administered by the states according to detailed federal rules. In the new system, the federal government sends its welfare funds to the states as block grants, requiring the states to design and operate their own welfare programs within broad federal guidelines. Each state has its own welfare system now, and some have in turn authorized their counties to design their own programs. Government welfare is now able to take into account not only the particular characteristics of the welfare populations in the different jurisdictions but also the specific mix of economic opportunities and barriers and the particular set of nongovernmental resources.

Second, as is suggested by the change of the name of the core welfare program to Temporary Assistance for Needy Families, the purpose of welfare has shifted from income maintenance to empowerment for self-sufficiency. Welfare is intended to prepare families to support themselves through employment rather than to be an alternative to work as a source of income. Certifying eligibility for cash benefits is no longer the dominant activity in welfare offices; instead, programs and rules are designed to provide both "help" and "hassle"—specific assistance such as job training, child care assistance, and life skills counseling coupled with pressure to move along: time limits on benefits, employment requirements, and the like.[38]

Third, public welfare is being transformed from a government-centered activity to a collaborative effort with civil society, specifically including religious organizations. If the aim of welfare is to help people attain self-sufficiency, officials need to make connections with employers to find out how to prepare recipients for employment and to secure jobs for them, with churches and neighborhood groups to find mentors, and with schools, businesses, religious congregations, and social groups to patch together transportation alternatives. This turn to collaboration has been fostered, as well, by the devolution of welfare to the state and local levels, where decisions about welfare programs and case management are made by government officials who are closer to the actual institutions of civil society. The officials' need to find effective programs for recipients facing the new time limits on benefits has also fueled the search for new partnerships with nongovernmental organizations, including religious organizations that long existed outside the view of many officials.

Congress, however, did more than give such indirect impulses to push public welfare into greater collaboration with civil society and with religious organizations. The federal welfare reform law contained a specific provision designed to expand the involvement of religious organizations in the public welfare effort. The law's Charitable Choice section specifically required state and local governments to open the door to faith-based organizations when buying services from nongovernmental sources. In reversing the trajectory of U.S. government welfare, legislators set in motion a process to bring religion back into public welfare.

Ironically, this legislative effort was not the result of pressure from the faith communities, nor did it receive much initial support from them.[39] Their chief concerns focused on different issues. In simplest terms, mainline and progressive religious leaders put assistance to the poor high on their agenda and, regarding government as society's agent for good, pressed for expanded welfare programs and expenditures. Conservative religious bodies, concerned that open-ended government welfare creates dependency and convinced that religious institutions bear the primary responsibility for assisting the poor, advocated shrinking public welfare as the way forward. Neither perspective had much to contribute to legislators concerned at least as much with the quality of government welfare as with the hoary dispute about the quantity of government's effort.

In the welfare reform debates, progressive religious forces focused on cuts in federal welfare spending, the narrowing of welfare eligibility, the end of the legal entitlement to federal welfare, and the devolution of welfare control to lower governments. In their view, the legislative majority was pursuing not so much welfare reform as welfare abolition; what the process represented was the federal government's abandonment of its responsibility for the nation's poor. Talk about engaging civil society in public welfare was a sideshow; mainline churches already operated government-funded programs and did not need legislative changes to encourage or facilitate such involvement. And such talk was hollow, at best, they argued, because cuts in government spending would actually reduce the resources available to such religiously affiliated programs. What the poor needed was more welfare help, not more religious charity.

On the conservative religious side, the focus of attention was the liberality of government welfare and not so much the movement to bring government and civil society closer together. The most active groups pushed to ensure that welfare would become more stringent, more focused on behavioral change and less on income support. For the Christian Coalition, the chief goal was the triumph of conservative social aims such as time limits on benefits and discouraging unwed motherhood. This was not merely a bias for less government spending nor a crude attack on the poor; the incentives and disincentives of welfare were to be redesigned to encourage good choices by those unable to support themselves. But what is most striking is that groups such as the Christian Coalition paid little attention to the congressional impulse to bridge the gap between public welfare and religious assistance programs. Religious and other conservatives were more inclined to see government welfare and the churches as alternatives than as potential partners.[40]

The Promise of Charitable Choice

Buried in the pages of the long federal welfare law was a small section of legal language about religious service providers that has come to be called the Charitable Choice provision. In the welfare reform debates, there had been a great deal of loose conservative talk about abolishing the government's role in welfare and turning the task over to churches and private charities. But Charitable Choice was a different idea. It had to do with how government itself would carry out its welfare task. It was a guideline about procurement: who could compete for government funds to provide welfare services, and on what terms. Charitable Choice did not substitute religious charities for government welfare. Instead, the new rules were meant to enable religious organizations to accept government funds without the pressure to sideline their religious character. The goal of Charitable Choice is to bring religion back into U.S. public welfare.

The Charitable Choice provision, by its own declaration, is designed to permit religious organizations to collaborate with public welfare "on the same basis as any other nongovernmental provider," but "without impairing [their] religious character" and "without diminishing the religious freedom of beneficiaries."[41] To enable religious organizations to come inside the welfare system without leaving their religion behind, the provision has four main features.

First, the new federal rule obligates state and local governments not to discriminate against religious organizations when making procurement decisions. That is, religious organizations, including churches and other congregations as well as religious nonprofit organizations, cannot be excluded from competing for contracts simply because they are religious, or too religious, or of the "wrong" religion.[42] But the aim is a level playing field, not one tilted in the opposite direction. Religious organizations get no preferences. Officials are to select whichever organization can best provide the services government has decided to offer to needy families.

Second, Charitable Choice obligates government to respect the religious character of religious organizations that do accept government funds to provide services. They do not become agents of government by winning contracts but retain their independent status as organizations defined and guided by religious belief. Specifically, Charitable Choice provides that the organizations have the right to display religious symbols and items in the places they provide government-funded services and, with some restrictions, to use moral and religious concepts and language in those services. Most important, religious organizations retain their right to hire only employees who agree with their religious principles. Though such "discrimination" is extremely controversial, control of staffing is obviously vital to any organization with a particular mission, as both courts and legislatures have clearly affirmed for religious organizations not involved in procurement.[43]

Third, though protecting the faith character of religious organizations, Charitable Choice explicitly protects as well the right of recipients to be assisted without religious coercion. Organizations may not use religion to discriminate against recipients seeking assistance. Recipients who enter a faith-based program can decline to take active part in any religious activities that are part of the program. And most important, the state or local government must be prepared to offer an alternative to any recipient who objects to receiving services from a religious provider. This requirement ensures that recipients are not forced to violate their convictions, makes it clear that government is not establishing any particular faith, and enables the religious organizations to manifest their convictions in their programs without fear of trampling on the rights of recipients.

Fourth, Charitable Choice maintains the separation of church and state by requiring religious organizations to use government funds for the public purpose of assisting needy families by providing specific services and not to divert such funds to confessional activities such as worship, sectarian instruction, or proselytization.[44] Staff members, of course, are free to respond to clients' religious questions, and inherently religious practices like prayer or Bible study can be offered if funded by private money. But such activities must be optional parts of a program.

These new procurement rules constitute a string or condition that accompanies federal funds to state and local governments. That is, Charitable

Choice established a new requirement for state and local procurement policy and thus also a new parameter for the redesign of state and local welfare services.[45] In the 1996 federal welfare law, Charitable Choice was attached to TANF funding—the core federal welfare money that can be spent on a wide variety of services. The next year, Congress attached the provision to special services for hard-to-employ welfare recipients by adopting the Welfare-to-Work program as an amendment to the 1996 welfare law. In 1998, when federal legislators reauthorized the Community Services Block Grant Program, they added Charitable Choice language to funding for services administered by community action agencies in low-income communities. In late 2000, Congress and President Clinton added Charitable Choice language to federal drug treatment funds when they reauthorized the Substance Abuse and Mental Health Services Administration.

Charitable Choice, of course, does not mark the start of government procurement from religious organizations. As noted, various levels of government in the United States have for many years funded religious agencies to provide services to needy families. But the legitimacy of such collaborations has been in doubt, and often the price of collaboration has been very high. Religious organizations seeking federal Community Development Block Grant funds, for example, have had to certify that they would hire staff without regard to religion, would "provide no religious instruction or counseling, conduct no religious proselytizing, and exert no other religious influence" in offering assistance, and would certify that the services would be provided in a place containing "no sectarian or religious symbols or decorations."[46]

Such rules exclude many religious providers and cause many others to exclude themselves. Those service organizations that do participate have to so downplay their religious elements that they have come to be identified as "religiously affiliated" or "religion-sponsored" agencies to emphasize that their specifically religious elements have had to be muted or eliminated. A religious motivation for service was officially acceptable, but a religious shaping or openness in the services was officially not. Some religious groups regarded the restrictions as acceptable; the opportunity to serve outweighed the limitations, or the specific services involved needed no overt religious content. But there could be no doubt that, as far as the official government policy went, religious providers were welcomed despite, and not because of, their religious character.

Charitable Choice holds a very different emphasis. Now eligible religious organizations are typically termed "faith-based" to underline their right to retain their faith characteristics and to offer programs that embody a religious perspective as a legitimate part of the public welfare effort. In this redesigned collaborative framework, government is charged with protecting, rather than suppressing, those religious characteristics that define the organizations and give their services their particular flavor. The presumption is that religious organizations have something unique to offer precisely because of their faith. If the government considers such an organization's services to be especially effective, then it is counterproductive to require the organization to strip away those things that define it and make it work. Charitable Choice ensures that religious organizations can bring their religion with them when they collaborate with the government welfare system, not leave faith behind as irrelevant or unacceptable.

The redesigned rules for procurement presume and exemplify a new church–state framework. In place of no-aid separationism, Charitable Choice rests on the constitutional concept of government neutrality, an alternative interpretative scheme that has found increasing favor with the Supreme Court.[47] Here the government's goal is not to avoid any possible assistance to religion, as if the First Amendment is intended to disadvantage people of faith and their institutions. What it must do, rather, is to treat on an equal basis people and organizations of any faith or none. When it selects service providers, it should not uniquely disqualify religious organizations on the ground that they are religious or "pervasively sectarian" but instead evaluate all competitors by their promise of good, cost-effective assistance.

No-aid separationism requires religion to be kept out of government-funded services so that no client will be subject to coerced belief. Neutrality lets religion in and protects clients by ensuring that they can choose a different provider, if their conscience requires it. And rather than exclude "pervasively sectarian" providers to prevent government endorsement or support of religion, neutrality allows faith-based providers to accept government funding as long as they use the funds for the designated purpose of serving the needy, rather than for inherently religious practices. The neutrality principle claims that, through rules such as Charitable Choice, government can accept faith-based organizations into the public welfare effort without returning to the old and unconstitutional practice of an informal or formal religious establishment.

Some religious leaders regard even these new terms of collaboration as too restrictive. Fearing that any close tie with government will erode the spiritual mission of social ministries, some conservative religious and political figures have promoted expanded tax benefits for donations to religious and private charities as a better way than Charitable Choice for government to increase the resources of the faith sector.[48] Some Evangelical and Fundamentalist leaders, arguing that sharing the Gospel is the heart of an authentic helping relationship, worry that the bar on using government funds for proselytizing signifies a covert government bias against robust faith-based service programs. Others have criticized the requirement that clients be allowed not to actively take part in religious activities. Programs designed to transform the lives of the addicted or persistently homeless, they argue, will lose their effectiveness if clients can refuse to be fully engaged in every part of a program. The high value of preventing coercion is already secured by the guarantee of an alternative provider.

Other critics, both religious and secular, have condemned Charitable Choice for allowing too much religion into public welfare and into government's collaboration with religious providers. Separationists worry that religious coercion is likely because, notwithstanding the provision's features to protect clients, it does not specifically require governments or religious agencies to inform recipients of their option not to actively participate in religious activities and their right to receive services from another provider (the latest enacted and proposed versions of Charitable Choice do require that notice be given). And even if notice is given, some worry that vulnerable clients may put up with objectionable practices for fear of losing benefits.

But these critics' most basic objection is to the very inclusion of faith-based providers in government-funded welfare. Such organizations cannot and will not separate out the (improper) religion from the (proper, i.e., secular) social services government wants to fund. Government will end up supporting religion; clients will end up indoctrinated, not assisted. The only solution is to exclude "pervasively sectarian" providers, allowing in only religious affiliated organizations, religious organizations that run separate, secular, social service programs.

But that, of course, was the status quo before Charitable Choice. It rests on an interpretation of the Constitution that demands that government welfare assistance be secular and any assistance that incorporates religion be kept out on the private margins of society. This is a public policy position that requires religious programs to be excluded from public welfare, no matter how effective they are. By the end of the twentieth century, it was no longer so obvious to policymakers, analysts, and the public that such exclusion constitutes good welfare policy or is dictated by the Constitution. On the campaign trail for the Democratic nomination for president in 1999, Vice President Al Gore made the case for including religion instead:

> As long as there is always a secular alternative for anyone who wants one, and as long as no one is required to participate in religious observances as a condition for receiving services, faith-based organizations can provide jobs and job training, counseling and mentoring, food and basic medical care. They can do so with public funds—and without having to alter the religious character that is so often the key to their effectiveness.[49]

These are just the features of Charitable Choice.

Religion and American Welfare in the Twenty-First Century

Charitable Choice is designed to make government welfare more inclusive by changing the policies that kept religion out. Government programs themselves have to be operated without reference to religion, but by purchasing services from faith-based providers government can bring religion back into public welfare. Procurement conducted according to Charitable Choice is designed to do just that: Religiously affiliated providers that have traditionally accepted government funding no longer need to sideline their faith commitments,[50] and faith-based organizations that always avoided government for fear of secularization—or that were prevented from participating because government officials rejected them as too religious—no longer need to remain outside the government-funded welfare system. The legitimacy of these new arrangements no doubt will be tested in the courts. Assuming they survive Supreme Court review, can we expect that public welfare in the new century will be markedly more inclusive of faith-based providers and programs?

It appears that Charitable Choice is not merely a momentary fancy of a few politicians desperate for something different. A public opinion poll by the centrist Democratic Leadership Council in early 1999 showed that very large majorities of Republicans, Democrats, and independents agreed that U.S. social problems can better be solved by "closer collaboration" between government and religious and charitable associations than by either government or civil society acting alone. More recent polls have similarly indicated strong public support for an expanded religious role in social services and for increasing government collaboration with faith-based programs.[51]

Federal legislators have continued to propose new applications for the principle—to programs for the homeless and addicted; to juvenile justice services and efforts to strengthen fatherhood; and even, in a "Charitable Choice Expansion Act," to all federal funds that flow to nongovernmental providers either directly or through lower governments.[52] In 2001, the House adopted H.R. 7, "The Community Solutions Act," proposed by J.C. Watts (Republican of Oklahoma) and Tony Hall (Democrat of Ohio), which extends the Charitable Choice language to new federal funding programs in additional departments. However, the House debate was heated and bitter, and few senators showed enthusiasm about taking up the bill. A notable aspect of the presidential primary campaign in 1999 and 2000 was the commitment of both Al Gore, the leading Democratic candidate, and George W. Bush, the top Republican contender, to implementing and expanding Charitable Choice.[53] Upon his election, President Bush immediately issued a statement, "Rallying the Armies of Compassion," which declared that making the federal government friendlier to faith-based (and community-based) assistance efforts would be a top priority for his administration, and he announced on January 29, 2001, two executive orders to set up a White House Office of Faith-Based and Community Initiatives and counterpart centers in five major cabinet departments.

Many religious leaders have real concerns, however, and state and local officials have been slow to come into compliance with Charitable Choice. In the faith communities, theological conservatives worry about the risks of secularization, despite the new rules; progressives fear that expanded religious involvement will allow government to abandon its own welfare role, even though Charitable Choice is about government procurement, not government load shedding. Yet, through the Christian Roundtable on Poverty and Welfare Reform, organized by the Call to Renewal movement of progressive Evangelicals, Protestant and Catholic leaders from all parts of the theological spectrum have endorsed Charitable Choice as one key tool in the fight against poverty,[54] and groups ranging from the National Association of Evangelicals to the Interfaith Community Ministries Network and the California Council of Churches have endorsed the concept. Despite the adamant opposition of most Jewish civil liberties groups, some Jewish leaders have urged that Charitable Choice offers an appropriate and welcome way for faith to become reintegrated into public social services.[55]

State and local officials, charged with redesigning their welfare systems, have often found other issues more pressing than the task of ensuring that their procurement practices comply with Charitable Choice. Some have been paralyzed by fears of litigation from separationist groups; many resist making the Charitable Choice exception to their antidiscrimination laws. In any case, under the logic of devolution, the new requirement was passed along to the states without any direct federal guidance or oversight. Nevertheless, state and local officials in many places—obligated to improve the effectiveness of welfare services, freed to experiment with new programs, and liberated by the national mood favoring involvement of the faith community—have actively pursued collaboration with faith-based organizations, often by constructing nonfinancial arrangements in which volunteers from congregations are enlisted to provide mentoring to recipients making the transition from welfare to employment.

Changes in actual contracting have been slower to take root. Research in nine states (California, Illinois, Massachusetts, Michigan, Mississippi, New York, Texas, Virginia, and Wisconsin) in 1999 showed that, three years after Charitable Choice was adopted, fifty-four new financial collaborations with faith-based organizations had been devised, many with groups that had never before worked with government.[56] Three years later, the number had mushroomed to 485.[57] Many of the contracts involve multiple congregations and religious nonprofit agencies. And, just as with many of the new nonfinancial collaborations, often what the religious organizations are bringing to the partnerships and to the welfare families is something new for public welfare: "up-close and personal" assistance—counseling, supportive networks, advice, intensive life skills and family management training—help not only to find employment but to organize a life off welfare.

The Bush administration is pressing federal officials and state and local governments to comply with existing Charitable Choice law. It is working with Congress to expand Charitable Choice to new areas of federal funding. And its cabinet centers will be continuously reviewing federal statutes, regulations, and practices to identify and remove barriers that hamper faith-based and community-based organizations.[58] Nevertheless, a large expansion of religious involvement in public welfare is necessarily a matter of decades and not years. Religious organizations need to change priorities, expand capacity, and develop new management capabilities; and government agencies need to learn how to reach out to faith communities and to redesign procurement practices to remove bureaucratic obstacles to new participants.

At this early stage, then, it is impossible to predict what ultimate effect Charitable Choice will have on the array of providers and programs that are part of American public welfare. Given current trends, the sweeping change in the trajectory of welfare, and the growing interest in the role of religion and spirituality in life and society, it seems safe to expect that, via Charitable Choice or some other innovation, religious organizations will play a significantly larger role in welfare in the new century. Such inclusion poses a series of challenges to faith communities, to the government welfare system, and to the Charitable Choice idea itself.

For the government, an inescapable issue is how to balance the autonomy rights of providers (Charitable Choice asserts their "independence from Federal, State, and local governments") with its duty to maintain high standards and to protect the poor who receive services from nongovernmental providers. When is the voluntary sharing of a religious message too insistent? How can the requirement of demonstrated competence be softened to allow new providers to win contracts, but without a loss of quality? Equally pressing is the challenge of assuring adequate services throughout a jurisdiction when the delivery system is increasingly made up of multiple providers offering a variety of services of varying quality in diverse locations. And, particularly in rural areas, the requirement of an alternative provider for clients who reject religious programs may become difficult to meet if government contracts with more and more faith-based organizations.[59]

Faith communities face the challenge of resisting co-optation as collaboration increases, a concern of both conservatives and progressives, albeit for different reasons.[60] Progressives worry that religious care for the poor may become confined to acts of charity, to the neglect of working for social justice, including pressing for adequate government social spending and programs. Conservatives worry that, even if government funds can be obtained without secularizing requirements, those funds may have two pernicious effects. Faith-based organizations may become habituated to government support, chasing after welfare funding even when their mission and competence do not match the government requirements and even if restrictive conditions are reintroduced. And even without such problems, the availability of government funds can make organizations lose their dependence on the communities of compassion that gave birth to them, as energy formerly devoted to communicating with supporters and raising funds from them is diverted to grant writing and government paperwork.[61]

Faith communities need to be concerned, as well, about becoming too identified with the ideology of welfare. Because not all life choices are equally positive for people and because it is a responsibility generally acknowledged by religious traditions that those able to do so should support themselves and contribute to others, faith communities generally seem to find it acceptable, at least in principle, that welfare assistance requires positive action by those requesting help. Nevertheless, unmerited help—mercy—is at the heart of the religious requirement to assist the neighbor in need. Faith-based organizations that choose to collaborate with government welfare, and the faith communities in which they are rooted, need to decide how they can cooperate with legitimate welfare requirements while still extending open arms of mercy to those unable or unwilling to meet the requirements.

A final set of challenges, for both government and religion, is to go beyond Charitable Choice. Charitable Choice is a rule for procurement, for government purchase of services. But the best response to need is a compassionate society and not only a generous and effective welfare system; a strong safety net includes assistance organizations in civil society that respond directly to crises without the orchestration of government. What then can government do to strengthen civil society? Is its only positive contribution to get out of the way, as libertarians urge? If there is an active role it can play, what is it? Charity tax credits, as some conservatives have proposed? Expanded deductions for charitable donations? Greater immunity from liability when mistakes are made in good faith? Technical assistance from government agencies?

A difficulty within Charitable Choice itself also requires attention. The concept presumes that religious organizations can best serve the poor if they are able to embody a particular religious vision. Effective services will be "sectarian"—not in the sense of demanding that clients learn esoteric dogma but because the programs reflect some particular religiously shaped diagnosis and remedy. To break free of a dependency on drugs or to accept the authority of some young upstart at work may require a narrative that is morally and religiously thicker than a general appeal to the American creed or the values of our consumer society.

And yet, when procurement officials select a provider, they are required by Charitable Choice to disregard religion, treating effectiveness as if it had no connection with religion at all, neither the religion of the provider nor the beliefs of those who are seeking assistance. It is as if a school system, understanding at last that robust values undergird effective education, were to give the contract for operating all the schools of the district to the Catholic parochial school authorities, forgetting that robust values are specific so that good education is configured differently by different communities of belief.

The appropriate alternative to banishing religion from education is to fashion a system of school choice that honors the variety of educational and religious convictions of the district's families.[62] In the same way, the full promise of Charitable Choice may require accepting a positive tie between effectiveness and religion. Officials should seek a variety of providers, secular and religious, when the services they want to procure touch directly on morality and faith—services such as life skills training, mentoring, substance abuse treatment, overcoming chronic homelessness, and abstinence education.

The goal is not a quota system; officials should not presume that religious and denominational differences will always generate different welfare services. It should be up to the various faith communities and faith-based providers to decide if some different variety of service needs to be offered. But government officials will be on safe ground if they assume that no one provider, no one style of a service, is unambiguously the best, the most effective, for every family and person needing assistance. Some form of religious or worldview pluralism may be the ultimate reform, going beyond religious neutrality in procurement, as a solution to enforced secularism in public welfare.[63]

Conclusion

Religion was a large part of American welfare before welfare became (federal) government welfare. The construction of that government welfare system was, in many ways, a great advance. A strong government role meant that care for the poor became more constant, less dependent on geographic location or the waxing and waning of moods of generosity. And with its presumption that poverty is largely a structural issue, the expanded government role redressed the overmoralization of the older approaches. But it was an unfortunate thing, for the poor, for religion, and for government, that in building the government welfare system religion was shoved to the margins.

The challenge for the United States is not to return to the days before the government became so extensively involved in welfare, but to move ahead to a new era in which religion will once again also be fully involved in welfare. Public welfare needs to be redefined not as the welfare government delivers, but as the joint effort of government and civil society, including faith-based organizations. What we need is a model of "equal partners,"[64] in the words of Luis Lugo.

The care of the needy is the "shared responsibility" of various social institutions, Lugo points out; government must play a key role, but the poor are not exclusively the government's responsibility. In particular, faith-based organizations have a major role to play. They "succeed because they minister to the needy in a way that is qualitatively different, one that addresses matters of the heart and draws on spiritual and moral resources largely beyond the reach of government," he argues. So collaboration is essential. But in that collaboration, faith must be given room. When faith-based organizations "cooperate with various levels of government in pursuit of common ends, [they must] guard jealously their religious identity, knowing that it is precisely because of it that they contribute to the common good."[65]

It is just such a collaborative relationship of respect that Charitable Choice institutes. The government's responsibility for the needy is not tossed out with a utopian hope that churches will miraculously reconstitute themselves as the national safety net. Instead religious organizations are brought into the public welfare effort—with their faith intact. But Charitable Choice does not replace the "naked public square"[66] with a theocratic welfare state. Instead, choice is structured into welfare so that the religious liberty of recipients, both those who reject religion and those seeking holistic help, can be respected. The promise of Charitable Choice is a public welfare system enlarged to include religious organizations and the faith dimension of life.

Notes

1. See, e.g., Michael Katz, *In the Shadow of the Poorhouse: A Social History of Welfare in America* (New York: Basic Books, 1986), who also proposes the "quasi-welfare state" characterization. On the "Europe envy" of this main story line, see, e.g., Ram A. Cnaan, with Robert J. Wineburg and Stephanie C. Boddie, *The Newer Deal: Social Work and Religion in Partnership* (New York: Columbia University Press, 1999), 86–87, and Theda Skocpol, *Protecting Soldiers and Mothers: The Political Origins of Social Policy in the United States*, papered. (Cambridge, Mass.: Belknap Press, 1995), 3ff.

2. Marvin Olasky, *The Tragedy of American Compassion* (Washington, D.C.: Regnery Gateway, 1992). See also James L. Payne, *Overcoming Welfare: Expecting More from the Poor—and from Ourselves* (New York: Basic Books, 1998).

3. Martin E. Marty, *The Modern Schism: Three Paths to the Secular* (New York: Harper & Row, 1969), 98.

4. On the concept of "de-privatization" see José Casanova, *Public Religions in the Modern World* (Chicago: University of Chicago Press, 1994).

5. Katz, *Shadow of the Poorhouse*, 14. In addition to Katz, particularly useful overviews of American welfare history for present purposes include Walter I. Trattner,

From Poor Law to Welfare State: A History of Social Welfare in America, 4th ed. (New York: Free Press, 1989); and June Axinn and Herman Levin, *Social Welfare: A History of the American Response to Need*, 3d ed. (New York: Longman, 1992).

6. These examples are drawn from Diana S. Richmond Garland, *Church Agencies: Caring for Children and Families in Crisis* (Washington, D.C.: Child Welfare League of America, 1994); Norris Magnuson, *Salvation in the Slums: Evangelical Social Work, 1865–1920*, paperback ed. (Grand Rapids, Mich.: Baker Book House, 1990); Diane Winston, *Red-Hot and Righteous: The Urban Religion of The Salvation Army* (Cambridge, Mass.: Harvard University Press, 1999); Olasky, *Tragedy of American Compassion*; and Dorothy M. Brown and Elizabeth McKeown, *The Poor Belong to Us: Catholic Charities and American Welfare* (Cambridge, Mass.: Harvard University Press, 1997).

7. For the struggle of Catholic organizations to be able to collaborate with public agencies, see Brown and McKeown, *Poor Belong to Us*.

8. See, e.g., C. Eric Lincoln and Lawrence H. Mamiya, *The Black Church in the African American Experience* (Durham, N.C.: Duke University Press, 1990), and Andrew Billingsley, *Mighty Like a River: The Black Church and Social Reform* (New York: Oxford University Press, 1999).

9. Cnaan, *Newer Deal*, 58ff; Andrew W. Dobelstein, *Moral Authority, Ideology, and the Future of American Social Welfare* (Boulder, Colo.: Westview Press, 1999), 60–75.

10. Cnaan firmly establishes this point in his *Newer Deal*.

11. Theda Skocpol quotes the "big bang" characterization from Christopher Leman, albeit by way of criticizing the notion for minimizing earlier federal action and the complexity of American welfare history. Skocpol, *Protecting Soldiers and Mothers*, 4.

12. Axinn and Levin, *Social Welfare*, 185–201; the rule is reprinted at 204–5. See Brown and McKeown, *Poor Belong to Us* , chap. 5, for Catholic Charities' battle to retain a public role despite the new rule.

13. Axinn and Levin, *Social Welfare*, 198.

14. Steven Rathgeb Smith and Michael Lipsky, *Nonprofits for Hire: The Welfare State in the Age of Contracting* (Cambridge, Mass.: Harvard University Press, 1993), 53ff; Lester M. Salamon, *Partners in Public Service: Government–Nonprofit Relations in the Modern Welfare State* (Baltimore: Johns Hopkins University Press, 1995).

15. Cf. Smith and Lipsky, *Nonprofits for Hire*.

16. Joe Loconte, *Seducing the Samaritan: How Government Contracts Are Reshaping Social Services* (Boston: Pioneer Institute for Public Policy Research, 1997). For more nuanced views, see Stephen V. Monsma, *When Sacred and Secular Mix: Religious Nonprofit Organizations and Public Money* (Lanham, Md.: Rowman & Littlefield, 1996); and especially Charles L. Glenn, *The Ambiguous Embrace: Government and Faith-Based Schools and Social Agencies* (Princeton, N.J.: Princeton University Press, 2000).

17. Dobelstein, *Moral Authority*, chap. 3; Cnaan, *Newer Deal*, chap. 4.

18. Cf. Dobelstein, *Moral Authority*, chaps. 3-4; Axinn and Levin, *Social Welfare*, 199–200.

19. Of course, welfare broadly includes assistance for those unable to work and benefits tied to employment. The persistent concern about dependency has to do with nonwork (and more generally, isolation from society) by those who could support

themselves and their dependents. On this aspect of the normative issue in welfare, see especially James W. Skillen, "The Question of Being Human in Assessing the Requirements of Welfare Policy Reform," in *Welfare in America: Christian Perspectives on a Policy in Crisis*, ed. Stanley W. Carlson-Thies and James W. Skillen (Grand Rapids, Mich.: Eerdmans, 1996), 119–44; Lawrence M. Mead, *Beyond Entitlement: The Social Obligations of Citizenship* (New York: Free Press, 1986); and Neal Gilbert, *Welfare Justice: Restoring Social Equity* (New Haven, Conn.: Yale University Press, 1995).

20. Mary Jo Bane and David T. Ellwood, *Welfare Realities: From Rhetoric to Reform* (Cambridge, Mass.: Harvard University Press, 1994), 2–7.

21. See, e.g., Mark A. Noll, *A History of Christianity in the United States and Canada* (Grand Rapids, Mich.: Eerdmans, 1992), chap. 14.

22. David O. Moberg, *The Great Reversal: Evangelism and Social Concern*, rev. ed. (Philadelphia: Lippincott, 1977).

23. Robert T. Handy, *A Christian America: Protestant Hopes and Historical Realities*, 2d ed. (New York: Oxford University Press, 1984), 142.

24. Presbyterian Church (USA), "'God Alone Is Lord of the Conscience': Policy Statement and Recommendations Regarding Religious Liberty," report of the Committee on Religious Liberty and Church-State Relations (adopted by the 200th General Assembly, 1989), 31.

25. Robert T. Handy, *Undermined Establishment: Church-State Relations in America, 1880-1920* (Princeton, N.J.: Princeton University Press, 1991), 7.

26. Charles Leslie Glenn Jr., *The Myth of the Common School* (Amherst: University of Massachusetts Press, 1988); and Brown and McKeown, *Poor Belong to Us*.

27. Useful dissections of no-aid separationism include Monsma, *When Sacred and Secular Mix*; idem, *Positive Neutrality: Letting Religious Freedom Ring* (Westport, Conn.: Greenwood Press, 1993); Carl E. Esbeck, "A Constitutional Case for Governmental Cooperation with Faith-Based Social Service Providers," *Emory Law Journal* 46, no. 1 (1997): 1–41; and Douglas Laycock, "The Underlying Unity of Separation and Neutrality," *Emory Law Journal* 46, no. 1 (1997) 43–74.

28. The case is *Bowen v. Kendrick* (1988). For commentary on the case and dispute about its outcome and about the validity of the "pervasively sectarian" concept, see, e.g., Carl H. Esbeck, "The Neutral Treatment of Religion and Faith-Based Social Service Providers: Charitable Choice and Its Critics," and Alan Brownstein, "Constitutional Questions about Charitable Choice," both in *Welfare Reform & Faith-Based Organizations*, ed. Derek Davis and Barry Hankins (Waco, Tex.: J.M. Dawson Institute of Church-State Studies, Baylor University, 1999), at 173–217 and 219–65, respectively.

29. This is the strong argument of Monsma, *When Sacred and Secular Mix*.

30. Cnaan, *Newer Deal*, 181.

31. Monsma, *When Sacred and Secular Mix*, chap. 3.

32. Mead, *Beyond Entitlement*; and idem, *The New Politics of Poverty: The Nonworking Poor in America* (New York: Basic Books, 1992).

33. U.S. General Accounting Office, *Welfare Reform: States Are Restructuring Programs to Reduce Welfare Dependence* , GAO/HEHS-98-109 (Washington, D.C.: U.S. General Accounting Office, 1998); and Richard P. Nathan and Thomas L. Gais, *Implementing the Personal Responsibility Act of 1999: A First Look* (Albany, N.Y.: Federalism Research Group, Nelson A. Rockefeller Institute of Government, State University of New York, 1999).

34. Charles Murray, *Losing Ground: American Social Policy, 1950–1980* (New York: Basic Books, 1984); and David T. Ellwood, *Poor Support* (New York: Basic Books, 1988).

35. Michael Novak et al., *The New Consensus on Family and Welfare: A Community of Self-Reliance* (Washington, D.C.: American Enterprise Institute for Public Policy Research, and Milwaukee: Marquette University Press, 1987).

36. Peter L. Berger and Richard John Neuhaus, *To Empower People: From State to Civil Society*, ed. Michael Novak, 2d ed. (Washington, D.C.: AEI Press, 1996); Don E. Eberly, ed., *Building a Community of Citizens: Civil Society in the 21st Century* (Lanham, Md.: University Press of America, and Commonwealth Foundation, 1994); and E.J. Dionne Jr., ed., *Community Works: The Revival of Civil Society in America* (Washington, D.C.: Brookings Institution Press, 1998).

37. For a summary of the law, see *Congressional Quarterly 1996 Almanac* (Washington, D.C.: CQ Press, 1997), 6-13 to 6-21; *Congressional Quarterly 1997 Almanac* (Washington, D.C.: CQ Press, 1998), 2-57 to 2-58, 6-31 to 6-36.

38. The "help and hassle" idea is from Lawrence M. Mead, "Welfare Employment," in *The New Paternalism: Supervisory Approaches to Poverty*, ed. Lawrence M. Mead (Washington, D.C.: Brookings Institution Press, 1997), 61–63.

39. However, Charitable Choice's sponsor, Senator John Ashcroft (Republican of Missouri); the author of the idea, Carl Esbeck, at the time professor of law at the University of Missouri-Columbia; and the two organizations that worked most closely to craft and promote the concept, the Center for Law and Religious Freedom of the Christian Legal Society and the Center for Public Justice, all belong to the Evangelical Protestant faith community.

40. Stanley W. Carlson-Thies, "'Don't Look to Us': The Negative Responses of the Churches to Welfare Reform," *Notre Dame Journal of Law, Ethics & Public Policy* 11, no. 2, "Entitlements" special issue (1997): 667–89.

41. Charitable Choice was section 104 of the federal welfare reform law, P.L. 104-193. The section is reprinted, with extensive commentary and guidance, in *A Guide to Charitable Choice: The Rules of Section 104 of the 1996 Federal Welfare Law Governing State Cooperation with Faith-Based Social-Service Providers* (Washington, D.C.: Center for Public Justice, and Annandale, Va.: Center for Law and Religious Freedom of the Christian Legal Society, 1997).

42. States may require houses of worship to establish separate 501(c)(3) organizations to receive the government funds and provide the services; states cannot require those separate organizations to be secular.

43. Stanley W. Carlson-Thies, "Faith-Based Institutions Cooperating with Public Welfare: The Promise of the Charitable Choice Provision," in *Welfare Reform and Faith-Based Organizations*, ed. Derek Davis and Barry Hankins (Waco, Tex.: J M. Dawson Institute of Church-State Studies, Baylor University, 1999), 34–5.

44. When the government funds arrive via voucher rather than direct government contract, Charitable Choice does not require inherently religious elements to be separated out. The Court recognizes that, in the case of vouchers, the choice of provider is made by the recipient and not by government, eliminating establishment concerns. Of course, here also the government funds have to be used to provide the government-mandated social services.

45. Charitable Choice is the rule governing the federal funds even in states with "Blaine" amendments forbidding state funding of religious organizations; if necessary,

such states have to keep the federal funds separate from their own funds and adhere to the Charitable Choice rules in expending the former. See *Guide to Charitable Choice*, 25–26. Charitable Choice is an option for states only in the sense that, as a rule governing procurement, it is moot if a state uses none of the funds to purchase services from outside providers.

46. Quoted in Carlson-Thies, "Faith-Based Institutions Cooperating with Public Welfare," 38. See also Monsma, *When Sacred and Secular Mix*, chaps. 3–5; Loconte, *Seducing the Samaritan*; and Carl H. Esbeck, *The Regulation of Religious Organizations as Recipients of Governmental Assistance* (Washington, D.C.: Center for Public Justice, 1996).

47. See, e.g., Esbeck, "Constitutional Case"; idem, "Neutral Treatment of Religion and Faith-Based Social Service Providers"; Monsma, *Positive Neutrality*; and Stephen V. Monsma and J. Christopher Soper, eds., *Equal Treatment of Religion in a Pluralistic Society* (Grand Rapids, Mich.: Eerdmans, 1998). In the *Mitchell v. Helms* decision, June 2000, a majority of the Supreme Court justices all but abandoned the no-aid doctrine while all but adopting the "neutrality" alternative.

48. E.g., Marvin Olasky, *Renewing American Compassion* (New York: Free Press, 1996). For other views, pro and con, on Charitable Choice, see especially Davis and Hankins, *Welfare Reform*. Differing viewpoints are summarized in Carlson-Thies, "'Don't Look to Us,'" and in Martha Minow, "Choice or Commonality: Welfare and Schooling after the End of Welfare as We Knew It," *Duke Law Journal* 49 (1999): 493–559.

49. "Remarks as Prepared for Delivery by Vice President Al Gore on the Role of Faith-Based Organizations," May 24, 1999.

50. Particularly noteworthy is how Charitable Choice has encouraged some in the Salvation Army to reconsider the acceptability of past government regulations. See Diane Winston, *Soup, Soap, and Salvation: The Impact of Charitable Choice on the Salvation Army* (Washington, D.C.: Center for Public Justice, 2000). The Army's constant emphasis on maintaining its integrity is emphasized in Glenn, *Ambiguous Embrace*, "Interlude: The Salvation Army."

51. Mark Penn, "The Community Consensus," *Blueprint: Ideas for a New Century (Democratic Leadership Council)*, spring 1999, 52–53; Public Agenda poll, Jan. 9, 2001, "For Goodness' Sake"; Pew Forum on Religion and Public Life poll, April 10, 2001, "Faith-Based Funding Backed, but Church-State Doubts Abound."

52. Then-senator John Ashcroft (Republican of Missouri), now attorney general in the George W. Bush administration, introduced this measure in both the 105th and 106th Congresses.

53. Gore, "Remarks"; George W. Bush, "The Duty of Hope," speech delivered in Indianapolis, July 22, 1999, and "'The Duty of Hope' Fact Sheet," July 22, 1999.

54. Jim Wallis, "Overcoming Poverty: A New Era of Partnership," in *Welfare Reform and Faith-Based Organizations*, ed. Derek Davis and Barry Hankins (Waco, Tex.: J M. Dawson Institute of Church-State Studies, Baylor University, 1999), 160–61.

55. Marshall Breger, "The Jewish Community and Its Liberal Allies Are Prepared to Sacrifice the Needy and Indigent on the Altar of Church-State Ideology," *Moment*, Aug. 1998, 18–19; Nathan J. Diament, "The Debate Over 'Charitable Choice': The Case for Gore's Proposal," *New York Jewish Week*, June 18, 1999. Notwithstanding their continued strong opposition to Charitable Choice, the American Jewish Committee and other separationist groups have taken part in "common ground" discussions that have issued statements supporting some forms of expanded collaboration between gov-

ernment and religious social-service programs. See, e.g., "In Good Faith: A Dialogue on Government Funding of Faith-Based Social Services" (Feinstein Center for American Jewish History, Temple University, Philadelphia, 2001), and "Finding Common Ground: 29 Recommendations of the Working Group on Human Needs and Faith-Based and Community Initiatives" (Search for Common Ground, Washington, D.C., 2002).

56. Amy L. Sherman, *The Growing Impact of Charitable Choice: A Catalogue of New Collaborations between Government and Faith-Based Organizations in Nine States* (Washington, D.C.: Center for Public Justice, March 2000). A "report card" on Charitable Choice compliance released by the Center for Public Justice in September 2000, gave failing grades to a large majority of states, which had admitted via a survey that their funding practices did not conform in one or more ways to the new federal rules.

57. Amy L. Sherman, "Collaborations Catalogue: A Report on Charitable Choice Implementation in 15 States: Executive Summary" (Charlottesville, Va.: Faith in Communities, A Hudson Initiative, 2002), chart 1.

58. In August 2001, the White House released a report based on program audits by the five centers, "*Unlevel Playing Field: Barriers to Participation by Faith-Based and Community Organizations in Federal Social Service Programs*."

59. On implementation issues, see Stanley W. Carlson-Thies, *Charitable Choice for Welfare & Community Services: An Implementation Guide for State, Local, and Federal Officials* (Washington, D.C.: Center for Public Justice, 2000), and Ryan Streeter, ed., *Religion and the Public Square in the 21st Century: Proceedings from the conference: The Future of Government Partnerships with the Faith Community* (Indianapolis: Hudson Institute, 2001).

60. For these and other concerns, see Davis and Hankins, *Welfare Reform*; Glenn, *Ambiguous Embrace*; and Amy L. Sherman, *Restorers of Hope: Reaching the Poor in Your Community with Church-Based Ministries That Work* (Wheaton, Ill.: Crossway, 1997), part 3.

61. In fact, faith-based organizations providing services under the charitable choice rules appeal to be well aware of these and other challenges and to be surmounting them. See the report of a survey of nearly 400 faith-based organizations: John C. Green and Amy L. Sherman, "Fruitful Collaborations: a Survey of Government-Funded Programs in 15 States" (The Hudson Institute/Hudson Faith in Communities, Sept. 2002). For practical guidance, faith groups can turn to Amy Sherman, *The Charitable Choice Handbook for Ministry Leaders* (Washington, D.C.: Center for Public Justice, and Indianapolis: Welfare Policy Center of the Hudson Institute, 2001).

62. Rockne M. McCarthy, James W. Skillen, and William A. Harper, *Disestablishment a Second Time: Genuine Pluralism for American Schools* (Grand Rapids, Mich.: Christian University Press, 1982); James W. Skillen, ed., *The School-Choice Controversy: What Is Constitutional?* (Grand Rapids, Mich.: Baker Books, 1993); Joseph P. Viteritti, *Choosing Equality: School Choice, the Constitution, and Civil Society* (Washington, D.C.: Brookings Institution Press, 1999); and Minow, "Choice or Commonality."

63. James W. Skillen, *Recharging the American Experiment: Principled Pluralism for Genuine Civic Community* (Grand Rapids, Mich.: Baker Books, 1994); Stanley W. Carlson-Thies, "The Meaning of Dutch Segmentation for Modern America," in *Sharing the Reformed Tradition: The Dutch-North American Exchange, 1846–1996*, eds.

George Harinck and Hans Krabbendam (Amsterdam: VU Uitgeverij, 1996), 159–175; Stephen V. Monsma and J. Christopher Soper, *The Challenge of Pluralism: Church and State in Five Democracies* (Lanham, Md.: Rowman & Littlefield, 1997).

64. Luis E. Lugo, *Equal Partners: The Welfare Responsibility of Governments and Churches* (Washington, D.C.: Center for Public Justice, 1998). The "equal partners" concept valuably emphasizes that faith-based providers are of no lesser value than government agencies, but it deemphasizes the enormous difference in power between the two kinds of institutions. An alternative term such as "collaborators" usefully connotes both working together and the potential for faith-based organizations to be co-opted (note that collaborator was the term in World War II for citizens who aided the enemy). Charles Glenn's notion of an "ambiguous embrace" is intended also to highlight both possibilities and dangers (Glenn, *Ambiguous Embrace*). Of course, the whole point of the Charitable Choice concept is to limit the government's distorting impact on faith-based organizations when the two sectors work together. In that sense, Charitable Choice is but one example of a global movement to recast the relationship between government and nongovernmental organizations. On that global trend, see Lester M. Salamon and Helmut K. Anheier, *The Emerging Nonprofit Sector: An Overview* (Manchester: Manchester University Press, 1996).

65. Lugo, *Equal Partners*, 15, 18, 19.

66. Richard John Neuhaus, *The Naked Public Square: Religion and Democracy in America* (Grand Rapids, Mich.: Eerdmans, 1984).

10

Public Education Changes Partners

Charles Glenn

Although actual classroom practice has changed far less than one might imagine during the past hundred years, the *function* and the *meaning* of American public education have become profoundly different. There are few occupations whose day-to-day activities have changed as little as have those of schoolteachers, but the relationship of schools and society has become very different than it was in 1900.

With the perfect hindsight of history, we can see that two possible directions were available to the public school a hundred years ago, as it became impossible to ignore that several generations of heavy immigration and urbanization had made the United States irreducibly pluralistic. Horace Mann, in the 1840s, had insisted that public schools could teach the "pure religion of heaven" and a distinct moral code upon which all could agree. The social consensus that made such claims reasonable no longer existed in 1900, at least in industrial cities and states.

Two choices were available. One would have been to redefine the "common school" as a school based upon the shared values of a particular group of parents or community, as was still the case in rural areas and in the growing Catholic, Lutheran, Dutch Reformed, and other alternative schools. This was the course then being followed in Belgium, England, Germany, and the Netherlands, all of which organized publicly supported schooling along denominational lines, with parents free to choose.

The other—the one taken with little debate—was to purge the public school, over time, of the explicit value commitments that Mann and his contemporaries took for granted. Thus John Dewey, writing in the 1890s and many decades thereafter, offered a vision of education in which norms and meanings would emerge from the interactions in the school. "The primary root of all educative activity," he wrote, "is in the instinctive, impulsive attitudes and activities of the child, and not in the presentation and application of external material."[1]

This understanding of education as oriented exclusively toward the future that it was itself creating fitted conveniently with changes in its organizational basis.[2] Schools a hundred years ago mirrored the society that they served, or at least its white, Protestant, middle-class mainstream. Public schools today, though they continue to be invoked as the symbols and bulwarks of democracy, are often deeply alienated from their public. Perhaps the most dramatic sign of this alienation is the dramatic expansion of homeschooling during the 1990s to what is now estimated to be more than a million children.[3] Although religious motivation has played an important part for many homeschooling parents, there are many others who simply do not trust the message communicated by how public schools operate as well as by the explicit teaching that they provide.

In 1900, public schools were strongly local institutions, controlled by more than a hundred thousand local elected school boards, some of which supervised a single school. Teachers also were often local, typically the daughters of prosperous farmers or businessmen who had gone off after high school for several years of training at a state 'normal school' or denominational college. The beloved children's classic *Anne of Green Gables* and its sequels capture this model in its Canadian form.

Schooling consisted largely of the first eight grades; in 1900, there were almost 15 million public school pupils in these elementary grades, compared with only a half-million in high schools. Though the South lagged well behind the rest of the country in the provision and quality of schooling, there were great efforts under way in North Carolina and elsewhere to make schooling universal and effective for white children, though the post-Emancipation push to educate black children had faltered from lack of conviction.[4]

There have been many changes in the scope and mission of schooling, but none is more significant than the fact that it is no longer the *local* enterprise it was for so long. Even though, by European standards, American public schooling is absurdly decentralized to some 15,000 autonomous districts, individual schools have come to have far less local flavor than they did seventy years ago. To an overwhelming extent, schools and those who work in them now respond to norms set by the education profession and by state and federal policymakers, and not to local norms and societal consensus.

This is not to call for a return to the old ways in American education. There have been many gains, as well as many losses, in the curriculum, in the quality of teaching, and in how pupils are treated. The close control of schools by local elected officials made it difficult to introduce new material and to expose pupils to broader perspectives. Children today receive a much broader, if also often much shallower, schooling than did those of a hundred years ago.

Among the losses, however, is the taken-for-granted engagement of parents with the content of their children's education. In no way is this more apparent than in the banning of religious themes from public schools. It is not an exaggeration to say that pupils who relied exclusively on what they were told in school and on their assigned readings could come out after twelve or thirteen years unaware that such a thing as religion existed in the contemporary world, much less that it continues to play a major role in American life.

In this chapter, I argue that a primary cause of this change in the relationship between public schools and the religious beliefs of the public is a long-standing fear of religion on the part of policy elites, a fear and consequent hostility that can be traced consistently over more than two hundred years of European and American history. I also contend that this fear is reinforced by a way of conceptualizing education that inevitably casts religion as its enemy.

Religion-Free Schools

Opposition to any hint of religion in public schools was illustrated a few years ago when the American Civil Liberties Union took a stand against a proposed state law calling for abstinence-based sex education on the grounds that "teaching that monogamous, heterosexual intercourse within marriage is a traditional American value is an unconstitutional establishment of a religious doctrine in public schools."[5]

The relentless secularization of the curriculum and daily life of American public schools is in stark contrast with the practice in other Western democracies, despite the fact most have a level of religious belief and practice outside of schools much lower than in the United States. Most Western European countries provide for regular religious instruction as part of the public school curriculum, as well as providing public funds for independent religious schools chosen by parents.[6]

Often, it is assumed that the religion-free character of American public schools is a consequence of the disestablishment of state churches during the early years of the Republic, and of the "wall of separation between Church and State" that Jefferson and others understood to be a feature of our constitutional order. The assumption is mistaken. Religion—specifically Christianity in some nondenominational form—was very much present in public schools throughout the nineteenth century and into the twentieth. A national survey in 1946 found that "Bible reading in the schools was required in thirteen states, and authorized for school districts as a local option in twenty-five more. In 1960 one-third of the Nation's schools reportedly began the school day . . . with devotional prayer, and 42 percent required reading the Bible."[7]

Support for religious practices in public schools was especially strong among those public school advocates who feared the growing competition of alternative religious schools, both Catholic and Protestant. Thus the National Teachers' Association (forerunner of the National Education Association, the 3-million-member union that is the most powerful force in American education today) expressed opposition, in 1869, to public funding for "'sectarian'" schools, but resolved that "the Bible should not only be studied . . . but devotionally read, and its precepts inculcated in all" elementary schools.[8]

What accounts for the change from public schools permeated with broadly Christian themes and practices only forty years ago to the exclusion of Christmas trees and Santa Clauses from many today? A quick answer might be that our society has become more respectful of cultural diversity, and that the exclusive presence of Christianity would no longer be considered acceptable. Though true, this is not an adequate explanation. It is routine, in other Western democracies, to give equal, or at least proportional, time to different religious traditions as they are represented in a particular school. Would not that be the appropriate "multicultural" thing to do? But few American public schools do so; their presentation of cultural diversity rarely includes religious themes in a serious way.

Now all expressions of religion as it is actually lived today are banned from most public schools. Children may do a unit on Greek gods and goddesses or on the beliefs of the ancient Egyptians, but what modern-day Greeks and Egyptians believe is unlikely to be mentioned. Native American spirituality is a partial exception, but pupils are unlikely to learn that many Sioux are Episcopalians and many Navajo are Catholics or Methodists.

As with most social phenomena, there is no single explanation for the exclusion of living religions from U.S. public schools. It would be easy to assume that it is an inevitable consequence of modernity and of a growing societal pluralism, leading to the secularization of public life. Public schools would, by this account, simply be following wider social trends. But this explanation does not work. In the first place, the American people are not growing more indifferent to religion than they were in the past, nor are they as "secularized" as the peoples of Western Europe, where religion continues to play a much more prominent part in public education. And, in the second, the public schools are not following a trend in public life, but leading it. Religion receives much more public recognition and support in Congress, in the military, in government-funded social and health services, in prisons, and in higher education than it does in public schools.[9] The schools are an island of secularity in a sea of varied but frequently dynamic religious expressions.

How do we explain the anomaly, then, that schools, which we would expect to be more intimately concerned with communicating an account of the nature of the Good than any other sphere of public life, are in fact the most rigorously purged of any such themes? Among the contributing factors to this development (for, like most social phenomena, it is overdetermined) is a way of thinking about education and religion that was originally held by a relatively small elite who saw universal schooling as a means of transforming society by "popular enlightenment." This way of thinking (which it would not be misleading to refer to as an ideology) has come to be widely accepted by teachers as a result of the norms absorbed during their professional training. It is possible to trace the expanding influence of this ideology during the course of the nineteenth and twentieth centuries, and to interpret some of the recent developments in American education as reactions by the broader public against this now-dominant set of assumptions within the rather closed world of public education.

It may seem strange to refer to an enterprise that employs several million adults and takes up half of the waking hours of tens of millions of children and youth as a closed world. But the leadership of the guild of professional educators—in the professional associations and the teacher-training institutions—has become very good at tuning out any signals from the wider culture that call its self-understanding into question.[10] Currently, for example, most criticisms of teaching methods or content are dismissed as coming from the Religious Right, whether or not those making them are especially religious or politically conservative.[11] Critics who can be so described are immediately deprived of any right to be heard.

In this chapter, we will be focusing primarily upon how thinking about education has evolved. But first it is important to set that analysis within the context of the structural changes that have occurred during the past century.

How American Public Education Has Evolved since 1900

First, some numbers. In 1900, 28.4 percent of the U.S. population was between the ages of five and seventeen years, compared with 18.2 percent in 1990. Although we are very conscious of the substantial proportion of school-age children who are recent immigrants or members of minority groups, the proportion was even higher in 1900. Then, without the socializing force of radio and television, the mission of the schools in teaching English and bringing these children into the productive mainstream of the society seemed even more crucial. American schools, both public and religious, were in their different ways intensely concerned with forming citizens.

As was noted above, there were almost 15 million public school pupils in the first through eighth grades in 1900; this number doubled to almost 30 million in 1990. Meanwhile, however, the total U.S. population had tripled. At the high school (grades nine through twelve) level, the change was much more dramatic, from about a half-million in 1900 to more than 11 million in 1990. Most of this expansion of the proportion of pupils going on to high school had been accomplished by 1940 (well ahead of most European countries), in part as a result of the unavailability of jobs for youth during the Depression. Higher education enrolments also grew between the wars and then took off after World War II, rising from 238,000 in 1900 to 1,494,000 in 1940, 3,640,000 in 1960, and 13,820,000 in 1990.

The first point to be made about these numbers is that schooling has come to be a much longer proposition for most pupils, extending over sixteen or more rather than eight or fewer years for many. The impetus for this extension of schooling was largely economic; in an information-based economy, the payoff for more years of formal education becomes much more significant. Not only did the nature of employment change, but there was a natural ratcheting effect: As more youth complete more years of schooling, those who do not find themselves at a competitive disadvantage in the labor market. A high school diploma has come to be the norm, and its lack an indication (whether fairly or not) of serious unfitness for employment. *Achievement*, what is actually learned in high school or college, has come to be in some ways less important than *attainment*, what level of education has been completed.

A second implication of these enrolment trends should also be noted. In 1900, the focus of education was largely upon what pupils learned in the elementary grades. Secondary and higher education—though more widespread than in other countries at the time—were the privilege of a small proportion of youth. One consequence was that the focus of the overall educational enterprise was less on preparation for employment and more on preparation for life as a citizen of good moral character and patriotic sentiments.

Although, as we will see, the governance of American public education was highly dispersed, there was broadly based agreement about this mission. David Tyack and Elizabeth Hansot noted that "the system of public education expressed an ideological coherence represented by established churches or centralized governments in other nations."[12] This coherence was broadly Christian, though avoiding what were regarded as divisive doctrines about the nature of God and the means of redemption. The precepts to which the National Teachers' Association resolution referred, in 1869, were moral rather than strictly theological; avoidance of the distinctive teachings of any Christian denomination was seen as the best guarantee of continuing to permeate public schools with a general Christian flavor.[13] As formal education has increasingly been extended until the student is of an age to enter directly into a career for which the education has ostensibly prepared him or her, this character-shaping mission has taken second place (often a very distant second place) to vocational or professional preparation.

A second development has been the consolidation of the governance of public education. In 1940, there were about 118,000 local school districts; today there are about 15,000. State governments regulate these districts much more closely than they did in 1900, and the federal government is also far more influential through regulations, enforcement actions, and categorical funding. During the past fifteen years, the states have greatly expanded their funding of local districts, and they have expanded even more vigorously the standards that local districts are expected to meet. What in 1900 was a loosely knit "system" of locally governed schools has become a complexly integrated system in which the voice of parents and voters and the authority of the school boards that they elect have much more limited effects. Although American public education is still, by European standards, highly decentralized and unstandardized, it has become less and less responsive to local values and priorities. Outsiders, including elected officials, find it very difficult to have any influence upon the actual functioning of schools.

This evolution is related in complex ways to a third development, the growing professionalization of teaching and educational administration. Bringing "trained intelligence"—what we would call expertise—to bear upon social problems was, for John Dewey and many of his contemporaries, the infallible route to social progress.[14]

Historian David Tyack has described the process of educational reform in the late nineteenth and early twentieth centuries, when "articulate professionals agreed on the remedies: consolidation of schools and transportation of pupils, expert supervision by county superintendents, 'taking the schools out of politics,' professionally-trained teachers . . . the result was to be a standardized, modernized 'community' in which leadership came from the professionals." These "new educational standards reflected an increasingly cosmopolitan rather than local scale of values among schoolmen, who sought to blur the differences between district and district, county and county, and even state and state."[15]

The "articulate professionals" who have increasingly provided the leadership for American education are big-city and state superintendents, professors of education, and officials of the educational associations and teachers' unions. They see little need to respond to the uninformed views of the general public and of parents, as was recently illustrated by a survey of "teachers of teachers," professors in teacher training institutions. Seventy-nine percent of the 900 professors surveyed agreed that "the general public has outmoded and mistaken beliefs about what good teaching means," and communication with parents was considered important, not to learn what parents wanted for the education of their children, but so they could be "educated or reeducated about how learning ought to happen in today's classroom." "What bothers me," one of the professors complained, "is for the public to make the decision of what I, the teacher, should do in the classroom. I really resent that. . . . They're getting into methodology, and what methodology [you can teach] they're going to tell you by law."[16] That is, by the democratic political process.

Now, of course majority opinion should not always prevail, and expertise has an important part to play in the complex world we and our children live in. Whether to teach reading by phonics or a "whole language" approach can most appropriately be decided by careful research (which, not unexpectedly, suggests that elements of both should be employed!). But much of what is referred to by this professor as "methodology" involves choices about how to teach that depend directly upon opinions about the goals of education. The professors of education surveyed were convinced, for example, that "the intellectual process of searching and struggling to learn is far more important . . . than whether or not students ultimately master a particular set of facts." Sixty percent of them called for less memorization in classrooms, with one professor in Boston insisting that it was "politically dangerous . . . when students have to memorize and spout back."[17] By contrast, according to another study by the same public-interest organization, "eighty-six percent of the public, and 73% of teachers, want students to memorize the multiplication tables and do math by hand before using calculators."[18]

These are not purely technical questions. They also reflect assumptions about the very nature of education, value judgments in which parents deserve a voice. The professors are expressing one form of the "cosmopolitan" values that have been promoted by American schooling increasingly during the past century, and that have made the exclusion of religion from the public schools seem not a matter of political convenience or respect for societal diversity, but essential to the mission of education. To understand how that has come about—considering that our educational institutions at all levels grew from religious initiatives—requires an exploration of the self-understanding of educators.

The Self-Understanding of Educators

Every profession has norms that describe its core mission and provide an idealized account of what it means to exercise it. Norms describe what it is to be a lawyer or a doctor or an accountant or a psychologist. Educators are no exception, and the dominant norm for the past two hundred years, it is fair to say, is that educators are *liberators*. What is perhaps the oldest and still one of the most influential accounts of education, in Plato's *Re-*

public, consists of a parable that begins with prisoners in a cave. Socrates offers, in this parable, "an image of our nature in its education and want of education":

> Behold! Human beings living in an underground cave, which has a mouth open towards the light and reaching all along the cave; here they have been from their childhood, and have their legs and necks chained so that they cannot move, and can only see before them, being prevented by the chains from turning round their heads. Above and behind them a fire is blazing at a distance, and between the fire and the prisoners there is a raised way; and you will see, if you look, a low wall built along the way, like the screen which marionette players have in front of them, over which they show the puppets. . . . And do you see men passing along the wall carrying all sorts of vessels, and statues and figures of animals made of wood and stone and various materials, which appear over the wall? Some of them are talking, others silent.
>
> You have shown me a strange image, [one of his interlocutors replies], and they are strange prisoners.
>
> Like ourselves, I replied; and they see only their own shadows, or the shadows of one another, which the fire throws on the opposite wall of the cave?

"Like ourselves," Socrates says; that is, we are also prisoners of the illusions which he has been describing. Education is the process by which one imprisoned in illusions of what appears to be reality is forced to look toward the light of the fire, which at first is painful, and then is led unwillingly up the path out of the cave to stand in the light of day, and at last look toward the sun itself. "Will he not fancy that the shadows which he formerly saw are truer than the objects which are now shown to him?" Of course, and this is why the educator is called literally to disillusion pupils from what parents and society have taught.

Plato's understanding of education was radical for its day, and continues to be radical today. Most people, and especially most parents, think of education as communicating a tradition and the skills to make use of it in confronting new challenges. For Plato, parents were part of the problem, and their influence should be minimized by sending out of the city all those over ten years old. Why? Because parents usually seek to convey to their children their own understanding of reality, of the goals of a good life, of how to treat other people, of all that can be brought together under the names of culture and religion. To take an example roughly contemporaneous with Plato, in Deuteronomy Moses tells the people of Israel:

> See, I have taught you decrees and laws as the LORD my God commanded me, so that you may follow them in the land you are entering to take possession of it. Observe them carefully, for this will show your wisdom and understanding to the nations . . . Only be careful, and watch yourselves closely so that you do not forget the things your eyes have seen or let them slip from your heart as long as you live. Teach them to your children and to their children after them. . . . These commandments that I give you today are to be upon your hearts. Impress them on your children. Talk about them when you sit at home and when you walk along the road, when you lie down and when you get up.[19]

There is no suggestion, here, that parents are chained in a darkness from which their children need to be set free. Not that parents are, in this account, the ultimate source of truth and authority; they, like their children, are subject to a tradition of moral obligation that they are expected to obey and to cherish.

The theme of education as liberation from the dead hand of the past and of parents in order to build society on a new foundation came to have canonical status among the nation-builders of the eighteenth and nineteenth centuries.[20] Jean-Jacques Rousseau wrote in 1755:

> That government which confines itself to mere obedience will find difficulty in getting itself obeyed. If it is good to know how to deal with men as they are, it is much better to make them what there is need that they should be. The most absolute authority is that which penetrates a man's inmost being, and concerns itself no less with his will than with his actions. It is certain that all peoples become in the long run what the government makes them. . . . Make men, therefore, if you would command men.[21]

It was through schooling that the authority of the state could establish itself in the "inmost being" of its citizens, making them into what one of the U.S. Founders, Benjamin Rush, called "Republican machines." Rousseau was one of the first, but by no means the last, social reformer since Plato to insist that the state should not "abandon to the intelligence and patriotism and prejudices of fathers the education of their children, as that education is of still greater importance to the State than to the fathers."[22]

The Jacobins of the extreme phase of the French Revolution articulated this ambition as clearly as it has ever been stated. "It is in national schools," Danton told the National Convention, "that children must suck republican milk. The Republic is one and indivisible; public instruction must also be related to this center of unity." Only in this way could the "total regeneration" of the French people called for by Robespierre and his allies be accomplished. But this could be accomplished only through resolute denial of the claims of parents. As a Jacobin orator warned his colleagues:

> You will lose the younger generation in abandoning it to parents with prejudices and ignorance who give it the defective tint which they have themselves. Therefore, let the Fatherland take hold of children who are born for it alone.[23]

John Dewey, the most significant education theorist of the twentieth century, explicitly aligned himself with this tradition of social change directed and accomplished by schools, writing that "all the educational reformers following Rousseau have looked to education as the best means of regenerating society. They have been fighting against the feudal and pioneer notion that the reason for a good education was to enable your children and mine to get ahead. . . . They have believed that the real reason for developing the best possible education was to prevent just this."[24]

Though his phrasing is characteristically more roundabout than that of Rousseau, Dewey believed just as firmly that "we must think and act upon the assumption that public education has a positive responsibility to shape those habits of thought and action which in turn shape organized conditions of social action. . . . I see no other way of rendering education in fact, and not just in name, the foundation of social organization."[25] Dewey insisted that religious and other "partial" viewpoints be banished from the school lest they compete with what he termed "state-consciousness."[26]

Using schooling to reshape "patterns of belief, desire and purpose," and thus to achieve "the clarification and development of the positive creed of life implicit in democracy and in science" that Dewey had written of as early as 1897 was a bold agenda for a society in which the institutions of democratic decisionmaking were by no means calling for such changes. But "Democracy," for Dewey, was by no means identified with the political system by which ordinary citizens, through their elected representatives, make decisions about schools and other public services.

Dewey justified his disregard for democratic politics by arguing that "school boards at present . . . are representative of a special class or group in the community, not of community interests."[27] And, again: "The reactionaries are in possession of force, in not only the army and police, but in the press and the schools."[28] Nor were school boards the only problem; parents and the general public joined in frustrating the intentions of social intelligence:

> Professional education has its results limited and twisted because of the general state of education. . . . Parents, school officials, taxpayers have the last word, and the character of that word is dependent upon their education. They may and do block or deflect the best laid plans.[29]

The only remedy was to strive for control of educational decisionmaking by teachers, through their professional organizations, that Dewey saw as "a constant and aggressive force in combating the efforts of various organized interests . . . to exploit the schools for their own ends."[30] Dewey did not appear to notice that critics could accuse him and other social progressives of a similar intention to use the schools to accomplish their social goals, but he expressed outrage at the activities of industry to influence public opinion about schooling, describing them as "efforts of special interests to control public and private education for their own ends. . . . In some respects, these revelations seem to me more sinister than those of the oil scandals, in that they represent an attempt at corruption of the source of public action."[31] He took for granted, by contrast, that the interests of teachers represented the "public interest" in the broadest, purest sense . . . if only the public knew what was good for it! He asserted

> the right of teachers to determine the subject-matter and methods employed in the schools. . . . If the teaching profession can educate itself and the public to the need of throwing off this incubus [of lay control of schools], genuinely educative forces will be released to do their work. In consequence, the freedom and impetus that result will enable the schools, without a centralized system, to develop a system of truly national education—by which I mean one animated by policies and methods that will help create that common purpose without which the nation cannot achieve unified movement.[32]

The distancing of children from the values represented by their families and communities was one of the aspects of the Russian educational system that Dewey found most intriguing when he visited in 1928. He was deeply impressed by the changes being brought about by the communist regime, and he told his American readers in the *New Republic* that "the main effort is nobly heroic, evincing a faith in human nature which is democratic beyond the ambitions of the democracies of the past."[33] He reported that, for the Soviet educational authorities, "the great task of the school is to counteract and transform those domestic and neighborhood tendencies that are still so strong, even in a nominally collectivistic regime," and he went on to note that

> to anyone who looks at the matter cold-bloodedly, free from sentimental associations clustering about the historic family institution, a most interesting sociological experimentation is taking place, the effect of which should do something to determine how far the bonds that hold the traditional family together are intrinsic and how far due to extraneous causes; and how far the family in its accustomed form is a truly socializing agency and how far a breeder of non-social interests.[34]

In Russia, Dewey was able to observe in action "the role of the schools in building up forces and factors whose natural effect is to undermine the importance and uniqueness of family life."[35] Although he does not mention it, he cannot have been unaware of the vigorous antireligious propaganda that marked the Soviet education system.[36]

Dewey himself mentions parents and families remarkably seldom in the thousands of pages that he wrote about education and human development. Typical of his thinking about families seems to be the statement, in 1922, that

> parents, priests, chiefs, social censors have supplied aims, aims which were foreign to those upon whom they were imposed, to the young, laymen, ordinary folk . . . men in authority have turned moral rules into an agency of class supremacy [but] any theory which attributes the origin of rule [*sic*] to deliberate design is false.[37]

It is the responsibility of teachers, Dewey argued, to help their pupils break free of these authorities, including their own parents. Teachers would have to constitute themselves an alternative source of authority to determine the direction of social change, given the conservative domination of school boards and the highly decentralized nature of American education. "We need an authority," he wrote, "that, unlike the older forms in which it operated, is capable of directing and utilizing change and we need a kind of individual freedom that is general and shared and that has the backing and guidance of socially organized intelligent control."[38] This authority would be that exercised by a self-aware educational profession:

> Teachers may be appointed by school boards and boards of trustees, but teachers are first and foremost responsible to "their moral employer," the public. They are "the servants of the community, of the whole community, and not of any particular class interest within it." Their "primary loyalty is to an idea, to a function and calling," which is "the pursuit and expression of truth," and they have a responsibility and right to organize to insure that they and their institutions carry out this social function.[39]

It is easy to applaud this high sense of the teacher's mission. But what does it mean to be servants of the whole community, if the will of that community is not expressed through the organs of democratic government? And are teachers as a collective body to decide for themselves what "idea" or "truth" they are to serve? Do parents—or students—have any say in this? Dewey seemed to have no doubts about the mission of educators:

> The schools will surely, as a matter of fact and not of ideal, *share* in the building of the social order of the future according as they ally themselves with this or that movement of existing social forces. This fact is inevitable . . . according as teachers and administrators align themselves with the older so-called "individualistic" ideals—which in fact are fatal to individuality for the many—or with the newer forces making for social control of economic forces. The teacher will . . . not be content with generalities about the desired future order. The task is to translate the desired ideal over into the conduct of the detail of the school in administration, instruction, and subject-matter.[40]

Like others before and after him who saw the mission of education as being to free the young from the traditions and superstitions of the past, Dewey recognized that a new set of beliefs would have to be put in place of those dismissed. For many of the education reformers, the substitute belief was some form of faith in science, in progress, in humanity itself, always advancing toward a brighter future. "By the 1850s," James Turner notes, "a great many Victorians on both Atlantic coasts invested science with power and promise, by the 1870s even with sacredness, hard now to credit. The belief became common that only science could make the world intelligible: science seemed the avatar of all knowledge."[41] As early as 1894, Dewey wrote that "it is because science represents a method of truth to which, so far as we can discover, no limits whatsoever can be put, that it is necessary for the church to reconstruct its doctrines of revelation and inspiration, and for the individual to reconstruct, within his own religious life, his conception of what spiritual truth is and the nature of its authority over him."[42]

As, a few years later, Dewey became deeply involved with experiments intended—and destined—to change how American educators thought about their work, he wrote of the need "to labor persistently and patiently for the clarification and development of the positive creed of life implicit in democracy and in science, and to work for the transformation of all practical instrumentalities of education till they are in harmony with these ideas."[43] The word "creed" was not chosen lightly; as he moved away from the liberal Protestantism of his early manhood, Dewey constantly employed its vocabulary to describe his new beliefs. "My Pedagogic Creed" (1897) was his earliest and still perhaps his most influential statement of the principles and assumptions of what would become Progressive Education.

Dewey was not at all shy about suggesting that science could take the place of traditional religion as the basis for an improved morality and system of belief. "A culture which permits science to destroy traditional values but which distrusts its power to create new ones," he warned, "is a culture which is destroying itself."[44] Some time later, he wrote specifically about religion:

> The root of the religious attitude of the future may lie immensely more in an improved state of science and of politics than in what have been termed religions. . . . The democracy and the science, the art of to-day may be immensely more prophetic of the religion which we would have spread in the future than any phenomena we seek to isolate under the caption of religions phenomena.[45]

We have lingered long over John Dewey because his thinking was at once highly representative of the direction in which nineteenth-century thinking about education had been moving, and profoundly influential upon what became, in the twentieth, received opinion in education circles. This is not to say that every teacher—or every education professor—has mastered the intricacies of Dewey's thought. But his emphasis on the experience of the pupil over the content of the curriculum, his confident rejection of the influence of tradition and the uninformed public, and his convictions about the culture-transforming mission of the school are essential to the self-understanding of public school educators.

To summarize this self-understanding, it is that educators know better than parents what is good for their children, and that what is good for them is to become "autonomous" in a Kantian sense—that is, not influenced by inherited beliefs or standards that they have not themselves reflected upon critically and arrived at independently of any external authority. The task of educators, then, is to lead children out of darkness into the light. Religion is part of the darkness of received belief out of which pupils should be led, not by antireligious propaganda, as in Soviet schools, but by consistently presenting a version of reality in which religion has no place at all. This can lead to a systematic distortion of both history and contemporary life, as when a National Education Association publication insisted that "when the Founding Fathers drafted the Constitution with its Bill of Rights, they explicitly designed it to guarantee a secular, humanistic state."[46]

What is so bad about educators having goals that are different from those of either parents or the society at large? The short answer is that, because children are especially vulnerable to influence, it is inappropriate for any group to use the authority of mandatory and state-funded schooling to seek to turn them against the convictions of their parents. Freedom of conscience ranks high among the guiding principles of a democratic society. Law professor John Coons points out that a free society should not proceed on the assumption that any group knows better than average parents what is best for those parents' children:

> The right to form families and to determine the scope of their children's practical liberty is for most men and women the primary occasion for choice and responsibility. One does not have to be rich or well placed to experience the family. The opportunity over a span of fifteen or twenty years to attempt the transmission of one's deepest values to a beloved child provides a unique arena for the creative impulse. Here is the communication of ideas in its most elemental mode. Parental expression, for all its invisibility to the media, is an activity with profound First Amendment implications.[47]

"Christian parents are often accused of indoctrinating" their children, of course, and this has served as a justification for the "liberating" role of teachers, "but this accusation is misguided because initiation is a necessary part of forming a self. Liberal parents, too, of necessity, initiate their children into a liberal tradition. . . . Children are not born autonomous, but need to be educated towards autonomy."[48]

The longer, more complex, answer is that the health of the civil society institutions—like families, religious communities, and ethnic and other voluntary organizations—upon which a free society so crucially depends is undermined if they cannot communicate distinctive ways of understanding the world and specific behavioral expectations. Public education, perhaps ironically, is in an unintended alliance with the mass media to communicate a version of reality purged of the virtues that ennoble human life and make for a healthy civil society. Neither makes an appeal to the "better angels of our nature"—the media because of pervasive cynicism, the public schools because of pervasive timidity. Neither celebrates nobility, self-sacrifice, obedience to duty, or love of and desire to know a Truth that transcends appearances.

At least Plato believed that the process of liberation would finally bring the pupil to see and understand a higher reality; at least Dewey believed that the right sort of schooling would produce citizens capable of cooperating to solve society's problems. Public education in our time has retained their emphasis upon liberation from the influence of family, tradition, and the common opinion, but has nothing to put in their place but careerism and self-esteem. It is as though Plato's educator abandoned the arduous journey out of the cave and began to enthrall the prisoners by displaying sitcoms on its walls! In fact, out of an instinct that much the same message is communicated by schools and by the mass media, many homeschooling families report that they throw away their television sets or use them only to show selected videos.

It is curious that many educators whose own lives have been shaped by their religious convictions have no difficulty compartmentalizing these from what they do as teachers or administrators in public schools. This is not to suggest that it would be appropriate, either ethically or legally, for them to seek to make converts or to persuade their pupils of the superior truth claims of their own beliefs. It would be enough, and entirely appropriate, for such educators to demonstrate in word and actions that faith is a factor of real—even central—significance in their own lives.

Similarly, all teachers should present the curriculum in ways that show how profoundly influential religious convictions and the behavior shaped by them have been and continue to be. Naturally, they should not conceal the fact that religion can have negative as well as positive effects. The goal should be to ensure that pupils have a balanced understanding of the role of religion and that, at least occasionally during their years of schooling, they encounter teachers and administrators who make no secret of the significance of religious or philosophical convictions in shaping their own lives. Pupils are unlikely to come away from their schooling with a mature and settled religious faith; nor should nurturing faith be the mission of the public schools. But schools should communicate that the themes of religion are important matters with which every fully experienced life must come to terms.

Education, rightly understood, is the lifelong process by which convictions are acquired and tested. A good school, a good teacher, a good book provide the resources from which an understanding of the world and its demands can be constructed. Taken together, the elements of a good education expose us to a variety of sources of meaning. And a good education also exposes us to models of coherent systems of meaning, not only in books but also in people worthy of admiration and emulation, including our teachers. It does so in a way communicating to us that achieving a stable set of beliefs and a settled disposition to act in ways consistent with these beliefs is not only possible but indeed the highest calling of men and women.

Perhaps the best metaphor to describe a good education is as a voyage of exploration that departs from the known into the unknown but knowable. Explorers are not aimless wanderers; they are purposeful and they go out searching in conviction that there is something real to be discovered. What is more, they see themselves as part of a shared enterprise, bringing back discoveries that must be fitted into what is already known and what others have found. That process of reconciling observations is a safeguard against purely idiosyncratic or delusional interpretations of individual experience. In other words, the exploration takes place within a context of already-established meaning; it is not free-floating, but is disciplined by the shared experience of a culture and, ultimately, of humanity in general.

Religious traditions are the repository of much that humanity has experienced, of how men and women have sought to come to terms with life and death, of how they have come to understand the nature of the good life. Children are cheated of much of what schools should contribute toward their education if they are presented with a version of reality that implies there is no need to raise such questions, and no value in learning about the various answers by which human beings have lived.

The Emerging U.S. Educational System . . . and Religion

There are some encouraging signs that the public education system in the United States will begin, once again, to do justice to the importance of religious questions and answers, and thus will not only serve its pupils better but also become more responsive to the concerns of parents.

The fundamental problem raised by controversies over education and religion cannot be addressed by simply doing justice to the history and present role of various faith traditions in the curriculum.[49] Desirable as that would be in the interest of accuracy, it would not remove the alienation that has grown up between public education and the public. The more basic problem—conflicts over religion are merely one of its more obvious manifestations—is the failure of American education to adapt to the changes in American society and culture.

One of the most significant of these changes is that most of us have come to accept a pluralistic understanding of our differences. People do not necessarily differ more than they ever did—indeed, they probably differ less—but we are more aware of each other and that many of those around us do not accept many of our own assumptions about the purpose (if any) of life and how it should be lived.

The pluralistic way of thinking about these differences is to be distinguished clearly from relativism, which denies that there is any such thing as ultimate truth. Instead, relativism insists that there are different perspectives, all of which are at least potentially true for those who hold them. The corollary of this apparently liberal, tolerant stance is that we have no common ground of right and wrong that we can count on sharing with others around us and upon whom we depend. Each of us, relativism claims, makes choices based upon our own "values," and the mark of personal authenticity is that these values are not accepted on the basis of anyone else's authority or of any tradition, but are simply our own. Pluralists, by contrast, "hold . . . that some values have rational and moral authority not only within but also outside of the context in which they are held. According to pluralists, not all values are context-dependent."[50]

A pluralistic understanding of society accepts, even celebrates, the organization of much of life by the autonomous associations, organizations, and relationships of the civil society, in which find expression "many reasonable conceptions of a good life. These conceptions are formed of the values provided by the agents' moral traditions and of the agents' efforts to fit some of them to their individual characters and circumstances."[51] Though all must play by certain common rules in the "public square" of society, they bring distinctive perspectives to bear on how they think about and respond to issues, and *that is just as it should be*, as long as they respect the common rules and one another.

This understanding of the nature of a healthy and free society differs profoundly from the assumption held by Dewey and others, that those who employ the "trained intelligence" that he identified with the scientific method would inevitably come to agree about the best course of action in all cases. That assumption now seems quaint; we have come to see that intelligent, well-meaning men and women can disagree profoundly because they have different fundamental assumptions. We have come also to have confidence that our society can live with these differences.

The idea that a public education system can and should promote a "common faith" has come to seem another of the quaint assumptions of Dewey's generation, midway in the transition from Protestant hegemony to our present pluralism. As I pointed out above, in 1900 there were two ways out of the no-longer-tenable dominance of American culture and its public education system by an ecumenical Protestantism that had largely lost its nerve.[52] One, the false path taken by Dewey and other educational leaders, was toward substituting a secularized orthodoxy, Dewey's common faith, "rescued through emancipation from dependence upon specific types of beliefs and practices, from those elements that constitute a religion."[53] The other path—the one not taken—was toward acceptance that no single alternative belief system could replace the old certainties.

Public education did indeed become more and more uniform during the course of the century, as we have seen. But at the same time (and as an inevitable consequence of the encounter with a diverse and diversifying society), the curriculum lost its old assurance. Rather than expressing a new, secular faith, it came to express a yawning emptiness.[54]

In recent years, however, there have been encouraging signs that American public education is becoming pluralistic, providing space for schools that express distinctive ways of understanding their goals and how to attain them. It is no longer possible to speak of a single model of public education, a "one best system" in Tyack's phrase. Those who organized and led the alternative schools of the 1960s, the thousands of magnet schools of the 1970s and 1980s, and the 2,000 charter schools founded during the past five years have made it their business to articulate distinctive profiles in order to attract parents who are no longer bound by residential assignments.[55] They have in a sense reinvented the local school, in a way that makes it responsive to those it serves. In the process, the monopoly system of public education, though still formally in place, has been subverted from within.[56]

Schools that must attract parents on the basis of distinctive educational offerings can no longer afford to see their mission as liberating children from the influence of their families and communities. Instead, they must seek to enable their students to move beyond without repudiating the achievements of those who have gone before them. To return to the metaphor used earlier in the chapter, they must launch them upon explorations that extend the map of human experience drawn by the explorations of earlier generations.

This enterprise of "bounded exploration" can best be undertaken, I contend, if it starts in schools and colleges that make no apology for expecting students to have mastered a common heritage and to know its contours well before they push off to discover new islands and continents on their own. Because an essential part of this exploration is concerned with how to live, it can best take its starting point from induction into a coherent set of moral convictions. These will be tested, called into question, and perhaps modified by individuals; but these students need at least a starting point and a compass to make that process fruitful. A school or college where ethical questions are avoided will not educate morally autonomous individuals.

Fortunately—for the health of our society and for serious engagement with important moral issues and questions of ultimate meaning—a new U.S. educational system is beginning to emerge. There is now an apparently irresistible drive toward more diversity in American education, whether through charter and other alternative public schools or through vouchers that make it possible for parents to choose nonpublic schools. Much of the educational establishment deplores this development, warning that it will divide the society in all sorts of harmful ways. Like Plato in the *Republic*, they perceive unity as the highest social good and fear that it is vulnerable to any alternative forms of education. They should have more confidence in the good sense of parents and teachers; there is little evidence of demand for weird or bigoted forms of schooling.

One of the great advantages of this new educational diversity is that it encourages schools and colleges to be distinctive rather than to provide a lowest-common-denominator education. Distinctive schools and colleges are more likely to be coherent, to stand for some tradition of culture and conviction that can be the starting-point for that exploration that alone can complete an education . . . not that it is ever completed! As Coons and his colleague Stephen Sugarman put it:

> The most important experience within schools of choice may be the child's observation of trusted adults gripped by a moral concern which is shared and endorsed by his own family. The content of that

> concern may be less important than its central position in the life of the institution. Even where particular values seem narrow and one-sided, a child's engagement with them at a crucial stage of his development might secure his allegiance to that ideal of human reciprocity which is indispensable to our view of autonomy. . . . This hypothesis seems as plausible as the traditional notion of professionals that compulsory and early severance of the child from his home culture is an act of merciful liberation.[57]

Public education does not have to be provided in schools operated by the government. Nor does it have to conform with the bureaucratic urge toward standardized operation. In most Western democracies, public education is provided in a mix of government-operated and "free" schools that are sponsored and controlled by churches and other private associations.

I have offered a metaphor for education as a deeply individual though shared process; let me offer another for the educational system that a free and just society requires. To borrow a phrase used cynically by Mao Tse-tung, "Let a hundred flowers bloom, let a hundred schools of thought contend." The sort of educational system that our society needs is like a garden with many different flowers. It is not like a neatly trimmed lawn from which all diversity—dandelions and crabgrass alike—has been carefully removed. A richly diverse garden is not promiscuous; the gardener removes what does not belong there, just as the state should ensure that no schools (or families) are allowed to brutalize children, and that all children have the opportunity to learn what is essential to their future participation in society.

Uniformity, however, is not sought in a garden. The eye and the soul are pleased by a rich diversity that expresses many different ways of being healthy and beautiful, of exploring and finding meaning. Among these are those rooted in religious traditions and experience. They have been too long missing from American public education. As Elmer John Thiessen points out, such pluralism is not inconsistent with requiring that every school, whatever its sponsor, teach the civic virtues that are essential for a flourishing society. After all,

> a monolithic state-maintained system of education [is] very much open to the charge of institutional indoctrination. A pluralistic system of education is best able to achieve the needed balance between teaching for specific commitments and also teaching for commitment to the common liberal values that are essential for the

> coexistence of peoples with various commitments in pluralistic liberal democracies.[58]

Most Western democracies foster a pluralistic educational system based upon parent choice by funding the schools that parents select for their children. At the same time, Sweden and Spain, France and Canada, and all the others require that these schools teach in a way consistent with internationally recognized human rights.[59]

"The cure for intolerance," Thiessen reminds us, "is not found in a relativistic elimination of convictions, but in a liberal education which combines teaching for commitment with the encouragement of respect for others. . . . It would seem that a stable and coherent primary culture is essential for children to develop a sense of identity, which is in turn a prerequisite to developing a tolerant and loving relationship with others. . . . Tolerance grows out of security and acceptance."[60]

But it is not from the individual teacher alone nor even from the school that this respect is learned. It is also learned from a political system that shows respect for individuals and groups whose religious commitments require that they initiate their children into those commitments. Respect for freedom and for diversity of worldview does not require, in a free society, that we abandon those convictions that lead precisely to this respect.

Notes

1. John Dewey, "The School and Society," in *The Child and the Curriculum and the School and Society* (Chicago: University of Chicago Press, 1956), 117.
2. The best account remains that of David Tyack, *The One Best System: A History of American Urban Education* (Cambridge, Mass.: Harvard University Press, 1974).
3. See National Center for Education Statistics, *Homeschooling in the United States: 1999* (Washington, D.C.: U.S. Department of Education, 2001); also Mitchell L. Stevens, *Kingdom of Children: Culture and Controversy in the Homeschooling Movement* (Princeton, N.J.: Princeton University Press, 2001).
4. James D. Anderson, *The Education of Blacks in the South, 1860–1935* (Chapel Hill: University of North Carolina Press, 1988); James L. Leloudis, *Schooling the New South* (Chapel Hill: University of North Carolina Press, 1996).
5. James Davison Hunter, *Culture Wars* (New York: Basic Books, 1991), 310.
6. Charles L. Glenn, *Choice of Schools in Six Nations* (Washington, D.C.: U.S. Department of Education, 1989).
7. A. James Reichley, *Religion in American Public Life* (Washington, D.C.: Brookings Institution Press, 1985), 145.
8. Hunter, *Culture Wars,* 134.
9. Charles L. Glenn, *The Ambiguous Embrace: Government and Faith-Based Schools and Social Agencies* (Princeton, N.J.: Princeton University Press, 2000).

10. A personal testimony: I was the manager for urban education and civil rights at the Massachusetts Department of Education for more than twenty years, attending hundreds of cabinet-level meetings. Not once was there discussion of the radical critiques of public education from both Left and Right, and not once mention of the fact that 12 percent of Massachusetts schoolchildren were in nonpublic schools. These realities were invisible.

11. Charles L. Glenn, "Outcome-Based Education: Can It Be Redeemed?" in *Curriculum, Religion and Public Education: Conversations for an Enlarging Public Square,* ed. James T. Sears with James C. Carper (New York: Teachers College Press, 1998).

12. David Tyack and Elisabeth Hansot, *Managers of Virtue: Public School Leadership in America, 1820–1980* (New York: Basic Books, 1982), 31.

13. Gerard V. Bradley, *Church–State Relationships in America* (New York: Greenwood Press, 1987), 127.

14. See, e.g., John Dewey, *Intelligence in the Modern World* (New York: Modern Library, 1939).

15. Tyack, *One Best System*, 23–25.

16. Steve Farkas and Jean Johnson, *Different Drummers: How Teachers of Teachers View Public Education* (New York: Public Agenda, 1997), 12.

17. Farkas and Johnson, *Different Drummers*, 10, 13.

18. Public Agenda, *Given the Circumstances: Teachers Talk About Public Education Today* (New York: Public Agenda, 1996, 19).

19. Deuteronomy 4:5–6, 9; 6:4–7.

20. Charles L. Glenn, *The Myth of the Common School* (Amherst: University of Massachusetts Press, 1988).

21. Jean-Jacques Rousseau, "Discourse on Political Economy" (1755), in *The Social Contract and Discourses*, trans. G.D.H. Cole (London: Everyman, 1993), 139.

22. Rousseau, "Political Economy," 148.

23. References for Danton, Robespierre, and Billaud-Varenne are found in Glenn, *Myth of Common School*, 291–92.

24. John Dewey, "Schools of To-Morrow" (1915), *Middle Works, Volume 8: Essays on Education and Politics 1915* (Carbondale: Southern Illinois University Press, 1979), 319.

25. John Dewey, "Education, the Foundation for Social Organization" (1937), in *Later Works, 1925–1953, Volume 11: 1935–1937* (Carbondale: Southern Illinois University Press, 1987), 235.

26. John Dewey, "Religion and Our Schools" (1908), in *Essays on Pragmatism and Truth, 1907–1909* (Carbondale: Southern Illinois University Press, 1977), 175.

27. John Dewey, "The Need for Orientation" (1935), in *Later Works, 1925–1953, Volume 11: 1935–1937* (Carbondale: Southern Illinois University Press, 1987), 165.

28. John Dewey, "The Future of Liberalism" (1935), in *Later Works, 1925–1953, Volume 11: 1935–1937* (Carbondale: Southern Illinois University Press, 1987), 294.

29. John Dewey, "Body and Mind" (1927), in *Later Works, 1925–1953, Volume 3: 1927–1928* (Carbondale: Southern Illinois University Press, 1988), 38.

30. John Dewey, "Why I Am a Member of the Teachers Union" (1927), *in Later Works, 1925–1953, Volume 3: 1927–1928* (Carbondale: Southern Illinois University Press, 1988), 273.

31. John Dewey, "A Critique of American Civilization" (1928), in *Later Works, 1925–1953, Volume 3: 1927–1928* (Carbondale: Southern Illinois University Press, 1988), 141.

32. John Dewey, "Toward a National System of Education" (1935), in *Later Works, 1925–1953, Volume 11: 1935–1937* (Carbondale: Southern Illinois University Press, 1987), 358–59.

33. John Dewey, "Impressions of Soviet Russia II: A Country in a State of Flux" (1928), *Later Works, 1925–1953, Volume 3: 1927–1928* (Carbondale: Southern Illinois University Press, 1988), 213.

34. John Dewey, "Impressions of Soviet Russia, IV: What Are the Russian Schools Doing?" (1928), *Later Works, 1925–1953, Volume 3: 1927–1928* (Carbondale: Southern Illinois University Press, 1988), 228.

35. Ibid., 230.

36. See Charles L. Glenn, Educational Freedom in Eastern Europe, 2d ed. (Washington, D.C.: Cato Institute, 1995), 33–38, 53–56.

37. Dewey, *Human Nature and Conduct* (1922), 5.

38. John Dewey, "Authority and Social Change" (1936), in *Later Works, 1925–1953, Volume 11: 1935–1937* (Carbondale: Southern Illinois University Press, 1987), 137.

39. Steven Rockefeller, *John Dewey: Religious Faith and Democratic Humanism* (New York: Columbia University Press, 1991), 286.

40. John Dewey, "Can Education Share in Social Reconstruction?" (1934), *in John Dewey: The Later Works, 1925–1953, Volume 9: 1933–1934* (Carbondale: Southern Illinois University Press, 1989), 207–8.

41. James Turner, *Without God, Without Creed: The Origins of Unbelief in America* (Baltimore: Johns Hopkins University Press, 1985), 137.

42. John Dewey, "Reconstruction," in *The Early Works, 1882–1898, Volume 4: 1893–1894* (Carbondale: Southern Illinois University Press, 1971), 103.

43. John Dewey, "Religion and Our Schools" (1908), *The Middle Works, Volume 4: Essays on Pragmatism and Truth, 1907–1909* (Carbondale: Southern Illinois University Press, 1977), 168.

44. John Dewey, "Freedom and Culture," in *Later Works, Volume 13: 1938–1939,* ed. Jo Ann Boydston (Carbondale: Southern Illinois University Press, 1991), 172.

45. John Dewey, "Some Thoughts concerning Religion" (1910), in *Later Works, Volume 17: 1885–1953,* ed. Jo Ann Boydston (Carbondale: Southern Illinois University Press, 1990), 379.

46. Mary Peek, *What Every Teacher Should Know about the New Right,* quoted in Hunter, *Culture Wars,* 113.

47. John E. Coons, "Intellectual Liberty and the Schools," *Journal of Law, Ethics & Public Policy* 1 (1985): 511.

48. Elmer John Thiessen, *Teaching for Commitment: Liberal Education, Indoctrination, and Christian Nurture* (Montreal: McGill-Queen's University Press, 1993), 128.

49. Charles L. Glenn and Joshua L. Glenn, "Making Room for Conviction in Democracy's Schools," in *Schooling Christians,* ed. Stanley Hauerwas and John H. Westerhoff (Grand Rapids, Mich.: Eerdmans, 1992).

50. John Kekes, *Against Liberalism* (Ithaca, N.Y.: Cornell University Press, 1997), 162.

51. Kekes, *Liberalism,* 170.

52. Thomas C. Reeves, *The Empty Church: The Suicide of Liberal Christianity* (New York: Free Press, 1996).

53. John Dewey, "A Common Faith" (1934), in *Later Works, Volume 9: 1933–1934,* ed. Jo Ann Boydston (Carbondale: Southern Illinois University Press, 1986, 11). It is striking how frequently, throughout his many decades of writing, Dewey the "secular humanist" uses the word "faith."

54. Charles L. Glenn, "Religion, Textbooks and the Common School," *The Public Interest*, July 1987, 28–47.

55. Chester E. Finn Jr., Bruno V. Manno, and Gred Vanourek, *Charter Schools in Action* (Princeton, N.J.: Princeton University Press, 2000).

56. Charles L. Glenn, "School Distinctiveness," *Journal of Education* 176, (1994): 73–103.

57. John E. Coons and Stephen D. Sugarman, *Education by Choice: The Case for Family Control* (Berkeley: University of California Press, 1978), 83.

58. Elmer John Thiessen, *In Defense of Religious Schools and Colleges* (Montreal: McGill-Queen's University Press, 2001), 196.

59. Charles L. Glenn and Jan De Groof, *Finding the Right Balance: Freedom, Autonomy and Accountability in Education*, vol. 1 (Utrecht, The Netherlands: Lemma, 2002), a study of laws and policies in 26 countries.

60. Thiessen, *In Defense of Religious Schools*, 52, 56.

11

With God on Their Side: Religion and U.S. Foreign Policy

William Martin

The United States, though far from perfect in its record of religious tolerance, has been remarkably successful at avoiding wars over differing faiths and, overall, at granting freedom to a wide variety of religious expressions and practices. That is a notable achievement in human history. The Framers of the Constitution were keenly aware of the threat to unity that religion could pose, and they set out to prove that a nation could exist and flourish without an established religion—a novel proposition in the eighteenth century. This sentiment did not arise from a hostility toward religion, but from a conviction that both religion and government, as well as individuals with their unalienable rights, would best flourish under such an arrangement. Throughout hundreds of years of recorded history, governments and

This chapter is an expansion of previous work by the author, some of which originally appeared in "The Christian Right and American Foreign Policy," *Foreign Policy*, spring 1999, 66–80; "With God on Their Side," *Georgetown Journal of International Affairs*, winter-spring 2000, 7–14; and "Religion and Statecraft," a paper prepared for the Inaugural Conference of the James A. Baker III Institute for Public Policy at Rice University, Houston, 1995.

religious institutions had struggled with each other for dominance, or at least parity, but neither had given much thought to the possibility that they might proceed independently of each other. Still, determined not to allow religion and government to infringe on the each other's territory, the Framers wrote a Constitution designed to accomplish that novel result.

As the other chapters in this book make clear, understandings of the proper relationship between religion and government, within the limits of the Constitution, have varied over more than two centuries of the Republic's life and continue to stimulate lively discussion and disagreement. Most of these essays focus on domestic politics. In a bit of a departure, I will give more attention to the role religion has played and continues to play in U.S. foreign policy and will contend that effective statecraft must therefore take account of religion's crucial role in human societies and, by extension, to the relations among them.

The United States clearly affirmed its secular status with respect to foreign policy shortly afterward when, in 1797, while John Adams was president, the government signed a treaty with Tripoli, a Muslim region of North Africa. Article 11 of the treaty states, "As the Government of the United States is not, in any sense, founded on the Christian religion; as it has in itself no character of enmity against the law, religion or tranquility of Musselmen [Muslims]; and as the states never have entered into any war or act of hostility against any Mohometan nation, it is declared by the parties that no pretext arising from religious opinion shall ever produce an interruption of harmony existing between the two countries."[1] This treaty, endorsed by the secretary of state and President Adams, was approved by the Senate without objection, apparently because it regarded its stipulations as accurate. That view was not undisputed, and statements to the contrary have been made by prominent leaders, but the basic position has held. Still, as other chapters in this book make abundantly clear, it should not be inferred that religion has not, does not, or should not play a significant role in shaping the nation's domestic and foreign policy. Indeed, examples of such religious influence abound.

A Long Tradition

From the day John Winthrop proclaimed to the passengers of the *Arbella* that God Almighty had dispatched them to New England to establish "a city upon a hill" for all humankind to behold and emulate, Americans have repeatedly manifested a confidence that they were on a divine mission and that God was on their side in their intercourse with other nations. Although the rationalism and optimism of the Enlightenment played a larger role in the thinking of most Founding Fathers than did biblical theology, the Great Awakening stirred by Jonathan Edwards, George Whitefield, and other revivalists earlier in the eighteenth century made its contribution to the movement for independence from England.

Men and women convinced that their direct relationship with God gave them the right and obligation to oppose any infringement on their religious liberties could easily transfer that same spirit of independence to the political realm. Consequently, they deemed illegitimate any authority they had not elected or that operated without their consent. Similarly, the Awakening generated millennial expectations that caused people to regard breaking free of England and founding a new republic not simply as a political experiment, but as part of God's great new work on earth.[2] To be sure, not all religious people subscribed to this view. Most notably, Anglicans were more likely to be loyalist, though substantial segments sided with Whiggish dissenters. But Puritan clergy voiced these sentiments so frequently and publicly that they came to be called the "Black Regiment," in recognition of their role in supporting the cause of independence and revolution.

It is not surprising that involvement by religious forces in matters of foreign policy has most often entailed issues of war and peace. The Mexican War at the midpoint of the nineteenth century had the support of Protestant Christians in the Southwest, but Catholics were troubled at the prospect of their nation's going to war against a Catholic country, and many Protestant clergy in the North and East opposed the war because Texas, a key prize in the war, was a slaveholding state. Catholics felt similar ambivalence at the Spanish-American War at the end of the century, but the dominant Protestant sentiment during that war viewed it as part of the missionary obligation inherent in America's Manifest Destiny. By liberating Cuba and gaining control of the Philippines, Guam, and Puerto Rico, the United States was helping oppressed people throw off Spain's Romish yoke.

Although some clergy criticized American arrogance in this war, it is likely that most Protestant church people saw little to criticize in President William McKinley's rationalization that "there was nothing left for us to do but to take them all and to educate the Filipinos and uplift and civilize and Christianize them and by God's grace do the very best we could by them, as our fellow men for whom Christ also died."[3] The high degree of consensus in favor of this war moved Sidney Ahlstrom to observe that "never have patriotism, imperialism, and the religion of American Protestants stood in such a fervent coalescence as during the McKinley-Roosevelt era."[4]

Numerous churches participated in a peace and anti-imperialism movement that arose in part as a reaction to the bellicosity of the Spanish-American War, but rampant patriotism resurfaced quickly as the United States prepared to take arms against Germany in World War I. In an episode that seems incongruous today, some of the most liberal Protestant church leaders, such as Shailer Matthews and Shirley Jackson Case of the Chicago Divinity School, attacked premillennial Fundamentalists for their early unwillingness to get involved in the war, at least in combat roles, even charging them with a lack of patriotism.[5] Eventually, most Fundamentalists came to support the war, and famed evangelist Billy Sunday, never a doubter on the matter, used his 1917 New York City revival to sell war bonds and urge young men to volunteer for military service.

Apart from Quakers, Mennonites, and a few conscientious objectors spread among other denominations, few churches raised objection to the war. The government supplied ministers with propaganda, and they transmitted it from their pulpits. So general was support for the war that William Warren Sweet observed, "At least for the period of World War I the separation of church and state was suspended."[6] The war led to another suspension on the part of Catholic bishops. To coordinate Catholic support for the war effort, the National Catholic War Council was formed in 1917. After the war, this coalition was transformed into National Catholic Welfare Council, providing bishops with an organizational platform from which they could speak out with a unified voice on social issues of national importance, something they had previously done only rarely.[7]

In the aftermath of World War I, reflection on the real and potential horrors of conflict among powerful nations gave rise to strong, often contradictory responses. Anger toward Germany led many ecclesiastical leaders to favor the harsh terms the Treaty of Versailles imposed upon that defeated nation, and xenophobic fear generated by the Bolshevik Revolution and the ensuing Red Scare moved many Protestants to speak out in favor of restrictions on immigration—particularly from non-Protestant lands. Along with such punitive and chauvinistic impulses, often from the same sources, came strong support for the League of Nations. When the Senate narrowly voted in 1919 to keep the United States out of the League, effectively dooming it to failure, the Federal Council of Churches (forerunner of the National Council of Churches) and other major ecclesiastical bodies reacted with sharp criticism and disappointment.[8]

Disillusionment with war also resuscitated a peace movement, undergirded by a strong spirit of pacifism, particularly in the mainline churches. The noninterventionist, isolationist spirit intrinsic to these convictions was inexorably eroded by German, Italian, and Japanese aggression during the 1930s, although the struggle between pacifists and interventionists roiled virtually every major denomination and church agency, at least until the Japanese attack on Pearl Harbor in 1941. Catholics, Jews, and Protestants—though chastened by an awareness of the hubris of nations, their own as well as others, and particularly within mainline Protestant circles influenced by Reinhold Niebuhr's insight that nations could not be expected to act with a purity of motive one might require of a moral individual and that earthly kingdoms could never become the Kingdom of God—quickly formed a united front in support of the war.

To a considerable extent, the conviction that had enabled American religious leaders to support war against the Axis powers in World War I provided similar support for U.S. efforts to fight communism in Korea, despite the less clear objectives in that conflict. No such consensus characterized the war in Vietnam. Concerned about the wisdom of supporting the South Vietnamese government and about tactics being used in the early stages of the war, as well as about the possibility of triggering nuclear war, some religious leaders—Reinhold Niebuhr, Episcopal bishop James Pike, Rabbi Julius Mark, and Stanford and Yale chaplains Robert McAfee Brown and William Sloane Coffin, among others—voiced opposition to the war, circulating petitions, placing advertisements in major newspapers, and calling on President Lyndon Johnson to initiate a cease-fire and begin peace negotiations.

The great majority of the nation's clergy, however, stayed on the sidelines, apparently reasoning that the government had sufficient knowledge and understanding to justify its policies. As knowledge of problematic aspects of the war—for example, the use of chemical defoliants, carpet bombing, and overrepresentation of African-American males in combat troops—opposition to the war began to mount sharply in 1965, and substantial numbers of clergy and laity formed groups such as the Clergyman's Emergency Committee for Vietnam and Clergy and Laymen Concerned about Vietnam. The National Council of Churches and the Synagogue Council of America called for a bombing halt and asked for a greater role for the United Nations.

African-American clergy were hesitant to criticize the president, given the help they needed on civil rights. But in August 1965, Martin Luther

King Jr. called on the administration to enter into negotiations with Hanoi and the National Liberation Front. As a denomination, Roman Catholics voiced only limited sharp criticism of the war, but the exceptions were dramatic. The Catholic Peace Fellowship criticized U.S. policy for failing to satisfy the criteria for a just war. A young man who doused himself with gasoline and set himself on fire in front of United Nations headquarters was a member of the Catholic Worker Movement. More notably, no individual opponents of the war attracted more publicity than the priest brothers, Philip and Daniel Berrigan, whose radical tactics included such actions as pouring blood over draft papers and setting draft files on fire with homemade napalm. Eventually, as the war continued to escalate, Richard Cardinal Cushing of Boston, who had previously sided with the administration, denounced the invasion of Cambodia.[9]

Obviously, religious involvement in matters of foreign policy is not restricted to times of war. Beginning in the late 1960s, mainline Protestant and Jewish groups began to mount serious opposition to South African apartheid, with students at New York's Union Theology Seminary, inspired by their dean, Henry P. Van Dusen, taking an important early role. By leading the first of peaceful protests against major banks and other institutions with branch operations in South Africa, these and other student religious groups played a significant role in encouraging the boycotts and sanctions that eventually led to the official dismantling of apartheid in South Africa. In 1983, during the early years of Ronald Reagan's administration, when U.S. defense policy assumed a more bellicose stance, U.S. Catholic bishops issued a widely publicized pastoral letter questioning the morality of nuclear war; in 1998, they issued an additional letter, assessing U.S. policy in the light of the earlier one.[10]

At the beginning of a new century, religious groups continue this long tradition of attempting to influence national policy. The United States Catholic Conference, a civil corporation closely tied to the National Conference of Catholic Bishops, lobbies Congress about public policy issues of concern to the church. Recent efforts have included calling on the United States to join in pressuring the Indonesian government to halt violence against the people of East Timor.[11] The National Council of Churches of Christ plays a similar role on behalf of the more theologically and socially liberal mainline Protestant denominations. Both bodies have encouraged Congress to boost efforts to "reduce poverty and assist growth and development" worldwide by taking the lead in forgiving the crushing burden of debt owed by dozens of poor and developing nations not only to the United States and other wealthy countries, but also to such international bodies as the African Development Bank, International Monetary Fund (IMF), and World Bank. Supportive church groups refer to this more and more popular campaign as Jubilee 2000, recalling the Biblical injunction to forgive all debts and obligations of servitude every fiftieth year—aptly named the "Year of Jubilee" (Leviticus 25:10).[12]

Individual mainline denominations also take positions on a variety of issues pertinent to foreign policy. A visit to the official Websites of such bodies as the United Methodist Church, Presbyterian Church (USA), or Episcopal Church, to choose just three prominent examples, will reveal resolutions and other efforts to persuade U.S. leaders to normalize relations with Cuba, oppose military aid to Colombia, lift sanctions against Iraq, be patient with Cambodia, resist Israeli expansion into Palestinian areas, and pay off the U.S. debt to the United Nations.[13]

Other religious bodies have also maintained a presence in Washington, speaking out on behalf of both broad and parochial interests. The Friends Committee on National Legislation has long informed Congress of the views of the Religious Society of Friends (Quakers) on such matters as the international ban on land mines and the Comprehensive Test Ban Treaty and has consistently called for redirecting monies in the defense budget to more humanitarian purposes. More narrowly, organizations representing immigrant communities in which religion and ethnicity overlap and reinforce each other have often lobbied for policies favorable to their ethnic and spiritual kin in other countries. Irish Catholics in the United States have supported the Irish Republican Army in its struggles against Protestant forces in Northern Ireland; the Greek lobby has enjoyed the support of the Greek Orthodox Church in its conflict with Islamic Turkey over control of Cyprus; and the (Christian) Armenian Assembly has played a significant role in persuading Congress to impose sanctions on Azerbaijan, a Muslim state.[14]

The most strikingly successful example of a religio-ethnic group's impact on U.S. foreign policy is undoubtedly that of the "Jewish Lobby," a coalition that has exercised decisive influence over the shape of U.S. policy toward the Middle East since the establishment of the State of Israel in 1947. To be sure, some involved in each of these efforts operate from purely, or mainly, secular motives. For many, however, culture and religion are inextricable. In any case, even when it is not fully believed, religion can support ethnic loyalty and heighten antipathy toward the other, often stoking long-burning fires of religious enmity in the process.

New Players

These veteran players do not have the political arena all to themselves. Whether operating from a position of strength, seeking to extend a growing influence, or from a defensive posture, seeking equal treatment for themselves and their co-religionists in other countries, new religious coalitions and communities have shown a growing determination to extend their influence beyond the water's edge. Two striking examples are the increasing effect of the conservative Christian movement known as the Religious Right and the nascent efforts of a diverse, growing American Muslim population to speak with a unified voice on matters of vital interest to Islamic peoples.

Christian Conservatives

The movement of politically active Christian conservatives (mostly Caucasian Protestants), commonly identified as the Religious Right, does not constitute a majority, moral or otherwise, but it is not a marginal phenomenon. Researchers who track this movement estimate that only about one-sixth of all eligible voters openly identify with the Religious Right; but that segment, on average, is better educated, better paid, and more likely to hold professional jobs than the U.S. population as a whole.[15] Moreover, by 1996, they had come to dominate or have substantial influence in Republican Party organizations in more than half of the states, a situation many conventional Republicans found incomprehensible and maddening.[16]

In the early 1980s, Evangelical preacher Jerry Falwell and his organization, the Moral Majority, with strong encouragement and assistance from New Right operatives, were the most visible representatives of the Religious Right. After Falwell closed down the Moral Majority in 1986, other leaders and groups came to the fore with better organization, greater political sophistication, and stronger connections to Washington insiders. The most prominent of these were the Christian Coalition, begun by religious broadcaster and cable television mogul Pat Robertson and political whiz kid Ralph Reed; Focus on the Family, led by radio broadcaster James Dobson; the Family Research Council, formerly headed by Gary Bauer; Grover Norquist's Americans for Tax Reform; Concerned Women for America; the American Family Association; and a legion of allied organizations, many of them focusing on a single cause, such as opposition to abortion or gay rights or support for educational vouchers.[17]

Leaders of these groups come together several times a year at meetings of the Council for National Policy (CNP), a low-profile organization whose membership includes heads of various radio, television, and print media organizations; key congressional figures such as representatives Dick Armey and Tom DeLay, senators Trent Lott and Jesse Helms; conservative ideologues and operatives such as Oliver North and Paul Weyrich (of the Free Congress Foundation); and major financial supporters of conservative causes, including members of the wealthy Coors and DeVos (founders of Amway) families.[18]

Christian conservatives compensate for their size by mastery of technology and organization. Radio and television, of course, play a major role. The United States alone has more than 1,600 Christian radio stations and nearly 250 Christian television stations, almost all of which are Evangelical and most of which carry at least some programs produced by Religious Right leaders or supporters. Jerry Falwell was urged to enter the political arena not only because of his views but because his *Old Time Gospel Hour* television program could be seen in 95 percent of American homes. Pat Robertson's *700 Club* has an aggregate weekly audience of about 7 million viewers and his Christian Broadcasting Network beams programs to about 90 nations in more than 50 languages. James Dobson's Focus on the Family uses part of its $114 million annual budget to produce eight radio programs, the most important of which—the daily half-hour *Focus on the Family*—can be heard on more than 4,000 outlets, reaching an estimated 5 million listeners each week. The American Family Association and Concerned Women for America reach hundreds of thousands with half-hour programs, and Gary Bauer's 90-second daily commentaries are aired on more than 400 stations. In addition to broadcast media, most of the major groups keep their active members informed by mail, facsimile, email lists, and telephone.

These specialized media deliver a clear, highly partisan theological and political message that is reinforced by the intense personal networks common in Evangelical and Pentecostal churches. Conservative Christian political leaders use these networks of churches and "parachurch" organizations to identify supporters, raise funds, and provide programs and candidates to rally around. When their candidates are elected, they supply them with a steady flow of research and position papers and, when the need arises, inundate their offices with a barrage of faxes, emails, letters, and telephone calls. These insular networks not only facilitate mobilization but also foster a missionary zeal seldom matched by those on the Left and almost never by the more moderate middle. The result is impressive. "A lot of groups have a great Washington presence and some have great grass roots," observed one member of Congress, "but few combine them both."[19] It is worth noting that more liberal religious bodies often lack precisely such grassroots approval and involvement, and frequently experience internal tension and dissent as lay people, and not a few clergy, register opposition to official stances formulated by denominational leaders holding political and economic views well to the left of their own.

The Religious Right first began to flex its political muscles during the Reagan years. To their considerable disappointment, because they had figured prominently in Reagan's 1980 election, his administration paid little attention to their list of primary concerns, most notably banning abortion and reinstating school prayer. Instead, most were mollified by having their photograph taken alongside the Great Communicator, which gave the illusion of access to power. Unable to accomplish much on the home front, several key players assumed substantial roles in support of conservative political and economic policies abroad. They found it natural to support Reagan's hard-line stance against godless communism.

Encouraged by special State Department briefings, Christian Right leaders offered both ideological and financial support to anticommunist forces in El Salvador, Guatemala, Honduras, and Nicaragua. Most notably, Robertson's Christian Broadcasting Network contributed between $3 million and $7 million to United States—backed anticommunist Contras in Honduras and Nicaragua. He also lionized Guatemalan military dictator (and Pentecostal Christian) General Rios Montt, whose brutal regime killed thousands of Indian tribes people and other civilians regarded as procommunist or, as at least one Guatemalan official charged, as "possessed by demons." Falwell, along with several other TV preachers, defended apartheid forces in South Africa by claiming they had been misportrayed by liberal media and by depicting the African National Congress as a Soviet puppet. More notoriously, Robertson forged strong ties with Zaire's corrupt dictator, Mobutu Sese Seko—an alliance the entrepreneurial broadcaster used to gain forestry and diamond-mining concessions for his African Development Corporation.[20]

More recently, with experience and enhanced organization, Christian conservatives have widened the scope of their agenda to include such causes as opposition to the Global Warming Treaty, support for the North American Free Trade Agreement, encouragement of stronger defense systems, opposition to the United Nations and the IMF, and support for Israel.

Some of these echo the interests of their allies and mentors among the not-necessarily-religious New Right or "movement conservatives" who have helped shift the nation's politics to the right in recent decades. But on most international issues, the motivation is the same as that driving the domestic agenda: distrust of secular government, determination to preach and practice their beliefs without hindrance or restriction, opposition to any perceived threat to "traditional family values," and—less obvious to most secular observers—a conviction that increasing globalization is a fulfillment of dire biblical prophecies foreshadowing the return of Christ and the onset of Armageddon.

Religious conservatives have vigorously lobbied for legislation that would impose sanctions on countries that persecute or limit the freedom of Christians to worship and evangelize, particularly in the "10/40 Window," a latitude belt that circles the globe and includes regions in Asia, Latin America, and the Middle East that have been designated as prime areas for Christian missionary work.[21]

In this connection, they have paid particular attention to China and were instrumental in pressuring Congress to pass the International Religious Freedom Act in late 1998. This act creates a White House office for reporting religious persecution worldwide and allows the president to choose from a variety of measures, ranging from diplomatic protest to economic sanctions, to punish offending countries. Though less stringent than the Religious Right wanted, this legislation could affect dozens of countries with less than exemplary records on religious freedom, including close U.S. trading partners such as Egypt, India, Saudi Arabia, and Turkey.

In 1998, religious and social conservatives in the House of Representatives nearly blocked $18 billion in appropriations for the IMF, in part because the IMF channels money to countries and organizations that regard abortion as an acceptable form of family planning or population control. The United Nations is another favorite whipping boy. Exponents of the Religious Right vehemently attacked the platform of the 1995 U.N. World Conference on Women in Beijing, charging that it placed too much emphasis on reproductive freedom and freedom of sexual expression, depicted marriage and motherhood in a negative light, and implicitly endorsed homosexuality. In the same vein, they have criticized the U.N. Convention on the Rights of the Child, arguing that the treaty contains dubious provisions that would guarantee children the right to access pornography and other age-inappropriate media or to express their sexuality without having to answer to their parents.

Similarly, the Christian Right not only sees the United Nations as a threat to the American family but as a mechanism that allows a secular élite to threaten family values worldwide. They deride programs that promote abortion, sterilization, or contraception. Abortion, in particular, is regarded as an anathema that reveals the hypocrisy of nations claiming to adhere to international norms such as the Universal Declaration of Human Rights, while simultaneously terminating the lives of unborn children (the "most vulnerable members of the human family").

The campaign against the United Nations has had an impact. In large measure because of opposition from the Religious Right, the United States did not contribute to the U.N. Population Fund in 1998, jeopardizing a program that provides contraceptives to nearly 1.4 million women in 150 countries. More telling, the billion or so dollars in U.N. arrears—the United States and the United Nations disagree on the amount— was long held hostage because of the insistence of House Republicans aligned with the Religious Right that funding be tied to legislative language barring aid to organizations that seek to legalize or fund abortions.[22]

Religious Right activists have also been critical of the International Criminal Court and other multinational or broad-scope organizations such as the European Union, the Trilateral Commission, the Council on Foreign Relations, the World Council of Churches, and, in some quarters, the Roman Catholic Church. This propensity stems from several sources, including standard-issue isolationism, a fear of sacrificing national sovereignty to a liberal international order, and a conviction that the United Nations and other efforts at global governance are controlled by Marxists, secular humanists, and radical (often homosexual) feminists bent on eradicating traditional Christian values—with, perhaps, a standing U.N. military force to back their goals.

Another important source of these concerns, however, is a theological doctrine widely shared in Fundamentalist and Pentecostal circles and known as Dispensationalist Premillennialism. This doctrine, spelled out in such books as Hal Lindsey's *The Late, Great Planet Earth*, the best-selling book of the 1970s, and fictionalized in the wildly popular *Left Behind* series of novels, holds that highly figurative apocalyptic passages in such biblical sources as Ezekiel, Daniel, and Revelation furnish a blueprint for the "Last Days," which are likely to come upon us at any moment. Dispensationalists believe that the imminent appearance and reign of the Antichrist will feature a unified political and economic dictatorship so complete that buying or selling will be impossible without his authorization. A mighty False Prophet will lead a global religion to bolster this regime.[23]

In an atmosphere permeated by such beliefs, terms such as "global governance" and "new world order" resonate with ominous overtones and any organization aspiring to multinational or global influence is sure to be viewed with suspicion. Over the decades, Dispensationalists have regularly identified prominent world leaders—Kaiser Wilhelm, Adolf Hitler, Benito Mussolini, Anwar Sadat, Josef Stalin, and even Henry Kissinger—as plausible Antichrists and trembled at the rise of the European Common Market, which they had identified as the Ten-Horned Beast in chapters 7 and 8 of Daniel. The identification suffered a bit when the beast grew a couple of extra horns (Portugal and Spain joined in 1986), but the European Union's growing power and newly unified currency make it a cause for anxiety once again.

Perhaps most important, Dispensationalism also underlies the unwavering support which virtually all segments of the Christian Right give to Israel. The key to understanding this phenomenon is the belief that a complete restoration of the nation of Israel, including the rebuilding of the Temple in Jerusalem, is a prerequisite to the end of the present age (or "dispensation"), which will usher in the Second Coming of Christ and the establishment of his millennial reign. Consequently, Christians must support Israel. While overlooking the irony that this scenario envisions a mass conversion of Jews, Jewish leaders have welcomed the efforts of U.S. Evangelical Christians to bolster Israel's defense against hostile neighbors. The Israeli government has assiduously wooed prominent Evangelical leaders, such as television evangelists and presidents and deans of seminaries, by bringing them to Israel at little or no cost and favoring the tour groups they lead with briefings by cabinet officers. And when an Israeli prime minister visits the United States, he is almost certain to meet with leaders of the Christian Right, both in public and private. In April 1998, when Benjamin Netanyahu addressed a Washington audience of 3,000 people attending a Voices United for Israel conference, at least two-thirds of whom were Evangelical Christians, he observed that "we have no greater friends and allies than the people sitting in this room."

In return for such attention, conservative notables such as Jerry Falwell and Pat Robertson arrange meetings between Evangelical leaders and Israeli officials, deliver passionately pro-Israel messages on their radio and television programs, and invite their followers to urge their members of Congress to support Israel. At one 1998 meeting, Falwell pledged to resist the efforts of Bill Clinton's administration' to pressure Israel into ceding more land back to the Palestinians. "There are about 200,000 Evangelical pastors in America," he observed, "and we're asking them all through email, faxes, letters, telephone, to go into their pulpits and use their influence in support of the state of Israel and the prime minister."

In an extensive October 1998 article in *Christianity Today*, Evangelical historian Timothy Weber noted that, in addition to such high-level efforts, "scores of small, grassroots, pro-Israel organizations that rarely get into the headlines [exist] to educate and mobilize their local communities to support Israel." Weber also called attention to "an enormous network of pro-Israel and Christian Zionist organizations" and noted that "Most of them have their own Web pages on the Internet, and they usually have links to one another." Many Evangelicals, Weber observed, have a strong tendency to idealize Israel and demonize the Palestinians, without much understanding of the history or complexity of the conflict, and need to be wary of allowing the ends to justify the means, "just because the ends have been prophesied."[24]

During the two decades since the Religious Right rose to public prominence during the 1980 election campaign, numerous scholars, journalists, and other observers of the political and religious scene have predicted again and again, and even claimed to see, the demise of the Religious Right. Those predictions, often tinged with fond hope, have thus far failed to come true. On the contrary, it seems clear that anyone who wants to make sense of American politics, domestic or foreign, over the short or long term, must accept that religious conservatives have become an enduring, important part of the social landscape.

This same American brand of conservative Christianity is also being transported across the globe. Most of the Christian mission work now occurring throughout the world is being done by Pentecostal and Fundamentalist Protestants, and it is meeting with extraordinary success. In Central America, a Pentecostal revival spurred by television broadcasts produced by Pat Robertson's Christian Broadcasting Network and the Jimmy Swaggart Evangelistic Association involved thousands of Evangelical and Protestant churches and helped generate support for regimes and rebel movements deemed hostile to communism. Indigenous evangelists and broadcasters have emulated their success in Brazil, Chile, and other South American countries. In several countries of Africa, missionaries prepared at Pentecostal training centers in Oklahoma and Arizona have built sprawling complexes resembling those in the United States, and their optimistic espousal of American capitalism and the promise of God-given prosperity have infiltrated hundreds of already existing churches and denominations.

All these missionaries and their indigenous coworkers would earnestly insist that their primary goal is to help their converts secure an eternal home in heaven. Inevitably, however, some fruits of their labors are decidedly this-worldly in their consequences. In their revealing book, *Exporting the American Gospel: Global Christian Fundamentalism*, Steve Brouwer, Paul Gifford, and Susan Rose delineate some of the most important of these. The combination of optimism and strict personal discipline that has helped millions of Pentecostals in this country achieve impressive upward mobility has often proved helpful to Christians in developing nations, particularly to those who perceive the advantages of the technology and organizational skills the American missionaries bring with them.

More problematically, Brouwer and his coauthors note that the premillennial conviction that nothing should stand in the way of the restoration of Israel nurtures anti-Islamic feelings and provides religious justification for U.S. policies that are viewed with hostility by some Middle Eastern countries. Similarly, the unquestioning acceptance of capitalism by most of these American missionaries leads to them to be highly critical of the small nations that have employed Marxist themes and rhetoric in their efforts to break free of colonialism. Since Catholic leaders in some of these countries sided with the liberation movements, Fundamentalists and Pentecostals have found it easy to revive long-standing suspicions of Catholicism, an easy reach for those who have long seen the Church of Rome in the apocalyptic images of the book of Revelation.

Finally, Brouwer and his coauthors contend that the patriarchal nature of much of conservative Christianity makes acceptance of authoritarian governments easy, particularly if those governments facilitate the missionaries' evangelistic efforts by providing access to state-owned radio and television facilities, in return for the symbolic blessing of their regimes. Thus, the dominant brand of Christianity being exported to developing nations is strongly supportive of American capitalism and is an effective vehicle for disseminating and gaining acceptance for such core American traits as optimism, belief in hard work and personal discipline, and confidence in technology. At the same time, however, it has the potential to raise false hopes, exacerbate political tensions, and help prop up authoritarian and corrupt regimes.[25]

The Muslim Community

Until quite recently, Muslims in the United States have shown little interest in organizing themselves to wield political influence. This appears to be changing, however, as thoughtful leaders recognize that strategic mobilization of an estimated—perhaps overestimated—6 million co-religionists could enable them speak with a louder voice. Most major cities have a few prominent Muslim activists and organizations. And in 1997, a group of national Islamic organizations formed the American Muslim Coordination Council, designed to provide consistent advice to Muslims about political issues and candidates and to "bring Muslims off the political sidelines and onto the political playing field."[26]

This trend is spreading through the American Muslim population. In the March 1998 issue of the *Washington Report on Middle East Affairs*, executive editor Richard H. Curtiss commended a plan to devise a questionnaire, to be sent to all candidates for U.S. federal office, with the results to be discussed "in every mosque in America." If candidates are aware of such a process, Curtiss contended, "they will start paying attention to the issues which concern the Islamic community," issues that would include, "an even-handed U.S. foreign policy in support of human rights, self-determination and fair play abroad." Such an initiative could be expected to have an effect on U.S. foreign policy. The point, he stressed, "is to become known as a community that votes, and can vote as a bloc when one candidate is judged better suited on the basis of Islamic standards."[27]

Some of these standards, particularly those supporting conservative family values, would mesh smoothly with those of the Religious Right. Others reflect distinctly Muslim concerns, such as greater religious tolerance toward the Islamic community (a concern greatly heightened by hostile acts and attitudes directed at Muslims after the terrorist attacks on the World Trade Center and the Pentagon on September 11, 2001), accommodation of religious observances and practices of Islamic workers, and securing chaplains for Muslims in the military. On foreign policy, key concerns include self-determination for Kashmir, support for the Muslim-led government of Bosnia, opposition to repression of the ethnic Albanian population of Kosovo by Serbian forces, cessation of Russian attacks on Muslim civilians in Chechnya, Palestinian self-determination, and opposition to the establishment of Jerusalem as the capital of Israel.[28]

Several Muslim leaders have imitated the tactics of the Religious Right and implored their co-religionists to become more politically active. They have encouraged the Islamic community to influence the political process by conducting voter registration drives, attending precinct caucuses of the political party of their choice, establishing personal contacts with members of Congress, and seeking elective and public office. Noting that Christians have risen to power in some predominantly Muslim countries, State University of New York–Binghamton professor Ali Mazrui asks, "Why should not Muslim minorities in non-Mulsim countries seek participation and increasing empowerment for themselves?" Though conceding that "American Muslims may never equal the power of the Jews in the U.S. system," he thinks it reasonable to hope that "Muslims may one day help provide some counterbalance in policy formation." For the Islamic community not to take advantage of the resources and opportunities for full participation in the U.S. political system, he says, "is an exercise in political castration."[29]

The number of Muslims in the United States is a matter of dispute. The frequently sided figure of 6 million was challenged in 2001 by several surveys that produced estimates ranging between 1.8 and 2.8 million. Muslims spokespersons challenge these estimates, noting that substantial numbers of Muslims are recent immigrants who are likely to be missed by (or refuse to participate in) random-sample telephone surveys. They contend that results of canvassing of mosques and Islamic centers by national Muslim organizations justify the claims of 6 to 7 million American adherents of Islam.

If the larger figure is accurate, the U.S. Muslim population is roughly equal to the Jewish community.[30] Even if that estimate is too high, the number of Muslims in the United States is clearly growing rapidly as a result of immigration. To be sure, even the highest estimate is a long way from a majority. Richard Curtiss noted, however, that it is difficult for a candidate to become president without winning California, and that the 700,000 or so Muslims in California, working together, could make it difficult for a candidate to win California without their vote.[31] Though the 2000 elections proved that this can be done, it did not invalidate the contention that, as both Jews and Christian Conservatives have shown, well-organized minority constituencies can wield power out of proportion to their numbers.

The challenge for Muslims will be to achieve a sufficient level of organization. James Zogby, director of the Arab-American Institute, which represents both Muslim and Christian Arabs, notes that to speak of "the Muslim community" as a homogeneous entity is to engage in "mythic construction." Zogby reckons that American Muslims of Pakistani origin are the most active and best organized component, but their primary motive has been to support self-determination for Kashmir. The Arab component, more concerned about the Middle East, is fairly well organized but makes up only about 10 to 15 percent of American Muslims. A large Iranian community shares a widespread displeasure with the current regime in Iran, but is itself sharply divided over what kind of government they would like to see in their homeland. The Turks have shown limited political activism and would likely refrain from uniting with Islamic community at large due to Turkey's secular orientation. And African-American Muslims—one of the largest constituencies in the U.S. Muslim community—have little historical reason to be concerned about any of the aforementioned issues.[32]

These disparate interests may hamper Muslim efforts to become significant players on the U.S. political scene, but the 2000 elections clearly demonstrated that the potential is there. In preparation for the spring primary campaign, the American Muslim Political Coordination Council organized a widespread voter registration drive, signing up voters in mosques and Islamic centers, on college campuses, and at community events. They followed this with workshops for campaign volunteers and voters and invited candidates to address Muslim gatherings in major cities. Overall, Muslims tended to favor Al Gore on domestic issues, but they were less pleased with his strong sympathies for Israel, and after he named Joe Lieberman as his running mate, they began to lean toward George W. Bush.

In September, at a well-attended meeting in Chicago, the council's proposal to encourage a bloc vote for one or the other of the two leading candidates got an overwhelmingly positive response, though which candidate would get the vote was still uncertain. On October 5, Bush met with Arab and Muslim leaders in Dearborn, Michigan, to discuss their concerns. No presidential candidate had ever done that. Less than a week later, during the second presidential debate, Bush warmed the hearts of Arab-Americans by decrying the profiling of Arabs at American airports and the use of "secret evidence" to detain or deport Arabs suspected of involvement with terrorists. Gore agreed to meet with Arab and Muslim leaders but canceled the meeting, ostensibly because he had to return to Washington to discuss the heightened conflict between Israel and the Palestinians. Ten days later, on October 23, at the National Press Club, the coalition announced its support of Bush.

On November 7, Muslim Americans voted overwhelmingly for George W. Bush. According to Muslim spokespersons, who subscribe to the higher estimates of the American Muslim population, about 4.7 million Muslims are eligible to vote, and 3.2 million are thought to have actually voted. The data from exit polls are less than fully satisfactory, but it appears that Bush got more than 70 percent of these votes. That was not enough to swing the election for Bush in California or Michigan, two states in which Muslims thought they might make a decisive difference. They did make a difference, however, in Florida. I have examined the Florida vote in some detail in another essay, but the key findings are that at least 40,000 Muslims went to the polls in Florida and that Bush got approximately 90 percent of those votes.

Even with more conservative estimates, it appears that Muslims surely gave Bush at least a 20,000-vote edge. Had Al Gore gotten 58 percent of those 40,000 votes, as Clinton did in 1996, or even the quarter of them it seemed he had sewn up in September, he would have registered a clear victory in Florida and would have become president. The dream of American Muslims to organize themselves into an effective counterweight to Jewish voters, in numbers if not in influence and expertise, appears to have become a reality. Whether they will remain in the Republican camp is another story, but it would be hard to deny that they have won a seat at the table. From that position, they will surely seek to have a stronger voice in American foreign policy. [33]

The events of September 11, of course, constitute a challenge to these aspirations. The attacks on the World Trade Center and the Pentagon by Islamic extremists and the subsequent rejoicing of a nontrivial minority of Muslims worldwide created a backlash that included some overt, even violent, anti-Muslim actions and wider, if unmeasurable, suspicion that increased Islamic presence in the United States may not be entirely benign. At the same time, political, religious, and other cultural leaders were at pains to discourage hostile behavior against Muslims, to assign blame for the attacks to a fanatical minority, and to corroborate Islamic spokespersons' characterization of Islam as "a religion of peace." But despite such calls for tolerance and restraint, it seems likely, even barring further terrorist activity, that Muslim dreams of amicable assimilation into the American political mainstream have suffered a significant setback.

Religion and Statecraft

What are the implications of the fervent and growing efforts of religious activists to affect U.S. foreign policy? How should legislators and other government officials respond to them? How seriously should diplomats and political analysts view their behavior and concerns? Will their participation in politics inevitably lead to increased hostility and conflict with lamentable results both at home and abroad? Given the faith-flavored potions that have poisoned so many regions, no realistic assessment can ignore the possibilities for harm. Still, careful attention to the "religious factor" is not only analytically indispensable, but can offer at least modest grounds for an optimistic reading of the roles religion can play in international relations.

The Reality of Religion

Because religion is often tightly interwoven with particular cultures and ethnic groups, it can be impossible to disentangle discrete components and label them correctly as secular or religious, sincere or manipulative, beneficial or dangerous. It is also true, however, that religion can be a powerful force in its own right, because in much of the world, including the United States, religious structures often exhibit enormous strength and resilience. In some areas, they are stronger than existing governments and may represent the true effective power, capable either of shoring up or bringing down a secular government. This important fact may be overlooked by political scientists, economists, sociologists, mainstream media, policymakers, and diplomats whose milieu is likely to be in an advanced stage of secularization. Within these circles, the spiritual, supernatural (or, more precisely, non-empirical) dimensions of life are shouldered out of the arena, both during professional preparation and on the job.

If religion is not taken seriously in one's own circle, it is easy to conclude that it is not to be taken seriously at all. When people profess or appear to be acting from religious motives, there is a temptation to ignore them as ignorant or insubstantial or to look for their "real" motive, which surely will involve money or power. When religious leaders and positions with which one is unfamiliar seem to have wide popular support, it may be easier to seek out and try to deal only with secular political or military leaders, who hold offices and have ranks, because one has talked to their kind before. Without proper glasses, some things are difficult to see.

Surely, the best-known example of that in recent years has been Iran. It is now widely accepted that the 1979 revolution was, in large measure, what it declared itself to be: a powerful reaction to Western modernization, orchestrated and led by clerics representing an extremist form of the Shi'ite sect, itself a minority within Islam. Extreme as it was, however, it bore a kinship to a much broader Islamic reaction to modernization in general and to its Western form in particular. For different reasons, not least of which was its atheism, communism did not offer a viable alternative to

Western modernization and the threat it is deemed to pose to piety and morality. The only well-developed and plausible alternative was to be found in Islam.

It may well be that a full and nuanced understanding of the situation on the part of the United States would have changed little. But it is also widely accepted that U.S. leaders were almost completely blind-sided by events in Iran. The revolution was attributed mainly to economic inequalities and to resentment of an autocratic, corrupt, and repressive regime. That Western culture might be the enemy seemed inconceivable. The United States urged the shah to stem corruption, to narrow the distribution of wealth, and to widen the distribution of power. As for those strange bearded men in black robes, proposing to lead a country while sitting on prayer rugs instead of the Peacock Throne, surely their demagogic appeal would be only momentary, and when the *real*—that is to say, the economic and political—causes of the uprising were attended to, what appeared to be religious enthusiasm would wane and the men wearing sharply tailored American and European suits, the men we knew, the men who looked, well, more like us, would be in charge.

In his 1988 book, *The Eagle and the Lion: The Tragedy of American-Iranian Relations*, James Bill reported that the lone proposal by the Central Intelligence Agency to pay close attention to the religious dimension of Iranian politics and to monitor "the activities and attitudes of the more prominent religious leaders" before the revolution "was vetoed on the grounds that it would amount to mere 'sociology,' a term used in intelligence circles to mean the time-wasting study of factors deemed politically irrelevant." The strategic, economic, and political factors typically considered when nations, particularly Western nations, face diplomatic challenges throughout the world, seemed to rule out what happened in Iran. But it happened, and the United States was not prepared for it.[34]

Despite two decades of heightened awareness of the capacity of religious extremism to upset political stability, particularly in Africa, Asia, and the Middle East, many Americans, at least initially, found it difficult to believe that Osama bin Laden and his al Qaeda disciples had acted from religious motives, but mounting evidence made that conclusion impossible to avoid. Though resentment of U.S. power and wealth undoubtedly played a role, religious conviction—however perverted—was a vital factor.

The motives of dead men are difficult to prove, but bin Laden had previously justified acts of terrorism on religious grounds, and a videotape of his discussion of the attacks with an associate indicates not only that he conceived of his handiwork as justified by Islamic teaching, but that he regarded them as an effective tool of evangelism, causing many non-Muslims to read the Qur'an and other literature in an effort to learn more about what he called "the true Islam." As Andrew Sullivan observed in his insightful and widely discussed article in the October 7, 2001, *New York Times Magazine*, "We cannot know the precise motive of bin Laden" when he claims to be engaging in a religious war against "unbelief and unbelievers," but "we can know that he would not use these words if he did not think they had salience among the people he wishes to inspire and provoke."[35]

Islam was not well designed for a pluralistic world, and certainly not for a world in which secular assumptions and values play demonstrably important roles—whether or not they are increasing in prevalence. The events and aftermath of September 11 may impel Muslims in this country and elsewhere to examine seriously how Islam can coexist peacefully with both unbelievers and believers in other religions in a world that is not going to become less complex and in which sustained isolation is impossible. By electing to participate in the political process in the United States, where they have no hope of seeing Islamic law, the Sharia, become the basis of public policy, Muslims in this country are trying to come to terms with pluralism and an officially secular state. Muslims in other regions struggle to find a viable relationship between religion and politics, with attempts ranging from Turkey to the Taliban. It is a formidable task, and Muslims find themselves more and more taking sides against each other, but modernity and the attendant pluralism are not likely to recede. American Catholics came to terms with a pluralistic nation in the latter decades of the nineteenth century. Perhaps American Muslims can make peace with pluralism and, in the process, provide guidance to Muslims elsewhere.

Religion's Influence in Other Situations

In other situations, the influence of religion has not been as enormous and unified as in Iran or other predominantly Muslim states. But it has nonetheless played a critical role. In the Philippines, during the struggle to oust Ferdinand Marcos, the Roman Catholic Church, led by Jaime Cardinal Sin, served to prevent communist elements from exploiting a possible power vacuum. In Nicaragua and in other Latin American countries, clerics—Protestants as well as Catholics—have been and will continue to be found on the left, on the right, and in the middle, with varying levels of success.

It is easy to multiply examples. Though other factors, including deeply entrenched habits of hatred that now operate independent of their roots, are unquestionably involved, the war in the former Yugoslavia; struggles between Protestants and Catholics in Northern Ireland; bloody clashes between Hindus and Sikhs and Muslims in India; the genocidal repression by the Chinese of Buddhism in Tibet; struggles between competing forces within El Salvador, Nicaragua, and other Latin American nations; the threats to order posed by Muslim fundamentalists in Algeria, Egypt, and elsewhere; tensions between believers and nonbelievers in countries of the former Soviet Union; the "Culture Wars" between the Religious Right and the Secular Left in this country—all these underscore the folly of imagining that, once we have looked carefully at the economic, political, and secular cultural variables in a given situation, we have learned all we really need to know. Quite to the contrary, in any such situation a person, organization, or government with a reliable understanding of the religious dimension will have a significant interpretive advantage.

No one doubts that a thorough knowledge of the culture with which one is dealing is vital to effective statecraft. We need to recognize that, in most of the world, religion is a vital, inextricable, perhaps even the defining component in a culture. Effective statecraft must not neglect it.[36]

The United States as a Religious Nation

A point worth emphasizing, to ourselves and to others, is that the official status of the United States as a secular *state*—a civil entity—has not produced a *nation* of secular people. Indeed, among modern industrial nations, the United States stands essentially alone at the top of measure after measure of religiosity, and by no means is all of that Christian or Judeo-Christian. In recent decades, multiplied thousands of Muslims, Buddhists, Hindus, and believers of every stripe and hue have come to these shores and brought their religions with them. Though certainly not free of religious bigotry, Americans have by our laws and our adherence to them encouraged and protected an impressive, even astonishing, array of religious belief and practice.

This vitality of American religious life should be viewed as a potentially valuable asset in our dealings with other religious people. Consider, as just one example, American interactions with Muslim countries. As was already noted, much of the resentment directed against the United States by some Muslim nations is generated by revivalist Muslims who view

Western modernization—"Westoxication"—as the primary threat not to their economic or political life, but the spiritual well-being of their communities and their children. Their fears, not greatly different from those voiced by religious conservatives in this country, are legitimate, real, and powerful. Instead of assuming that other, "real" motives are the only ones that need attention, diplomats need to face these fears openly, acknowledge their seriousness, make it clear that the same concerns are shared by millions of Americans, and offer whatever reassurance is required to help them believe that the United States is not an enemy of Islam.

The U.S. government has made it clear that it objects to and opposes the extremism and terrorism that have sometimes been associated with Islamic movements, but it has no quarrel with mainstream Islamic theology and has high respect for its long-standing concern for a just, ethical public order. That message needs to be repeated and elaborated in many contexts, until religious people throughout the world understand that the United States does not intend, certainly not as a matter of policy, to threaten the religious faith of any people.

More positively, American diplomats should constantly be on the alert for opportunities to consult and enlist the support of religious leaders in other countries, or to find opportunities for cooperation between religious leaders of various countries. As has been noted, religious leaders may have more broadly based, more stable support than political or military leaders. But beyond that, religious leaders may be able to draw on the best of their respective traditions to create something positive that might otherwise have been missed.

An old story, perhaps apocryphal, tells of an occasion on which former secretary of state John Foster Dulles met with an Arab and a Jewish leader and began by saying, "Why can't we all sit down together and work this thing out like Christian gentlemen."[37] The story, whether true or not, can be interpreted in two ways. It is easy, when people of different cultures interact, for each of them to think more highly of and draw more heavily on their native tradition than may be appropriate. Perhaps they are truly ethnocentric, believing that the axis of the universe runs through their own hometown and that all those who differ with them are to some degree inferior. More charitably, and perhaps more commonly, they may simply be insufficiently aware of other cultures to understand and appreciate their strengths.

But a second interpretation is possible. Perhaps Secretary Dulles, or the many people he represents in this story, may not know all we could wish they knew, or may express themselves a bit naively or inelegantly, and yet have an ecumenical instinct, a broad sense of kinship with other men and women of goodwill, and a desire to summon forth the highest and best in all parties to the discussion. It would be fatuous to imagine that this second interpretation will fit every situation in which people of differing faiths meet at any table. But it would be tragic to be so cynical as to believe it is never accurate.

Not all peacemaking efforts by religious parties involve well-known persons. A useful book, *Religion: The Missing Dimension of Statecraft*, which grew out of something called the Religion and Conflict Resolution Project, chronicles in considerable detail the work of the Moral Re-Armament Movement in reducing hostility between France and Germany after World War II; the role of East German churches in promoting peaceful change in the years building up to the collapse of the former Soviet Union; the unassuming yet persistent work of Quakers in defusing civil war in Nigeria; the positive contribution made by various religious actors in the transition of Rhodesia to Zimbabwe; and the role of Moravians in effecting conciliation between the Sandinistas and the East Coast Indians of Nicaragua. These are fascinating accounts, perhaps all the more because, with few exceptions, they have received so little attention.[38]

Several factors contribute to the ability of religious institutions and individual religious figures to play a positive role in conciliation. In regions where nationhood is a relatively underdeveloped concept, ethnic group and religious affiliation are apt to provide more powerful and stable ties for the majority of people. And even in countries with a strong sense of nationhood and a well-developed political apparatus, religious institutions may still be regarded so positively by large numbers of people that their endeavors will be trusted and taken more seriously than those of other institutions. In these and intermediate situations, religious institutions may be so highly respected that political leaders, whatever their own level of piety, dare not completely ignore or severely repress them. Further, though history is replete with examples of corrupt clerics, the relative independence these circumstances provide can give widely trusted religious leaders some leverage in brokering disputes—leverage that purely secular leaders may lack.

Another helpful role religious institutions and leaders can play is to provide an "off the hook" excuse that can enable conflicting parties to reach an agreement that would otherwise be publicly indefensible. At the time of the passage of the Civil Rights Act in 1964, many "reluctant discriminators" in the American South, feeling guilty about their behavior but unwilling to risk loss of friends or face, were relieved to be able to say, "I don't really want Negroes in my restaurant, but what can I do now that the law says I have to serve them?" Similarly, parties in conflict may have gone so far in their statements and behavior that, whatever their true feelings, they cannot back down without risking disillusion or rebellion in their ranks. If, however, they can be seen to accede to the urgings and authority of religious leaders—leaders also admired by their own supporters—they may be able to accept otherwise unacceptable compromises.

Religion, of course, cannot provide all the answers or solve every conflict. The world's many religions cannot be fully harmonized so as to remove all barriers among them. They are not all the same once we get beneath some superficial veneer. And yet most have in common a preference for peace over war and for nonviolence over violence, a tradition of compassion, however unequally directed, an admiration for ethical integrity, for the keeping of promises, and a consistent reminder of the imperfections of human nature. Religious leaders may be able to draw upon the best of their respective traditions to create something positive that might have been missed had matters been left entirely to political or military leaders.

Congress, the president, and other key policymakers cannot answer all of the prayers of equally devout but diverse religious communities. Neither can they fashion a one-size-fits-all approach to nations or peoples with a strong religious orientation. And sometimes the differences may be so great and intense that religion would best be omitted from the discussion. But those who would shape U.S. policy and who would take the lead in forging relations among nations must be aware of the resources for compassion, reconciliation, justice, and peace that exist within religious traditions and should not hesitate to explore their possibilities when the opportunity arises.

The Value of Religious Freedom

A further point with important implications for U.S. foreign policy is the enormous value Americans place on religious freedom. Many of the first settlers from Europe came because they wanted freedom to worship as they chose. To be sure, they did not initially feel a strong need to grant that same freedom to others, but it eventually came to that. When the Bill of Rights was added to the Constitution in 1789, the first freedom secured was free exercise of religion, according to the dictates of one's conscience.

And as I have noted, the record on this score, though not perfect, is truly remarkable—unprecedented in human history and one of the nation's most admirable achievements. Even the most secular Americans are likely to recognize and honor the importance of this freedom. The leaders of other nations need to understand that, however cynical and manipulative their private attitudes may be, their success in dealing with the United States will be enhanced by their taking care to guarantee and protect the religious freedom of their own people.

Though not always praised for his diplomatic acumen, Billy Graham has consistently used his unique entrée to world leaders to emphasize this point. During his several visits to the Soviet Union in the early 1980s, for example, he stressed to Soviet leaders that trying to control the religious beliefs and practices of so many people created a complicated and unnecessary problem for government and cast it in an unfavorable light internationally, particularly in the United States, whose people found it hard to feel much kinship for a society that attempted to establish atheism as its official philosophical position. In a conversation with Boris Ponomarev, chief of the International Affairs Department of the Central Committee of the Communist Party and a member of the Politburo, Graham explained that "a major reason the American public does not support closer ties with the Soviet Union is because of what is perceived as religious discrimination and even oppression, especially of [Christians] and Jews. You will never reach a satisfactory understanding with the United States as long as you keep up this anti-Semitic and anti-Christian thing."

Graham specifically urged that larger numbers of Jews be permitted to emigrate to Israel, that churches be permitted to operate seminaries and other institutions for theological training, that rabbinical training and language teaching in Hebrew be expanded, that young people of all faiths be allowed to practice their religion openly without fear of being barred from universities or desirable occupations, that restrictions on the publication of Bibles and other religious literature be lifted, and that believers be permitted to construct or alter buildings as needed. Four years after this conversation, Ponomarev told Graham, "I will never forget the things that you said. We have deeply appreciated it and have discussed it many times."[39]

Graham was wise enough not to take full credit for the changes that have occurred since those conversations. But it is a fact that, in the former Soviet Union as well as in other Warsaw Pact nations, some of the earliest manifestations of a wider ranger of religious freedoms were directly connected to Graham's visits to those countries. In a conversation I once had with Georgi Arbatov, then director of the U.S.–Canada Institute and also a member of the Soviet Central Committee, Arbatov gave primary credit for the changes to the Soviet Union's long-standing (but little-known) policy of religious freedom. He acknowledged, however, that Graham's visits and influence had played a role in improving the situation for religious people. This illustrates not only the suasive power of the appeal for religious freedom, but also the positive role that a single religious leader can sometimes play.

Separation of Church and State

When the Framers of the Constitution, led by James Madison and encouraged by Thomas Jefferson's well-known views, managed to write a document that made no mention of God and forbade the federal government either to support or impede religion, it launched a bold experiment. Critics were certain that God himself would bring down any nation that dared affront him in such cavalier fashion.[40] Madison and his colleagues thought it likely that both state and church would fare best with a wall between them. History gives the Framers the nod. Virtually all serious historians and social scientists who deal with religion agree that a large measure of the extraordinary vitality of American religion can be attributed to this initially unique arrangement. Americans cannot, of course, require other nations to follow this example. I see no problem, however, in our being willing to acknowledge the success of our arrangement and to invite others to inspect it, leaving it to them to assess its merits and act as they see fit.

In Andrew Sullivan's aforementioned article, he notes that, following John Locke's argument "that true salvation could not be a result of coercion, that faith had to be freely chosen to be genuine, and that any other interpretation was counter to the Gospels," the founders had seen to it that "a central element of the new American order" would be a provision "ensuring that no single religion could use political means to enforce its own orthodoxies." They did this, he said, "to preserve peace above all—but also to preserve true religion itself." To be sure, many devoutly religious people, of widely differing faiths, would deny the Founders or Andrew Sullivan the right to define the content of "true religion itself." Still, Sullivan contends, correctly I think, that what is at issue in the present and quite likely future struggle with Islamic and other religious foes of the United States is "the simple but immensely difficult principle of the separation of politics and religion." Though acknowledging that renewed and widespread reverence for the flag can be stirring, he concludes that "the symbol of this conflict should not be Old Glory. . . . We are fighting not for our country as such or for our flag. We are fighting for the universal principles of our Constitution, and the possibility of free religious faith it guarantees."[41]

We must take great care that we do not underestimate the value of this historic wall of separation and allow it to be dismantled—or bulldozed. People of faith absolutely have a right to be politically active, and they cannot be expected to leave their religious convictions behind when they enter the political arena. They have a right to organize themselves to work effectively for the good of their country as they understand it, and that understanding will inevitably be informed by their religious faith, as religious faith has undergirded those who fought for the abolition of slavery and for civil rights, and who now fight for debt relief and a sustainable environment. Christians—Catholics, mainline Protestants, Fundamentalists, Mormons, and Jehovah's Witnesses—and also Buddhists, Hindus, Jews, Muslims, and even secular humanists, may all legitimately work, drawing on the values and beliefs of their religious or secular traditions, to shape public policy, within the limits of a Constitution whose protection of religious pluralism has served so admirably in avoiding society-rending religious conflict.

There are, however, real and reasonable limits to that shaping process. The most important of these is that a religious body should not expect to accord its specifically religious doctrines a privileged position in the effort to mold public policy. This applies equally to domestic and foreign policy. It is not appropriate to attempt to shape U.S. policy in the Middle East on the basis of a belief that Jews should be allowed to inhabit "all the land," including "Judea and Samaria," because God promised it to the descendants of Abraham; or a belief that the Dome of the Rock and the Al Aqsa Mosque must be removed from the Temple Mount in Jerusalem, one of the holiest sites in Islam, so that the Messiah can come (whether for the first or second time); or a belief that efforts to achieve peace are futile, even perverse, because that goal will be achieved by the Mahdi (the expected one), a messianic figure who will one day return to usher in a perfect Islamic society.

Such beliefs, dependent as they are upon revelation thought to be divine and peculiar to specific religious communities, are simply not a viable basis for the foreign policy of a multicultural democracy in a pluralistic world. Many members of the various religious communities discussed in this chapter understand and accept that. Others do not. The U.S. government should pay close attention to those who do, and who assert their opinions on the basis of justice, fairness, and collective welfare of the involved parties and the global community. It should also recognize that, given the diversity within and among the traditions represented in the United States, no group can claim to speak for any of these communities as if there were no dissenting voices. That recognition should leave policymakers in a better position to weigh competing claims with greater care.

Concluding Note

My aim in this chapter has not been to suggest that legislators need to become experts in comparative religions or that diplomats should spend three years in seminary before assignment to a foreign post, though informed sensitivity to the offenses Western ideas about such matters as sexuality, gender roles, population control, and freedom of expression can pose for the religions and traditions of other cultures does not seem to much to ask. Nor do I mean to suggest that religious factors will be of crucial importance in every situation, or that thorough knowledge of the religious situation will always result in improved relations, or that religion may not be an intractable part of the problem rather than an ingredient in a solution. But I am quite willing to assert that religion is, and is likely to remain, a fundamental dimension of human life, and that it is often of considerable, sometimes critical importance in a situation involving statecraft. And I am willing to claim that legislators and diplomats who appreciate that fact and deal with it sensitively will more accurately represent the United States than those who do not.

Notes

1. Morton Borden, *Jews, Turks, and Infidels* (Chapel Hill: University of North Carolina Press, 1984), 76–79.

2. This paragraph is taken largely from William Martin, *With God on Our Side: The Rise of the Religious Right in America* (New York: Broadway Books, 1996), 3.

3. Charles S. Olcott, *The Life of William McKinley*, vol. 2 (Boston: Houghton Mifflin, 1916), 110–11. Quoted in Sidney E. Ahlstrom, *A Religious History of the American People* (New Haven, Conn.: Yale University Press, 1972), 879.

4. Ahlstrom, *Religious History*, 880.

5. George M. Marsden, *Fundamentalism and American Culture: The Shaping of Twentieth-Century Evangelicalism 1870–1925* (New York: Oxford University Press, 1980), 142–47.

6. William Warren Sweet, *The Story of Religion in America* (New York: Harper & Brothers, 1950), 402.

7. Ahlstrom, *Religious History*, 891.

8. Ibid., 892–900.

9. For an extensive treatment of the role of religious leaders in connection with the Vietnam War, see Michael B. Friedland, *Lift Up Your Voice Like a Trumpet: White Clergy and the Civil Rights and Anti-War Movement 1954–1973* (Chapel Hill: University of North Carolina Press, 1998).

10. See the U.S. Catholic bishops' statements on nuclear war at <http://www.nonviolence.org/archivedsites/pages/13.htm>.

11. For information about the United States Catholic Conference and the National Conference of Catholic Bishops, see <http://www.nccbuscc.org/faithfulcitizenship/ citizenship.htm>.

12. For information regarding Jubilee 2000, see <http://www.j2000.org>.

13. For details regarding the political and economic stances of the National Council of Churches, use the "search" feature at <http://www.ncccusa.org/> Methodist, Presbyterian, and Episcopal positions are described, respectively, at <http://www.umc.org/faithinaction/justice/>, .<http://www.pcusa.org> , and <http://www.dfms.org>.

14. For information on positions advocated by the Friends Committee on National Legislation, see <http://www.fcnl.org/issues.htm>. Armenian Assembly positions are described at <http://www.aaainc.org>.

15. James Davison Hunter and Carl Bowman, "The State of Disunion: 1996 Survey of American Political Culture (Ivy, Va.: Media Res Educational Foundation, 1996), 51–57.

16. John Persinos, "Has the Christian Right Taken Over the Republican Party?" *Campaigns and Elections*, Sept. 1994, 21–24. John Green and his colleagues at the Ray C. Bliss Institute of Applied Politics at the University of Akron offer two qualifications to these findings. First, in some states, social issue conservatives not ordinarily viewed as part of the Christian Right contribute to this strength. Second, about half the states in both the "dominant strength" and "substantial influence" categories are in the South, where religious conservatives are largely unopposed. In the remaining states, mostly in the Midwest and on the West Coast, more moderate Republicans provide stiff opposition, (Conversation and correspondence with John Green, May 1996.)

17. All of these conservative organizations have easily located Websites.

18. Various investigative reporters and other journalists have compiled lists of the CNP's membership. This one is taken from "Council for National Policy Members Hold Cloistered Session in Saint Louis," published by the Institute for First Amendment Studies, an organization that keeps a close watch on religious conservatives in politics, see <http://www.ifas.org/fw/9401/cnp.html>.

19. This statement was provided to me by a researcher at the journal *Foreign Policy,* in which I published "The Christian Right and American Foreign Policy," spring 1999, 66–80. When I later tried to ascertain the precise source, I was unsuccessful in locating the researcher in question and therefore cannot provide the name of a speaker. I regard the statement as unexceptional and see no reason to doubt its authenticity.

20. Material on Pat Robertson is taken from Sara Diamond's review of David Edwin Harrell Jr., *Pat Robertson: A Personal, Political and Religious Portrait* (San Francisco: Harper & Row, 1987), in *The Nation*, Feb. 13, 1988; Sara Diamond, *Spiritual Warfare: The Politics of the Christian Right* (Boston: South End Press, 1989), esp. 161–229; and idem, *Roads to Dominion: Right Wing Movements and Political Power in the United States* (New York: Guilford Press, 1995), 237–41.

21. For information regarding the "10/40 Window," see <http://1040window.org>.

22. For one account of the conservative Republican resistance to paying U.N. dues, see Romesh Ratnesar, "Superpower Stiff," *Time*, Nov. 15, 1999, 52.

23. Hal Lindsey, *The Late Great Planet Earth* (Grand Rapids, Mich.: Zondervan, 1970); and Tim LaHaye and Jerry B. Jenkins, *Left Behind* and several sequels (Wheaton, Ill.: Tyndale House Publishers, 1995). For information about this and the sequels, see <http://www.leftbehind.com>. For a reasonably concise introduction to Dispensationalist theology, see William Martin, "Waiting for the End," *The Atlantic*, June 1982, 31–37.

24. Timothy Weber, "How Evangelicals Became Israel's Best Friend," *Christianity Today*, Oct. 5, 1998, 38.

25. Steve Brouwer, Paul Gifford, and Susan D. Rose, *Exporting the American Gospel: Global Christian Fundamentalism* (New York: Routledge, 1991).

26. Richard H. Curtiss, "U.S. Muslims May Put Themselves on American Political Map in 1998," *Washington Report on Middle East Affairs* 18 (1998): 76–77.

27. Ibid.

28. For examples of positions advocated by American Muslim organizations, see the Websites of the American Muslim Council <http://www.amconline.org>; the Council on American Islamic Relations <http://cair-net.org>; and the Washington Report <http://www.washington-report.org>. For a fatwa, a formal Muslim legal opinion, regarding Muslim participation in American politics, see <http://www.amconline.org/newamc/fatwa.shtml>.

29. Ali A. Mazrui, "A New Cultural Constituency: American Muslims & the Crisis of Political Participation," American Muslim Council Website <http://www.amconline.org/publications>.

30. For a good summary account of this dispute, see Gustav Niebuhr, "Studies Suggest Lower Count for Number of U.S. Muslims," *New York Times*, Oct. 25, 2001, sec. A, 16, col. 4. The two most thorough studies were conducted by the Graduate Center of the City University of New York and the American Jewish Committee (AJC). The first, the American Religious Identification Survey 2001, directed by Egon Mayer and Barry Kosmin, involved random interviews with 50,000 people, a huge sample for a national survey. The second, written by Tom W. Smith, director of the General Social Survey at the National Opinion Research Center (NORC) at the University of Chicago, was commissioned by AJC and based on several NORC surveys.

31. Curtiss, "U.S. Muslims."

32. Interview with James Zogby, Oct. 15, 1999.

33. See William Martin, "Muslims—A New Force in American Politics?" Paper presented at the James A. Baker III Institute for Public Policy at Rice University, Houston, Feb. 1, 2001; and "Reflections on Elections: The Role of Religion in the 2000 Elections" <http://riceinfo.rice.edu/projects/baker/>.

34. James E. Bill, *The Eagle and the Lion: The Tragedy of American–Iranian Relations* (New Haven, Conn.: Yale University Press, 1988), 417. Cited by Edward Luttwak, in "The Missing Dimension in Douglas Johnson and Cynthia Sampson, eds. *Religion: The Missing Dimension in Statecraft* (New York and London: Oxford University Press, 1994), 12. The quotation is from Luttwak.

35. Andrew Sullivan, "This Is a Religious War," *New York Times Magazine*, Oct. 7, 2001, 44–57, 52–53. This article may also be available at <http://www.andrewsullivan.com>.

36. For a useful discussion of a number of these situations, as well as others not mentioned here, see Johnson and Sampson, eds., *Religion: The Missing Dimension in Statecraft.*

37. The most recent reference I have seen to the story is by Harvey Cox, in "World Religions and Conflict Resolution," in *Religion: Missing Dimension in Statecraft*, 266.

38. Johnson and Sampson, *Religion: Missing Dimension in Statecraft.*

39. For a detailed account of Billy Graham's relations with Soviet bloc leaders, see William Martin, *A Prophet with Honor: The Billy Graham Story* (New York: Morrow, 1991), chaps. 29–31.

40. I am quite aware that, in some circles, it is thought improper to assign gender to God. Because the Founding Fathers did not share this sensibility, I defer to their mode of reference on this occasion.

41. Sullivan, "This Is a Religious War."

Contributors

Stanley W. Carlson-Thies is acting director of the Civitas Program in Faith and Public Affairs and a fellow of the Center for Public Justice, a Washington, D.C.-area nonpartisan Christian think tank. He was on the policy staff of the White House Office of Faith-Based and Community Initiatives during its first fifteen months. He is the author of *Charitable Choice for Welfare & Community Services: An Implementation Guide for State, Local, and Federal Officials*, and a co-editor of and a contributor to *Welfare in America: Christian Perspectives on a Policy in Crisis*.

José Casanova is professor of sociology and chair of the Committee on Historical Studies at the New School for Social Research in New York. He is the author of *Public Religions in the Modern World*, a prize-winning reconsideration of relations between religion and modernity. He is directing a research project on religion and immigrant incorporation in New York.

John A. Coleman, S.J., is Casassa Chair in Social Values at Loyola Marymount University in Los Angeles. A former Wilson Center fellow, Coleman is an authority on the history of Catholic social teaching. His books include *The Evolution of Dutch Catholicism*; *An American Strategic Theology;* and *One Hundred Years of Catholic Social Teaching*.

E.J. Dionne Jr. is a senior fellow at the Brookings Institution, where he focuses on American politics, civil society, and faith and public life. A syndicated columnist with the *Washington Post* and co-chair of the Pew Forum on Religion and Public Life, he is author of *Why Americans Hate Politics* and editor or co-editor of several Brookings volumes, among them: *Community Works: The Revival of the Civil Society in America; Sacred Places, Civic Purposes: Should Government Help Faith-Based Charity?;* and *What's God Got to Do with the American Experiment?* with John DiIulio. He is also working on the volume *United We Serve: National Service and the Future of Citizenship,* with Kayla Drogosz.

Charles Glenn teaches educational policy and history at Boston University and is an authority on education policy in America and Europe. The most recent of his six books, *Finding the Right Balance: Freedom, Autonomy, and Accountability in Education* (with Jan De Groof) was a two-volume study of how twenty-six nations balance educational freedom with common standards and accountability.

D. G. Hart is academic dean and professor of church history at Westminster Theological Seminary in California. He holds a Ph.D. in American history from The Johns Hopkins University and is the author of *That Old Time Religion in Modern America* (2002), *The Lost Soul of American Protestantism* (2002), *The University Gets Religious* (1999), and *Defending the Faith* (1994). Hart is an elder in the Orthodox Presbyterian Church.

Hugh Heclo is Robinson Professor of Public Affairs at George Mason University in Fairfax, Virginia, and a former professor of government at Harvard University. His prize-winning books include *Modern Social Politics in Britain and Sweden* and *A Government of Strangers: Executive Politics in Washington*. A former Wilson Center fellow, he is a member of the International Scholars' Council advising the Librarian of Congress. In 2002 he was the recipient of the John Gaus Award given by the American Political Science Association for exemplary lifetime scholarship in the joint tradition of political science and public administration.

William Martin is the Harry and Hazel Chavanne Professor of Religion and Public Policy in the Department of Sociology and a senior scholar in the James A. Baker III Institute for Public Policy at Rice University, where he has taught since 1969. His most recent book, *With God on Our Side: The Rise of the Religious Right in America*, is the companion volume to the PBS miniseries of the same name. He is currently writing about U.S. drug policy.

Wilfred M. McClay holds the SunTrust Bank Chair of Excellence in Humanities at the University of Tennessee at Chattanooga, where he is also professor of history. He co-edits Rowman and Littlefield's book series entitled "American Intellectual Culture," serves on the editorial boards of *The Wilson Quarterly* and *The American Quarterly*, and is a member of the National Council on the Humanities. He is a frequent contributor to *The*

Public Interest, First Things, American Scholar, and *Commentary*, among other journals. A former Wilson Center fellow, McClay is author of the prize-winning study *The Masterless: Self and Society in Modern America.*

Wilson Carey McWilliams is professor of political science at Rutgers University, where he teaches American politics and political thought. He is the author of *The Idea of Fraternity in America* and most recently, *Beyond the Politics of Disappointment? American Elections, 1980–1998*. He is a frequent contributor to *Commonweal* and other journals of opinion.

A. James Reichley is senior fellow at the Graduate Public Policy Institute at Georgetown University. A former member of the Wilson Center's Board of Trustees, he is an authority on the history of American political parties and the role of religion in public life. His books include *Religion in American Public Life*, *Faith in Politics*, and *The Values Connection.*

Charles J. Reid Jr. is associate professor of Law at the University of St. Thomas in Minneapolis. With degrees in law and canon law from the Catholic University of America and a Ph.D. in the history of medieval law from Cornell University, his research interests center on the history of Western conceptions of rights, including the rights of conscience.

Index